UPGRADING TO FORTRAN 90

Springer
New York
Berlin
Heidelberg
Barcelona
Budapest
Hong Kong
London
Milan
Paris
Tokyo

Cooper Redwine

UPGRADING TO FORTRAN 90

With 298 Illustrations

Springer

Cooper Redwine
Northrop Grumman Corporation
Pico Rivera, CA 90660, USA

Library of Congress Cataloging in Publication Data
Redwine, Cooper.
    Upgrading to Fortran 90 / Cooper Redwine.
        p. cm.
    Includes bibliographical references and index.
    ISBN-13:978-0-387-97995-3   e-ISBN-13:978-1-4612-2562-1
    DOI:10.1007/978-1-4612-2562-1

    1. FORTRAN 90 (computer program language) I. Title.
QA76.73.F28R43   1995
005.13'3—dc20   95-12917

Printed on acid-free paper.

Production managed by Terry Kornak; manufacturing supervised by Jacqui Ashri.
Typeset in TeX from the author's Microsoft Word files.

9 8 7 6 5 4 3 2 1

ISBN-13:978-0-387-97995-3

*To my teachers at Union College,
especially Dr. Edward Craig*

PREFACE

Fortran 90 is a general-purpose programming language that provides superior facilities for dealing with numerical data, and it is far and away the best language for most applications that are dominated by mathematical, engineering, or scientific analysis. Of course, Fortran 90 supports a free source form, as well as modern control-flow and data structures, but it offers much more. Fortran 90's array-handling capabilities are outstanding, and it provides a rich collection of intrinsic procedures. Also, Fortran 90 provides excellent mechanisms for partitioning large programs into smaller, more manageable pieces. Furthermore, it supports features that facilitate data hiding and data abstraction. Yet even with these dramatic enhancements to previous versions of Fortran, an exceptionally high degree of backward compatibility is maintained. However, the price that is paid for all this is that Fortran 90 is a sprawling, untidy language whose complexity is roughly comparable to that of Ada or C++.

Like any important but complicated subject, Fortran 90 merits many books from many points of view. This book is a tutorial geared to the needs of the reader who already has a working knowledge of some dialect of Fortran based on the FORTRAN 77 standard, although no specific knowledge of that or any other language standard is assumed. Moreover, great proficiency in Fortran is not prerequisite. Also, because many people today have been exposed to C, C++, Pascal, and Ada, comparisons are sometimes drawn in this book to these languages, but no familiarity with any of them is presupposed.

Not only does this book present the big ideas surrounding those Fortran 90 features not traditionally available in Fortran, but it goes beyond that to give detailed explanations of what these features are and what they are not, as well as their interrelationships with the rest of the language. Nearly every new feature is demonstrated in a small, but complete, program. The intent of presenting the material in this fashion is to avoid, on the one hand, the confusion that can be created by code fragments, and on the other hand, the obscuring of fundamental language principles that often results from long, involved examples. The terminology of the Fortran 90 standard is emphasized throughout the book in order to provide the reader with the vocabulary needed to understand reference documentation.

Perhaps a few words are in order regarding the organization of the book. Chapter 1 merely establishes the background for the methodical treatment that follows, and although some of the most important features are previewed, the reader is not necessarily expected to be able to understand the details of these introductory examples in a first pass through the book. Chapters 2 through 8 give a detailed presentation of the more elementary features introduced by Fortran 90, and a few features that are not new are reviewed along the way. The more advanced features of Fortran 90 are then covered in Chapters 9 through 13. Finally, the last chapter gives a thorough discussion of the new input/output features.

As the preparation of this book neared its final stages, I was looking over some of the advanced examples that appear toward the end of the text when I started to think back to how it was that I ever became involved with Fortran in the first place. I was employed as a young engineer in 1966 when my technical lead assigned me the task of writing a program to find solutions to a complicated equation. He wanted to use the program to carry out some parametric studies. Rather than admit that I knew nothing about Fortran, I went to the library and checked out a slim volume on the subject by Daniel McCracken, and I managed to bumble my way through the assignment. Both Fortran and I have come a very long way since.

Cooper Redwine
Cypress, California
December 1994

CONTENTS

CHAPTER 1

GETTING READY

1.1 OVERVIEW OF THE CHAPTER

This tutorial presents a description of Fortran 90 tailored to meet the needs of a reader who feels reasonably comfortable developing programs using any of the popular implementations of Fortran available in the late 1980s or early 1990s, that is, a reader who already has a working knowledge of arrays, DO loops, subroutines, CHARACTER variables, and simple I/O. The discussion here focuses on those Fortran 90 features that were not generally available in earlier versions of the language, although occasionally some of the less popular traditional features will be described briefly. But before beginning a methodical presentation of the new features, which will occupy Chapters 2 through 14 of the tutorial, this first chapter will prepare the way by introducing some fundamental terminology, showing how some of the most important of the new features look and feel, and describing a few conventions that will be used throughout the tutorial. The heart of the tutorial is made up of approximately 150 complete Fortran 90 programs, all of which can be compiled and executed, and this approach is established in this chapter by the presentation of the first 9 of these programs.

The focus of this tutorial is on gaining a working knowledge of those features of Fortran 90 that are new to the Fortran language, and any discussion of language standards here is more or less incidental. However, it is difficult to frame sensibly the discussion of the new features without frequent reference to two standards: the new Fortran 90 standard and the older FORTRAN 77 standard. The following two sections give a little background on these two standards and cover the matter of the shift from upper to lower case in all but the first letter in the official name of the language.

Sections 1.4 through 1.12 of this chapter center around short, but complete, example programs that are intended to impart the flavor of some of the new features of Fortran 90. Presumably, most readers will not be able to follow all of the details of these examples, but it is enough at this point in the tutorial to begin to develop a feel for Fortran 90. The purpose of the examples in this chapter is merely to preview some of the big ideas before embarking on the detailed presentation given in Chapters 2 through 14.

The presence of certain new features in Fortran 90 has motivated the development of some new terminology, as well as changes in meaning to some old terminology. An example of important new terminology is the phrase "scoping unit," which is previewed in Section 1.12. Later, this tutorial will build up a full explanation of scoping units in sections scattered from Chapter 5 through Chapter 13. Examples of some old terminology with a changed meaning are "variable" and "array," and this topic is discussed in Section 1.13.

While the emphasis in this tutorial is on examples and concepts rather than on rules, it will sometimes be helpful to specify syntax forms. The syntax specifications show such things as where keywords must appear, where programmer-chosen names may appear, which parts of statements are mandatory and which are optional, and the like. The final section of this chapter will describe the conventions that are employed throughout the remainder of the tutorial in specifying syntax forms.

1.2   FORTRAN, FORTRAN 77, FORTRAN 90, FORTRAN

In the mid-1950s, a team led by John Backus of IBM developed a new language that made the task of programming a computer an order of magnitude easier. One of the major achievements of the new language was that it provided a much more intuitive way of coding mathematical formulas than had previously been available, and so it was named FORTRAN, taken from the first few letters of the words "*For*mula *Tran*slation." At the time, it was customary that all letters in acronyms be written in upper case, no matter from which part of a word a particular letter in the acronym derived.

In the late 1950s and early 1960s, the new language flourished in a computer world going through a period of rapid change. Important improvements were made to the language in its early years, but dialects were proliferating. In the 1960s, an organization called the American Standards Association (ASA) developed a short document delineating a standard set of features that any implementation of the language should possess. The language described in the document was a version of what was then popularly called "FORTRAN IV." Some years later, the language specified by the document came to be known as "FORTRAN 66," so designated because of the completion of that standard in 1966.

Because the version of the language specified by the FORTRAN 66 standard was so restrictive, the popular compilers of the late 1960s included implementation-peculiar, advanced processing facilities that were not covered by the standard. A feature supported by a compiler but not specified by the standard on which the compiler is based is often referred to as an **extension**. The extensions provided by the compilers based on the FORTRAN 66 standard greatly increased the scope of applicability and ease of use of the language, but did so at the expense of decreasing portability.

In the 1970s, the American National Standards Institute (ANSI), the successor organization to the ASA, developed a new standard that was eventually published as *American National Standard Programming Language FORTRAN* (ANSI X3.9–1978). The newer standard was designated as "FORTRAN 77" because its technical content was completed in 1977. While maintaining a high degree of backward compatibility with the older standard, FORTRAN 77 supported major new features, such as the CHARACTER data type, the IF ... THEN ... ELSE control construct, and standardized I/O facilities, that overcame some of the worst weaknesses of the language described in the FORTRAN 66 standard. In 1980 the ANSI FORTRAN 77 standard was also adopted as an international standard by the ISO (International Organization for Standardization). Compilers based on the FORTRAN 77 standard started becoming widely available around 1981, and a relatively easy transition from FORTRAN 66-based compilers to compilers based on the newer standard was largely completed by the mid-1980s.

The 1980s proved to be yet another period of rapid change in technical computing environments. The FORTRAN 77 implementations were quite popular, but more powerful languages such as C, C++ (which contains C as a subset), and Ada were increasingly being chosen for software development. An ANSI committee struggled to formulate a successor to the FORTRAN 77 standard that would provide power comparable to that of C++ and Ada, maintain backward compatibility with the previous standard, and gain widespread acceptance. Along the way, the committee discontinued the tradition of using only capital letters in the official name of the language and instituted the practice of referring to it as "Fortran" with only the initial letter in upper case. The technical work on the new standard was declared to have been completed in 1990, and the language described in that standard was designated "Fortran 90." The ISO adopted the new standard as described in *Information Technology—Programming Languages—Fortran* (ISO/IEC 1539:1991), and ANSI published the same standard as *American National Standard Programming Language Fortran 90* (ANSI X3.198–1992).

Throughout the remainder of this tutorial, the word "FORTRAN" in all uppercase letters will appear only as part of the phrase

"FORTRAN 77," which refers to the FORTRAN 77 standard discussed previously. The phrase "Fortran 90," refers, of course, to the Fortran 90 standard just described. The word "Fortran," with only the initial letter capitalized and no number following, will be used in this tutorial as a generic term to denote any version of the language from the 1950s through the present.

1.3 FORTRAN 90 COMPARED WITH FORTRAN 77

Figure 1.1 depicts a high-level conceptual view of the makeup of Fortran 90. Fortran 90 is firmly rooted in FORTRAN 77 with roughly two-thirds of the content of the new standard relating to features supported by the older standard. Thus, the workhorse data types are still INTEGER, REAL, and CHARACTER; IF and DO statements remain the bases of most control structures; I/O is fundamentally unchanged, although there are a few enhancements; and breaking a large program into smaller pieces is still a matter of using subroutine subprograms and function subprograms. In fact, most programmers will find that if they write Fortran routines exactly as they did before Fortran 90 became

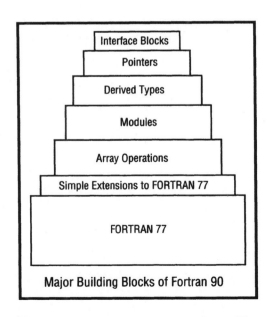

FIGURE 1.1. High-level conceptual view of the makeup of Fortran 90.

available, their routines will usually still work on the compilers based on the new standard. Actually, this tutorial does not have much to say about the Fortran 90 features carried over from FORTRAN 77, concentrating instead on those features specified by the new standard that were not supported by the old.

As indicated by Figure 1.1, some of the new features of Fortran 90 are simple extensions to FORTRAN 77. A noteworthy example is the free source code form, which permits any part of a statement to appear anywhere on a line. Also, a new form of type declarations, characterized by the presence of a double colon (::), makes it possible to specify all attributes of a variable in a single statement. Furthermore, Fortran 90 supports control constructs that make it possible (and usually desirable) to code lengthy and complicated programs without using labels (also known as "statement numbers"), and therefore it is never necessary to use any form of a GO TO statement. Hence, the look and feel of a lot of Fortran 90 code is somewhat different from that written for most FORTRAN 77 implementations. Some of the standard Fortran 90 features representing simple extensions to the FORTRAN 77 standard are illustrated in the example program of Section 1.5.

Figure 1.1 also indicates some additional Fortran 90 features that have not usually been provided by FORTRAN 77 implementations. Among these are array operations, which can often perform simple array manipulations in place of the short DO loops that have traditionally been required. Another major new feature is the module, which permits separately compiled program units to share data in a manner that is less error-prone than that provided by the common block. In addition, because the module can contain subprograms as well as data specifications, it thus becomes the basis for important new ways to partition large programs. A third new feature is the interface block, which permits interfaces between an external subprogram and its caller to be more complex than in previous versions of Fortran. And the final two features shown in Figure 1.1, derived types and pointers, support much more sophisticated data structures than have traditionally been available in Fortran, including linked lists. It is worth noting that the Fortran 90 support for dynamic storage allocation, derived types, pointers, and a new intrinsic function named TRANSFER makes nearly all uses of the EQUIVALENCE statement unnecessary. The example programs given in Sections 1.6 through 1.11 illustrate some of the Fortran 90 capabilities mentioned in this paragraph.

A remarkable aspect of the language specified by the Fortran 90 standard is that it contains as a subset the language described by the FORTRAN 77 standard; thus, any program that complies with the older standard also complies with the new standard. However, because most of the popular compilers include extensions to the standards, it is important to realize that a given Fortran 90 implementation may not support a particular extension to the FORTRAN 77 standard. For example, the older standard did not support giving a variable an initial value in its type declaration, but many FORTRAN 77 compilers permit this by using syntax like the following:

```
INTEGER COUNT / 0 /
```

The above syntax is not supported by the FORTRAN 77 standard, and it is also not supported by the Fortran 90 standard. But, of course, a vendor who supported the above syntax in its compiler(s) based on the FORTRAN 77 standard will in many cases continue support for the syntax in its Fortran 90 compiler(s) in order to maintain backward compatibility with its own previous products.

As is done in the preceding paragraph, departures from the Fortran 90 standard will be mentioned in this book from time to time, but this should not be construed as encouragement to write code that does not conform to the new standard. On the contrary, the author strongly recommends that programmers adhere strictly to the standard unless there is some compelling reason to do otherwise. For example, the effect of the preceding type declaration can be achieved in standard Fortran 90 by the following statement:

```
INTEGER :: COUNT = 0
```

Thus, even when using a Fortran 90 compiler that supports as an extension the former syntax in type declarations, the latter is to be preferred since it conforms to the standard. Compliance with the standard promotes portable skills and portable code, and any decision to deviate from the standard should not be made lightly.

1.4   FORTRAN 90 VERSION OF THE "HELLO, WORLD" PROGRAM

Figure 1.2 gives the source listing for a simple program[1] that a programmer can use to confirm that he or she is able to compile Fortran 90 source code successfully when first encountering an unfamiliar compiler. When compiled and executed, the program of Figure 1.2 displays

```
Hello, World
```

on a default output device. Throughout the remainder of this tutorial, it will be assumed that programs are executed interactively at a terminal

---

[1] Based on a similar program in C in the classic book *The C Programming Language* by B.W. Kernighan and D.M. Ritchie (Prentice-Hall, Englewood Cliffs, NJ, 1988).

```
! The following may be used to confirm the capability
! of a given human/software/hardware configuration to
! compile and execute Fortran 90 programs.

PROGRAM display_hello_world
                                ! Displays "Hello, World"
    PRINT "(A)", &              ! (without quote marks).
          " Hello, World"       ! Output is to screen
                                ! on most computers.
END PROGRAM display_hello_world
```

FIGURE 1.2. Complete Fortran 90 program in free source form.

and that program output to the default output device is displayed on the screen of that terminal.

The source code in Figure 1.2 is in the new free source form. Any part of a statement may appear anywhere on a line. A statement may start in position 1 or any other position. A trailing ampersand (&) indicates that the statement on the current line is continued on the following line, as illustrated by the PRINT statement. An exclamation point (!) indicates that the rest of the line is a comment.

The programmer has chosen the name display_hello_world for the program of Figure 1.2. The Fortran 90 standard permits any programmer-chosen name to contain as many as 31 characters, and the underscore (_) may appear in a name. Next, note in Figure 1.2 that the quotation mark (") may be used to delimit a character string, but the alternative of using the apostrophe (') to delimit a character string is also permissible. Finally, observe that the END statement contains information that unambiguously pairs it with the PROGRAM statement.

Note in Figure 1.2 that some letters are capitalized, while others are not. The Fortran language has never been case sensitive, and Fortran 90 maintains that tradition. Thus, a Fortran 90 compiler permitting the presence of lowercase letters is required by the standard to treat a the same as A, b the same as B, and so on, unless they appear within a quoted string (such as "Hello, World"). This tutorial will assume that the example programs presented are to be used with a compiler supporting lower case and will employ the convention that, except for quoted strings, the presence of lowercase letters indicates a programmer-chosen name. The only programmer-chosen name in Figure 1.2 is display_hello_world. Observe that the statement keywords PROGRAM, PRINT, and END, and the edit descriptor A are entirely in upper case, indicating that they are not programmer-chosen names. The use of this convention throughout this tutorial is intended to improve the readability of the code.

1.5 PREVIEW: SIMPLE EXTENSIONS OF *FORTRAN* 77

Quite a few features supported by the Fortran 90 standard are relatively simple extensions of the FORTRAN 77 standard, and in many cases these features represent capabilities that were provided in some form by one or more of the popular compilers based on the older standard. The preceding section illustrated three such features: long names, quotation mark delimiters for character constants, and free source form. This section will discuss several more features that are standard in Fortran 90 but that reflect only a modest departure from the FORTRAN 77 standard.

The standard Fortran 90 program in Figure 1.3 exhibits quite a number of features that lie outside the FORTRAN 77 standard, but the program should still be rather easy to follow for someone with a good working knowledge of traditional Fortran. The program is intended to be run interactively at a terminal. The user is expected to enter a sequence of names at the keyboard, pressing the Return key (or its equivalent) after each name is entered. The user signals end of input by entering the end-of-file indication at the keyboard, which varies from system to system, but is typically something like CTRL-Z or CTRL-D. The program then displays the line

```
List of names input:
```

on the screen, followed by a listing of the names entered previously by the user.

The IMPLICIT NONE statement in Figure 1.3 makes mandatory the explicit declaration of each variable in the main program. This widely available extension to the FORTRAN 77 standard has been found to be quite helpful in detecting programming errors and has been made standard in Fortran 90. It is good practice in a production environment to place an IMPLICIT NONE statement in each program unit, but to avoid cluttering the examples, this tutorial will not follow this practice.

Type declarations are permitted to have a more general form in Fortran 90 than they were in FORTRAN 77, and this is illustrated by the type declarations near the beginning of the program in Figure 1.3. First, observe that each type declaration may contain a double colon (::). Next, note that the equal sign (=) may appear in a type declaration, and that it is used in Figure 1.3 to give the values 0 and 100 to num_ names and Max_names, respectively. Further, observe that not only may data types (INTEGER, CHARACTER, etc.) be specified in a type declaration, but additional attributes, such as PARAMETER and DIMENSION, may be specified as well. Finally, note that Fortran 90 permits the length of a CHARACTER variable to be specified by enclosing it in parentheses—

```
PROGRAM read_and_store_names

  IMPLICIT NONE                 ! IMPLICIT NONE now standard

  INTEGER :: read_status, i   ! double colon in
                              ! type declarations

  INTEGER :: num_names = 0    ! new form of initialization

  ! New way to declare a constant follows.
  INTEGER, PARAMETER :: Max_names = 100

  ! New way to dimension an array follows.
  CHARACTER(132), DIMENSION(Max_names) :: names

  CHARACTER(132) :: buffer   ! new way to specify length
                             ! of CHARACTER variable


  DO                                          ! new form of DO
     ! ADVANCE = "NO" suppresses line feed here.
     WRITE (*, "(A)", ADVANCE = "NO")               &
                 " Enter name (or EOF to quit): "
     READ (*, "(A)", IOSTAT = read_status) buffer
     ! < is synonym for .LT.
     IF (read_status < 0) EXIT               ! EXIT is new.
     ! >= is synonym for .GE.
     IF (num_names >= Max_names) THEN
        PRINT *, "Too many input names."
        STOP
     END IF
     num_names = num_names + 1
     names(num_names) = buffer
  END DO                                      ! END DO now standard


  PRINT "(//A)", " List of names input:"

  DO i = 1, num_names        ! no label required in indexed DO
     PRINT *, TRIM (names(i)) ! TRIM is new intrinsic func.
  END DO

END PROGRAM read_and_store_names
```

FIGURE 1.3. Program illustrating simple extensions of FORTRAN 77.

a minor variation of the FORTRAN 77 form that requires the length specification to be preceded by an asterisk (*).

The executable part of the program in Figure 1.3 consists almost entirely of two DO loops, each of which is terminated by an END DO statement. The END DO is a widely available extension to FORTRAN 77 that becomes standard in Fortran 90. The first DO illustrates a form of the DO that will be known as the "simple DO" in this tutorial, although some people prefer to call it the "DO forever." The actions specified by the statements between the simple DO statement and its corresponding END DO are performed repeatedly until a new variety of statement, the EXIT statement, is executed, causing an immediate exit from the loop. The second DO loop illustrates a standard form of the indexed DO, which is essentially the same as the classic Fortran DO loop, except that no label is required. Note that when an END DO terminates an indexed DO, it need not be labeled in Fortran 90 as is required by some of the more restrictive FORTRAN 77 implementations.

The two IF statements in Figure 1.3 demonstrate a minor Fortran 90 feature that has sometimes been provided as a FORTRAN 77 extension. In the first IF statement, the symbol < is used as a synonym for .LT., and >= is used as a synonym for .GE. in the second IF. Fortran 90 supports similar synonyms for the other relational operators.

Fortran 90 provides only a few enhancements to I/O as described in the FORTRAN 77 standard. The WRITE statement of Figure 1.3 illustrates the most important of these enhancements, which is known as "nonadvancing I/O." The ADVANCE = "NO" specifier causes the line feed that ordinarily accompanies the execution of a WRITE to be suppressed. On the other hand, the READ statement utilizes only features that are carried over from the FORTRAN 77 standard. The variable read_status takes on a negative value only if the end of file is detected when the READ is executed, in which case the EXIT statement is executed, breaking the read loop.

In most implementations of Fortran 90, the output from the WRITE statement of Figure 1.3 and the echo of the response entered by the user at the keyboard will be on the same line of the screen, but this behavior is not absolutely guaranteed by the new standard. In this connection, it should also be mentioned that the widely available extension to FORTRAN 77 of suppressing advancement to a new line by specifying the dollar sign ($) in a format remains nonstandard in Fortran 90. Thus, there is unfortunately no standard way of specifying that a prompt/response pair must appear on the same line of the screen that is guaranteed to work in all Fortran 90 implementations. Nevertheless, since the ADVANCE = "NO" specification in the WRITE conforms to the new standard while the dollar sign specification in the format does not, the former is to be generally preferred over the latter in those implementations supporting both.

The new standard intrinsic function TRIM appears in the last PRINT statement in Figure 1.3. TRIM returns a copy of its CHARACTER argument with any trailing blanks trimmed off. TRIM is only 1 of 75 new intrinsic procedures: The Fortran 90 standard lists 70 intrinsic functions and 5 intrinsic subroutines that were not in the FORTRAN 77 standard.

As mentioned in the preceding section, all programmer-chosen names in Figure 1.3 contain lowercase letters. All of the letters in variable names, such as buffer and read_status, are in lower case. But the initial letter of the name Max_names is capitalized to emphasize that since it has the PARAMETER attribute, it cannot be changed during execution and should therefore be considered a constant. Note that statement keywords, such as INTEGER, DO, and so on, as well as the name of the intrinsic function TRIM, are entirely in uppercase letters to indicate that they are not programmer-chosen names.

1.6 PREVIEW: ARRAY OPERATIONS

Fortran 90 supports many new array facilities, some of which are illustrated in the program in Figure 1.4. Each of the names a, b, and c is declared to be a one-dimensional array with subscripts in the range

```
PROGRAM demo_array_operations

   ! Declare an array and give it initial values.
   REAL, DIMENSION(3) :: a = (/ 2.0, 8.0, 18.0 /)


   REAL, DIMENSION(3) :: b, c



   b = 2.0 * a   ! Multiply a scalar constant times an array.

   c = SQRT (b) + (/ 1.0, 2.0, 3.0 /)    ! Take square root of
                                         ! each element of
                                         ! array b & add array
                                         ! constant to result.
   PRINT "(F6.1)", c

END PROGRAM demo_array_operations
```

FIGURE 1.4. Program illustrating some new array facilities.

1 through 3. Each of the array elements is of data type REAL. The entities (/ 2.0, 8.0, 18.0 /) and (/ 1.0, 2.0, 3.0 /) in Figure 1.4 are examples of a new variety of data object known as the "array constructor." The entity (/ 2.0, 8.0, 18.0 /) is a constant one-dimensional array with three elements whose values are listed between the delimiters (/ and /). Similarly, the entity (/ 1.0, 2.0, 3.0 /) is a different constant one-dimensional array having three elements.

The elements of array a—a(1), a(2), and a(3)—are initialized to the values 2.0, 8.0, and 18.0, respectively, in the type declaration for a. Then the assignment statement

```
b = 2.0 * a
```

causes each element of a to be multiplied by the scalar constant 2.0, and the value of the product is assigned to the array b. Thus, after this assignment statement is executed, b(1) holds the value 4.0, b(2) holds 16.0, and b(3) holds 36.0.

In the second assignment statement in Figure 1.4, the old SQRT intrinsic function is used in a new way. Note that the argument of SQRT is an array, and so the square root of each element of that array is taken. Hence, the result of the expression SQRT (b) is a one-dimensional array with three elements whose values are 2.0, 4.0, and 6.0.

Also, in the second assignment statement in Figure 1.4, the three-element array returned by the SQRT function is added to the array constant (/ 1.0, 2.0, 3.0 /), which means that corresponding elements of the two arrays are added. This results in the elements of c—c(1), c(2), and c(3)—taking on the values 3.0, 6.0, and 9.0, respectively. Hence, when the PRINT statement is executed, the following is displayed:

```
3.0
6.0
9.0
```

The example program in Figure 1.4 illustrates the general principle that some operators, including +, − (or-), *, and /, may be used with a pair of arrays in Fortran 90, but the arrays must have the same number of dimensions and the same extent along each dimension. The operator is then applied to corresponding elements on an element-by-element basis. Not only is it permissible for such operators to have two operands that are both arrays, but, as illustrated by the first assignment statement of Figure 1.4, it is also permitted for one operand to be an array and the other to be a scalar. Also, many Fortran 90 intrinsic functions, such as SQRT, ABS, SIN, and so on, may be used with an array argument, in which case the function is applied independently to each element of the array and returns an array result.

In addition to the array features illustrated in the foregoing example, Fortran 90 provides a new way to refer to a subset of array elements. For instance, if arr is a one-dimensional array whose valid subscripts range from 1 through n, then the expression arr(i:m) refers to the collection of array elements arr(i), arr(i+1), . . . , arr(m). arr(i:m) is an example of what is known as an "array section." Array sections play an important role in code that manipulates data stored in arrays.

1.7 PREVIEW: SHARING DATA BY WAY OF A MODULE

The **module**, a major new Fortran 90 feature, brings several capabilities to the language, including an improved mechanism for sharing data. For example, in FORTRAN 77 implementations, COMMON blocks in INCLUDE files are a popular way of facilitating shared access to data. But COMMON blocks in INCLUDE files are not necessarily portable, while the module offers a mechanism that is governed by the Fortran 90 standard. This, along with its generality and ease of use, makes the module the preferred method of sharing data in Fortran 90, and the use of both COMMON blocks and INCLUDE files should generally be avoided. By way of illustration, this section will present a main program and a subroutine that share access to data stored in arrays through the use of a module.

Figure 1.5a gives a simple example of a Fortran 90 module named arrays_to_be_shared. Two one-dimensional REAL arrays named x and y are to contain data to be shared. Each of these arrays is capable of containing as many as Max_size values, where the value of Max_size is set at 100. The name Max_size is specified with the PARAMETER attribute, and so it is actually a constant since it cannot be changed at execution time. Observe that there is sufficient information in the END statement of Figure 1.5a to pair it with the preceding MODULE statement.

```
MODULE arrays_to_be_shared

    INTEGER, PARAMETER :: Max_size = 100     ! maximum size
                                             ! of each array

    REAL, DIMENSION(Max_size) :: x, y    ! arrays to contain
                                         ! data to be shared

END MODULE arrays_to_be_shared     ! new form of END stmt
```

FIGURE 1.5A.   A simple example of a module.

```
              ! Load values into arrays x and y.


SUBROUTINE load_arrays (num_values, status_code)

   USE arrays_to_be_shared   ! Access x, y, Max_size.

   ! INTENT indicates if dummy args are input or output.

   INTEGER, INTENT (IN)  :: num_values    ! number of
                                          ! values to load

   INTEGER, INTENT (OUT) :: status_code   ! 0 = OK,
                                          ! 1 = not OK


   INTEGER :: i   ! loop index


   IF (num_values <= Max_size) THEN
      DO i = 1, num_values
         x(i) = +i             ! Load x with positive values.
         y(i) = -i             ! Load y with negative values.
      END DO
      status_code = 0          ! Everything is OK.
   ELSE
      status_code = 1          ! Arrays are too small.
   END IF

END SUBROUTINE load_arrays   ! new form of END statement
```

FIGURE 1.5B. Subroutine that uses the module of Figure 1.5a.

Figure 1.5b gives a subroutine named load_arrays, which stores values into the arrays x and y. The subroutine accesses x and y, as well as Max_size, by way of the statement

```
USE arrays_to_be_shared
```

where arrays_to_be_shared matches the name in the MODULE statement in Figure 1.5a. The attribute INTENT (IN) specified for the dummy argument num_values means that its value is an input to the subroutine, while the attribute INTENT (OUT) specified for status_code indicates that its value will be output by the subroutine. If the value input for num_values is less than or equal to Max_size, then positive values are loaded into x, negative values are loaded into y, and the subroutine returns with status_code set to 0. If the value input for num_values is greater than Max_size, no values are stored in either x or y, and the subroutine returns with status_code set to 1. Incidentally, note that the END statement in Figure 1.5b contains enough information to pair it unambiguously with the SUBROUTINE statement at the beginning of the subroutine.

Figure 1.5c lists a main program that asks a user at a terminal how many values are desired to be loaded into each of the arrays x and y, calls the subroutine of Figure 1.5b to load the requested number of values into the arrays, and then displays those values at the terminal. The USE statement gives the main program access to x, y, and Max_size in the module of Figure 1.5a. Incidentally, in Figure 1.5c, note the use of == as a synonym for the relational operator .EQ. in the IF statement.

Each of the collections of source code in Figures 1.5a, 1.5b, and 1.5c constitutes a Fortran 90 program unit and may, in most implementations, be placed in a file by itself and compiled separately. However, the module of Figure 1.5a must ordinarily be compiled before either the

```
PROGRAM demo_shared_arrays

   USE arrays_to_be_shared      ! Access x, y, Max_size.

   INTEGER :: num_vals_desired
   INTEGER :: load_status
   INTEGER :: i


   WRITE (*, "(A)", ADVANCE = "NO")                            &
                            " How many values per array? "
   READ *, num_vals_desired


   CALL load_arrays (num_vals_desired, load_status)


   IF (load_status == 0) THEN       ! == is synonym for .EQ.
      DO i = 1, num_vals_desired
         PRINT "(2F12.3)", x(i), y(i)
      END DO
   ELSE
      PRINT "(A)",     " Error: Too many values requested."
      PRINT "(A, I5)", " Maximum array size = ", Max_size
   END IF

END PROGRAM demo_shared_arrays
```

FIGURE 1.5c. Main program that uses the module of Figure 1.5a.

subroutine of Figure 1.5b or the main program of Figure 1.5c. If the code given in Figures 1.5a, 1.5b, and 1.5c is contained within a single file, implementations are likely to require that the source for the module precede that of the other two program units. Such implementation details are left unspecified by the Fortran 90 standard and will vary somewhat from implementation to implementation. For compilers intended primarily for training, it may be compulsory for the code given in Figures 1.5a, 1.5b, and 1.5c to be contained within a single file.

Suppose that the program composed of the main program of Figure 1.5c, the subroutine of Figure 1.5b, and the module of Figure 1.5a is executed, and the user enters 5 in response to the prompt issued by the program. Then the following would be displayed at the terminal:

```
1.000      -1.000
2.000      -2.000
3.000      -3.000
4.000      -4.000
5.000      -5.000
```

As has been traditional in Fortran, the subprogram of Figure 1.5b is not contained within any other program unit. But Fortran 90 introduces two additional varieties of subprogram, known as the "module subprogram" and the "internal subprogram," that always constitute only a part of a program unit. The traditional, standalone Fortran subprogram is now designated as the "external subprogram" to distinguish it clearly from the two new varieties of subprogram. One of the new varieties of subprogram—the module subprogram—will be previewed in the next section.

1.8 PREVIEW: MODULE SUBPROGRAMS

The preceding section gave an example of a module that consisted only of data specifications, but a module may contain subprograms—either subroutines or functions—as well. A simple example is given by the module of Figure 1.6a, which contains only one subprogram, a function named identity_matrix. Note that a statement consisting only of the keyword CONTAINS precedes the source code for the function. When a positive integer n is input to identity_matrix, it returns a two-dimensional n × n array of type REAL that has ones along the diagonal and zeros elsewhere. Thus, the function returns an array of values, a capability not traditionally available in Fortran.

Figure 1.6b shows a main program that can be used as a test driver for the function of Figure 1.6a. Because identity_matrix is a module sub-

```
MODULE identity_matrix_maker

CONTAINS  ! Indicates subroutine(s) and/or function(s) follow.

   FUNCTION identity_matrix (n)

      INTEGER, INTENT (IN) :: n
      REAL, DIMENSION(n,n) :: identity_matrix  ! This func
                                               ! returns an
                                               ! n x n array.

      INTEGER :: j   ! local loop index


      identity_matrix = 0.0   ! Set each element to zero.

      DO j = 1, n                      ! Change value of
         identity_matrix(j,j) = 1.0    ! each element along
      END DO                           ! diagonal to unity.

   END FUNCTION identity_matrix

END MODULE identity_matrix_maker
```

FIGURE 1.6A. Example of a module subprogram.

program, the main program does not automatically have access to it as would be the case for (say) a traditional external subprogram, and this access is gained in Figure 1.6b by the USE statement that specifies the module identity_matrix_maker of Figure 1.6a. In Figure 1.6b, when the assignment statement

```
u = 3.0 * identity_matrix (4)
```

is executed, identity_matrix is invoked with an argument of 4, and the function returns a two-dimensional 4 × 4 array whose elements have the value 1.0 along the diagonal and 0.0 off the diagonal. The scalar constant 3.0 is then multiplied by each element of the result returned by the function, and the product is stored in the array u.

When the module of Figure 1.6a and the main program of Figure 1.6b are compiled, linked, and executed, the following is displayed:

```
3.0   0.0   0.0   0.0
0.0   3.0   0.0   0.0
0.0   0.0   3.0   0.0
0.0   0.0   0.0   3.0
```

```
PROGRAM test_identity_matrix

    USE identity_matrix_maker    ! Gain access to module
                                 ! function identity_matrix.


    REAL, DIMENSION(4,4) :: u
    INTEGER :: i



    u = 3.0 * identity_matrix (4)   ! Invoke module function.

    DO i = 1, 4
        PRINT "(4F5.1)", u(i,1:4)    ! Display ith row of u.
    END DO

END PROGRAM test_identity_matrix
```

FIGURE 1.6B. Test driver for the module procedure of Figure 1.6a.

One row of the two-dimensional array u is displayed each time the PRINT statement of Figure 1.6b is executed. Note the expression u(i,1:4) in the output list for the PRINT statement. This expression denotes the ith row of the array u and is an example of the new Fortran 90 feature known as the "array section" mentioned previously at the end of Section 1.6.

In general, anything that can be accomplished with an external sub-program can also be accomplished with a module subprogram, and these two varieties of subprogram are competing mechanisms for seg-menting a large, complicated program into smaller, more manageable pieces. However, sometimes a module subprogram will have the ad-vantage of being easier to use than its external counterpart, and this is the case with the example of this section. This comes about because identity_matrix is a function that returns an array result. If identity_matrix were an external subprogram, the availability of an additional block of code known as an "interface block" would be required in the main program of Figure 1.6b, a requirement that programmers might well find unexpected.

The example of this section illustrates a module containing only a subprogram, while that of the preceding section gave a module con-sisting only of data specifications, but much of the usefulness of the module derives from its capability of combining data specifications and subprograms that are intimately interrelated in the same compila-tion unit. Examples of such modules will be given later in the tutorial in Chapters 7, 9, and 12.

1.9 PREVIEW: DERIVED TYPES

Fortran programmers are quite accustomed to declaring an array and then being able to refer either to individual elements by using subscripts or to the whole array by using its name with no subscript. This is a powerful capability, but the individual pieces that make up an array must all be of the same data type. A major new feature in Fortran 90 is its support for data aggregates made up of individual pieces of data that may be of different data types. The programmer can refer either to individual components of the aggregate or to the aggregate as a whole. The programmer defines the composition of such an aggregate, and in standard Fortran 90, each such definition is considered as creating a new data type. Ultimately, of course, the components of any of the programmer-defined data types are of type INTEGER, REAL, CHARACTER, and so forth, so the programmer-defined data types are known as "derived types" while the data types built into the language are now called "intrinsic types."

The program of Figure 1.7 illustrates a derived type named employee_type. The programmer defines employee_type as having four components, name, age, salary, and is_married, where the data type of each component is one of the intrinsic types. The component definitions are rather similar in form to type declarations, although it turns out that there are many more restrictions on derived-type component definitions than there are on type declarations.

In Figure 1.7, the statement

```
TYPE (employee_type) :: an_employee
```

declares an_employee to be a variable of the data type employee_type. Thus, this statement is a type declaration and is similar in form and function to type declarations for intrinsic types, such as INTEGER and CHARACTER. It is important to recognize that before declaring variables of a derived type, the programmer must establish the type definition. This is not the case for declaring variables of intrinsic type, where the type definition is automatically built into the language.

Each of the first four assignment statements in Figure 1.7 assigns a value to one of the individual components of the variable an_employee. Note that a component of a variable of a derived type is referenced in standard Fortran 90 by the variable name, followed by the percent sign (%), followed by the component name. On the other hand, the first PRINT statement shows that the name an_employee with no component name following can be used to refer to the variable's whole collection of components.

Now focus attention on the final assignment statement in Figure 1.7:

```
PROGRAM demo_derived_type

   TYPE :: employee_type
      CHARACTER(75) :: name            ! Define a
      INTEGER       :: age             ! derived type
      REAL          :: salary          ! named
      LOGICAL       :: is_married       ! employee_type.
   END TYPE employee_type

   TYPE (employee_type) :: an_employee  ! Declare a variable
                                        ! named an_employee
                                        ! to be of type
                                        ! employee_type.


   ! Individual components of an_employee can be referenced.
   an_employee%name       = "John Doe"  ! Assign values
   an_employee%age        = 56          ! to individual
   an_employee%salary     = 987.65      ! components of
   an_employee%is_married = .TRUE.      ! an_employee.


   ! The group of values can be referred to collectively.
   PRINT "(1X, A, /, I3, F9.2, 2X, L1)", an_employee


   ! Structure constructor used to right of equal sign below.
   an_employee =                                            &
           employee_type ("Mary Roe", 32, 1234.56, .FALSE.)


   ! Display values, referencing individual components.
   PRINT "(1X, A)",              an_employee%name
   PRINT "(I3, F9.2, 2X, L1)", an_employee%age,        &
                               an_employee%salary,     &
                               an_employee%is_married

END PROGRAM demo_derived_type
```

Figure 1.7. Program illustrating a derived type.

```
an_employee =                                            &
        employee_type ("Mary Roe", 32, 1234.56, .FALSE.)
```

The values listed inside the parentheses on the right-hand side of the equal sign are assigned on a component-by-component basis to the variable an_employee. The right-hand side expression here is an example of what is called a "structure constructor," which is coded by specifying the name of a derived type followed by a parenthesized list of component values. The final two PRINT statements display the values just assigned to an_employee, but observe that, unlike in the first PRINT statement, individual components are specified in the output lists.

When the program of Figure 1.7 is executed, the following is displayed:

```
John Doe
56    987.65   T
Mary Roe
32   1234.56   F
```

1.10 PREVIEW: POINTERS

In the 1970s, Pascal, C, and other languages demonstrated how the presence of pointers in a language greatly expands its breadth of applicability. Still, pointers remain unfamiliar to many Fortran programmers since pointers were available as extensions in only a handful of FORTRAN 77 implementations. But under the new standard, pointers become part of the official language, providing the Fortran programmer with a powerful tool that can be used in a portable way. The Fortran 90 pointer is rather similar to pointers in other languages and those offered as extensions to FORTRAN 77, but the reader should be advised that there are significant differences as well.

Conceptually, an ordinary variable contains data, while a pointer, rather than contain data, in some manner points to a storage area that does. Although no implementation methodology for pointers is specified in the new standard, it is perhaps most useful to think of a Fortran 90 pointer as containing the address of a data storage area, along with a description of that storage area sufficient to access any individual piece of data that may be stored there. In Fortran 90, a pointer usually points to an array of values or to a value of a derived type since it is seldom worth the trouble to employ pointers to scalar values of intrinsic types. This section will present a short program illustrating some of the elementary aspects of the use of the Fortran 90 pointer in pointing to an array. Later in the tutorial, two entire chapters will be devoted to the topic of pointers.

The program of Figure 1.8 declares p to be a pointer to a one-dimensional array of type REAL. Note that the declaration of a pointer is similar to that of an ordinary variable, except that the

```
PROGRAM demo_pointer

   REAL, DIMENSION(:), POINTER :: p     ! Declare a pointer to
                                        ! a one-dimensional
                                        ! array of type REAL.


   REAL, DIMENSION(4), TARGET :: a      ! Declare arrays that
   REAL, DIMENSION(3), TARGET :: b      ! may be pointed to.

   INTEGER :: i   ! loop index


   a = (/ 1.0, 2.0, 3.0, 4.0 /)
   p => a                               ! Cause p to point to a.
   PRINT "(4F7.1)", p


   b = (/ -1.0, -2.0, -3.0 /)
   p => b                               ! Cause p to point to b.
   PRINT "(3F7.1)", p



   ALLOCATE (p(4))          ! Create storage area for 4 REALs
                            ! and cause p to point to it.

   DO i = 1, SIZE (p)       ! SIZE is an intrinsic function.
      p(i) = 1000.0 * i     ! Put values in storage area.
   END DO
   PRINT "(4F7.1)", p

   DEALLOCATE (p)           ! Free storage area.

END PROGRAM demo_pointer
```

FIGURE 1.8. Program illustrating a pointer to an array.

POINTER attribute is specified. The colon (:) in parentheses following
the keyword DIMENSION means that the range of subscripts at a given
stage of program execution will be those of whatever target p is pointing
to at the time.

Two ordinary, one-dimensional REAL arrays, a and b, are also declared
in Figure 1.8. a has four elements, and b has three. The Fortran 90
standard requires that if a named array is pointed to by a pointer, then
the TARGET attribute must be specified for that named array. Hence, the
TARGET attribute is specified for a and b so that it will be legal to point
to them with p later in the program.

In the first executable statement in Figure 1.8, values are assigned to each element of the array a by using an array constructor. Now, pay particular attention to the second executable statement:

```
p => a
```

This is an example of a new variety of statement known as the "pointer assignment statement," which causes the address of a, along with other descriptive information about a, to be stored in p. The symbol => is made up of the equal sign (=) followed immediately by the greater than (>) sign. After the statement is executed, p points to the storage area containing the values of a.

Later in Figure 1.8, execution of the pointer assignment statement

```
p => b
```

causes p to point to b, which means that the address of b, along with other descriptive information about b, is stored in p. p no longer points to a and now points instead to the storage area containing the values of b. This illustrates a capability of a pointer that is not shared by an ordinary variable: An ordinary variable is always associated with the same storage area throughout the execution of the program, but the programmer can associate a pointer with one area of storage at one stage of program execution and a different area of storage at another stage of program execution.

The ALLOCATE statement of Figure 1.8 illustrates another facet of using pointers. Execution of this statement creates a storage area of sufficient size to contain a one-dimensional REAL array of four elements and causes p to point to the newly created storage area. The DO loop that follows then puts values in the newly created storage area. The new intrinsic function SIZE can be used to determine the number of elements in an array, and here it accepts the pointer p as an argument and returns 4, the size of the target of p. After the final PRINT statement, execution of the DEALLOCATE statement disassociates p from its target storage area and frees that storage area for possible other uses.

When the program of Figure 1.8 is executed, the following is displayed:

```
   1.0     2.0     3.0     4.0
  -1.0    -2.0    -3.0
1000.0 2000.0 3000.0 4000.0
```

Note that in the first PRINT statement in Figure 1.8, p can be considered an alias for a, and in the second PRINT statement, p can be thought of as an alias for b. After the ALLOCATE statement, p can be regarded as an array name of a dynamically allocated storage area that otherwise has no name. Observe that even though p is a pointer, when it is associated with a target, its name can be used in almost any way that an ordinary, one-dimensional array name can be used—in appropriate contexts, a reference to p is treated as a reference to its current target.

1.11   PREVIEW: INTERFACE BLOCKS

Subprograms—subroutines and functions—have been a major feature of the Fortran language from very early times. In Fortran 90, the notion of the subroutine has been broadened to encompass *module* subroutines (which are subroutines contained within a module as illustrated in Section 1.8) and *internal* subroutines (which are subroutines contained within other subprograms or main programs). To distinguish the old FORTRAN 77-style subroutine (that is, those subroutines not contained within another program unit) from module subroutines and internal subroutines, the older subroutines have been redesignated as "*external* subroutines." Fortran 90 treats the function subprogram in an analogous fashion.

Of the three varieties of Fortran 90 subprogram—module, internal, and external—only the external subprogram offers the possibility of independent compilation, and this suggests that the external subprogram will continue to play an important role in decomposing large programs into smaller, more manageable pieces—especially in programs that are developed and maintained by teams of programmers. But some of the new Fortran 90 features demand more elaborate interfaces between subroutines and the routines that invoke them than traditionally have been available in the language, and the same is true for functions as well. For example, Fortran 90 permits an array argument to carry the number of subscripts allowed for each dimension along with the beginning address of the array, a function to return an array of values, and subprogram arguments and function results to be pointers. These advanced features present no particular problems for module subprograms and internal subprograms, but when these features are used with external subprograms, a new mechanism known as the "interface block" must be employed.

This section will give an example of an interface block in the context of a convenient Fortran 90 feature known as the "assumed-shape array," which is a new variety of dummy argument. The new capability illustrated by the example is that it is now possible to arrange things so that, at entry to a subroutine, the size of an array used as a dummy argument is available, even though the caller does not pass the size as an argument or communicate it to the subroutine by any other

means traditionally available in Fortran. Of course, the same capability
is provided for functions, as well as for subroutines.

Figure 1.9a gives the listing of a subroutine that finds the line that
best fits a set of points using the method of least squares. As shown in
many books, if the set of points (x_1, y_1), (x_2, y_2), ..., (x_n, y_n) is given,
then the slope m and the intercept b of the best fitting line $y = mx + b$
can be found from the equations

$$ m = \frac{\sum_{i=1}^{n}(x_i - x_{\text{avg}})(y_i - y_{\text{avg}})}{\sum_{i=1}^{n}(x_i - x_{\text{avg}})^2}, $$

$$ b = y_{\text{avg}} - mx_{\text{avg}}. $$

Here x_{avg} is the average of the x_i, and y_{avg} is the average of the y_i. The
choice of variable names in Figure 1.9a directly reflects the preceding

```
!!!!!!!!!!!!!!!!!!!!!!!!!!!!!!!!!!!!!!!!!!!!!!!!!!!!!!!!
! Note: Caller must supply an interface body when !
!        using find_best_fit_line as an external   !
!        subroutine because it has dummy arguments !
!        that are assumed-shape arrays.            !
!!!!!!!!!!!!!!!!!!!!!!!!!!!!!!!!!!!!!!!!!!!!!!!!!!!!!!!!

SUBROUTINE find_best_fit_line (x, y, m, b)

  REAL, DIMENSION(:), INTENT (IN)  :: x, y   ! assumed-shape
                                             ! dummy array
                                             ! arguments
  REAL,              INTENT (OUT) :: m, b

  REAL :: x_avg, y_avg


  x_avg = SUM (x) / SIZE (x)   ! Find avg of elements in x.
  y_avg = SUM (y) / SIZE (y)   ! Find avg of elements in y.

  ! Compute slope m.
  m = SUM ((x - x_avg) * (y - y_avg)) /                    &
                              SUM ((x - x_avg) ** 2)

  b = y_avg - m * x_avg   ! Compute intercept b.

END SUBROUTINE find_best_fit_line
```

FIGURE 1.9A. External subroutine requiring caller to use interface body.

symbology. Note that Fortran 90 array operations as described in Section 1.6 are used in Figure 1.9a so that the code is a straightforward representation of the previous equations.

Two new Fortran 90 intrinsic functions, SUM and SIZE, are illustrated in Figure 1.9a: SUM is used to sum the elements of arrays, and SIZE is used to determine the number of elements in arrays. But since the size of the arrays x and y is not passed to find_best_fit_line as an argument, how then is it available in the subroutine? The answer lies in the fact that x and y are examples of a new variety of array known as the "assumed-shape array," which is indicated in Figure 1.9a by the presence of x and y in the argument list, together with the attribute specification DIMENSION(:) in the type declaration for those two arrays. The parenthesized colon (:) following the keyword DIMENSION signifies that the permissible subscript ranges for x and y will be determined at execution time from the subscript ranges of their corresponding actual arguments appearing in the CALL statement invoking find_best_fit_line.

A main program that calls the subroutine of Figure 1.9a is given in Figure 1.9b. Note first in Figure 1.9b that the main program has two one-dimensional REAL arrays, u and v, each containing four elements. Each of these arrays is given a set of initial values by using an array constructor as mentioned earlier in Section 1.6. When the subroutine of Figure 1.9a is called, the dummy array x takes on the size of u, and the dummy array y takes on the size of v.

On most systems, the code given in Figures 1.9a and 1.9b can be placed in two separate files or in a single file, but in either case, note that find_best_fit_line is being used as an external subroutine because its source code is not contained inside any other source code. When the program given by Figures 1.9a and 1.9b is executed, the output is as follows:

```
slope     =   3.371
intercept = -3.886
```

Thus, the program tells us that the least-squares linear fit for the set of points (5,14), (4,9), (6,16), and (8,23) is the line y = 3.371x − 3.886.

The principal new feature illustrated in Figure 1.9b is the interface block, which is delimited by the INTERFACE and END INTERFACE statements. Note that the interface block contains a description of the interface with the subroutine find_best_fit_line; that description, which is known as an "interface body," consists of copies of the SUBROUTINE and END SUBROUTINE statements with a copy of the type declarations for the subroutine's arguments in between. It is mandatory under Fortran 90 rules that an interface body be supplied for find_best_fit_line because the subroutine has dummy arguments that are assumed-shape arrays. The presence of the interface body informs the compiler that it must set up the interface with the subroutine in such a way that the range of the

```
PROGRAM test_least_squares

  ! Interface block containing one interface body follows.
  INTERFACE

    ! Interface body for subroutine of Figure 1.9a follows.
    SUBROUTINE find_best_fit_line (x, y, m, b)
      REAL, DIMENSION(:), INTENT (IN)  :: x, y
      REAL,               INTENT (OUT) :: m, b
    END SUBROUTINE find_best_fit_line

  END INTERFACE


  REAL, DIMENSION(4) :: u = (/  5.0, 4.0,  6.0,  8.0 /)
  REAL, DIMENSION(4) :: v = (/ 14.0, 9.0, 16.0, 23.0 /)

  REAL :: slope, intercept


  CALL find_best_fit_line (u, v, slope, intercept)

  PRINT "(A, F6.3)", " slope     = ", slope
  PRINT "(A, F6.3)", " intercept = ", intercept

END PROGRAM test_least_squares
```

FIGURE 1.9B. Main program calling the subroutine of Figure 1.9a.

(this is done automatically with modules)

array argument subscripts will automatically be passed each time the subroutine is called.

An interface body is permitted for any external subprogram, but if no new Fortran 90 features are involved, the presence of an interface body is optional so that backward compatibility is maintained. In Figure 1.9b, an interface body is compulsory because an external subroutine having an assumed-shape array argument is called, and as will be discussed in Chapter 13, there are several other circumstances that require the use of an interface body. But the author recommends always supplying an interface body for every external subroutine and function, even when it is not required. This permits a Fortran 90 compiler to make a consistency check of the specifications given in the interface body against the statement invoking the subroutine or function, which helps in the prevention of nasty execution-time errors caused by argument mismatches.

In addition to containing interface bodies for external subprograms as illustrated in this section, the interface block can be used to associate module subprograms with programmer-defined meanings for language components such as +, .OR., =, and the like. The former usage of interface blocks will be detailed in Chapter 13, while the latter will be covered in Chapter 9.

1.12   PREVIEW: SCOPING UNITS

The "scope" of a name is the region of a program over which that name must have the same interpretation. This notion has played a role in Fortran from its early years, but new features in Fortran 90 make the issue of scope much more complex than it has been traditionally. To deal with the increased complexity, the Fortran 90 standard introduces the term "scoping unit," which, roughly, refers to a collection of code throughout which each name must have a single meaning. Since the term "scoping unit" pops up frequently in Fortran 90 literature, this section will illustrate how to use the formal definition of the term to identify each scoping unit in a complete Fortran 90 program.

In FORTRAN 77, it suffices to define scope in terms of "program units," where a program unit is either a main program, a subroutine subprogram, or a function subprogram (or possibly a unit of code delimited by a BLOCK DATA statement and its corresponding END statement). For the most part, the scope of a variable name in a FORTRAN 77 program is a program unit, so that the same variable name may appear in, say, a main program and a subroutine subprogram with a different interpretation in each of the two program units.

The introduction of new features in Fortran 90 renders inadequate the definition of scope in terms of program units, and so the notion has been redefined in terms of collections of code known as "scoping units." Among the new features that motivated the change in characterization are derived-type definitions, interface blocks, modules, module subprograms, and internal subprograms. Also, Fortran 90 classifies the module as a new variety of program unit, so that in Fortran 90, the term "program unit" refers to one of the following: a main program, an external subroutine subprogram, an external function subprogram, or a module (or possibly, as in FORTRAN 77, to a unit of code delimited by a BLOCK DATA statement and its corresponding END statement).

With this bit of background, it is possible to present the full definition of a Fortran 90 scoping unit. A **scoping unit** is one of the following:

(1) a derived-type definition;

(2) an interface body, excluding any derived-type definitions and interface bodies contained within it;

(3) a subprogram, excluding derived-type definitions, interface bodies, and subprograms contained within it;

(4) a program unit, excluding derived-type definitions, interface bodies, and subprograms contained within it.

A little thought reveals that for a program conforming to the FORTRAN 77 standard, the scoping units are simply the program units.

A better understanding of scoping units can be achieved by applying the above definition to a program, and this is illustrated by the program of Figure 1.10.[2] First, any derived-type definition is a scoping unit, and so the definition of derived_type is designated as scoping unit 1. Second, any interface body, minus any derived-type definitions and other interface bodies contained within it, is a scoping unit. Thus, the interface body for external_sub is a scoping unit and is designated as scoping unit 2. Third, any subprogram, minus derived-type definitions, interface bodies, and internal subprograms contained within it, is a scoping unit. Hence, subroutine internal_sub, which contains none of these things, is a scoping unit and is designated as scoping unit 3. By the same token, the portion of the subroutine external_sub remaining after excluding the definition of derived_type and the internal subroutine internal_sub is a scoping unit and is designated as scoping unit 4. Finally, a main program is a program unit, and so a main program minus derived-type definitions, interface bodies, and internal subprograms is a scoping unit. Thus, the portion of the main program outside the interface body for external_sub is a scoping unit and is designated as scoping unit 5. Hence, the program of Figure 1.10 can be broken down into five nonoverlapping scoping units. Furthermore, note that, as shown by scoping units 4 and 5, the code in a scoping unit is not necessarily contiguous.

It is worth noting in Figure 1.10 that the name n appears at least once in each of the five scoping units. In scoping unit 1, the name n appears in a component definition in a derived-type definition. In scoping unit 2, n plays the role of a dummy argument in an interface body. In scoping unit 3, the name n appears twice—one time as a local variable in the internal subroutine and another time as the name of a component of a variable named struct of data type derived_type. In scoping unit 4, n appears as the name of a local variable in the external subroutine and also as the name of a component of struct. Finally, in scoping unit 5, n appears as the name of a local variable in the main program.

---

[2]The idea for this example was suggested by a figure in *Fortran 90 Explained* by M. Metcalf and J. Reid (Oxford University Press, Oxford, England 1990).

```
PROGRAM demo_scoping_units            ! scoping unit 5
    INTEGER :: n = 5                  ! scoping unit 5
    INTERFACE                         ! scoping unit 5

        SUBROUTINE external_sub (n)   ! scoping unit 2
            INTEGER, INTENT (IN) :: n ! scoping unit 2
        END SUBROUTINE external_sub   ! scoping unit 2

    END INTERFACE                     ! scoping unit 5
    CALL external_sub (89)            ! scoping unit 5
    PRINT "(I3)", n                   ! scoping unit 5
END PROGRAM demo_scoping_units        ! scoping unit 5


SUBROUTINE external_sub (i)           ! scoping unit 4
    INTEGER, INTENT (IN) :: i         ! scoping unit 4
    INTEGER :: n = 4                  ! scoping unit 4

    TYPE :: derived_type              ! scoping unit 1
        INTEGER :: n                  ! scoping unit 1
        REAL    :: x                  ! scoping unit 1
    END TYPE derived_type             ! scoping unit 1

    TYPE (derived_type) :: struct     ! scoping unit 4
    struct%n = 3                      ! scoping unit 4
    struct%x = 67.0                   ! scoping unit 4
    CALL internal_sub                 ! scoping unit 4
    PRINT "(2I3)", n, i               ! scoping unit 4
CONTAINS                              ! scoping unit 4

    SUBROUTINE internal_sub           ! scoping unit 3
        INTEGER :: n = 3              ! scoping unit 3
        PRINT "(2I3)", struct%n, n    ! scoping unit 3
    END SUBROUTINE internal_sub       ! scoping unit 3

END SUBROUTINE external_sub           ! scoping unit 4
```

FIGURE 1.10.   Program illustrating scoping units.

When the program of Figure 1.10 is executed, the following is displayed:

```
3  3
4 89
5
```

The first line is displayed by the PRINT statement in scoping unit 3, the second line by the PRINT statement in scoping unit 4, and the third line by the PRINT statement in scoping unit 5. The compiler has no difficulty distinguishing the various interpretations of the name n in the five scoping units, but human readers may be confused by such a poor choice of names.

1.13 TERMINOLOGY: CONSTANT, VARIABLE, ARRAY

While it is true that the language described in the Fortran 90 standard contains as a subset the language described in the FORTRAN 77 standard, it does not necessarily follow that the terminology used in the older standard automatically carries over to the new standard. There are a few terms that appear in both standards, but with different meanings. This section will briefly discuss three such terms: constant, variable, and array. As always, the intent in this tutorial is to impart a working knowledge of the terminology, rather than to give airtight, legalistic definitions.

The FORTRAN 77 standard places most of the data in a program in one of three categories: constant, variable, or array. These categories do not overlap, because a constant is a scalar whose value must not change, a variable is a scalar whose value may change, and the value(s) in an array may change. It is permissible to give a constant a name (by using a PARAMETER statement), and a variable or an array must always have a name. This characterization, although not entirely intuitive, turns out to be serviceable in FORTRAN 77, even though certain varieties of data that arise in programs do not fit any of the three categories. Examples of data items that lie outside this classification scheme are array elements and substrings of character variables, which do not meet the definitions because they are considered not to have names.

The definitions of some FORTRAN 77 terms are modified by the Fortran 90 standard to fit in better with the enhanced capabilities of the new version of the language; constant, variable, and array are among those terms whose meanings have been altered. The primary difference is that the Fortran 90 standard classifies a data item as being either a variable or a constant based on whether or not the programmer can cause its value(s) to be changed at execution time, no matter whether it is a scalar or an array or whether it is considered to be named or unnamed. The underlying idea in Fortran 90 is quite straightforward: If a value or aggregate collection of values must not be changed during execution, it is a constant, while if a value or aggregate collection of values can be changed by an assignment statement, it is a variable.

The Fortran 90 terminology is closer to everyday technical usage, but years of living with documentation based on the older classification may make the Fortran 90 approach seem vaguely foreign at times.

In Fortran 90, a constant may be a scalar, such as 9.8, or it may be an array, like (/ 1.0, 2.0, 3.0 /). A constant having no name, such as 5, 'ABC', or 9.8, is called a **literal constant**. Also, a constant may be given a name by specifying the PARAMETER attribute. For example, if the declarations

```
REAL,                    PARAMETER :: Pi   = 3.1416
INTEGER, DIMENSION(3), PARAMETER :: Order = (/ 1, 2, 3 /)
```

are made, then Pi and Order are examples of what are known in Fortran 90 as **named constants**.

In Fortran 90, anything that can be placed to the left of the equal sign in an assignment statement is called a **variable**, irrespective of whether it is a scalar or an array or whether it is named or unnamed. For example, suppose the following declarations are made:

```
CHARACTER(5) :: c
INTEGER, DIMENSION(4) :: k
```

Then the scalar variable c, the substring c(2:4), the array variable k, the array element k(2), and the array section k(1:3) are all referred to as variables in Fortran 90. Note that k, a named array, is a variable, as are the data objects c(2:4), k(2), and k(1:3), which are considered to be unnamed. Also, an individual component of a variable of a derived type is itself a variable, even though it is considered to be unnamed.

In Fortran 90, the term "array" is used much more broadly than in FORTRAN 77. Conceptually, a Fortran 90 array is any set of scalar data, all of the same type, whose individual elements are arranged in a rectangular pattern, whether named or unnamed, constant or variable. Thus, an array variable, such as k above, is an array, but an array section like k(1:3) is itself an array as well. Moreover, an array may be some unnamed storage area set up by the compiler. For example, if b is an array, then the expression b + 3 represents an array, as does the function result represented by SQRT (b), where SQRT is the intrinsic square root function. But note that the arrays represented by b + 3 and SQRT (b) are not variables because these expressions cannot appear on the left-hand side of an assignment statement.

1.14 CONVENTIONS USED IN SPECIFYING SYNTAX

This tutorial is intended to impart the spirit of Fortran 90 rather than to give detailed language rules. Nevertheless, it is sometimes helpful to specify the syntax of a statement in a way that indicates which words may be chosen by the programmer, which portions of the statement may be omitted, and so on. This section describes the conventions used in syntax specifications throughout the book. A summary of these conventions is presented in Figure 1.11.

In Fortran, a **statement keyword** is a word that is part of the syntax of a statement. Familiar examples are INTEGER, DO, and READ. In FORTRAN 77, all varieties of statements, except the assignment statement and the statement function statement, begin with a statement keyword. In Fortran 90, all varieties of statements begin with a statement keyword, except for the two carryovers from FORTRAN 77 and the new pointer assignment statement. A list of statement keywords is given in Appendix A.

In a syntax specification in this tutorial, statement keywords will be in uppercase, plain letters while placeholders for those parts of a statement where the programmer can make a choice will be in lowercase italics. For example, the syntax specification for the PROGRAM statement is

PROGRAM *program-name*

Here, PROGRAM is a statement keyword while *program-name* indicates that the programmer must supply a name in this part of the statement. An example of a valid PROGRAM statement is

```
PROGRAM produce_calibration_report
```

If an italicized portion of a specification ends in *-list*, it indicates that the programmer may specify more than one item, but each adjacent pair of items must be separated by a comma. For example, the syntax specification for the INTRINSIC statement is

INTRINSIC *intrinsic-procedure-name-list*

An example of a valid INTRINSIC statement is

```
INTRINSIC ABS, LOG, SQRT
```

Of course, it is valid for the list to contain only one item, for example,

```
INTRINSIC MAX
```

- Lowercase italics indicate where programmer has freedom of choice.
- Lowercase italics ending in *-list* indicate programmer may choose more than one item, but each adjacent pair of items must be separated by a comma.
- An item enclosed in brackets ([ ]) may be omitted.

Figure 1.11. Conventions used in syntax specifications in this book.

Another convention used in syntax specifications is that brackets ([ ]) are employed to indicate portions of a statement which may be omitted. Consider, for example, the syntax specification for the PRINT statement:

PRINT *format* [, *output-list*]

Thus, a valid PRINT statement with an output list is

```
PRINT '(A, I5)', city_name, zip_code
```

However, there are valid PRINT statements where there is no output list, for example,

```
PRINT '(/)'
```

It is not unusual for a syntax specification to employ one pair of brackets inside another pair of brackets. Consider, for example, the CALL statement

CALL *subroutine-name* [([*argument-list*])]

Thus, a subroutine named solve_linear_system that requires arguments might be invoked by a statement such as

```
CALL solve_linear_system (a, x, b)
```

However, a subroutine named read_input_file that has no arguments can be invoked by either

```
              CALL read_input_file ()
```

or

```
              CALL read_input_file
```

Thus, the parentheses in the CALL statement are required only if *argument-list* is present.

CHAPTER 2

Laying the Foundation

2.1 *Overview of the Chapter*

The following two sections present the rules governing programmer-chosen names and free source form as dictated by the Fortran 90 standard. These rules are fundamental to every example in this tutorial. But it should be noted that the Fortran 90 free source form is not backwardly compatible with FORTRAN 77. This issue is dealt with in the new standard by provisions for an alternate Fortran 90 source form, which is described in Appendix D.

Section 2.4 will give the general form of a Fortran 90 main program. The form is basically the same as in FORTRAN 77, except that a Fortran 90 main program may contain internal subprograms. Also, the END statement may carry more information in Fortran 90 than is permitted by the FORTRAN 77 standard.

Sections 2.5 through 2.9 are taken up by a description of Fortran 90 type declaration statements. Type declarations are, of course, used mostly for variables, but it must not be forgotten that they may also be used for named constants and functions. Any type declaration conforming to the FORTRAN 77 standard is valid in Fortran 90, but the new standard supports a more general form of the type declaration statement that permits the specification of more properties of the entities being declared. As illustrated throughout this tutorial, the hallmark of the Fortran 90 type declaration is the double colon (::), which precedes the list of names being declared.

For an intrinsic data type (INTEGER, REAL, CHARACTER, etc.), a Fortran 90 type declaration statement begins in the same way as a FORTRAN 77 type declaration, namely with the keyword(s) specifying the data type. For a programmer-defined derived type, a Fortran 90 type declaration starts out with the keyword TYPE, followed by the programmer-chosen name of the derived type in parentheses. This chapter will discuss only type declarations involving intrinsic types, deferring the description of derived types until Chapter 5.

Section 2.6 discusses the standard Fortran 90 syntax for specifying an initial value for a variable in its type declaration statement. The new syntax employs the equal sign (=) to set the variable to a value at compile time. The support in the Fortran 90 standard for setting initial values in type declarations makes it possible to avoid nearly all of the DATA statements that are required in programs conforming to the FORTRAN 77 standard. Actually, many versions of Fortran permit initial values to be specified in type declarations by placing them between slashes (/), but this syntax is not supported by either the FORTRAN 77 standard or the Fortran 90 standard.

Section 2.7 shows how the Fortran 90 type declaration statement allows the programmer to specify more information about a variable than just its data type and initial value—the programmer may also specify other properties of the variable, known as "attributes." For example, the programmer may specify that the variable is an array for which storage can be dynamically allocated (the ALLOCATABLE attribute), or that the variable is a pointer (the POINTER attribute), or that the variable is to be inaccessible outside the module in which it is declared (the PRIVATE attribute), and so on. Many of the attributes relate to new features, and so a full discussion of the meaning of most attributes must be deferred until later chapters. The discussion of attributes in this chapter focuses primarily on the role that they play in the syntax of the type declaration statement.

The Fortran 90 standard introduces the notion of "kind" to deal with the possibility that an implementation may support more that one internal representation for an intrinsic data type, and Section 2.8 takes a first cut at discussing some aspects of this major topic. Many Fortran programmers are at least somewhat familiar with some of the related ideas already since most of the popular FORTRAN 77 implementations support type declarations for INTEGER*2 and INTEGER*4 variables. This form of type declaration is not standard in FORTRAN 77, and it remains nonstandard in Fortran 90. In the Fortran 90 standard, the issues raised by this form of nonstandard type declaration are addressed in a more general way: The new standard takes the point of view that INTEGER*2 and INTEGER*4 correspond to two kinds of data type INTEGER, rather than being two separate data types as they are usually characterized in FORTRAN 77-oriented literature. The Fortran 90 concept of kind provides the basis for greatly improved portability, particularly between computers employing different internal numeric representations. As will be discussed in Section 2.8, the notion of kind affects the syntax of type declarations and gives rise to variant forms for literal constants.

The final two sections of this chapter discuss the Fortran 90 syntax rules for type declaration and attribute specification. In practice, programmers should find it reasonably easy to handle type declaration and attribute specification, but the detailed, generalized rules related

to these matters are quite difficult to follow as set forth in the new
standard. The difficulty stems largely from the fact that the standard
supports several alternative ways of writing code that will achieve the
same effect. Thus, rather than try to cover every possible variation,
this tutorial will present slightly simplified descriptions that should be
adequate for most practical purposes.

2.2 PROGRAMMER-CHOSEN NAMES

When writing a Fortran program, a programmer must choose a variety
of names. Familiar examples of programmer-chosen names are names
of variables and names of subroutines. Figure 2.1 summarizes the
rules as set forth in the Fortran 90 standard that govern any sort of
programmer-chosen name. Basically, all of the rules are carried over
from the FORTRAN 77 standard, except that the old standard restricts
names to a maximum length of six characters and does not permit the
underscore (_) to appear in names.

As indicated in Figure 2.1, the Fortran 90 standard requires that
compilers permit names of up to at least 31 characters in length. The
first character must be 1 of the 26 letters of the English alphabet. Each
additional character must be a letter, an underscore or one of the digits
0 through 9. The new standard does not require that lowercase letters
be permitted in the source, but it seems certain that all popular implementations will support them. If an implementation does support
lowercase letters in the source, the new standard requires that upper-
and lowercase letters be distinguished only within a quoted character
string; thus, in names, a and A are equivalent, b and B are equivalent,
and so on. The underscore is intended to be used primarily as a separa-
tor to improve readability, but a name may have a trailing underscore
as well as two or more consecutive underscores.

```
■   Names may be up to 31 characters long.
■   First character must be a letter.
■   Only letters, underscores, and digits are allowed.
■   Names are not case sensitive.
■   Names may be the same as a keyword.
■   Names may be the same as the name of an intrinsic procedure.
```

FIGURE 2.1. Rules governing a programmer-chosen name.

Also, it should be mentioned that unlike many other popular languages, Fortran has never had "reserved words," which are words that cannot be used for programmer-chosen names because they are reserved by the compiler for its own use. However, Fortran does have what are known as **statement keywords**, which are words that may have special meaning in a Fortran program, depending on context. DO and READ are familiar examples of statement keywords. If the implementation supports lowercase letters in the source, keywords may be in upper case, lower case, or a mix of the two cases. A complete list of the 111 standard Fortran 90 statement keywords is given in Appendix A, and most implementations will have additional statement keywords. Approximately 60 percent of the standard Fortran 90 keywords are also keywords in standard FORTRAN 77. Fortran rules have always permitted the programmer to choose a name that is identical to a keyword, and Fortran 90 preserves that tradition.

Fortran 90 rules also allow the programmer to choose a name that duplicates that of an intrinsic procedure. A list of 113 standard Fortran 90 intrinsic procedures is given in Appendix C, and implementations may provide additional intrinsic procedures. As in FORTRAN 77, an intrinsic procedure whose name is duplicated by a programmer is not available over the region of code where the programmer-chosen name conflicts with it. (Nevertheless, an intrinsic procedure name remains available when duplicated by a programmer-chosen generic name, as described in Section 9.2, provided that the intended usage of the name is unambiguous, because of such things as the number, types, kinds, or ranks of the arguments.)

Figure 2.2 gives a complete program that illustrates some programmer-chosen names conforming to the Fortran 90 standard. As throughout the tutorial, it is assumed that an implementation supporting lowercase letters in the source is being used. All programmer-chosen names in Figure 2.2 and throughout the book contain one or more lowercase letters, while a word entirely in upper case is something other than a programmer-chosen name, such as a statement keyword or the name of an intrinsic procedure. No type declarations are made in Figure 2.2, and so the names starting with i through n default to type INTEGER, while the other variable names default to type REAL, as has always been true in Fortran.[1] When the program of Figure 2.2 is executed, the following is displayed:

```
     1
    2.0
     3
    4.0
```

[1]This rule gave rise to the old witticism, "GOD IS REAL (UNLESS DECLARED INTEGER)."

```
PROGRAM demo_valid_Fortran_90_names

    names_may_contain_underscores = 1
    PRINT "(I6)", names_may_contain_underscores

    consecutive_underscores__are_OK = 2.0
    PRINT "(F6.1)", consecutive_underscores__are_OK

    may_end_with_an_underscore_ = 3
    PRINT "(I6)", may_end_with_an_underscore_

    digits_are_gr8_4_names_2 = 4.0
    PRINT "(F6.1)", digits_are_gr8_4_names_2

    longest_supported_by_Fortran_90 = 31
    PRINT "(I6)", longest_supported_by_Fortran_90

    print = 132.0              ! Name may duplicate a keyword.
    PRINT "(F6.1)", print

    sqrt = 25.0 ** 0.5         ! Name may duplicate that
    PRINT "(F6.1)", sqrt       ! of an intrinsic procedure.

END PROGRAM demo_valid_Fortran_90_names ! New form of END stmt
```

FIGURE 2.2. Program with names conforming to Fortran 90 standard.

```
     31
  132.0
    5.0
```

2.3 FREE SOURCE FORM

The Fortran 90 free source form, which is described in this section, is incompatible with the traditional Fortran source form. Thus, the new standard supports an alternate source form—the fixed source form—to satisfy the requirement of maintaining backward compatibility with FORTRAN 77. Details of the Fortran 90 fixed source form are presented in Appendix D. However, the new free source form will be used for all complete programming examples in this tutorial.

The basic rules governing the free source form are summarized in Figure 2.3. Most of these rules are illustrated in the complete Fortran 90

- ■ Statements may be placed anywhere on line.
- ■ Exclamation mark (!) indicates rest of line is comment.
- ■ Ampersand (&) indicates statement continues on following line.
- ■ Multiple statements, separated by semicolon (;), may be on same line.
- ■ Blanks are significant.

FIGURE 2.3.   Basic rules governing free form source.

program shown in Figure 2.4. The style in which the example program of Figure 2.4 is coded is intended to bring out certain aspects of the free source form and is not recommended for general use.

In free form, source lines as long as at least 132 characters must be supported by a standard-conforming compiler, and no character position in a line of source code has any special usage. A statement may start in the first character position or in any other position. If a label (statement number) is present, it may start in any position.

An exclamation mark (!) that is not part of a quoted string indicates that the rest of the line is a comment. The exclamation mark is the only way to indicate a comment in free source form—neither an asterisk (*) nor a C in position 1 can be used to indicate a comment in this form. A line that has no characters at all, is all blank, or whose first nonblank character is an exclamation mark is called a **comment line**.

If a statement is started on a line, it must be finished on that same line unless a trailing ampersand (&) follows the partial statement. A simple example of continuing a statement is

```
CALL clean_up (dirty_data,  &
               clean_data)
```

The trailing ampersand indicates that the statement is continued on the next line that is not a comment line. The continuation begins with position 1 of the next noncomment line unless the first nonblank character of that line is an ampersand, in which case continuation begins immediately following the leading ampersand. This rule permits, for example, convenient continuation of strings:

```
PRINT "(A)", "Watch out &
          &for long strings."
```

The display resulting from this PRINT statement is

```
Watch out for long strings.
```

Observe that the ampersands themselves are not part of the string. By the way, when a character string is continued in the manner just il-

```
!!!!!!!!!!!!!!!!!!!!!!!!!!!!!!!!!!!!!!!!!!!!!!!!!!!!!!!!!!!!!!!!!!
!    Warning: The style of this program is not exemplary.    !
!!!!!!!!!!!!!!!!!!!!!!!!!!!!!!!!!!!!!!!!!!!!!!!!!!!!!!!!!!!!!!!!!!

PROGRAM demo_free_source_form  ! Stmts may start in column 1.

   IMPLICIT NONE  ! Blank required between IMPLICIT and NONE.

   INTEGER var_1, &   ! Ampersand indicates continuation.
           var_2, &
           var_3

   INTEGER very_long_variable_name


   PRINT 1234," Position of statement numbers not restricted."
          1234 FORMAT (A)    ! Label may be anywhere on line.

     PRINT "(A)",  " This is &
                   &standard."       ! one way to continue
                                     ! a string

     PRINT "(A)",  " This is " // &  ! second way to
                   "also standard."  ! continue a string

     very_long_variable_name = 4
     PRINT '(I5)',  very_long_vari&  ! example of
                   &able_name        ! continuing a name

   var_1 = 1; var_2 = 2; var_3 = 3  ! Semicolon separates
                                    ! multiple stmts on line.

     PRINT '(3I5)', var_1, var_2, var_3

END PROGRAM demo_free_source_form    ! new form of END stmt
```

FIGURE 2.4.   Program illustrating free source form.

lustrated, the standard does not permit the trailing ampersand to be
followed by commentary.

The combination of a trailing ampersand on one line followed by
a leading ampersand on the next noncomment line can also be used
to continue a name across a line boundary. However, continuation of
a name to another line should be avoided because it makes programs

difficult to read. Nevertheless, this feature is illustrated in Figure 2.4 for the name very_long_variable_name.

A Fortran 90 compiler must permit at least 39 continuation lines in free source form, and comment lines do not count toward this limit. This allowance is sufficiently generous so that, except for unusual situations such as a lengthy list of values to be used in initializing an array, programmers almost never need to be concerned about exceeding it.

Note that an ampersand is simply part of a comment if it follows an exclamation mark that is not part of a quoted string. This is important in situations like the following:

```
CALL clean_up (dirty_data,  &  ! Get rid of bad data.
               clean_data)
```

It would be an error here to place the ampersand indicating continuation to the right of the words "bad data"—it must be placed to the left of the exclamation mark as shown. In this connection, observe that the ampersand cannot be used to continue a comment across a line boundary. This presents no problem, however, since if commentary runs too long to be handled as a trailing comment, part of it can be placed on a comment line:

```
d = b ** 2 - 4.0 * a * c  ! Compute the
                          ! discriminant.
```

Fortran 90 permits more than one statement to be placed on a line, provided a semicolon (;) is used to separate statements. As a matter of style, only very closely related statements should ordinarily be placed on the same line. An example of this feature is given toward the end of the program in Figure 2.4.

A final point to be made about the Fortran 90 standard free source form is in regard to the significance of blanks, a topic that may be unfamiliar to many readers. The background to this topic is that blanks in positions 7 through 72 traditionally have not been syntactically significant in Fortran. Thus, the following code meets the FORTRAN 77 standard:

```
*       Warning: This code fragment not in
*                Fortran 90 free source form.
        IN TEGERVAR(100)
        DO200J=1,100
  200 V AR(J) = 0
```

This code declares a one-dimensional array named VAR to be of type INTEGER and uses a DO loop to set each element to zero. Note that the keyword INTEGER is coded with an embedded blank and later the array name VAR is coded with an embedded blank. Also, observe that there is no blank between the keyword INTEGER and the name VAR, and later there is no blank between the keyword DO and the label 200, nor is there a blank between the label 200 and the name J. The reason that many Fortran programmers are unfamiliar with the traditional syntactical insignificance of blanks is that deliberate use of this feature has been generally avoided since the early 1960's.

It must be understood that, unlike in traditional Fortran, blanks *are* syntactically significant in the Fortran 90 free source form. In free form, blanks must not appear within names or keywords. Also, each name, constant, or label must be separated from any adjacent name, constant, label, or keyword by one or more blanks or end-of-line indicators. Note that this rule does not state that an adjacent pair of statement keywords must be separated, because this is not always required. In some instances (for example, IMPLICIT NONE, DO WHILE, CASE DEFAULT), the Fortran 90 standard requires separation, while in many cases the separation is optional, as indicated by Figure 2.5. For consistency, all examples in this book will separate pairs of adjacent statement keywords with one blank.

As discussed in the preceding two paragraphs, blanks in Fortran 90 are syntactically significant in many places in free source form, but one place where they are not is within a format specification. Hence, in a statement such as

BLOCK DATA	or	BLOCKDATA
DOUBLE PRECISION	or	DOUBLEPRECISION
ELSE IF	or	ELSEIF
END BLOCK	or	ENDBLOCK
END DO	or	ENDDO
END FILE	or	ENDFILE
END FUNCTION	or	ENDFUNCTION
END IF	or	ENDIF
END INTERFACE	or	ENDINTERFACE
END MODULE	or	ENDMODULE
END PROGRAM	or	ENDPROGRAM
END SELECT	or	ENDSELECT
END SUBROUTINE	or	ENDSUBROUTINE
END TYPE	or	ENDTYPE
END WHERE	or	ENDWHERE
GO TO	or	GOTO
IN OUT	or	INOUT
SELECT CASE	or	SELECTCASE

FIGURE 2.5. Keyword pairs where separation is optional.

```
PRINT "( A 6 , I 5 )", c, n
```

none of the blanks between the parentheses is syntactically significant. Blanks within a format specification have no effect on its interpretation (except, of course, when they are within a character string inside the parentheses delimiting the format specification).

2.4 THE GENERAL FORM OF A MAIN PROGRAM

As every Fortran programmer knows, each Fortran program has exactly one main program, and program execution always begins in that main program. The general form of a Fortran 90 main program as dictated by the new standard is given in Figure 2.6. The form of the Fortran 90 main program is essentially the same as that of the FORTRAN 77 main program, except that a Fortran 90 main program may contain one or more internal subprograms.

Note in Figure 2.6 that a main program is not required by the standard to start with any particular variety of statement, but it is good style to place a PROGRAM statement at the top of a main program. Also, observe that the END statement is the only statement whose presence is mandatory in a main program. Furthermore, the optional statement keyword PROGRAM may appear in the Fortran 90 END statement to indicate that it marks the end of a main program, as opposed to, say, the end of a subroutine subprogram or the end of a function subprogram. In addition, if the keyword PROGRAM is specified in the END statement, the *program-name* may also be specified in the END statement. The *program-name* may appear in the END statement only if the optional PROGRAM statement is present, and the name in the END statement must be identical to the name in the PROGRAM statement.

The details of the order of Fortran 90 statements are given in Appendix B, but most of the statements fall into one of two broad cate-

```
[PROGRAM program-name]
    [specification-part]
    [execution-part]
[CONTAINS
    internal-subprogram(s)]
END [PROGRAM [program-name]]
```

FIGURE 2.6. The general form of a main program.

gories indicated in Figure 2.6: the *specification-part* or the *execution-part*. The *specification-part* consists of statements, such as IMPLICIT statements and type declarations, that describe the data environment. The *execution-part* consists of statements, such as assignment statements, READ statements, and IF statements, that describe the actions to be performed when the program is executed.

The only important difference in the description of the form of a main program in the Fortran 90 standard and that of the FORTRAN 77 standard is that a Fortran 90 main program may contain one or more internal subprograms. As shown in Figure 2.6, if any internal subprograms are present, the new standard requires that the CONTAINS statement must precede them. Each Fortran 90 internal subprogram looks basically the same as a classic Fortran subroutine subprogram or function subprogram. However, the details of internal subprograms will not be discussed until Chapter 8. The only facts that need to be understood about internal subprograms at this point in the tutorial are that they exist and that they may be contained within a main program.

Figure 2.7 presents an example that illustrates all of the constituent parts that can go into making up a Fortran 90 main program. The program reads in a sequence of positive numerical values input by the user, one value per line. The DO loop is exited when the user enters a number less than or equal to 0.0. The main program constitutes a complete Fortran 90 program that computes the average of the sequence of input values. For example, suppose the user enters the following:

```
1.0
3.0
2.0
4.0
0.0
```

Then the program of Figure 2.7 displays

```
2.500
```

The CONTAINS statement in Figure 2.7 indicates that one or more internal subprograms follow. In this example, the main program contains two internal subprograms, an internal subroutine named accumulate_sum and an internal function named find_avg. Observe that, except for the fact that they are contained within the main program, the internal subprograms look basically the same as traditional Fortran subprograms. Note in Figure 2.7 that the form of the END statement for a subroutine or a function in Fortran 90 is analogous to that of the END statement for a main program as discussed above. There is much more to be said about internal subprograms, and the topic will be discussed at some length in Chapter 8. The principal reason for previewing internal

```
PROGRAM demo_form_of_main_program        ! program-stmt

   IMPLICIT NONE                         ! specification-part
   REAL       sum                        ! specification-part
   INTEGER    count                      ! specification-part
   REAL       x                          ! specification-part
   REAL       average                    ! specification-part

   count = 0                             ! execution-part
   sum = 0.0                             ! execution-part
   DO                                    ! execution-part
      READ *, x                          ! execution-part
      IF (x <= 0.0) EXIT                 ! execution-part
      CALL accumulate_sum                ! execution-part
   END DO                                ! execution-part
   average = find_avg (sum, count)       ! execution-part
   PRINT "(F12.3)", average              ! execution-part

CONTAINS                                 ! contains-stmt

   SUBROUTINE accumulate_sum             ! internal-subprogs
      sum = sum + x                      ! internal-subprogs
      count = count + 1                  ! internal-subprogs
   END SUBROUTINE accumulate_sum         ! internal-subprogs
   FUNCTION find_avg (total, n)          ! internal-subprogs
      REAL       find_avg                ! internal-subprogs
      REAL       total                   ! internal-subprogs
      INTEGER  n                         ! internal-subprogs
      find_avg = total / n               ! internal-subprogs
   END FUNCTION find_avg                 ! internal-subprogs

END PROGRAM demo_form_of_main_program    ! end-program-stmt
```

FIGURE 2.7.   Program illustrating form of a Fortran 90 main program.

subprograms at this early stage of the tutorial is to establish the form of the Fortran 90 main program in full generality.

2.5   SIMPLE TYPE DECLARATIONS FOR INTRINSIC TYPES

Although the Fortran 90 version of the type declaration statement is quite a bit more complex than that of FORTRAN 77, it is nevertheless straightforward. A Fortran 90 type declaration is never tricky or fancy like some type declarations seen in C. However, a complete description of the syntax of the Fortran 90 type declaration statement is fairly lengthy. This section is the first of several in this tutorial discussing this topic. For now, only type declarations for intrinsic types are considered. Type declarations involving derived types will be presented in Chapter 5.

A variety of elementary Fortran 90 type declaration statements are illustrated by the program made up of the main program of Figure 2.8a and the external function subprogram of Figure 2.8b. The main program and the external function are given in separate figures to emphasize that they will be independently compiled. Each type declaration begins with the statement keyword(s) designating one of the six data types in the FORTRAN 77 standard: INTEGER, REAL, DOUBLE PRECISION, COMPLEX, LOGICAL, or CHARACTER. These data types, minus DOUBLE PRECISION, are referred to collectively in the Fortran 90 standard as the "intrinsic types." When DOUBLE PRECISION appears in a type declaration in the role of the type specifier, the new standard regards it not as a data type, but as a synonym for a kind of data type REAL. The Fortran 90 standard places every data type in one of two broad categories: An "intrinsic type" denotes a data type that is built into the language, while a "derived type" is a programmer-defined data type that is derived from the intrinsic types.

Observe in Figures 2.8a and 2.8b that each type declaration contains a double colon (::). Actually, it is permissible to omit the double colon in all of the type declarations in Figures 2.8a and 2.8b, but the following sections of the tutorial will illustrate type declarations where the presence of the double colon is mandatory. For purposes of consistency and readability, a double colon will appear in every type declaration statement for the remainder of the tutorial.

Now focus attention on the declarations of the CHARACTER variables in Figure 2.8a. Note that the statements

```
CHARACTER*3 :: p
CHARACTER   :: q*3
```

would conform to the FORTRAN 77 standard if the optional double colons were omitted. Similarly, consider the following variants of the above two type declarations:

```
CHARACTER*(3) :: p
CHARACTER     :: q*(3)
```

These are also legal Fortran 90 type declarations that would be valid in standard FORTRAN 77 if the optional double colons were absent. All four of these FORTRAN 77-like ways of declaring a CHARACTER variable are supported in Fortran 90 for backward compatibility.

```
PROGRAM type_decls_for_intrinsic_types

  ! Type declarations for variables:

    INTEGER          :: int_var
    REAL             :: real_var
    DOUBLE PRECISION :: dble_var    ! not a type, but
                                    ! a kind of REAL

    COMPLEX          :: cmplx_var
    LOGICAL          :: log_var

    CHARACTER*3      :: p           ! based on FORTRAN 77 style
    CHARACTER        :: q*3         ! based on FORTRAN 77 style
    CHARACTER(LEN=3) :: r           ! verbose Fortran 90 style
    CHARACTER(3)     :: s           ! terse Fortran 90 style
    CHARACTER        :: one_char    ! length defaults to 1

  ! Type declaration for named constant:

    REAL    :: Pi                   ! can be expressed in
    PARAMETER (Pi = 3.1416)         ! only one statement

  ! Type declaration for external function:

    INTEGER :: double_int    ! not needed if interface body


    int_var   = 1;           PRINT "(I6)",     int_var
    real_var  = 2.0;         PRINT "(F6.1)",   real_var
    dble_var  = 3D0;         PRINT "(F6.1)",   dble_var
    cmplx_var = (4.0, 5.0);  PRINT "(2F6.1)",  cmplx_var
    log_var   = .TRUE.;      PRINT "(5X, L1)", log_var

    p = "ABC"; q = "DEF"; r = "GHI"; s = "JKL"; one_char = "M"
    PRINT "(1X, A)", p // q // r // s // one_char

    PRINT "(F9.4)", Pi

    PRINT "(I6)", double_int (8)    ! Invoke external function.

END PROGRAM type_decls_for_intrinsic_types
```

FIGURE 2.8A. Program illustrating some simple type declarations.

```
                ! Double a value of type INTEGER.

        FUNCTION double_int (int_in)

            INTEGER :: double_int        ! result variable
            INTEGER :: int_in            ! dummy argument


            double_int = 2 * int_in

        END FUNCTION double_int
```

FIGURE 2.8B.   Function invoked by main program of Figure 2.8a.

In addition to supporting forms of type declarations for data type CHARACTER that are similar to those supported by the FORTRAN 77 standard, the Fortran 90 standard introduces the form

```
CHARACTER(LEN=3) :: r
```

to declare a CHARACTER variable named r to be of length 3. This form is more consistent with those of other Fortran 90 type declarations and better reflects the Fortran 90 mind-set. The LEN= specifier is optional here, and so this type declaration can be written more succinctly as

```
CHARACTER(3) :: r
```

Thus, it turns out that the Fortran 90 standard supports more than half a dozen variant ways to declare a CHARACTER variable. For consistency and brevity, length specifications in CHARACTER type declarations in this tutorial will follow the form of the variable s in Figure 2.8a:

```
CHARACTER(3) :: s
```

Incidentally, if the length is not specified in a CHARACTER type declaration as illustrated for one_char in Figure 2.8a, the length defaults to 1 in Fortran 90, as it does in FORTRAN 77.

Although type declaration statements are used predominantly for variables, it is important to recognize that type declarations can also be used for named constants and functions. To reinforce this, the named constant Pi and the function name double_int appear in type declarations in Figure 2.8a. As will be illustrated in Section 2.7, Fortran 90 provides a way to include the information in the PARAMETER statement in the type declaration for Pi. Also, the type declaration statement for the external function double_int would be unnecessary if, as recommended in Chapter 13, an interface body were supplied instead. However, as things stand in Figure 2.8a, the type declaration for double_int is essential to avoid having the type default to REAL since the name does not begin with one of the letters i through n. The treatment here of the function is the same as would usually be given in FORTRAN 77.

When the program consisting of the main program of Figure 2.8a and the external function subprogram of Figure 2.8b is executed, the following is displayed:

```
   1
 2.0
 3.0
 4.0    5.0
   T
ABCDEFGHIJKLM
 3.1416
  16
```

2.6 SPECIFYING INITIAL VALUES IN A TYPE DECLARATION

Although the FORTRAN 77 standard does not permit a name to be given an initial value in a type declaration, many FORTRAN 77 implementations provide an extension to the standard that permits the effect of a DATA statement to be combined with a type declaration. For example,

```
REAL factor / 1.0 /  ! not standard
```

Even though many Fortran 90 compilers will support this feature for backward compatibility, it remains nonstandard in Fortran 90. As will be shown, this extension offers no significant advantage over the new standard Fortran 90 syntax, and so to promote portability it is recommended that use of this extension be abandoned.

In the new Fortran 90 syntax, a variable name may be given a value in a type declaration by using the equal sign (=). For example,

```
REAL :: factor = 1.0  ! standard in Fortran 90
```

The double colon (::) is required when a name is given an initial value in this manner. Here, factor is a variable of type REAL which is given an initial value of 1.0. Except for the special case of binary, octal, and hexadecimal constants, which is discussed in Appendix E, the new Fortran 90 mechanism for initializing variables makes use of the DATA statement unnecessary.

Figure 2.9 shows a program illustrating the standard Fortran 90 syntax for setting initial values in type declaration statements. The program reads a sequence of numerical values input by the user. When end of file

```
PROGRAM demo_initialization

    INTEGER :: count = 0                  ! count of input vals
    INTEGER :: ios                        ! I/O status

    REAL :: sum = 0.0                     ! sum of input vals
    REAL :: val_read                      ! input val just read
    REAL :: smallest_val = HUGE (0.0)     ! smallest input val
                                          ! so far

    CHARACTER(7) :: out_fmt = "(F12.3)" ! format for display


    DO
        READ (*, *, IOSTAT = ios) val_read
        ! /= is a synonym for .NE. (not equal)
        IF (ios /= 0) EXIT                ! Exit on EOF or err.
        count = count + 1                 ! Count input values.
        sum = sum + val_read              ! Sum input values.
        IF (val_read < smallest_val)  &   ! if smallest so far,
            smallest_val = val_read       !     then save value
    END DO

    IF (ios < 0) THEN
        ! end of file detected
        PRINT out_fmt, sum / count    ! Print avg of input vals.
        PRINT out_fmt, smallest_val   ! Print smallest val input.
    ELSE
        ! error detected on read
        PRINT *, "Error on read."
    END IF

END PROGRAM demo_initialization
```

FIGURE 2.9. Program illustrating initialization in type declarations.

is detected, the average of the input values and the smallest input value are displayed. Suppose, for example, that the user enters the following values:

2.0
4.0
1.0
3.0

Then the program displays

```
2.500
1.000
```

Under either the Fortran 90 standard or the FORTRAN 77 standard, the value of a variable is undefined unless that variable is explicitly given a value. Thus, in Figure 2.9, the variables count, sum, and smallest_val must be given values before the DO loop is entered. This is accomplished by initializing their values at compile time in type declarations. Also, the CHARACTER variable out_fmt must be given a value before the first PRINT statement is executed, and it is also initialized in its type declaration statement. Actually, the value of out_fmt is never changed, and so it would be better style to make it a constant, rather than to treat it as a variable as is done in Figure 2.9.

Note the reference to HUGE in the type declaration of smallest_val in Figure 2.9. HUGE is the new standard intrinsic function that returns a very large value that at least approximates the implementation's largest value having the same data type as its argument. Since that argument is the constant 0.0, which is of type REAL, the result returned by HUGE (0.0) is roughly the largest value of type REAL that the implementation on which the program is being compiled can represent. This type declaration illustrates that it is possible for intrinsic functions to be invoked in initialization expressions. Of course, such usage is limited to quantities that can be determined at compile time. The Fortran 90 standard places some restrictions on the intrinsic functions that can appear in initialization expressions, and these will be described in detail in Section 2.9.

2.7 ATTRIBUTE LIST IN A TYPE DECLARATION

In addition to data type and possibly initial value, the Fortran 90 standard permits certain other special properties to be specified in a type declaration statement. Consider, for example, the following type declaration:

```
REAL, DIMENSION(100), SAVE :: local_array
```

This declares local_array to be of type REAL and specifies two special properties of local_array: DIMENSION(100) and SAVE.

The Fortran 90 standard supports only 12 special properties that can be specified between the data type and the double colon in a type declaration statement, and these are summarized in Figure 2.10. In this tutorial, the term **attribute** will refer to 1 of the 12 keywords given in all uppercase letters in the left column of Figure 2.10. Even though 5 of

Attribute	Keyword in FORTRAN 77 Standard?	Usage
ALLOCATABLE	No	Indicates that array subscript bounds will not be determined until execution time.
DIMENSION(*array-spec*)	Yes	Indicates subscript bounds along each array dimension or that subscript bounds are to be determined at execution time.
EXTERNAL	Yes	Indicates that a function is defined by either: (1) a Fortran function subprogram that is not contained in a main program, another subprogram, or a module; or (2) a means other than Fortran.
INTENT(*intent-spec*)	No	Indicates whether dummy argument is input, output, or both.
INTRINSIC	Yes	Indicates that a function or subroutine is built into the implementation.
OPTIONAL	No	Indicates for a dummy argument that its associated actual argument may be omitted.
PARAMETER	Yes	Indicates that name takes on a constant value at compile time which cannot be changed at execution time.
POINTER	No	Indicates that a variable is not thought of as containing data, but rather as pointing to an area of storage holding the data of interest.
PRIVATE	No	Indicates that name inside a module is not accessible outside the module.
PUBLIC	No	Indicates that name inside a module is accessible outside the module.
SAVE	Yes	Specifies that a variable must retain all its properties, including its value, after exit from a subprogram.
TARGET	No	Indicates that name refers to an area in storage that may be pointed to by a variable with the POINTER attribute.

FIGURE 2.10. Complete list of standard Fortran 90 attributes.

the 12 keywords are carried over from the FORTRAN 77 standard, most of the attributes in Figure 2.10 are probably unfamiliar to a majority of Fortran programmers. However, this is unimportant at this point in the tutorial—the focus here is on developing an understanding of the syntax of the type declaration statement.

The program made up of the main program of Figure 2.11a and the external function subprogram of Figure 2.11b illustrates the use of five of the attributes listed in Figure 2.10: PARAMETER, DIMENSION, EXTERNAL, INTENT, and INTRINSIC. Discussion of the remaining attributes will be deferred until later in the tutorial. The ALLOCATABLE attribute

```
PROGRAM demo_attributes

    INTEGER, PARAMETER :: Max_vals = 100    ! named constant

    REAL, DIMENSION(Max_vals) :: vals    ! one-dimensional array
                                         ! with subscripts
                                         ! 1 through Max_vals


    REAL, EXTERNAL :: mean     ! external function


    REAL    :: val_read
    INTEGER :: count = 0
    INTEGER :: ios


    DO
        READ (*, *, IOSTAT = ios) val_read      ! Read a numer-
                                                ! ical value.
        ! /= is a synonym for .NE. (not equal)
        IF (ios /= 0) EXIT              ! Exit on EOF or error.
        IF (count <= Max_vals) THEN
            count = count + 1           ! Count values read.
            vals(count) = val_read      ! Store values in array.
        ELSE
            PRINT *, "Error: Too many input values."
            STOP
        END IF
    END DO

    IF (ios < 0) THEN
        PRINT "(/A, F12.3)", " Average =",  &
                        mean (count, vals)    ! Invoke external
                                              ! function mean.
    ELSE
        PRINT "(/A)", " Error on read."
    END IF

END PROGRAM demo_attributes
```

FIGURE 2.11A. Main program illustrating the use of attributes.

will be treated in Section 4.10. The SAVE attribute will be discussed in Sections 6.6 and 7.7. Chapter 10 describes the POINTER and TARGET attributes, while the PRIVATE and PUBLIC attributes will be treated in Chapter 12. Finally, the OPTIONAL attribute will be discussed in Section 13.10.

Consider the first type declaration in Figure 2.11a:

```
INTEGER, PARAMETER :: Max_vals = 100
```

This declares Max_vals to be of type INTEGER, specifies the PARAMETER attribute for Max_vals, and gives it a value of 100. The same effect as the single type declaration statement given above can be achieved with the following two statements:

```
INTEGER    Max_vals
PARAMETER (Max_vals = 100)
```

However, the readability is better when all of the information about Max_vals is combined in a single statement. In either case, Max_vals is set to 100 at compile time and cannot be changed at execution time. An entity such as Max_vals whose name is declared in a type declaration statement with the PARAMETER attribute specified or whose name appears in a PARAMETER statement is called a **named constant**.

```
FUNCTION mean (n, x)

   REAL                                :: mean  ! result variable

   INTEGER,            INTENT (IN) :: n      ! input dummy arg

   REAL, DIMENSION(n), INTENT (IN) :: x      ! input dummy arg
                                             ! that is one-dim
                                             ! array with
                                             ! subscripts
                                             ! 1 through n


   ! Standard permits typing intrinsic function, but not
   ! recommended by author.  Following may produce warning.
   REAL, INTRINSIC :: SUM   ! SUM is new intrinsic function.


   mean = SUM (x) / n    ! Compute average of n elements of x.

END FUNCTION mean
```

FIGURE 2.11B. Function invoked by main program of Figure 2.11a.

Now look at the second type declaration in Figure 2.11a:

```
REAL, DIMENSION(Max_vals) :: vals
```

This declares vals to be of type REAL and specifies the DIMENSION attribute for vals. The specification DIMENSION(Max_vals) means, of course, that vals is a one-dimensional array with subscripts ranging from 1 through Max_vals. Alternatively, the type declaration statement

```
REAL vals(Max_vals)
```

achieves the same effect. Another acceptable alternative is the following pair of statements:

```
REAL vals
DIMENSION(Max_vals) vals
```

Thus, the Fortran 90 standard supports at least three different ways to specify the subscript bounds for each dimension of an array. In this tutorial, the DIMENSION attribute in a type declaration statement will always be used for specifying arrays since it is the most readable of the available alternatives.

Examine the third type declaration in Figure 2.11a:

```
REAL, EXTERNAL :: mean
```

This declares mean to be of type REAL, and the EXTERNAL attribute identifies mean as a function that is defined by either: (1) a Fortran function subprogram that is not contained in a main program, another subprogram, or a module; or (2) by a language or mechanism other than Fortran (for example, assembly language, C, etc.). Here, mean is the external function subprogram given in Figure 2.11b. Actually, unless the implementation on which the program is being run happens to have an intrinsic function named mean, which would be nonstandard, the EXTERNAL attribute can ordinarily be omitted in the preceding type declaration. However, the information that the name mean is of type REAL must be specified since otherwise a default of type INTEGER will be assumed based on the fact that the initial letter is in the range i through n.

In Figure 2.11b, the attribute INTENT (IN) is specified for both dummy arguments n and x, indicating that they are expected to hold values at entry to mean and that those values must not be changed inside the subprogram. In fact, the INTENT attribute could be omitted both places and the function would still work. However, specification of the attribute improves readability and permits compilers to make more cross-checks.

The DIMENSION(n) attribute specified for dummy argument x in Figure 2.11b indicates that x is a one-dimensional array with bounds 1 through n, where n is also a dummy argument. An alternative declaration for x that would achieve the same effect as that given in Figure 2.11b is

```
REAL, INTENT (IN) :: x(n)
```

If the INTENT attribute and the double colon are omitted, it can be seen that the array x is an example of what has been called the "adjustable array" in FORTRAN 77. However, this terminology is not present in the Fortran 90 standard, and the characterization of this variety of array in the new standard will be deferred until Section 6.3.

Finally, in Figure 2.11b, the INTRINSIC attribute is specified for the new standard intrinsic function SUM, which can be used to find the sum of the elements in an array. It seems quirky to specify a data type for an intrinsic function, and the author recommends against it. However, this is permitted by the Fortran 90 standard, although some compilers may issue a warning. On the other hand, it often makes sense to use the INTRINSIC statement, a carryover from FORTRAN 77, to confirm that a name is that of an intrinsic procedure. For example,

```
INTRINSIC SUM
```

The main program of Figure 2.11a gets a sequence of values from the user and stores them in the array vals. Each time a new value is read, the variable count is incremented by 1. The DO loop is exited when either end of file is detected or a read error occurs. If the DO loop is exited because of the detection of end of file, the main program invokes the external function mean, whose listing is given in Figure 2.11b, to compute the average of the values stored in vals. Suppose, for example, that when the program is executed, the user enters

```
3.0
1.0
4.0
2.0
```

Then the following is displayed:

```
Average =    2.500
```

2.8 THE FORTRAN 90 CONCEPT OF KIND

According to the FORTRAN 77 standard, there are exactly six data types: INTEGER, REAL, DOUBLE PRECISION, COMPLEX, LOGICAL, and CHARACTER. But a typical FORTRAN 77 implementation supports type declarations that begin with something like INTEGER*2, REAL*16, and so on, and the accompanying vendor-supplied reference documentation often refers to each of these as a "data type" as well. The number following the asterisk (*) in such type declarations typically indicates the number of eight-bit bytes of storage to be occupied by a value of the "data type." For example, INTEGER*2 signifies a representation of integer values that occupies two bytes, while INTEGER*4 indicates a representation of integer values that occupies four bytes. In most implementations, simply specifying INTEGER results in four bytes of storage being consumed, in which case INTEGER and INTEGER*4 are synonymous.

FORTRAN 77 implementations introduced these variant "data types" as extensions to the standard because programmers have found it to be useful to have storage-conserving short integers and packed logicals and high-precision representation of real and complex values. For example, a type INTEGER variable typically consumes 4 bytes of storage and can take on values with a magnitude as large as approximately 2 billion, while an INTEGER*2 variable consumes only 2 bytes of storage, but can still take on values with a magnitude somewhat greater than 32 thousand. Thus, for arrays having many elements of integer values of moderate magnitude, INTEGER*2 offers considerable savings in storage over INTEGER. On the other side of the coin, a REAL*16 "data type" typically provides at least four times the precision of the default REAL data type, but the additional precision comes at the expense of consuming four times the amount of storage (and usually, slower execution as well).

It might be naively thought that the Fortran 90 standard should have somehow standardized the concept of variant "data types" as it has typically been implemented in FORTRAN 77-based compilers, but portability cannot be achieved using this approach because of hardware differences among the various computers on which Fortran programs must be executed. Hence, the framers of the Fortran 90 standard chose a different approach, known as **parameterized data types**, to address the issues raised by the desirability of short integers, high-precision reals, and so forth. As a result, type declarations such as INTEGER*2 and REAL*8 are not supported by the Fortran 90 standard, although vendors whose FORTRAN 77 implementations supported such declarations will generally continue to support them in their Fortran 90 implementations for reasons of backward compatibility.

The Fortran 90 standard divides data types into two broad classes: intrinsic types, which are built into the language, and derived types, which are defined by programmers based on the intrinsic types. The new standard takes the position that there are exactly five intrinsic types: INTEGER, REAL, COMPLEX, LOGICAL, and CHARACTER. Thus, the Fortran 90 intrinsic types are the same as five of the six FORTRAN 77 data types. The sixth FORTRAN 77 data type, DOUBLE PRECISION, is not considered to be a data type in Fortran 90 and instead is characterized as a variety of the intrinsic type REAL. In effect, many FORTRAN 77 implementations accept this characterization anyway, as evidenced by their permitting REAL*8 as a synonym for DOUBLE PRECISION.

The striking new feature in the Fortran 90 standard regarding data types is the recognition that an implementation may provide more than one internal representation for any of the five intrinsic types. This encompasses the old idea that an implementation running on a computer with 32-bit word length might offer one internal representation of integer values occupying 32 bits (4 bytes) and another internal representation of integer values occupying 16 bits (2 bytes). In Fortran 90 terminology, each different internal representation of a data type is known as a **kind** of that type. Hence, while FORTRAN 77 implementations often characterize INTEGER*2 and INTEGER*4 as two different data types, the Fortran 90 standard considers these as corresponding to two kinds of type INTEGER. However, it should be recognized that, unlike the byte-length scheme, the Fortran 90 concept of kind does not depend on the amount of storage required to represent a value. If, for example, a Fortran 90 implementation supports two different internal representations of real values, where each of the representations requires four bytes to represent a value, each representation would be considered a kind of REAL.

Even though the Fortran 90 standard permits an implementation to support more than one kind of any of the five intrinsic types, it does not require support for more than one kind of INTEGER, LOGICAL, or CHARACTER. The new standard does, however, require support for at least two kinds of REAL, one providing a default precision and the other providing precision greater than the default. In practice, one kind of REAL in most Fortran 90 implementations can be expected to provide a precision that is approximately twice that of the default, and this kind of REAL will play the same role as is played by the DOUBLE PRECISION data type in FORTRAN 77. Also, the keywords DOUBLE PRECISION remain available for use in a Fortran 90 type declaration as a synonym for one of the kinds of REAL providing greater than default precision in representing real values. (For convenience, the phrase "double precision kind of REAL" will be used elsewhere in the book to refer to the kind of REAL employed by an implementation when the programmer declares a variable to be of type DOUBLE PRECISION.) In addition, the new standard requires support for at least two kinds of COMPLEX, where each of the real and imaginary parts of a complex value is of the default REAL kind for one kind of COMPLEX and of the greater precision REAL kind for the other.

In a given Fortran 90 implementation, each kind of each intrinsic type is identified by a nonnegative integer value known as a **kind type**

parameter. The programmer may then employ the new KIND= specifier in a type statement to indicate which kind of a data type is to be used. For example,

```
INTEGER(KIND=2) :: short_int_var
```

The KIND= specifier is optional in the above type declaration statement, and so it can be coded more succinctly as

```
INTEGER(2) :: short_int_var
```

Either version of this type declaration statement indicates that the variable short_int_var is of data type INTEGER with kind type parameter 2. The choice of variable name here suggests that the programmer expects that for this implementation kind 2 of type INTEGER is some sort of short integer. But it is important to understand that the values that can be taken on by the kind type parameters and the precise meaning of each of the values are implementation-dependent. Thus, in many implementations, INTEGER(2) is a synonym for INTEGER*2, but this is not guaranteed by the Fortran 90 standard.

Another example of a type declaration specifying a kind type parameter is the following:

```
REAL(KIND=2) :: dble_prec_var
```

Again, the KIND= specifier is optional. Thus, the preceding type declaration could alternatively be coded as follows:

```
REAL(2) :: dble_prec_var
```

Again, the choice of variable name implies that the programmer expects kind 2 of type REAL to be the double precision kind of REAL. In practice, this is sometimes the case, but it is not required by the standard. However, the new standard does provide an intrinsic function KIND, which returns the value of the kind type parameter of its argument. Then, since 0D0 is a way (carried over from FORTRAN 77) of expressing the double-precision constant zero, KIND (0D0) is always the implementation's kind type parameter for the kind of REAL corresponding to DOUBLE PRECISION. Hence, the type declaration

```
REAL(KIND (0D0)) :: x
```

is guaranteed by the standard to be equivalent to the following:

```
DOUBLE PRECISION :: x
```

Incidentally, in the previous type declaration, as well as in all the other type declarations in this section, the double colon is optional.

The foregoing discussion might leave the impression that the parameterized data types introduce only a change in syntax: INTEGER*2 changes to INTEGER(2), REAL*8 changes to REAL(2), and so on. However, the main significance of the Fortran 90 concept of kind is that it provides the basis for improving portability. As will be illustrated ahead, an important aspect of the parameterization of data types is that new intrinsic functions are provided to aid in dealing with the problem of achieving portable control over numeric precision specification.

The program of Figure 2.12 illustrates some of the ideas related to the concept of kind. Note that the named constant Short is defined by the type declaration

```
INTEGER, PARAMETER :: Short = SELECTED_INT_KIND (4)
```

SELECTED_INT_KIND is a new intrinsic function that returns a value of a kind of type INTEGER for the implementation on which the program is being compiled. In this example, its argument is 4, and so SELECTED_INT_KIND will return the value of the kind of type INTEGER representing integers in the range between -10^4 and $+10^4$, that is, from $-9,999$

```
PROGRAM demo_kind

   INTRINSIC SELECTED_INT_KIND, SELECTED_REAL_KIND

   INTEGER, PARAMETER :: Short = SELECTED_INT_KIND (4)
   INTEGER, PARAMETER :: High  = SELECTED_REAL_KIND (11, 30)

   INTEGER        :: n    ! default kind of INTEGER
   INTEGER(Short) :: i    ! kind of INTEGER ranging between
                          ! -(10 ** 4) and +(10 ** 4)

   REAL           :: r    ! default kind of REAL
   REAL(High)     :: x    ! kind of REAL with precision of
                          ! 11 digits and ranging between
                          ! -(10.0 ** 30) and +(10.0 ** 30)


   n = 56789                    ! INTEGER const of default kind
   i = 1234_Short               ! INTEGER const of kind Short
   PRINT "(2I7)", n, i

   r = 0.1234546E+10             ! REAL const of default kind
   x = 0.12345678901E+25_High    ! REAL const of kind High
   PRINT "(2E19.11)", r, x

END PROGRAM demo_kind
```

FIGURE 2.12. Program illustrating parameterized data types.

through $+9,999$. Later in Figure 2.12, note that the variable i is declared to be an INTEGER with the kind specified by Short. Still later in Figure 2.12, examine the expression 1234_Short. This means that the literal constant 1234 is to be stored using the representation for the kind of type INTEGER indicated by the value of Short. In many implementations, Short will hold the value 2, and if this were true, the same storage result could be achieved by coding the literal constant as 1234_2. The main point to grasp here is that kind type parameters can be used with literal constants as well as with named entities.

Now look at the second type declaration in Figure 2.12:

```
INTEGER, PARAMETER :: High = SELECTED_REAL_KIND (11, 30)
```

SELECTED_REAL_KIND is a new intrinsic function that does for REAL values what SELECTED_INT_KIND does for INTEGER values. In this example, the arguments of SELECTED_REAL_KIND are 11 and 30, so it will return the value of the kind of type REAL capable of representing real numbers with a precision of at least 11 significant (decimal) digits and a range from at least -10^{30} to $+10^{30}$. Later, observe that the variable x is declared to be a REAL with the kind specified by High. Near the end of the program, a literal constant of this kind of REAL is assigned to x. By the way, the INTRINSIC statement in Figure 2.12 is not required, and it is included to improve program readability in the context of a tutorial presentation.

When the program of Figure 2.12 is executed, something like the following is displayed:

```
56789    1234
0.12345600000E+10   0.12345678901E+25
```

An interesting aspect of the Fortran 90 concept of kind is that it extends even to the CHARACTER data type. For example, the type declaration

```
CHARACTER(LEN=40, KIND=2) :: char_var
```

means that char_var is a type CHARACTER variable of length 40 characters and has kind type parameter value 2. The character set which is indicated by kind type parameter 2 is implementation-dependent. An important use for this capability is to support multibyte character data for (human) languages with large character sets, such as those in Asian languages. However, discussion of this facility lies beyond the scope of this tutorial. Of course, virtually all FORTRAN 77 implementations assume that only one internal representation of character data is to be supported, and ordinarily no provision of any sort is made within the language to support an alternate character set.

2.9 *SYNTAX OF THE TYPE DECLARATION STATEMENT*

As indicated in the last few sections, the type declaration statement not only specifies data type, but may also specify kind, attributes, and initialization expressions. The entities whose types are being declared may be variables, named constants, external functions, or possibly intrinsic functions. Also, the syntax rules for Fortran 90 type declarations are complicated by the requirement to maintain backward compatibility with FORTRAN 77. Furthermore, as will be discussed later, there are additional complexities when arrays, variables of derived types, and pointers are declared. As a result, the complete Fortran 90 rules specifying the syntax of the type declaration statement are rather intricate. But in practice, Fortran 90 type declarations are nearly always straightforward, and the slightly simplified syntax rules given in this section should be adequate for most purposes.

The syntax rules given in the Fortran 90 standard for the type specification part of a type declaration statement are shown in Figure 2.13. A kind may be specified for the intrinsic types INTEGER, REAL, COMPLEX, LOGICAL, and CHARACTER. If no kind is specified, the implementation's default representation for the data type will be used. Also, a length may be specified for the CHARACTER type, and if no length is specified, the length defaults to 1. The type specifier may be DOUBLE PRECISION, in which case no kind specification is permitted. In addition, the type specifier may be of the form TYPE (*type-name*), where *type-name* is the name of a programmer-defined derived type. No kind may be specified for a derived type.

The form of the type specification part of a type declaration statement is exactly one of the following:

    INTEGER [([KIND=] *kind-spec*)]
    REAL [([KIND=] *kind-spec*)]
    DOUBLE PRECISION
    COMPLEX [([KIND=] *kind-spec*)]
    LOGICAL [([KIND=] *kind-spec*)]
    CHARACTER [([LEN=] *length-spec*[,[([KIND=] *kind-spec*)])]
    TYPE (*type-name*)

Note: Although not shown above, any form supported by the FORTRAN 77 standard may also be used to declare entities of the default kind of type CHARACTER.

FIGURE 2.13. Syntax for type specification part of a type declaration.

The syntax rules set forth in the Fortran 90 standard governing type declaration statements defining named constants are summarized in Figure 2.14. The role of *type-spec* may be played by any of the forms appearing in Figure 2.13. Note that the PARAMETER attribute must be present and that only a maximum of two additional attributes may be specified. Observe also that the double colon is mandatory.

Each named constant being declared must be given a value by an expression indicated in Figure 2.14 by *initialization-expr*. Of course, an initialization expression may be nothing more than a literal constant, but Fortran 90 allows the use of operators in data initializations, permitting somewhat more complicated initialization expressions than have been traditionally available. For example, consider the following:

```
REAL, PARAMETER :: Pi = 3.14159
REAL, PARAMETER :: Radius = 1.0
REAL, PARAMETER :: Area = Pi * Radius ** 2
```

Look at the third statement: The named constant Area is given an initial value determined by an expression using operators, specifically the multiplication operator (*) and the exponentiation operator (**). The principal restriction on Fortran 90 initialization expressions is that no variables can be used; however, named constants (such as Pi and Radius in the preceding code) are acceptable, as are, of course, literal constants (such as 3.14159, 1.0, and 2 in the previous code). Any of the intrinsic operator symbols +, -, *, /, **, //, .AND., .OR., and so on may appear in initializations, provided that they have their intrinsic meanings (as opposed to programmer-defined meanings). However, if the exponenti-

---

> *type-spec, attribute-list* :: *named-constant-def-list*
>
> where
>
> - *type-spec* is as given by Figure 2.13
> - *attribute-list* is as follows:
>   Must contain PARAMETER
>   May contain DIMENSION(*array-spec*)
>   May contain at most one of PRIVATE or PUBLIC
> - *named-constant-def-list* has items of the form *named-constant = initialization-expr*
>
> *Disclaimer.* The Fortran 90 standard permits some variations in the specification of named constants not shown here.

FIGURE 2.14. Syntax of type declaration for named constants.

ation operator is used, the power must be an integer. Also, parentheses may be used in initialization expressions.

Another useful Fortran 90 feature is that initialization expressions may invoke standard intrinsic functions. The following summarizes the rules governing the use of intrinsic functions in initialization expressions:

1. Except for ALLOCATED, ASSOCIATED, and PRESENT, any intrinsic function listed in Appendix C as being in the inquiry category may be used.
2. The intrinsic functions REPEAT, RESHAPE, TRANSFER, TRIM, SELECTED_INT_KIND, and SELECTED_REAL_KIND may be used. Any other intrinsic function listed in Appendix C as being in the transformational category may *not* be used.
3. Any intrinsic function listed in Appendix C as being in the elemental category may be used, provided that all the arguments and the result are of type integer or character.

Figure 2.15 summarizes the rules for type declaration statements for variables as given in the Fortran 90 standard. The general form of type declarations for variables is more or less the same as that for named constants as discussed earlier, except that the choice of attributes is much wider. However, as detailed in reference works, the standard places some restrictions on the combinations of attributes that can appear in the same type declaration statement, but these restrictions are not likely to cause much trouble in practice. Of course, the PARAMETER attribute never appears in a type declaration for a variable.

Note in Figure 2.15 that while an initialization expression may appear for a variable in a type declaration statement, this is not required. If an initialization expression does appear, the rules governing it are the same as those for a named parameter as discussed before. But note that the presence of an initialization expression is prohibited if any of the attributes ALLOCATABLE, INTENT, OPTIONAL, or POINTER is specified. Finally, observe that the double colon is optional unless either an attribute list or an initialization expression is present.

The type specification part of a type declaration for a function is the same as that for a variable or named constant, but, of course, an initialization expression is never permitted. Also, the possibilities for the attribute list are extremely limited. Either PRIVATE or PUBLIC, but not both, may be specified as an attribute. Also, either EXTERNAL or INTRINSIC, but not both, may be in the attribute list. If INTRINSIC is not specified, then it is possible for OPTIONAL to appear under the highly unusual circumstance that the name being declared is that of a dummy procedure (an old Fortran feature that is described in Appendix G) whose associated actual argument may be omitted.

type-spec[, *attribute-list* ::] *var-name-list*

where

■   *type-spec* is as given by Figure 2.13
■   *attribute-list* is drawn from the following:
    ALLOCATABLE
    DIMENSION(*array-spec*)
    INTENT(*intent-spec*)
    OPTIONAL
    POINTER
    PRIVATE
    PUBLIC
    SAVE
    TARGET

Warning: Some combinations of attributes are invalid. Consult appropriate reference works.

■   *var-name-list* has items of the form
    var-name [= *initialization-expr*]

Notes:
(1)   Double colon required if any *initialization-expr* present.
(2)   If ALLOCATABLE, INTENT, OPTIONAL, or POINTER appears in *attribute-list*, *initialization-expr* must not be present.

Disclaimer: The Fortran 90 standard permits some variations in the specification of variables not shown here.

FIGURE 2.15.   Syntax of type declaration statement for variables.

2.10 ATTRIBUTE SPECIFICATION STATEMENTS

Among the specification statements supported by the FORTRAN 77 standard are a DIMENSION statement, an EXTERNAL statement, an INTRINSIC statement, a PARAMETER statement, and a SAVE statement. Observe that the 5 keywords for these statements are among the 12 keywords listed in Figure 2.10 that may appear in the attribute list of a type declaration statement. The five FORTRAN 77 statements mentioned earlier are, of course, carried over to Fortran 90, and in addition, the new standard contains provisions that make each of the remaining seven keywords in Figure 2.10 the initial word of a specification statement. For example,

```
INTEGER      :: n
REAL         :: x
INTENT (IN) :: n, x
```

The above three statements have the same effect as the following:

```
INTEGER, INTENT (IN) :: n
REAL,    INTENT (IN) :: x
```

Thus, the INTENT attribute may be specified either in the attribute list of a type declaration statement or in an INTENT statement, but for a given name it must not be specified both ways. The general idea illustrated here for the INTENT attribute is applicable to all 12 attributes given in Figure 2.10.

As a general guideline, the readability of a collection of data specifications is best when all information about each name is given in its type declaration statement. For this reason, the author recommends that the following attributes always be specified in a type declaration statement and never in a specification statement: ALLOCATABLE, DIMENSION, INTENT, PARAMETER, POINTER, TARGET. This tutorial will not give the syntax rules for these six varieties of specification statements—the interested reader can consult appropriate reference materials.

When either of the attributes SAVE or OPTIONAL is specified for a name that can legally appear in a type declaration statement, then the attribute list mechanism is recommended over that of the specification statement. However, specification of these attributes may be needed under circumstances where type declaration statements play no role. For example, as in FORTRAN 77, SAVE may be specified for a named COMMON block, while the new OPTIONAL keyword could conceivably be specified for a subroutine. But since these attributes arise only in rather special situations, discussion of each will take us too far afield at this stage of the tutorial. For now, the general guideline will simply be reiterated: Whenever possible, prefer specifying SAVE or OPTIONAL as attributes in type declarations rather than in specification statements.

The new statement keywords PUBLIC and PRIVATE can be used by module authors to specify precisely to what module users do and do not have access. Although this tutorial will present examples of PUBLIC and PRIVATE appearing as attributes in type declaration statements, the author believes that code is usually easier to understand when accessibility is specified by means of PUBLIC and PRIVATE statements. This issue is explored in some depth in the first few sections of Chapter 12.

The EXTERNAL keyword continues to have the same meaning in Fortran 90 that it has in FORTRAN 77. As in FORTRAN 77, EXTERNAL can only be a property of some sort of subroutine or function or possibly a BLOCK DATA program unit. If EXTERNAL is explicitly specified for a function, then it is preferable in Fortran 90 to specify it as an attribute in the type declaration of the function. If EXTERNAL is explicitly specified for a subroutine or a BLOCK DATA program unit, then the EXTERNAL statement must be used. The syntax of the Fortran 90 EXTERNAL statement is unchanged from FORTRAN 77: It consists simply of the keyword EXTERNAL followed by a list of names.

As in FORTRAN 77, the INTRINSIC keyword is used in Fortran 90 to indicate that a procedure is built into the implementation. The INTRINSIC statement is always favored over specifying this attribute in a type declaration statement. Figure 2.11b in Section 2.7 uses the INTRINSIC attribute in a type declaration statement for purposes of illustration, but it is recommended that this property never be specified in this manner. In fact, some compilers will issue a warning if the programmer specifies a data type for an intrinsic procedure name. The syntax of the Fortran 90 INTRINSIC statement remains the same as in FORTRAN 77: It is comprised of the keyword INTRINSIC followed by a list of names of intrinsic procedures.

CHAPTER 3

CONTROL CONSTRUCTS

3.1 *OVERVIEW OF FORTRAN CONTROL STRUCTURES*

By the 1970s there was widespread agreement among software professionals that code that relies on GO TO statements is generally harder to understand and maintain than code without GO TOs. But all of the popular Fortran implementations of the day required heavy use of GO TO statements since they lacked even such basic control structures as IF–THEN . . . END IF and WHILE. To overcome this weakness, a number of organizations independently developed computer programs known as "structured programming precompilers" (or "preprocessors"). The programmer then interspersed statements such as IF–THEN, CASE, WHILE, and REPEAT UNTIL with traditional Fortran code, and the precompilers translated the mixture into ordinary Fortran. The resulting translation was then compiled in the usual way. However, these precompilers were incompatible with one another, and when the FORTRAN 77 implementations became available in the 1980s, the structured programming precompilers faded away. Nevertheless, the precompilers have had a lasting influence on the thinking of those who used them and on the design of subsequent versions of the language, including Fortran 90.

The IF–THEN . . . END IF control structure is supported by the FORTRAN 77 standard, but the DO WHILE . . . END DO is not, although the latter has been a widely available extension in FORTRAN 77 implementations since about 1981. But in the 1980s, few FORTRAN 77 implementations supported a CASE control structure and, more importantly, most still required the use of a GO TO statement to break out of the middle of a DO loop. Thus, most of the popular Fortran implementations available in the 1980s did not provide all of the control structures that are generally thought to be needed to promote good programming practices.

The Fortran 90 standard features a set of statements for controlling the flow of execution which compares favorably with those of other popular languages. In particular, it is not difficult to write long, complicated

programs in standard Fortran 90 without ever using any form of a GO
TO statement. In order to make this possible, Fortran 90 needed to introduce only one statement not traditionally available in the popular
FORTRAN 77 implementations: The Fortran 90 EXIT statement, which
is somewhat similar to the Ada exit statement and the C break statement,
causes an immediate exit from a DO loop. In addition to the EXIT statement, Fortran 90 provides the related CYCLE statement, which transfers
control to the end of a DO loop, thus permitting the next iteration to
be initiated immediately. Furthermore, Fortran 90 generalizes the DO
statement in a manner similar to that of the loop statement in Ada:
In addition to the FORTRAN 77 indexed form of the DO statement,
Fortran 90 makes standard the DO WHILE and also supports the simple DO—a form sometimes called the "DO forever"—which consists of
the single word "DO." An EXIT statement is typically employed to break
out of a loop begun by a simple DO statement. Finally, Fortran 90 also
provides a CASE control structure. Incidentally, the Fortran 90 standard
does not directly support a control structure like Pascal's REPEAT UNTIL,
although, of course, the idea can be implemented using the simple DO
and the EXIT.

The FORTRAN 77 standard requires that a DO statement specify the
label (statement number) that terminates the loop. The terminating
statement can then be any of a variety of FORTRAN 77 statements
carrying that label, although many careful programmers followed the
practice of terminating each DO loop with a CONTINUE statement. However, most of the popular FORTRAN 77 implementations supported the
END DO statement as a means of indicating the end of a DO loop, usually
dropping the requirement for the label. The unlabeled END DO is standard in Fortran 90, and for purposes of readability and consistency, it
is recommended that only the unlabeled END DO be used to indicate the
end of any form of the DO loop.

For some purposes, it is convenient to treat as a unit a contiguous
group of Fortran 90 statements starting with a control statement (such
as DO or IF) and extending through the statement terminating the group
(such as END DO or END IF). The Fortran 90 standard calls such a group
of statements a **construct**. In addition to a DO construct and an IF
construct, Fortran 90 supports a CASE construct, which begins with a
SELECT CASE statement and terminates with an END SELECT statement.
(There is also a WHERE construct, which will be discussed in the next
chapter.)

A nice feature in Fortran 90, which was not supported by any popular language during the 1980s, is the **construct name**. Any DO, IF,
or CASE construct may be given a name by the programmer. Giving
names to constructs permits more compiler cross-checks and can improve readability, especially when constructs are nested and/or extend
over many lines of code. Moreover, a construct name provides a means

of exiting more than one level of nested DO loops without using a GO TO statement.

3.2 LOGICAL EXPRESSIONS

A typical standard FORTRAN 77 logical expression is something like

```
(X .LT. 1.0) .AND. (M .EQ. N)
```

This expression evaluates to true if the value of X is less than 1.0 *and* the value of M is equal to the value of N; otherwise, it evaluates to false. The symbols .LT. and .EQ. are examples of **relational operators**. For improved readability, the Fortran 90 standard supports the use of special symbols as relational operators, as shown in Table 3.1. Thus, the preceding logical expression can be coded in standard Fortran 90 as

```
(X < 1.0) .AND. (M == N)
```

Incidentally, the parentheses are not required here since any relational operator has precedence over any logical operator, such as .AND., and the precedence of operators is basically the same in Fortran 90 as it is in FORTRAN 77. The precedence of all Fortran 90 operators is given in Section 9.9.

For backward compatibility the old FORTRAN 77 relational operators are still valid in Fortran 90, but their use is discouraged for reasons of style. Incidentally, one might expect that the Fortran 90 standard would support also using suggestive symbols for logical operators, such as && for .AND. and || for .OR., but this is not the case—the only changes from the FORTRAN 77 standard regarding operator symbology are given in Table 3.1. By the way, some vendors provide FORTRAN 77 implementations that support most of the Fortran 90 relational operators listed in Table 3.1 but use <> (as in Pascal and BASIC) instead of /=

TABLE 3.1   The Relational Operators

Fortran 90 Operator	FORTRAN 77 Operator	Meaning
<	.LT.	Less than
<=	.LE.	Less than or equal to
==	.EQ.	Equal to
/=	.NE.	Not equal to
>	.GT.	Greater than
>=	.GE.	Greater than or equal to

(as in Ada) to represent not equal to. These vendors will no doubt continue to support this alternative in their Fortran 90 implementations, but as always, the author recommends compliance with the standard.

In standard FORTRAN 77, everything in a logical expression is required to be a scalar, but Fortran 90 permits array logical expressions. For example, if a is an array, evaluating the expression

```
a > 0
```

yields an array of values having the same number of dimensions and the same number of elements along each dimension as a, and each element of the resulting array is true or false, depending on whether the corresponding element of a is positive. Array logical expressions will come into play later in the tutorial. For now, it is enough to realize that array logical expressions exist in Fortran 90, but only scalar logical expressions can appear in an IF or DO WHILE statement.

3.3 The IF Construct

The Fortran 90 IF construct exhibits almost no features that were not present in FORTRAN 77. Figure 3.1a gives a complete Fortran 90 program that contains three IF constructs. Some of the Fortran 90 symbolic relational operators given in Table 3.1 are illustrated in the logical expressions of Figure 3.1a.

As was mentioned in Section 3.1, a construct name may optionally be used with a Fortran 90 IF construct. Construct names are illustrated in Figure 3.1b, which is identical to Figure 3.1a except that the construct names outer_test, inner_test_1, and inner_test_2 are given to the IF constructs. A construct name follows the rules for any Fortran 90 name as given in Figure 2.1. When an IF construct is given a name, the construct name followed by a colon (:) must precede the IF–THEN statement. If an IF–THEN statement is identified by a construct name, it is mandatory that the same construct name follow the corresponding END IF statement. If desired, each ELSE IF and ELSE statement may also be followed by the construct name, as is done with the name outer_test in Figure 3.1b.

It is interesting to compare the readability of the program of Figure 3.1a where the IF constructs do not have names against that of Figure 3.1b with the IF construct names. Perhaps most observers would conclude that the code in Figure 3.1a is easier to read. However, the presence of construct names can improve readability for deeply nested constructs or in instances where there is a lot of code between an IF–THEN statement and its corresponding END IF.

```
PROGRAM demo_if_construct

   INTEGER :: control_1, control_2, control_3


   READ *, control_1, control_2, control_3

   IF (control_1 < 0) THEN

      IF (control_2 >= 0) THEN
         PRINT *, "control_1 < 0 & control_2 >= 0"
      END IF

   ELSE IF (control_1 == 0) THEN

      PRINT *, "control_1 is zero"

   ELSE

      IF (control_3 /= 0) THEN
         PRINT *, "control_1 > 0 & control_3 not zero"
      END IF

   END IF

END PROGRAM demo_if_construct
```

FIGURE 3.1A. Program illustrating the IF construct.

The syntax for the Fortran 90 IF construct is given in Figure 3.2. There may be as many ELSE IF statements as desired in an IF construct. If *construct-name* appears, it must be present on both the IF–THEN and END IF statements, but its presence on ELSE IF and ELSE statements is optional. As indicated in Figure 2.5, the blank between the adjacent keywords ELSE IF is optional, as is the blank between the adjacent keywords END IF. If the ELSE statement is present, exactly one *block-of-statements* will be executed; otherwise, at most one *block-of-statements* will be executed. But note that a *block-of-statements* may be omitted, and an empty *block-of-statements* may be thought of as being executed with no effect, much like the traditional CONTINUE statement.

Although the Fortran 90 term "IF construct" does not appear in the FORTRAN 77 standard, all the features of a collection of source code designated by this term are carried over from the older standard with the exception of the construct name. However, some of the related terminology in the new standard differs slightly from that in the old. For

```
PROGRAM demo_if_construct

    INTEGER :: control_1, control_2, control_3


    READ *, control_1, control_2, control_3

    outer_test: IF (control_1 < 0) THEN

        inner_test_1: IF (control_2 >= 0) THEN
            PRINT *, "control_1 < 0 & control_2 >= 0"
        END IF inner_test_1

    ELSE IF (control_1 == 0) THEN outer_test

        PRINT *, "control_1 is zero"

    ELSE outer_test

        inner_test_2: IF (control_3 /= 0) THEN
            PRINT *, "control_1 > 0 & control_3 not zero"
        END IF inner_test_2

    END IF outer_test

END PROGRAM demo_if_construct
```

FIGURE 3.1B. IF constructs with construct names.

example, the initial statement of such a collection of code is known as a "block IF" statement in the FORTRAN 77 standard, but this designation is not used in the Fortran 90 standard.

3.4 INTRODUCTION TO THE CASE CONSTRUCT

Several languages, including Pascal, have provided a CASE control structure, which programmers typically use to select the execution of one of three or more mutually exclusive blocks of code. Traditionally, few Fortran implementations have offered a CASE construct, although many programmers encountered some version of it in the structured programming precompilers of the 1970s. The purpose of this section is merely to give an introduction to the CASE construct to those not en-

```
[construct-name:] IF (scalar-logical-expression) THEN
                [block-of-statements]
[ELSE IF (scalar-logical-expression) THEN [construct-name]
                [block-of-statements]]
[ELSE IF (scalar-logical-expression) THEN [construct-name]
                [block-of-statements]]
                        .
                        .
                        .


[ELSE [construct-name]
                [block-of-statements]]
END IF [construct-name]
```

FIGURE 3.2. General form of the IF construct.

tirely comfortable with the concept. Details of the syntax of the CASE construct will be given in the following three sections.

A first look at the CASE construct is given by the program of Figure 3.3. When the program is run, exactly one of the four PRINT statements will be executed, depending upon what integral value the user inputs. Note that this example could easily be implemented using an IF construct instead of the CASE construct, and in fact, it is true in general that any Fortran 90 CASE construct can be replaced with an IF construct. But notice in Figure 3.3 how clearly the syntax of the CASE construct reflects the way that people think about a menu selection situation, and then mentally compare that with the somewhat murkier IF . . . ELSE IF . . . ELSE IF . . . ELSE . . . END IF implementation. There are situations where the CASE construct provides clearer, more intuitive code than an IF construct, and so its inclusion in Fortran 90 increases the expressive power of the language.

3.5 A MORE GENERAL EXAMPLE OF THE CASE CONSTRUCT

Consider the complete Fortran 90 program of Figure 3.4a. The notation 2:5 indicates the range of values 2, 3, 4, 5, and so if the user inputs 2, 3, 4, or 5, the program displays

```
Monday through Thursday hours: 9 AM - 9 PM.
```

If the user inputs 6, the program displays

```
Friday hours: 9 AM - 5 PM.
```

```
PROGRAM demo_case

  INTEGER :: choice


  PRINT *, "Enter an integer from 1 through 3:"
  READ *, choice

  SELECT CASE (choice)
  CASE (1)
     PRINT *, "You chose option one."
  CASE (2)
     PRINT *, "You chose option two."
  CASE (3)
     PRINT *, "You chose option three."
  CASE DEFAULT
     PRINT *, "Illegal input value."
  END SELECT

END PROGRAM demo_case
```

FIGURE 3.3.   A first look at the CASE construct.

If the user inputs 7 or 1, the program displays

```
Closed Saturday and Sunday.
Call 1-800-555-1234 for information.
```

If the user inputs an integer that is less than 1 or greater than 7, the program displays

```
Illegal day code entry.
The valid entries are 1, 2, 3, 4, 5, 6, or 7.
```

This example illustrates that the case selector is not restricted to being only a single value. It may be a range of values, specified by a low value and a high value, separated by a colon (:); it may also be a list of values with each pair of adjacent list items separated by a comma. Although not illustrated in the example, a case selector list of values may contain both single values and ranges. For example,

```
CASE (1, 3:5, 7)
```

means the same thing as

```
CASE (1, 3, 4, 5, 7)
```

A CASE construct may be given a name in a manner analogous to that of giving an IF construct a name. This is illustrated in Fig-

```
PROGRAM demo_case_day

   INTEGER :: day_code


   READ *, day_code

   SELECT CASE (day_code)

   CASE (2:5)
      PRINT *, "Monday through Thursday hours: 9 AM - 9 PM."

   CASE (6)
      PRINT *, "Friday hours: 9 AM - 5 PM."

   CASE (7, 1)
      PRINT *, "Closed Saturday and Sunday."
      PRINT *, "Call 1-800-555-1234 for information."

   CASE DEFAULT
      PRINT *, "Illegal day code entry."
      PRINT *,                                              &
           "The valid entries are 1, 2, 3, 4, 5, 6, or 7."

   END SELECT

END PROGRAM demo_case_day
```

FIGURE 3.4A. A more general example of the CASE construct.

ure 3.4b, where the CASE construct is given the name day_case. The program of Figure 3.4b is the same as that of Figure 3.4a except that the CASE construct is given a construct name.

3.6   CASE SELECTOR OF TYPE CHARACTER

The Fortran 90 CASE selector can be of type CHARACTER, as illustrated by the complete program consisting of the main program of Figure 3.5a and the external subroutine subprogram of Figure 3.5b. In this program, the user inputs the name of the day of the week in any combination of upper- and lowercase letters. The subroutine is then called to strip off the first two nonblank characters of the user input

```
PROGRAM demo_case_day

   INTEGER :: day_code


   READ *, day_code

   day_case: SELECT CASE (day_code)

   CASE (2:5)   day_case
      PRINT *, "Monday through Thursday hours: 9 AM - 9 PM."

   CASE (6)     day_case
      PRINT *, "Friday hours: 9 AM - 5 PM."

   CASE (7, 1)  day_case
      PRINT *, "Closed Saturday and Sunday."
      PRINT *, "Call 1-800-555-1234 for information."

   CASE DEFAULT day_case
      PRINT *, "Illegal day code entry."
      PRINT *,                                              &
            "The valid entries are 1, 2, 3, 4, 5, 6, or 7."

   END SELECT day_case

END PROGRAM demo_case_day
```

FIGURE 3.4B. An example of a CASE construct with a construct name.

and, if necessary, changes lowercase letters to upper case. The case selection is then done based on the resulting two-letter abbreviation of the name of the day of the week.

The subroutine get_day_abbrev in Figure 3.5b illustrates several Fortran 90 features. As is easy to guess based on a knowledge of FORTRAN 77, the asterisk (*) specified for the length of the CHARACTER dummy argument day_name means that its length will be taken from the length of its corresponding actual argument. The INTENT attributes of the dummy arguments indicate that the first is input while the second is output. ADJUSTL is a new standard Fortran 90 intrinsic function that returns a left-justified copy of its argument.

The standard intrinsic function INDEX, a carryover from FORTRAN 77, is used in Figure 3.5b to find the position of an input character in the lowercase alphabet stored in Lower. If INDEX returns zero, it means that the input character is not a lowercase letter.

In Figure 3.5b, take particular note of the expression

```
PROGRAM demo_case_char

   CHARACTER(9) :: day_name
   CHARACTER(2) :: day_abbrev


   READ "(A)", day_name

   ! Get two-character abbreviation for day of week.
   CALL get_day_abbrev (day_name, day_abbrev)


   SELECT CASE (day_abbrev)    ! Selector is type CHARACTER.

   CASE ("MO", "TU", "WE", "TH")
      PRINT *, "Monday through Thursday hours: 9 AM - 9 PM."

   CASE ("FR")
      PRINT *, "Friday hours: 9 AM - 5 PM."

   CASE ("SA", "SU")
      PRINT *, "Closed Saturday and Sunday."
      PRINT *, "Call 1-800-555-1234 for information."

   CASE DEFAULT
      PRINT *, "Illegal day of week entry."
      PRINT *,                                                &
             "Valid entries are: MO, TU, WE, TH, FR, SA, SU"

   END SELECT

END PROGRAM demo_case_char
```

FIGURE 3.5A. An example of a CASE selector of type CHARACTER.


```
Upper(position:position)
```

When position is 1, this expression has the value A; when position is 2, it has the value B; and so on. Since Upper possesses the PARAMETER attribute, it is a named constant, and so the preceding expression illustrates that it is permissible to reference a substring of a constant. This expression is used in Figure 3.5b in converting a character from lower case to upper case. (Observe that the method used to effect the case conversion will work for ASCII, EBCDIC, or any other scheme of internal representation for the English alphabet.)

All the other interesting aspects of this example aside, the most important point to be made is that, unlike many other languages,

```
          ! Get first two nonblank input characters and
          ! convert to upper case if input in lower case.

SUBROUTINE get_day_abbrev (day_name, day_abbrev)

   CHARACTER(*), INTENT (IN)  :: day_name
   CHARACTER(2), INTENT (OUT) :: day_abbrev

   ! Named constant strings containing lowercase
   ! and uppercase letters of English alphabet in
   ! one-to-one correspondence.
   CHARACTER(26), PARAMETER ::                            &
                   Lower = "abcdefghijklmnopqrstuvwxyz", &
                   Upper = "ABCDEFGHIJKLMNOPQRSTUVWXYZ"

   INTEGER :: position   ! position of letter in alphabet
                         ! (1 = a or A, 2 = b or B, etc.)

   INTEGER :: i   ! loop index over characters in string


   ! Left-justify input string & strip off first two nonblanks.
   day_abbrev = ADJUSTL (day_name)

   ! If first two characters are lower case, change to upper.
   DO i = 1, 2
      position = INDEX (Lower, day_abbrev(i:i))
      IF (position /= 0)                                  &
                   day_abbrev(i:i) = Upper(position:position)
   END DO

END SUBROUTINE get_day_abbrev
```

FIGURE 3.5B. Subroutine called by the main program of Figure 3.5a.

Fortran 90 permits the CASE selector to be of type CHARACTER (any length). In some instances the selector range feature can be used to express a range of CHARACTER values, for example, "0000":"9999".

3.7 THE GENERAL FORM OF THE CASE CONSTRUCT

The general form of the CASE construct is indicated in Figure 3.6. There may be as many CASEs as desired, and it is optional to have a CASE DEFAULT. The optional *construct-name* is similar in form and concept

```
[construct-name:] SELECT CASE (case-expression)
[CASE (case-value-range-list) [construct-name]
                block-of-statements]
[CASE (case-value-range-list) [construct-name]
                block-of-statements]

                      .
                      .
                      .

[CASE DEFAULT [construct-name]
                block-of-statements]
END SELECT [construct-name]
```

FIGURE 3.6. General form of the CASE construct.

to the construct name described in Section 3.3 for the IF construct. If *construct-name* appears, it must be present in both the SELECT CASE and END SELECT statements, but its presence on any CASE statement is optional. As indicated in Figure 2.5, the blank between the adjacent keywords SELECT CASE is optional, as is the blank between the adjacent keywords END SELECT. However, the Fortran 90 standard requires that the adjacent keywords CASE DEFAULT be separated by one or more blanks.

The *case-expression* in Figure 3.6 is required to evaluate to a scalar value of type INTEGER, CHARACTER, or LOGICAL, and the values specified in each *case-value-range* must be of the same type as that of *case-expression*. In general, each *case-value-range* is a list of values and ranges separated by commas. A range of values is indicated by a lower bound and an upper bound separated by a colon (:). Thus, the range -2:1 is equivalent to the list of values -2, -1, 0, 1. It is perhaps unexpected that in expressing a range, either the lower bound or the upper bound, but not both, may be omitted. Thus, :-1 indicates all negative integers, and 1: means all positive integers.

3.8 DO Construct with Loop Index

The classic Fortran DO looks something like

```
C  Warning: FORTRAN 77 follows.
      DO 100 I = 1, 16, 2
         A(I) = 0.0
100   CONTINUE
```

For backward compatibility, the above code is still valid in standard Fortran 90, but its use is discouraged in favor of the nonlabel DO construct with a loop index:

```
DO i = 1, 16, 2        ! preferred
    a(i) = 0.0         !     in
END DO                 ! Fortran 90
```

Most readers are probably already familiar with this idiom because, although the nonlabel indexed DO and END DO statements are not standard in FORTRAN 77, most of the popular implementations have provided them as extensions for years.

For an elementary example of a DO construct with a loop index, consider the complete Fortran 90 program of Figure 3.7. If the user enters a value of 10 for n when this program is executed, the resulting value of sum displayed will be 55.

As with the IF and CASE constructs, Fortran 90 permits a construct name to be used with a DO construct. If the DO construct in Figure 3.7 were given the name accumulate_sum, the code for the loop might look like

```
accumulate_sum: DO i = 1, n
    sum = sum + i
END DO accumulate_sum
```

```
! Program to sum the integers from 1 through n
! for a user-specified value of n

PROGRAM sum_integers

    INTEGER :: i, n, sum = 0


    READ *, n

    DO i = 1, n
        sum = sum + i
    END DO

    PRINT *, sum

END PROGRAM sum_integers
```

FIGURE 3.7. DO construct with a loop index.

[*construct-name:*] DO [,] *index* = *num-expr-1, num-expr-2* [*,num-expr-3*]
                   [*block-of-statements*]
END DO [*construct-name*]

Disclaimer. The Fortran 90 standard supports forms of the indexed DO using labels (statement numbers) which are not reflected in the above description.

FIGURE 3.8.   General form of the DO construct with loop index.

The general form of the DO construct with nonlabel indexed DO statement is given in Figure 3.8. If *construct-name* appears, it must be present in both the DO and END DO statements. As indicated in Figure 2.5, the blank between the adjacent keywords END DO is optional. There is an optional comma between the keyword DO and the programmer-chosen variable *index*. The Fortran 90 standard requires that *index* must be a scalar variable of type INTEGER or of the default kind of REAL or of the double-precision kind of REAL. However, it is strongly recommended that variables of any kind of type REAL *not* be used in the role of *index* because this usage has been classified as **obsolescent**, which means that the Fortran 90 standard recommends that support for it be dropped in the next Fortran language standard. (See Appendix F for additional discussion of obsolescent features.)

Each of the numerical expressions *num-expr-1, num-expr-2,* and *num-expr-3* must evaluate to scalar values of type INTEGER or REAL (or DOUBLE PRECISION, which is considered a kind of REAL in Fortran 90). It is permitted, as in FORTRAN 77, that the value of *num-expr-1* be larger than the value of *num-expr-2*, in which case *block-of-statements* is not executed at all. Thus,

```
DO j = 5, 1
   PRINT *, "You'll never see this output!"
END DO
```

is valid, and the PRINT statement is never executed. As in previous versions of Fortran, the value of *num-expr-3* may not be zero. Of course, if *num-expr-3* is omitted, its value defaults to 1. As in FORTRAN 77, the value of *num-expr-3* may be negative, in which case the loop index variable decrements at each iteration. For example,

```
DO k = 8, 1, -2
   PRINT *, k
END DO
```

This loop causes the following to be displayed:

```
8
6
4
2
```

3.9 DO WHILE CONSTRUCT

Although the FORTRAN 77 standard does not support the DO WHILE statement, it is available in standard Fortran 90, and it works the same way as it does in popular FORTRAN 77 implementations: The block of statements between the DO WHILE and its corresponding END DO are executed repeatedly as long as the logical expression in the parentheses following the keyword WHILE is true. A complete standard Fortran 90 program illustrating the use of the DO WHILE is given in Figure 3.9.

The program of Figure 3.9 solves the following problem: Suppose you have some starting amount, say $1,000, and you are able to double

```
! This program determines number of years required to reach
! a specified goal when starting with a specified amount of
! money and doubling one's money each year.

  PROGRAM double_your_money

     INTEGER, PARAMETER :: starting_amount = 1000,   &
                           goal            = 1000000

     INTEGER            :: year = 0, amount


     amount = starting_amount

     DO WHILE (amount < goal)
        year = year + 1
        amount = 2 * amount
        PRINT "(2I10)", year, amount
     END DO

  END PROGRAM double_your_money
```

FIGURE 3.9. DO construct with a DO WHILE statement.

your money every year. How many years would it take to reach some goal, say one million dollars?[1]

When executed, the program of Figure 3.9 displays

```
 1        2000
 2        4000
 3        8000
 4       16000
 5       32000
 6       64000
 7      128000
 8      256000
 9      512000
10     1024000
```

Thus, if the assumption of doubling your money yearly could be met, one million dollars would be accumulated in only ten years.

As illustrated in Figure 3.9, the symbolic relational operators given in Table 3.1 can be used in the logical expression of the Fortran 90 DO WHILE statement. Also, a construct name may be used, and if the name count_years were given to the DO construct of Figure 3.9, the loop would look something like

```
count_years: DO WHILE (amount < goal)
    year = year + 1
    amount = 2 * amount
    PRINT "(2I10)", year, amount
END DO count_years
```

The general form of the nonlabel DO construct beginning with a DO WHILE statement is given in Figure 3.10. As usual, if *construct-name* appears, it must be in both the DO WHILE and END DO statements. There is an optional comma between the keywords DO and WHILE; if the comma is omitted, the standard requires a blank between these two keywords,

---

[*construct-name:*] DO [,] WHILE (*scalar-logical-expression*)
                    [*block-of-statements*]
END DO [*construct-name*]

Disclaimer. The Fortran 90 standard supports forms of the DO WHILE using labels (statement numbers) that are not reflected in the above description.

FIGURE 3.10.   General form of the DO construct with DO WHILE.

[1]This example is based on "How long before I'm a millionaire?" in *Ada from the Beginning* by J. Skansholm (Addison-Wesley, Reading, MA, 1988).

although few implementations are likely to enforce the requirement of the blank for reasons of backward compatibility. The *block-of-statements* executes as long as *scalar-logical-expression* evaluates to true, so if *scalar-logical-expression* is false at entry to the construct, then *block-of-statements* is never executed at all.

Although not indicated in Figure 3.10, the new standard permits a label (statement number) to appear in a DO WHILE. For example,

```
DO 20 WHILE (n < 50)
   total = 2 * total
   n = n + 1
20 END DO
```

Here, the END DO could also be replaced with CONTINUE, and in fact, the standard permits a wide variety of statements to be employed to terminate the DO WHILE (or, for that matter, any form of the DO) if a label is used. However, the author recommends against using a label in any form of the DO.

3.10 *THE SIMPLE DO AND THE EXIT*

In addition to supporting DO constructs that begin with the indexed DO statement and the DO WHILE statement, Fortran 90 also provides a form of the DO construct whose first statement consists simply of the single word "DO." An example of this form of DO construct is illustrated in the program of Figure 3.11, which computes the average of a sequence of nonnegative values input by the user. Input is terminated by entering a negative value.

Figure 3.11 exhibits a form of the DO loop, sometimes called a "DO forever," which few traditional Fortran implementations have supported, namely a form in which the block of statements between the DO and its corresponding END DO is executed repeatedly until the execution of some control transfer statement within that block causes an exit from the loop. Figure 3.11 also demonstrates the use of the EXIT statement, which is provided in Fortran 90 for the purpose of causing the termination of the execution of a DO loop. The Fortran 90 construct starting with the simple DO statement provides great flexibility in loop control when used in conjunction with the EXIT statement. This will be illustrated in subsequent examples.

Like the IF, CASE, indexed DO, and DO WHILE constructs, a Fortran 90 simple DO construct can be given a construct name. The presence of the construct name in the DO statement and in the corresponding END DO statement provides better compiler checking and may improve read-

```
PROGRAM find_average

   INTEGER :: number_of_values = 0
   REAL    :: value, sum_of_values = 0.0, average


   DO                              ! simple DO statement
      READ *, value
      IF (value < 0.0) EXIT        ! Break out of loop.
      number_of_values = number_of_values + 1
      sum_of_values = sum_of_values + value
   END DO


   average = sum_of_values / number_of_values
   PRINT *, average

END PROGRAM find_average
```

FIGURE 3.11. DO construct with a simple DO statement.

ability. Moreover, in the case of nested DOs, construct names provide
a convenient mechanism for simultaneously terminating more than
one loop. This is illustrated by the complete Fortran 90 program of
Figure 3.12.

Note that the program of Figure 3.12 has nested DO constructs,
named outer_loop and inner_loop. Observe that when inner_loop_index
exceeds 3, the statement

    EXIT inner_loop

will be executed, and the inner loop will be exited. Also, note that
when the product of outer_loop_index times inner_loop_index exceeds 8, the
statement

    EXIT outer_loop

will be executed, and the outer loop will be exited. Recall that in Figure 3.11 the EXIT statement consisted solely of the word EXIT, meaning
exit the innermost loop containing the EXIT statement. But here in Figure 3.12, the word EXIT is followed by construct names both times it
appears. This indicates that execution of the EXIT statement is to exit
the named loop. Thus, the first EXIT statement causes only the inner
loop to be exited, while the second causes the outer loop to be exited,
thereby exiting the inner loop as well.

The program of Figure 3.12 produces the following output:

```
PROGRAM demo_exit_followed_by_name

   INTEGER :: outer_loop_index = 2, inner_loop_index


   outer_loop: DO
      inner_loop_index = 1

      inner_loop: DO
         IF (inner_loop_index > 3) EXIT inner_loop

         PRINT "(3I4)", outer_loop_index, inner_loop_index, &
                        outer_loop_index * inner_loop_index

         IF ((outer_loop_index * inner_loop_index) > 8)      &
                                          EXIT outer_loop

         inner_loop_index = inner_loop_index + 1
      END DO inner_loop

      outer_loop_index = outer_loop_index + 1
   END DO outer_loop

END PROGRAM demo_exit_followed_by_name
```

FIGURE 3.12. Examples of EXIT followed by a DO construct name.

```
2   1   2
2   2   4
2   3   6
3   1   3
3   2   6
3   3   9
```

The general form of the DO construct starting with the simple DO statement is given in Figure 3.13. As always, if *construct-name* appears, it must be present in both the DO and END DO statements. If, as is usually the case, it is desired to stop the looping gracefully at some point, *block-of-statements* must contain some statement, such as EXIT, RETURN, STOP, or GO TO, which transfers control out of the DO construct. The EXIT statement usually provides the most readable way to terminate the execution of a simple DO construct, but there are exceptions to this general guideline.

The EXIT statement may be employed not only with the simple DO as just illustrated, but with other forms of the DO construct as well. The

```
[construct-name:] DO
        block-of-statements
END DO [construct-name]
```

Disclaimer. The Fortran 90 standard supports forms of the simple DO using labels (statement numbers) that are not reflected in the above description.

FIGURE 3.13. General form of the DO construct with simple DO.

form of the EXIT statement is given in Figure 3.14. An EXIT statement may appear only within a *block-of-statements* contained inside a DO construct. If *construct-name* is present in an EXIT statement, it specifies which DO construct enclosing the EXIT is to be exited. If no *construct-name* is specified in an EXIT statement, the EXIT terminates execution of the innermost DO construct within which it is enclosed.

It should be noted in Figure 3.12 that the construct name inner_loop is optional in the first EXIT statement because the inner loop would be exited anyway, even if the construct name were omitted. However, the construct name outer_loop in the second EXIT statement is required since if it were omitted, the EXIT statement would cause exit only from the inner loop, and the program would be caught in a so-called infinite loop.

3.11 THE CYCLE STATEMENT

It occasionally happens that in the middle of the body of a long and/or complicated DO loop, the programmer would like to begin the next iteration of the loop immediately, skipping the execution of the rest of the body of the loop. Fortran 90 provides the CYCLE statement as a mechanism for handling this situation gracefully. This section presents a contrived program that illustrates the use of the CYCLE statement.

The program of Figure 3.15 repeatedly reads lines of user input until the end of file is encountered (or an error occurs during the read). Each

```
EXIT [construct-name]
```

FIGURE 3.14. General form of the EXIT statement.

```
PROGRAM demo_cycle

   CHARACTER(80) :: buffer
   INTEGER :: i, rd_stat, nonblanks


   process_line: DO

      READ (*, "(A)", IOSTAT = rd_stat) buffer

      IF (rd_stat /= 0) EXIT process_line

      nonblanks = 0

      count_nonblanks: DO i = 1, 80

         IF (buffer(i:i) == "*") CYCLE process_line

         IF (buffer(i:i) /= " ") nonblanks = nonblanks + 1

      END DO count_nonblanks

      PRINT "(I5)", nonblanks

   END DO process_line

END PROGRAM demo_cycle
```

FIGURE 3.15. Program illustrating the CYCLE statement.

line of user input is not to exceed 80 characters in length. The program stores each line read in the variable named buffer and then passes through each character in buffer, looking for blanks and asterisks. A count of the number of nonblank characters in the line is kept in the variable nonblanks. If no asterisk appears in the line, the total number of nonblank characters in the line is displayed and then the next user input is read. However, if an asterisk appears anywhere in the input line, further processing of the line is abandoned, no program output is produced, and the next user input is read immediately.

A sample run of the program might look something like the following:

How many nonblanks in this line?
  27
No program output produced for this line *

The count of nonblanks in this line displayed below.
   44
From the point of the *, processing of the line stops.
Count of nonblanks follows.
   24

In the above sample program session, **boldface type** is used for user input while plain type is used for program output.

Observe in the program of Figure 3.15 that there are two DO loops: The outer DO is given the construct name process_line, and the inner DO is given the construct name count_nonblanks. The outer loop, which is the read loop controlled by a simple DO statement, is broken when the EXIT statement is executed. This occurs when an end-of-file condition (or perhaps an error condition) is raised during the read. The inner loop, which is the loop over the 80 characters in buffer, is controlled by an indexed DO statement. If an asterisk is encountered in buffer, the program immediately initiates a fresh iteration of the outer loop. This is accomplished by the statement

```
IF (buffer(i:i) == "*") CYCLE process_line
```

The syntax of the CYCLE statement, which is analogous to that of the EXIT statement, is given in Figure 3.16. Like the EXIT statement, the CYCLE statement may appear only within a DO construct. If *construct-name* is present in a CYCLE statement, it specifies the DO construct enclosing the CYCLE for which a new iteration is to be immediately initiated. If no *construct-name* is specified in a CYCLE statement, the CYCLE causes a new iteration to begin for the innermost DO construct within which it is enclosed.

It is interesting to note in the program of Figure 3.15 where the construct names are optional and where they are required. The inner loop name count_nonblanks could be omitted since it is never referred to. In the EXIT statement, the construct name process_line is optional because it refers to the innermost (and here, the only) DO construct enclosing the EXIT. However, a construct name must appear on the CYCLE statement since otherwise it would cause a fresh iteration of the indexed DO to be initiated. Thus, to achieve the desired effect, the same construct name must appear on the CYCLE statement, the simple DO statement, and the END DO terminating the simple DO; in this example, the construct name process_line has been chosen for this purpose. It is a

```
CYCLE [construct-name]
```

FIGURE 3.16.   General form of the CYCLE statement.

matter of judgment as to whether the presence of the construct names where not required in Figure 3.15 improves readability, but it seems likely that most would agree that they do.

3.12 Choosing the "Right" Control Structure

Fortran 90 provides the programmer with a variety of ways to control the flow of program execution, and it is not always clear how to choose a combination of statements that results in the code being easy for others to understand quickly. While it is well known that merely observing some set of rules does not guarantee clear programs, there are guidelines that, when followed, tend to improve the readability of code. This section will discuss some of the considerations in choosing control statements in such a way as to enhance readability.

In traditional Fortran, the classic GO TO was a mainstay control statement. An example of this kind of statement is

```
GO TO 1000
```

where 1000 is the label of another statement within the same routine. The collective experience of the Fortran community has been that the undisciplined use of GO TO statements usually results in code that is difficult to understand. Fortran 90 makes it possible to code without ever employing a GO TO statement or a label, but situations do arise, particularly in handling errors, where the clarity of the code may be improved by the judicious use of a GO TO statement. However, the careful programmer will want to reserve the use of GO TO for those unusual circumstances where every other alternative results in muddier code.

The simple GO TO statement described in the preceding paragraph is actually only one of three standard FORTRAN 77 statements containing the keywords "GO TO." The other two are the computed GO TO and the assigned GO TO, and both are supported by the Fortran 90 standard for backward compatibility. A typical use of the computed GO TO statement is as follows:

```
      GO TO (100, 200, 300) i
100 CONTINUE
      . . .
      GO TO 400
200 CONTINUE
      . . .
      GO TO 400
300 CONTINUE
      . . .
400 CONTINUE
```

If i is 1, control is transferred to the statement with label 100; if i is 2, control is transferred to 200; and if i is 3, control is transferred to 300. In Fortran 90, the preceding control construct is much more clearly expressed by a CASE construct:

```
SELECT CASE (i)
CASE (1)
  . . .
CASE (2)
  . . .
CASE (3)
  . . .
END SELECT
```

However, some uses of the computed GO TO cannot be so easily replaced by a CASE construct because there is no way to fall from one CASE block into another CASE block. Nevertheless, the computed GO TO is almost never the clearest way of doing things in Fortran 90.

An example of the third form of GO TO statement, the assigned GO TO, is

```
GO TO some_label (100, 200, 300)
```

where some_label is a variable name that has been given one of the values 100, 200, or 300 by a previous ASSIGN statement such as

```
ASSIGN 200 TO some_label
```

The assigned GO TO and ASSIGN statements are designated in the Fortran 90 standard as obsolescent, which means they are recommended for deletion in the next language standard. Hence, it is recommended that these statements be avoided. (See Appendix F for some additional discussion.)

Fortran 90 still supports the three forms of the IF statement that are available in FORTRAN 77: the IF–THEN statement, which begins an IF construct; the logical IF statement; and the arithmetic IF statement. An example of the old arithmetic IF statement is

```
IF (x) 100, 200, 300
```

If x is negative, control is transferred to the statement labeled 100; if x is zero, control is transferred to 200; and if x is positive, control is transferred to 300. The arithmetic IF statement is another example of an obsolescent feature, and its use is not recommended. (Some additional discussion is given in Appendix F.)

An example of a logical IF statement is

```
IF (a(i) > 0) count = count + 1
```

The equivalent IF construct is

```
IF (a(i) > 0) THEN
   count = count + 1
END IF
```

In isolation, either form is readily understandable. However, the presence of the IF–THEN version in a long section of code may contribute to spreading the code out vertically so much as to hamper overall readability of the section. On the other hand, the logical IF can be troublesome to a reader who is trying to match IF/END IF pairs. On balance, the logical IF is perhaps preferable in situations like that given here, where only one short statement is or is not to be executed depending on the outcome of a test.

For purposes of selecting one of two or more alternatives, there is often a choice between the IF construct and the CASE construct. However, in situations where the selection is based on a value of type REAL, the IF construct must be used because the CASE selector is restricted to types INTEGER, CHARACTER, and LOGICAL. Also, the choice of a LOGICAL selector for a CASE construct is usually dubious. For example, consider the valid CASE construct:

```
SELECT CASE (j == 1)
CASE (.TRUE.)
   . . .
CASE (.FALSE.)
   . . .
END SELECT
```

Now compare the above CASE construct with an equivalent IF construct:

```
IF (j == 1) THEN
   . . .
ELSE
   . . .
END IF
```

It seems reasonably clear that the IF construct is preferable here.

For purposes of executing a collection of statements many times, Fortran 90 supports a remarkable number of variants of the DO construct. A DO statement may or may not contain a label, and either the label DO or the nonlabel DO statement may be an indexed DO, a DO WHILE, or a simple DO. It is permitted to terminate a label DO with any one of several varieties of statements, including the CONTINUE. However, it seems obvious that the END DO statement is the clearest way to terminate a DO construct because it is the only statement having no other usage. Also, consider a label DO such as the following:

```
        DO 100 i = 1, n
               .

               .

               .

100 END DO
```

This form is certainly no clearer than the equivalent nonlabel DO with a construct name:

```
loop_over_subscripts: DO i = 1, n
             .

             .

             .

END DO loop_over_subscripts
```

Also, construct names are associated exclusively with control constructs, while statement labels have many uses. And, in general, labels do not fit in well with the standard Fortran 90 free source form. Since label DOs offer no advantage over their nonlabel counterparts, it is recommended that only the nonlabel forms of the DO statements be used.

When choosing among the nonlabel forms of the DO, the indexed DO is to be preferred over either the DO WHILE or the simple DO when the number of times the body of the loop is to be executed is known at entry to the loop. Also, when a repeatedly executed block of statements contains a variable that starts at some value and is incremented each time the block is executed until it reaches some maximum value (or is decremented each time until it reaches some minimum), the indexed DO is usually the best choice for a control structure.

Both the DO WHILE and the simple DO are ordinarily used where the number of times the body of the loop is to be executed is unknown at loop entry. Without considering specific example loops, it might seem that DO WHILE loops would generally be easier to grasp quickly since they usually specify a condition for exit at the top of the loop while the condition for exit from a simple DO may be buried deep inside the body of the loop. However, when attention is focused on specific examples, it is surprisingly difficult to find instances where using the DO WHILE yields clearer code than using the simple DO along with an EXIT statement. In fact, many experts believe that the expressiveness added to Fortran 90 by the DO WHILE is not sufficient to justify its inclusion in the language. No doubt this will be jarring to some readers, since in some ways it runs counter to what many have been taught about structured programming.

To focus ideas on the issue of whether the DO WHILE results in clearer code than the simple DO, it may be helpful to think of a classic

application, namely the read loop. Using the simple DO, the skeleton of
a Fortran 90 read loop might look like

```
DO
    READ (..., IOSTAT = rdstat) buffer
    IF (rdstat == End_of_file) EXIT
    ! process buffer
          . . .
END DO
```

Using the DO WHILE, a read loop that achieves the same effect as the
preceding one might be written as follows:

```
READ (..., IOSTAT = rdstat) buffer
DO WHILE (rdstat /= End_of_file)
    ! process buffer
          . . .
    READ (..., IOSTAT = rdstat) buffer
END DO
```

In the DO WHILE version, note the awkwardness of the initial READ statement being outside the loop. Also, there is the fact that, except for the
first buffer, each buffer is read at the bottom of the loop and then control is passed back up to the top to actually process it. Finally, testing
that the READ status is not end of file is the negative of the way that
most would naturally pose this question. But many have become so
accustomed to this idiom that they may have difficulty seeing anything
peculiar about it. However, the author believes that in most cases the
simple DO should be preferred over the DO WHILE. Nevertheless, there
are situations, for example, the program of Figure 3.9, where the DO
WHILE serves nicely.

It is worth observing that the Fortran 90 EXIT statement can be characterized as a restricted form of GO TO statement. But unlike the classic
GO TO statement, which permits control to be transferred to almost any
other point in the routine, the EXIT permits branching only in the forward direction and can cause control to be transferred only to the next
executable statement following the end of a DO construct. Nevertheless,
programmers who wish to write code that is easy to understand will
need to exercise some restraint in using the EXIT statement. Code will
usually be clearest if the number of EXIT statements appearing in each
DO construct is kept to a minimum.

Fortran 90 rules permit the EXIT statement to be employed not only
with the simple DO, but with the indexed DO and the DO WHILE as well.
However, it should be recognized that using EXIT with the latter two
forms of the DO defeats one of their most admired features, namely
that the loop control mechanism can be made evident at the top of the
construct. This suggests that use of the EXIT statement should usually

be avoided within an indexed DO or a DO WHILE construct. Nevertheless, when a loop control mechanism is chosen, alternatives should always be explored, and it seems to the author that there are situations where using EXIT with an indexed DO yields the most readily understandable code. For example, a linear search of a list containing a known number of items is perhaps most clearly expressed by an indexed DO whose execution is terminated by an EXIT statement if the item being searched for is found.

Of course, all of the foregoing discussion has been from the point of view that the sole criterion in choosing control structures is readability. But there are situations where readability is less important than other considerations, such as achieving unusually high execution efficiency or closely modeling the structure of another system. Nevertheless, the decision to ignore programming practices that ordinarily enhance readability is one that the serious programmer will not make lightly.

CHAPTER 4

ARRAYS

4.1 OVERVIEW OF ARRAY FEATURES

The array has always played a central role in Fortran programming, and in recognition of this, the Fortran 90 standard supports many new features to facilitate array handling. Traditionally, in Fortran expressions like a + 3 * SQRT (b), a and b have been restricted to taking on scalar values, but in Fortran 90, a and b may be arrays in such an expression, in which case the expression evaluates to an array of values. In this connection, Fortran 90 permits every element of an array to be given a value using a single statement. For example, if a and b are arrays that have previously been given values, then all the elements of array c may be given values using an assignment statement such as

```
c = a + 3 * SQRT (b)    ! a, b, c are arrays.
```

The Fortran 90 array-to-array assignment statement replaces the one or more DO loops required to effect this sort of assignment in traditional Fortran, thus providing enhanced readability and, in some implementations, improved execution efficiency. In addition to the capability of assigning values to all array elements using a single statement, as illustrated above, Fortran 90 supports an unusual form of array assignment, known as "masked array assignment," in which only some of the elements of an array may be assigned values depending on the result of an array logical expression. The masked array assignment involves the use of the new keyword WHERE.

In traditional Fortran, there is no compact notation for referring to a collection of elements that comprise only a portion of an array. But Fortran 90 provides mechanisms that permit restricting operations to a programmer-specified subset of array elements. For example, if a is a one-dimensional array whose subscripts range from 1 through 6, then a(2:4) refers to the subset of elements consisting of a(2), a(3), and a(4). Such a subset of array elements is called an "array section." Details of how array sections may be specified will be given later in the chapter.

Another useful Fortran 90 feature is the "array constructor," which permits the programmer to give the values of the elements of a one-dimensional array simply by specifying the list of values between the symbols (/ and /). For example, if x is a one-dimensional REAL array with four elements, values will be assigned to each element of x by a statement such as

```
x = (/ 1.1, 2.2, 3.3, 4.4 /)   ! Right-hand side is
                               ! array constructor.
```

An important use of the array constructor is to express a literal array constant in a program, but it is permitted to use variable names as well as constants between the symbols (/ and /). Also, even though the array constructor cannot by itself specify values for elements of an array of dimension greater than one, it can be used in conjunction with the new standard intrinsic function RESHAPE to specify values for elements of an array of two or more dimensions.

In traditional Fortran, the amount of storage required by each array had to be specified before the program was compiled. But Fortran 90 supports dynamic storage allocation, that is, storage may be allocated and freed during program execution. This is particularly useful for those times when the size of a data structure is not known until after data are read and/or computations are performed. One of several ways that Fortran 90 supports dynamic storage allocation is by providing what is known as the "allocatable array." The programmer must give the number of dimensions of an allocatable array before compilation, but specification of the range of subscripts for each dimension is deferred until execution. The new keywords ALLOCATABLE, ALLOCATE, and DEALLOCATE are used when working with allocatable arrays.

4.2   INTRODUCTION TO FORTRAN 90 ARRAYS

In FORTRAN 77, an array is typically declared with syntax such as

```
REAL array(2,3)
```

or, alternatively, with syntax like

```
REAL array
DIMENSION array(2,3)
```

For backward compatibility, Fortran 90 still supports these forms, but for consistency with other data specifications, it is preferred that the new forms employing the double colon (::) be used. Thus, the preferred way to declare an array in Fortran 90 is

```
REAL, DIMENSION(2,3) :: array
```

or, more concisely,

```
REAL :: array(2,3)
```

For tutorial purposes, the form of array declaration containing both the double colon and the keyword DIMENSION will be used throughout this book.

As in FORTRAN 77, array subscripts are permitted to be nonpositive. Thus,

```
REAL, DIMENSION(-1:0,-1:1) :: x
```

indicates that x is an array with elements x(-1,-1), x(0,-1), x(-1,0), x(0,0), x(-1,1), and x(0,1). The **bounds** of an array are the limits within which the values of its subscripts must lie. For the array x declared above, the bounds in its first dimension are -1 and 0 and the bounds in its second dimension are -1 and 1. If, as is usually the case, the lower bound for a dimension of an array is 1, then the lower bound need not be specified. The **size** of an array is, of course, the total number of elements in the array. Here the size of x is 6. The size of one dimension of an array is known as the **extent** in that dimension. For our array x, the extent in the first dimension is 2 and the extent in the second dimension is 3.

In addition to carrying over the FORTRAN 77 terminology mentioned in the preceding paragraph, the Fortran 90 standard introduces some array nomenclature that traditionally has not been used in the Fortran world. In order to consider specific examples of the new nomenclature, suppose the following declarations are made:

```
REAL, DIMENSION(6)       :: a
REAL, DIMENSION(2,3)     :: b
REAL, DIMENSION(0:1,5:7) :: c
REAL, DIMENSION(3,2)     :: d
REAL, DIMENSION(3,4,5)   :: e
```

Now, the number of dimensions of an array is called its **rank**. Thus, a has rank 1, each of b, c, and d has rank 2, and e has rank 3. The Fortran 90 standard, like the FORTRAN 77 standard, specifies that the rank of an array may not exceed 7, but implementations may support arrays of higher rank. Incidentally, scalars are considered to have rank 0. Also, the **shape** of an array is specified by an ordered list of its extents. Two arrays have the same shape if and only if they have the same rank and the same extents along each dimension. Hence, while arrays a, b, c, d above are all of size 6, only b and c have the same shape since they are both of rank 2 and have an extent of 2 in the first dimension and an extent of 3 in the second dimension.

Fortran 90 permits each of the elements of an array to be given a common scalar value simply by using the equal sign (=). Similarly, the value of each element of an array may be assigned to the corresponding element in another array of the same shape using the equal sign. An example of each of these varieties of array assignment is given in the complete program of Figure 4.1.

There are two REAL arrays of rank 2 declared in Figure 4.1, and their names are a_1 and a_2. For each array, the extent along the first dimension is 2 and along the second dimension is 3, and so they have the same shape.

When the program of Figure 4.1 is executed, the following is displayed:

```
-1.0  -1.0  -1.0
-1.0  -1.0  -1.0
 1.0   3.0   5.0
 2.0   4.0   6.0
```

Observe that the assignment statement

```
a_1 = -1.0
```

```
PROGRAM demo_array_assignment

    REAL, DIMENSION(2,3)        :: a_1
    REAL, DIMENSION(-1:0,-1:1) :: a_2
    INTEGER                     :: row, col

    a_1 = -1.0            ! scalar assigned to array

    DO row = 1, 2
        PRINT "(3F6.1)", (a_1(row,col), col = 1, 3)
    END DO

    a_2(-1,-1) = 1.0;  a_2(-1,0) = 3.0;  a_2(-1,1) = 5.0
    a_2( 0,-1) = 2.0;  a_2( 0,0) = 4.0;  a_2( 0,1) = 6.0

    a_1 = a_2             ! array assigned to array

    DO row = 1, 2
        PRINT "(3F6.1)", (a_1(row,col), col = 1, 3)
    END DO

END PROGRAM demo_array_assignment
```

FIGURE 4.1. Program illustrating array assignments.

causes the scalar value –1.0 to be assigned to each of the elements of a_1. The assignment of a scalar to an array is not standard in FORTRAN 77, but some implementations have provided this capability.

Also, observe in Figure 4.1 that the statement

```
a_1 = a_2
```

causes a_1(1,1) to take the value of a_2(–1,–1), a_1(2,1) to take the value of a_2(0,–1), a_1(1,2) to take the value of a_2(–1,0), and so on. This illustrates that Fortran 90 permits the values of one array to be assigned to another array, provided that the array expression to the right of the equal sign has exactly the same shape as the array to the left of the equal sign.

Incidentally, suppose that there was a third array declared as follows in the program of Figure 4.1:

```
REAL, DIMENSION(3,2) :: a_3
```

Then the following array to array assignment would *not* be legal:

```
a_3 = a_1   ! invalid
```

The array a_1 cannot be directly assigned to a_3 because the two arrays do not have the same shape—the extents along corresponding dimensions are not the same. Even though this sort of assignment cannot be made directly, Fortran 90 does provide a way to copy values between arrays of different shapes by using the intrinsic function RESHAPE. This will be illustrated in Section 4.8.

4.3   INTRINSIC OPERATORS AND FUNCTIONS USED WITH ARRAYS

Fortran 90 permits the intrinsic + operator to be used to add corresponding elements of two arrays with the same shape. Also, a scalar value can be added to each element of an array by using the + operator. Fortran 90 permits all the other intrinsic operators, such as *, /, –, to be used in a similar fashion. Moreover, most of the intrinsic functions, such as ABS, SQRT, and so on, are permitted to take array arguments, in which case they operate independently on each array element and return an array of values. These features are illustrated in the program of Figure 4.2. When executed, the program of Figure 4.2 displays

```
Adding 2 to array_a yields:
        3     4     5
        6     7     8
```

```
PROGRAM demo_array_intrinsics

  INTEGER, DIMENSION(2,3) :: array_a
  INTEGER, DIMENSION(2,3) :: array_b
  INTEGER :: i, j

  array_a(1,1) = 1;  array_a(1,2) = 2;  array_a(1,3) = 3
  array_a(2,1) = 4;  array_a(2,2) = 5;  array_a(2,3) = 6

  array_a = array_a + 2  ! Add a scalar to an array.

  PRINT "(A)", " Adding 2 to array_a yields:"
  DO i = 1, 2
     PRINT "(13X, 3I5)", (array_a(i,j), j = 1, 3)
  END DO

  array_b(1,1) = -2;  array_b(1,2) =  3;  array_b(1,3) = 2
  array_b(2,1) =  1;  array_b(2,2) = -1;  array_b(2,3) = 0

  array_a = array_a * array_b  ! Mult. corresponding elements.

  PRINT "(A)", " Multiplying each element of array_a times"
  PRINT "(A)", " corresponding element of array_b yields:"
  DO i = 1, 2
     PRINT "(13X, 3I5)", (array_a(i,j), j = 1, 3)
  END DO

  array_a = ABS (array_a)  ! Take abs value of each element.

  PRINT "(A)", " Taking absolute value of array_a yields:"
  DO i = 1, 2
     PRINT "(13X, 3I5)", (array_a(i,j), j = 1, 3)
  END DO

END PROGRAM demo_array_intrinsics
```

FIGURE 4.2. Intrinsic operators and functions used with arrays.

```
Multiplying each element of array_a times
corresponding element of array_b yields:
          -6   12   10
           6   -7    0
Taking absolute value of array_a yields:
           6   12   10
           6    7    0
```

Observe first in Figure 4.2 that the scalar value 2 is added to array_a. As indicated by the program output, this results in 2 being added to each element of array_a.

The second operation in Figure 4.2 is to use the intrinsic operator * to multiply each element of array_a times the corresponding element of array_b. When a Fortran 90 binary intrinsic operator such as * is used with array operands, it always operates on corresponding elements of the two arrays. Pay particular attention to the fact that the asterisk in the expression array_a * array_b does ***not*** indicate the sort of matrix multiplication usually discussed in books on matrix manipulations. In fact, ordinary algebraic matrix multiplication is not defined for array_a and array_b since array_a has three columns while array_b has two rows. In this connection, it should perhaps be mentioned that standard Fortran 90 provides the intrinsic function MATMUL, which supports the capability of performing algebraic multiplication of a pair of two-dimensional arrays. (An example of the use of MATMUL will be given in Section 4.8.)

The third operation in Figure 4.2 is to apply the intrinsic function ABS to array_a, and as indicated by the program output, ABS takes the absolute value of each element of array_a and returns these values in an array having the same shape as array_a. In general, all of the Fortran 90 intrinsic functions listed in Appendix C as being in the class "Elemental Function" (SQRT, REAL, INT, LOG, SIN, etc.) can be used with array arguments: Such a function will operate on each array element (one element at a time) and will return an array of values that will be the same as would have been obtained if the function had been applied separately to corresponding elements of each argument.

4.4   MASKED ARRAY ASSIGNMENT

The term "mask" has been used in computing for years to designate a computer word that specifies the bits of another computer word on which to operate. In the Fortran 90 standard, the term is applied in a similar way: A **mask** is an array that specifies the elements of another array on which to operate. An array used as a mask must be of type LOGICAL. An array to be operated on under the control of a mask may be of any data type, but generally it must have the same shape as the mask. This section will describe only the use of such masks in the new WHERE statement and WHERE construct. However, it should be mentioned in passing that the use of such masks also may arise in connection with certain of the new standard intrinsic functions, such as SUM, MAXLOC, and MINVAL.

In much the same way that Fortran provides the logical IF statement as well as the IF construct, Fortran 90 supports both the WHERE statement and the WHERE construct. Both the WHERE statement and the WHERE construct are illustrated by the program of Figure 4.3. When executed, the program of Figure 4.3 displays

```
1   0   3   0   5
2   0   2   0   2
```

The statement

```
WHERE (a < 0) b = 0
```

in Figure 4.3 illustrates the WHERE statement, and each negative element of the array a causes the corresponding element of the array b to be assigned the value 0. Note that the array subscripts of a are 1, 2, 3, 4, and 5, while the array subscripts of b are –1, 0, 1, 2, and 3. Since a(2) and a(4) are negative, the second and fourth elements of b, b(0) and b(2), are assigned the value 0.

The WHERE statement can be used to specify a test for each element of an array, and for each element of that array which passes the test (or for corresponding elements in another array of the same shape), a value from a programmer-specified array or scalar can be assigned.

```
PROGRAM demo_where

   INTEGER, DIMENSION(5)    :: a
   INTEGER, DIMENSION(-1:3) :: b

   a(1)  = 2;   a(2) = -4;   a(3) = 6;   a(4) = -8;   a(5) = 10
   b(-1) = 1;   b(0) =  2;   b(1) = 3;   b(2) =  4;   b(3) =  5

   WHERE (a < 0) b = 0     ! the WHERE statement

   PRINT "(5I4)", b

   WHERE (b /= 0)          ! the WHERE construct
      a = a / b
   ELSEWHERE
      a = 0
   END WHERE

   PRINT "(5I4)", a

END PROGRAM demo_where
```

FIGURE 4.3. The WHERE statement and the WHERE construct.

WHERE (*array-logical-expr*) *array-assignment-statement*

FIGURE 4.4. Syntax of the WHERE statement.

The general form for the WHERE statement is given in Figure 4.4. The shape of the array to the left of the equal sign in *array-assignment-statement* must be the same as that yielded by *array-logical-expr*.

The WHERE statement allows manipulation only of portions of arrays corresponding to elements passing a test, but the WHERE construct allows manipulations of portions of arrays corresponding to elements failing the test as well. In Figure 4.3 the WHERE construct is illustrated by

```
WHERE (b /= 0)
   a = a / b
ELSEWHERE
   a = 0
END WHERE
```

At this point in the program execution, the nonzero elements of the test array b are b(–1), b(1), and b(3), which have the values 1, 3, and 5, respectively. Since these are the first, third, and fifth elements of the test array b, the divisions performed in the assignment statement will be a(1) / b(–1), a(3) / b(1), and a(5) / b(3). The second and fourth elements of the test array b, b(0) and b(2), hold values of zero, and so the assignment statement a = 0 will cause both a(2) and a(4) to be assigned the value zero.

The WHERE statement permits only a single array assignment to be made under the control of the mask, but the WHERE construct extends this to any number of array assignments, although this is not illustrated in Figure 4.3. The general form of the WHERE construct is given in Figure 4.5. Each block of *array-assignment-statements* consists of one or more array assignment statements. In each array assignment statement, the shape of the array to the left of the equal sign must be the

```
WHERE (array-logical-expr)
    [array-assignment-statements]
[ELSEWHERE
    [array-assignment-statements]]
END WHERE
```

FIGURE 4.5. Syntax of the WHERE construct.

same as the shape of *array-logical-expr*. The only sort of statement that can appear in each block of *array-assignment-statements* is an array assignment statement as described in Section 4.2, and so it follows that the Fortran 90 standard does not support nested WHERE constructs. The blank between the keywords END and WHERE is optional.

4.5 ARRAY CONSTANTS

In traditional Fortran, a literal constant has always been a scalar quantity, such as 36, 1.98, or 'PRESSURE (PSI)'. But Fortran 90 permits rank 1 array literal constants to be specified simply by listing the values of the array elements between the delimiters (/ and /). For example, the following is a one-dimensional array literal constant of type default REAL containing four elements:

```
(/ 1.01, 0.98, 1.13, 0.87 /)
```

The program of Figure 4.6 illustrates the use of some rank 1 array literal constants. When executed, the program of Figure 4.6 displays

```
1.0   -3.0    2.0    4.0
```

Note that Figure 4.6 illustrates the use of array literal constants in type declaration statements, assignment statements, and array expressions. In general, Fortran 90 places no unexpected restrictions on the use of array constants.

Not only does Fortran 90 support array literal constants, but by using the PARAMETER attribute, a programmer can give a name to an array

```
PROGRAM demo_array_literal_constants

  REAL, DIMENSION(4) :: a
  REAL, DIMENSION(4) :: b = (/ 1.0, -1.0, -2.0, 3.0 /)

  a = (/ -1.0, 2.0, -3.0, 1.0 /)

  b = a * b + (/ 2.0, -1.0, -4.0, 1.0 /)

  PRINT "(4F6.1)", b

END PROGRAM demo_array_literal_constants
```

FIGURE 4.6. Program illustrating rank 1 array literal constants.

```
PROGRAM demo_array_named_constants

   INTEGER :: i

   CHARACTER(9), DIMENSION(12), PARAMETER :: Month_name =   &
         (/ "January  ", "February ", "March    ",          &
            "April    ", "May      ", "June     ",          &
            "July     ", "August   ", "September",          &
            "October  ", "November ", "December " /)

   INTEGER, DIMENSION(12), PARAMETER :: Days_in_month =     &
         (/ 31, 28, 31, 30, 31, 30, 31, 31, 30, 31, 30, 31 /)

   DO i = 1, 12
      PRINT "(1X, A, I5)", Month_name(i), Days_in_month(i)
   END DO

END PROGRAM demo_array_named_constants
```

FIGURE 4.7. Program illustrating array named constants.

constant. This is illustrated by the program of Figure 4.7. When executed, the program of Figure 4.7 displays the following:

```
January     31
February    28
March       31
April       30
May         31
June        30
July        31
August      31
September   30
October     31
November    30
December    31
```

As is the case with scalar named constants, array named constants are used in any situation where the programmer wants to be sure that subsequent code cannot change the values given to the name.

Note in Figure 4.7 that the trailing blanks in the names of months are explicitly coded. The Fortran 90 standard requires that each value have the same type and type parameters, but this requirement may not be strictly enforced in many implementations.

Actually, the array literal constant is only the most important special case of what is called the "array constructor," which will be discussed in greater generality in Section 4.7.

4.6 ARRAY SECTIONS

Fortran 90 provides new mechanisms for referring to a selected portion of an array, called an **array section**. This is illustrated by the program of Figure 4.8a. The declaration of the name array in Figure 4.8a specifies a rank 1 array and initializes array(1) to 11, array(2) to 22, array(3) to 33, array(4) to 44, and array(5) to 55. Each of the five PRINT statements displays a different array section, and the program output looks like this:

```
22   33   44
33   44   55
11   22   33
11   33   55
22   44   55
```

```
PROGRAM demo_sections_1

    INTEGER, DIMENSION(1:5) ::                                    &
                            array = (/ 11, 22, 33, 44, 55 /)

    PRINT "(3I5)", array(2:4)          ! subscript triplet--
                                       ! default stride

    PRINT "(3I5)", array(3:)           ! subscript triplet--
                                       ! default upper bound

    PRINT "(3I5)", array(:3)           ! subscript triplet--
                                       ! default lower bound

    PRINT "(3I5)", array(1:5:2)        ! subscript triplet--
                                       ! no defaults

    PRINT "(3I5)", array((/ 2, 4, 5 /)) ! vector subscript

END PROGRAM demo_sections_1
```

FIGURE 4.8A. Program illustrating array sections.

The first four PRINT statements illustrate the **subscript triplet** mechanism for specifying a sequence of subscripts for an array section. In general, the syntax for a subscript triplet is

[*lower-bound*]:[*upper-bound*][:*stride*]

Each of *lower-bound*, *upper-bound*, and *stride* must be expressions that evaluate to scalar integer values. If *stride* is omitted, it defaults to one, as is the case in the first PRINT statement in Figure 4.8a. An omitted *lower-bound* or *upper-bound* will default to the lower bound or upper bound for the corresponding dimension of the array from which the section is derived, as illustrated by the second and third PRINT statements in Figure 4.8a. The full form of the subscript triplet is illustrated by the fourth PRINT statement in Figure 4.8a.

In the first PRINT statement, 2:4 specifies a range of values, namely 2, 3, and 4, and so array(2:4) refers to the array section consisting of the elements array(2), array(3), and array(4). In the second PRINT statement, the upper bound is omitted in the expression 3:, which means that the upper bound defaults to 5, and so array(3:) refers to the array section consisting of the elements array(3), array(4), and array(5). Similarly, in the third PRINT statement, the omission of the lower bound in the expression array(:3) means that this refers to the array section consisting of the elements array(1), array(2), and array(3). In the fourth PRINT statement, 1:5:2 specifies a subscript range of 1 through 5, moving the subscript forward by 2 each time to obtain the next value in sequence. Thus, array(1:5:2) refers to the array section consisting of elements array(1), array(3), and array(5).

It would be valid in the program of Figure 4.8a to specify the expression array(:), which would be the same as coding array(1:5:1), an array section that is identical with the whole array. Also, it would be valid to specify a negative stride: For example, array(5:1:–2) would refer to an array whose elements would be array(5), array(3), and array(1), in that order. Of course, it is never valid to specify a subscript triplet with a stride of zero.

The last PRINT statement in Figure 4.8a illustrates the second mechanism for specifying a sequence of subscripts for an array section, the **vector subscript** mechanism. A vector subscript is simply a rank 1 array, each element of which takes on an integer value. In the final PRINT statement, the array literal constant (/ 2, 4, 5 /) is the vector subscript, and so here the array section consists of array(2), array(4), and array(5).

For simplicity of exposition, the array sections in Figure 4.8a were specified using constants, but, as is illustrated in Figure 4.8b, array sections may be specified using variables as well. The output of the program of Figure 4.8b is the same as that for the program of Figure 4.8a.

In much the same way that in set theory a subset is itself a set, an array section is itself an array. A subtle consequence of this is that

```
PROGRAM demo_sections_2

    INTEGER, DIMENSION(1:5) ::                        &
                array = (/ 11, 22, 33, 44, 55 /)

    INTEGER :: i, j, k
    INTEGER, DIMENSION(3) :: vector_subscript

    i = 2; j = 4
    PRINT "(3I5)", array(i:j)

    j = 3
    PRINT "(3I5)", array(j:)
    PRINT "(3I5)", array(:j)

    i = 1; j = 5; k = 2
    PRINT "(3I5)", array(i:j:k)

    vector_subscript(1) = 2
    vector_subscript(2) = 4
    vector_subscript(3) = 5
    PRINT "(3I5)", array(vector_subscript)

END PROGRAM demo_sections_2
```

FIGURE 4.8B. Array sections specified using variables.

the storage for the elements of a Fortran 90 array is not necessarily contiguous. In Fortran 90, unlike in traditional Fortran, the programmer must exercise caution in writing code that relies on array elements being stored sequentially.

4.7 ARRAY CONSTRUCTORS

As mentioned in Section 4.5, Fortran 90 supports a mechanism, known as the **array constructor**, for expressing a one-dimensional array. Simple illustrations of this mechanism were given in Figures 4.6 and 4.7, and this section will describe array constructors in more generality.

Consider the Fortran 90 program of Figure 4.9. When executed, the program displays

```
1.0    2.0    3.0    4.0    5.0
1.5    2.5    3.5    4.5    5.5
```

```
PROGRAM demo_array_constructor

    ! array constructor used in initialization
    REAL, DIMENSION(5) :: a = (/ 1.0, 2.0, 3.0, 4.0, 5.0 /)

    REAL :: x, y
    REAL, DIMENSION(2,3) :: b, c
    INTEGER :: i = 2, j = 3
    INTEGER, DIMENSION(5) :: m

    PRINT "(5F6.1)", a

    x = 2.5;  y = 4.5

    ! scalar expressions used to specify array constructor
    a = (/ 1.5, x, 3.5, y, 5.5 /)

    PRINT "(5F6.1)", a

    b(1,1) = 10.0;  b(1,2) = 12.0;  b(1,3) = 14.0
    b(2,1) = 11.0;  b(2,2) = 13.0;  b(2,3) = 15.0
    c(1,1) = 16.0;  c(1,2) = 18.0;  c(1,3) = 20.0
    c(2,1) = 17.0;  c(2,2) = 19.0;  c(2,3) = 21.0

    ! array expressions used to specify array constructor
    a = (/ b(i,1:3), c(1:2,j) /)

    PRINT "(5F6.1)", a

    ! implied DO used to specify array constructor
    m = (/ (i, i = 1, 5) /)

    PRINT "(5I6)", m

    ! intrinsic function used in specifying array constructor
    a = (/ (REAL (i), i = 1, 5) /)

    PRINT "(5F6.1)", a

END PROGRAM demo_array_constructor
```

FIGURE 4.9. Program illustrating array constructors.

```
11.0  13.0  15.0  20.0  21.0
   1     2     3     4     5
 1.0   2.0   3.0   4.0   5.0
```

First, note in the declaration of the array a that an array constructor can be used to initialize a one-dimensional array. These initialized values are displayed by the first PRINT statement. Then observe that scalar variables x and y are assigned the values 2.5 and 4.5, respectively, and the array constructor (/ 1.5, x, 3.5, y, 5.5 /) is assigned to the array a. This illustrates that any sequence of scalar values, constant or variable, can be used in an array constructor. The result of assigning this array constructor to a is displayed by the second PRINT statement.

The next feature illustrated by Figure 4.9 is given by the array constructor (/ b(i,1:3), c(1:2,j) /), which shows that array expressions can be used to specify an array constructor. Since i has the value 2, b(i,1:3) specifies the array section consisting of b(2,1), b(2,2), and b(2,3). Similarly, since j has the value 3, c(1:2,j) specifies the array section consisting of c(1,3) and c(2,3). Thus, the result of assigning (/ b(i,1:3), c(1:2,j) /) to a is displayed by the third PRINT statement.

Next, the array constructor (/ (i, i = 1, 5) /) illustrates that an array constructor can be specified using an implied DO syntax. The result of assigning this array constructor to the array m is displayed by the fourth PRINT statement.

Finally, the array constructor (/ (REAL (i), i = 1, 5) /), which also employs an implied DO, shows that intrinsic functions can be used in specifying an array constructor. The intrinsic function REAL, which is part of both the FORTRAN 77 and Fortran 90 standards, converts an INTEGER argument to its equivalent floating-point form. The result of assigning this array constructor to the array a is displayed by the fifth (and last) PRINT statement. Incidentally, the result would be the same if the REAL intrinsic function were not used here, because the ordinary mixed mode rules would apply, even for the array constructor.

Figure 4.9 has illustrated some different forms that the array constructor can take, but bear in mind the limitation that the values for an array constructor can be defined along only one dimension. However, this restriction can be worked around by using the standard intrinsic function RESHAPE, as will be shown in the next section.

4.8　THE RESHAPE INTRINSIC FUNCTION

There are several situations where a programmer would like to copy the values of the elements of an array of one shape to the elements of an array of a different shape, and Fortran 90 provides the RESHAPE intrinsic function to facilitate such copies. RESHAPE constructs an array of a specified shape from the elements of a given source array. In its simplest use, RESHAPE takes two arguments: The first is the source array, and the second is the shape of the target array to be constructed.

```
PROGRAM demo_reshape

  INTRINSIC RESHAPE, MATMUL

  ! Set initial values for array of rank greater than one.
  REAL, DIMENSION(2,3) :: a =                                      &
          RESHAPE ( (/ 1.0, 2.0, 3.0, 4.0, 5.0, 6.0 /),  &
                      (/ 2, 3 /)                      )

  REAL, DIMENSION(3,2) :: b
  REAL, DIMENSION(2,2) :: c
  INTEGER              :: i

  ! Copy values from a to b, even though shapes differ.
  b = RESHAPE (a, (/ 3, 2 /))

  ! Multiply a times b using matrix mult as in math
  ! texts and add 2 x 2 result to constant 2 x 2 array.
  c = MATMUL (a, b) +                                  &
          RESHAPE ( (/ 1.0, 2.0, 3.0, 4.0 /), (/ 2, 2 /) )

  DO i = 1, 2
     PRINT "(2F6.1)", c(i,:)   ! Display one row of c.
  END DO

END PROGRAM demo_reshape
```

Figure 4.10. Program illustrating the RESHAPE intrinsic function.

Simple uses of RESHAPE are illustrated by the program of Figure 4.10, which when executed results in the following display:

```
23.0  52.0
30.0  68.0
```

Note in Figure 4.10 that RESHAPE is used to set initial values in array a, whose shape is 2×3. The source array is the array constructor (/ 1.0, 2.0, 3.0, 4.0, 5.0, 6.0 /), which, like all array constructors, is a rank 1 array. The shape of the target is specified by the array constructor (/ 2, 3 /).

The second use of RESHAPE in Figure 4.10 is to copy the values of the elements from the 2×3 source array a to the 3×2 array b. RESHAPE may be used in either executable or nonexecutable statements, and there are no restrictions on the shape of the source array argument. However, the argument specifying the shape of the target array must be a rank 1 array.

The third (and last) use of RESHAPE in Figure 4.10 constructs a 2 × 2 array from the array constructor (/ 1.0, 2.0, 3.0, 4.0 /) and illustrates that RESHAPE may be used in array expressions. Also illustrated is the use of the new standard intrinsic function MATMUL, which performs matrix multiplication as usually defined in mathematics textbooks on a pair of rank 2 arrays. Recall that since a is 2 × 3 and b is 3 × 2, the result of performing matrix multiplication of a times b is a 2 × 2 array.

A final noteworthy aspect of Figure 4.10 is the use of the array section c(i,:) in the PRINT statement used to display each row of the array c. As discussed in Section 4.6, c(i,:) is equivalent to c(i,1:2). The Fortran 90 array section often provides a convenient alternative to the implied DO of traditional Fortran.

It should be mentioned that RESHAPE has two optional arguments, in addition to the two mandatory arguments illustrated earlier in this section. Usage of these optional arguments is straightforward and is left as an exercise for the reader.

4.9 ZERO-SIZED ARRAYS

The fundamental reason that the array exists in computer languages is to provide a convenient mechanism for handling a collection of two or more data items of the same type, and so it comes as something of a surprise to some people that there are situations in programming where it is useful for a language to support the notion that an array may contain only a single element or even no elements at all. While traditional Fortran does permit an array to have only one element, the Fortran 90 concept of the **zero-sized array**, that is, an array having no elements, is foreign to most Fortran programmers. But the zero-sized array is really just another example in a series of concepts that have been introduced into the language so that additional code treating zero as a special case is not required.

In older Fortran, it was not unusual to find code like the following:

```
C  Warning: Archaic Fortran follows.
      IF (J .GT. K) GO TO 200
      DO 100 I = J, K
      A(I) = I
  100 CONTINUE
  200 CONTINUE
```

In archaic Fortran, if a DO loop was encountered during execution, the body of that DO loop was always executed at least once. Thus, the IF

statement above was needed to prevent execution of the body of the
loop in the special case where the value of the initial parameter (J in
the above code) was greater than that of the terminal parameter (K in
the above code) at loop entry. Of course, the FORTRAN 77 standard
changed the language rules, and it is now permitted that the body of
a DO loop be executed zero times so that it is no longer necessary to
clutter a program with code such as the IF statement above.

But FORTRAN 77 also introduced the CHARACTER data type into the
language, and a new problem emerged regarding the treatment of zero-
length character strings. Suppose, for example, that S is a variable of
type CHARACTER and the expression S(J:K) is encountered during execution. The FORTRAN 77 standard states that the value of J must be less
than or equal to that of K but gives no indication of what should happen
if this condition is not met. Some FORTRAN 77 implementations have
treated execution of a statement referencing S(J:K) with J greater than
K as a fatal error, causing programmers to sometimes write defensive
code such as

```
T = ' '
IF (J .LE. K) T = S(J:K)
```

Of course, when the length of a target of a CHARACTER assignment is
less than that of the source, blanks are padded on the right of the target,
and so T will consist of all blanks here if J exceeds K. However, most
of the popular FORTRAN 77 implementations in use in the late 1980s
treated S(J:K) with J greater than K as if it were a valid string with zero
length, and so the single line of code

```
T = S(J:K)
```

would have the same effect as the preceding two-line code fragment. In
Fortran 90, the notion of the zero-length string has been made standard
so that this is now another situation in which programmers need not
be concerned about treating zero as a special case.

This finally brings us around to the topic of the zero-sized array,
which is somewhat analogous to the zero-length string. Note that in
Fortran 90 if a is a rank 1 array of type REAL, then the expression a(j:k)
denotes an array section. And just as it turns out to be desirable to treat
a character substring s(j:k) as a valid zero-length string if j exceeds k, it
also turns out to be desirable to designate the array section a(j:k) to be
a valid zero-sized array if j exceeds k.

The Fortran 90 handling of a zero-sized array is illustrated by the
contrived program of Figure 4.11. Observe there that when the loop
index i is 1, the array section x(i+1:4) consists of the elements x(2), x(3),
x(4); when i is 2, x(i+1:4) consists of x(3), x(4); when i is 3, x(i+1:4) consists
of x(4); and when i is 4, x(i+1:4) is a zero-sized array of rank 1. The new

```
PROGRAM demo_zero_sized_array

   INTRINSIC SUM
   INTEGER, DIMENSION(4) :: x = (/ 4, 3, 2, 1 /)
   INTEGER           :: i, total

   DO i = 1, 4
      total = SUM (x(i+1:4))    ! When i is 4, x(i+1:4) is
                                ! a zero-sized array.
      PRINT "(2I5)", i, total
   END DO

END PROGRAM demo_zero_sized_array
```

FIGURE 4.11. Program illustrating a zero-sized array.

standard intrinsic function SUM returns the sum of the elements of its array argument, and so when executed, the program of Figure 4.11 displays

```
1    6
2    3
3    1
4    0
```

Note that the program gives no special treatment to the zero-sized array and that the intrinsic function SUM behaves appropriately by returning zero when given a zero-sized array as its argument.

The zero-sized array in Figure 4.11 occurs in a highly contrived context, but the focus of this section has been merely to present the rationale for the existence of zero-sized arrays in Fortran 90. More natural occurrences of zero-sized arrays will be illustrated in Sections 7.9 and 7.10.

4.10 ALLOCATABLE ARRAYS

In traditional Fortran, the programmer had to specify the amount of storage required by each array before the program was compiled. But Fortran 90 supports **dynamic storage allocation**, that is, storage can be allocated and freed during program execution. One of the ways that array storage can be allocated dynamically is illustrated by the program

```
PROGRAM demo_allocatable_array

   INTEGER, DIMENSION(:), ALLOCATABLE :: a_vector

   INTEGER :: length_of_vector, loop_index

   READ *, length_of_vector                 ! Get size of array.

   ALLOCATE (a_vector(1:length_of_vector))  ! Get storage and
                                            ! declare subscript
                                            ! bounds for array.

   DO loop_index = 1, length_of_vector
      a_vector(loop_index) = loop_index     ! Put vals in array.
   END DO

   PRINT *, a_vector                         ! Display array vals.

   DEALLOCATE (a_vector)                     ! Free array storage.

END PROGRAM demo_allocatable_array
```

FIGURE 4.12. An example of an allocatable array.

of Figure 4.12. Suppose that when the program of Figure 4.12 is executed, the user enters 5. Then the program will display something like

```
1 2 3 4 5
```

First, note that the keyword ALLOCATABLE appears in the attribute list of a_vector in Figure 4.12, indicating that a_vector is an allocatable array. Next, observe the colon inside the parentheses following the keyword DIMENSION in the declaration of a_vector. Fortran 90 syntax uses one colon inside the parentheses following the keyword DIMENSION for each dimension of an allocatable array, and if the array has two or more dimensions, the colons corresponding to the dimensions are separated by commas. Thus, a_vector in Figure 4.12 is being declared as a rank 1 allocatable array. The declaration for a two-dimensional allocatable array would look something like

```
REAL, DIMENSION(:,:), ALLOCATABLE :: a_matrix
```

Observe that the subscript bounds along each dimension of an allocatable array are not part of its declaration—these will be indicated later in the executable part of the program in an ALLOCATE statement. Since the number of elements along each dimension of an allocatable array is not indicated in its declaration, such an array is one of two categories of arrays known as "deferred-shape arrays." (The other category involves the use of pointers and will be discussed in Chapter 10.)

The array a_vector in Figure 4.12 has been allocated no storage and has no subscript bounds specified until the statement

```
ALLOCATE (a_vector(1:length_of_vector))
```

is executed. Upon successful execution of the ALLOCATE statement, contiguous storage for length_of_vector INTEGER values will be allocated, and the a_vector subscript will have been declared to have a lower bound of 1 and an upper bound of the value of length_of_vector. The ALLOCATE statement could have been coded simply as

```
ALLOCATE (a_vector(length_of_vector))
```

since, as always, omitting a lower bound in the specification of array bounds causes the lower bound to default to 1. A typical ALLOCATE statement for a rank 2 array looks something like

```
ALLOCATE (a_matrix(m,n))
```

If an error condition occurs during execution of the ALLOCATE statement in the program of Figure 4.12, the Fortran 90 standard calls for execution to be terminated. While this may be acceptable in some programs, there are situations where it is desirable for the programmer to handle the error more gracefully, and for this reason provision is made for the ALLOCATE statement to return a status. An ALLOCATE statement that returns status from an attempt to allocate storage for a rank 2 array named a_matrix will look something like

```
ALLOCATE (a_matrix(m,n), STAT = alloc_status)
```

where STAT is a keyword and alloc_status is a programmer-chosen scalar INTEGER variable. The idea here is somewhat similar to that of returning status in an OPEN statement. After the above ALLOCATE statement is executed, the value returned in alloc_status should be checked. If the value of alloc_status is anything other than zero, an error occurred during execution of the ALLOCATE statement, and the programmer should provide for handling the error gracefully.

The syntax for the ALLOCATE statement used to allocate storage dynamically for allocatable arrays is given in Figure 4.13. Note that storage for more than one allocatable array may be allocated with a single ALLOCATE statement. Each item in the *array-bounds-list* is of the form

   [*lower-bound:*]*upper-bound*

where if *lower-bound* is omitted, it defaults to 1. If the STAT= specifier is present and an error occurs during execution of the ALLOCATE

ALLOCATE (*allocation-list* [, STAT = *scalar-integer-variable*])

where each item in *allocation-list* is:

allocatable-array(*array-bounds-list*)

FIGURE 4.13. Syntax of **ALLOCATE** statement for allocatable arrays.

statement, *scalar-integer-variable* takes on an implementation-dependent positive value; if there is no error, *scalar-integer-variable* takes on the value 0. It should also be mentioned that the ALLOCATE statement is used not only with allocatable arrays, but also with pointers, but discussion of this latter usage will be deferred until Chapter 10.

When program execution reaches a point where storage that has been allocated is no longer needed for an allocatable array, it is good programming practice to free that storage by using a DEALLOCATE statement as illustrated for a_vector in Figure 4.12. The syntax for a DEALLOCATE statement that frees storage for allocatable arrays is given in Figure 4.14. The syntax of the DEALLOCATE statement is similar to that of the ALLOCATE statement, except *allocatable-array-list* consists simply of allocatable array names—the list of bounds is not present in the DEALLOCATE statement as it is in the ALLOCATE statement. Here is an example of a DEALLOCATE statement:

```
DEALLOCATE (a, b, temp, STAT = dealloc_stat)
```

Of course, if no DEALLOCATE statement is given for an allocatable array, the storage will ultimately be freed anyway, but the point in the execution where deallocation will occur is determined by a reasonably complicated set of rules, which will not be given here. It often makes no difference whether storage for an allocatable array remains allocated until the program terminates, in which case it is perhaps unimportant if a DEALLOCATE statement is present, but the careful programmer will usually want to use a DEALLOCATE statement to identify explicitly the point where deallocation occurs, both to maintain tighter control over storage and to make the program clearer to readers.

DEALLOCATE (*allocatable-array-list* [, STAT = *scalar-integer-variable*])

FIGURE 4.14. The DEALLOCATE statement for allocatable arrays.

4.11 INVERTING A MATRIX

Recall that for an $n \times n$ matrix A, there may exist another $n \times n$ matrix A^{-1} such that

$$A\,A^{-1} \;=\; A^{-1}\,A \;=\; I\,,$$

where I is the $n \times n$ matrix having ones along its diagonal and zeros elsewhere. I is called the "identity matrix," and the matrix denoted by A^{-1} is known as the "inverse" of A. This section will present a complete program that finds the inverse of a matrix. The solution technique employed utilizes a version of the approach known as "Gauss–Jordan elimination." The code presented here is intended merely to illustrate Fortran 90 array features. Possible error conditions and execution efficiency are ignored, and the resulting program is unsuitable for production use.

The matrix inversion method to be pursued in this section involves first appending an $n \times n$ identity matrix to the right of the $n \times n$ matrix whose inverse is sought, thereby creating an $n \times 2n$ matrix that will be referred to here as the "augmented matrix." Suppose, for example, that it is desired to find the inverse of the following 3×3 matrix:

$$\begin{bmatrix} 1 & 2 & 5 \\ 2 & 3 & 8 \\ -1 & 1 & 2 \end{bmatrix}.$$

Then the 3×3 identity matrix is appended to the right of this matrix, and the augmented matrix is the resulting 3×6 matrix:

$$\begin{bmatrix} 1 & 2 & 5 & 1 & 0 & 0 \\ 2 & 3 & 8 & 0 & 1 & 0 \\ -1 & 1 & 2 & 0 & 0 & 1 \end{bmatrix}.$$

If the inverse of the original matrix exists, it can be found by performing a sequence of manipulations on the $n \times 2n$ augmented matrix. The manipulations transform the left half of the augmented matrix into the $n \times n$ identity matrix and its right half into the desired inverse. To continue the example, a sequence of such manipulations can be applied to the above 3×6 matrix that will transform it into the following

$$\begin{bmatrix} 1 & 0 & 0 & 2 & -1 & -1 \\ 0 & 1 & 0 & 12 & -7 & -2 \\ 0 & 0 & 1 & -5 & 3 & 1 \end{bmatrix}.$$

The left half of the transformed augmented matrix is the 3×3 identity matrix, and the right half contains the inverse of the original matrix. Hence, the inverse of the initial matrix given in this section is

$$\begin{bmatrix} 2 & -1 & -1 \\ 12 & -7 & -2 \\ -5 & 3 & 1 \end{bmatrix}.$$

The manipulations used to carry out the transformation of the augmented $n \times 2n$ matrix will be restricted here to what are known as "row operations," where a row operation is one of the following:

1. Exchange two rows.
2. Divide a row by a nonzero scalar.
3. Subtract a scalar multiple of one row from another row.

It has been shown that if the inverse of the original matrix exists, performing these three row operations on the augmented matrix in any sequence that transforms its left half into the identity matrix will simultaneously transform its right half into the desired inverse.

A systematic procedure for applying the preceding row operations has been discovered that has proven to be highly reliable and is reasonably efficient. If a_{ij} represents the element in the ith row and jth column of the $n \times 2n$ matrix that starts out as the augmented matrix and is transformed into a matrix whose left half is the $n \times n$ identity matrix and whose right half is the desired inverse, this procedure can be described as follows:

Gauss–Jordan Elimination
> For each column j, $j = 1$ through n:
>> In column j, find the row index m of the element
>>> having the largest magnitude in rows j through n.
>> Exchange row m with row j.
>> Divide row j by a_{jj}.
>> For each row i, $i = 1$ through n:
>>> If $i \neq j$, subtract a_{ij} times row j from row i.

When attempting to divide row j by a_{jj} in the above procedure, it is possible for a_{jj} to turn out to be zero. This means that the inverse of the original matrix does not exist, and the procedure is terminated.

Figure 4.15 gives a program that reads in the elements of a square matrix whose inverse is desired, appends the appropriate identity matrix to the right of the input matrix, and determines the inverse using Gauss–Jordan elimination as detailed earlier. In the program, a

```
PROGRAM invert_matrix
   REAL, DIMENSION(:,:), ALLOCATABLE :: a
   INTEGER :: i, j, m, n
   REAL, DIMENSION(:), ALLOCATABLE :: temp

   PRINT "(A)", " Enter number of rows (= number of cols):"
   READ *, n

   ALLOCATE (a(n,2*n), temp(2*n))

   ! Get elements of matrix to be inverted.
   DO i = 1, n
      DO j = 1, n
         PRINT "(2(A, I3))", " Enter value of element" // &
                             " in row ", i, " col ", j
         READ *, a(i,j)
      END DO
   END DO

   a(:,n+1:2*n) = 0.0       ! Append identity
   DO i = 1, n              ! matrix to right
      a(i,n+i) = 1.0        ! of matrix to
   END DO                   ! be inverted.

   !*********** Perform Gauss-Jordan elimination. ***********!

   DO j = 1, n  ! Loop over first n columns of matrix.

      ! Find row index m of element with largest magnitude.
      m = j            ! Start on the diagonal.
      DO i = j + 1, n  ! Loop over rows below diagonal.
         IF (ABS (a(i,j)) > ABS (a(m,j))) m = i
      END DO

      ! Exchange row m with row j.
      temp = a(j,:);  a(j,:) = a(m,:);  a(m,:) = temp

      a(j,:) = a(j,:) / a(j,j)   ! Divide row j by a(j,j)

      DO i = 1, n  ! Loop over each row of matrix.
                   ! Subtract a(i,j) times row j from row i.
         IF (i /= j) a(i,:) = a(i,:) - a(i,j) * a(j,:)
      END DO
   END DO

   PRINT "(/A)", " The inverse is"
   DO i = 1, n                          ! Display
      PRINT *, a(i,n+1:2*n)             ! each row
   END DO                               ! of inverse.
END PROGRAM invert_matrix
```

FIGURE 4.15. Program to find the inverse of a matrix.

is the name of the matrix that starts out as the augmented matrix and undergoes transformation as the procedure progresses, and the names i, j, m, and n have the same meanings as in the description of Gauss–Jordan elimination. The name temp is used in Figure 4.15 to designate a rank 1 array of sufficient size to store one row of the augmented matrix during the step where rows are exchanged. Note that array sections provide an ideal mechanism for expressing the row operations required by the solution procedure. Also, observe that storage for arrays is not allocated in Figure 4.15 until after the user has specified the size of the matrix to be inverted.

As an example, suppose that it is desired to find the inverse of the 3×3 matrix given near the beginning of the section. When correct responses are made to all prompts given by the program of Figure 4.15, output along the lines of the following will be displayed

```
The inverse is
   1.9999989  -0.9999993  -0.9999998
  11.9999981  -6.9999995  -1.9999996
  -4.9999990   2.9999995   0.9999998
```

Note that the inverse computed by the program is in good agreement with the manually computed inverse given earlier in this section, although there is a slight loss of precision due to floating-point representation.

A serious weakness of the program of Figure 4.15 is that no provision is made to handle gracefully an input matrix whose inverse does not exist. As the code stands, trying to invert such a matrix can be expected to result in an attempt to divide by zero, which usually constitutes an execution-time error on most systems. Before dividing by a(j,j), its value should be checked, and if it is found to be very small in magnitude, an appropriate message should be displayed; this is not done here for simplicity of exposition.

CHAPTER 5

DERIVED TYPES

5.1 INTRODUCTION TO DERIVED TYPES AND STRUCTURES

There are many situations in programming where it is desirable that a programmer be permitted to group a collection of related pieces of data, possibly of different types, under a single name. Several languages, including COBOL, PL/I, C, Pascal, and Ada, provide this capability. But despite widespread agreement as to the usefulness of this capability in organizing complicated data, it is supported in only a few FORTRAN 77 implementations (notably Digital's). The terminology used in dealing with a data aggregate containing different types is not uniform throughout the software world, and both the term "record" and the term "structure" have been associated with such a collection. The Fortran 90 standard employs only the latter term in this context. And while the Fortran 90 structure is conceptually similar to such data aggregates in other languages and in pre-1992 FORTRAN 77 implementations, the Fortran 90 standard embraces some differences in vocabulary, syntax, and rules of usage.

Now, in traditional Fortran, the programmer never specifies a data type definition since the only data types supported are the intrinsic ones, such as INTEGER, REAL, COMPLEX, CHARACTER, and LOGICAL, which are automatically defined. But Fortran 90 permits the programmer to specify definitions for data types categorized as "derived types," so-called because, rather than being fundamental data types, they are derived from the intrinsic types. With the definition of a derived type established, the programmer can use variables, constants, and other data objects (such as the result of applying operators or a result returned by a function) of that derived type, and such a data object is called a "structure."

But the Fortran 90 derived type enhances the language with capabilities that go beyond simply providing the mechanism for treating a collection of related pieces of data as a unit. One important use of the derived type is in building sophisticated dynamic data structures, known as "linked lists," which have a variety of applications. This will be elaborated on in Chapter 11 in conjunction with the discussion of pointers. Another important use of the derived type arises when a programmer creates an application-specific data type, known as an "abstract data type," with a programmer-specified set of permissible values and operations. This typically involves placing a derived-type definition in a module containing subprograms that specify operations on structures of the derived type. Chapters 7, 9, and 12 will discuss the relationship that exists between derived types and modules in Fortran 90. The remainder of this chapter will be devoted to the presentation of the more elementary aspects of derived types and structures.

5.2 DEFINING A DERIVED TYPE AND USING STRUCTURES

Figure 5.1 gives a simple Fortran 90 program illustrating a derived type. When executed, the program of Figure 5.1 displays

```
Maria Johnson       21  3.4
```

Note first in Figure 5.1 the series of statements beginning with

```
TYPE :: student_type
```

and ending with the END TYPE statement. This series of statements defines a **derived type**, that is, a data type created by a programmer which describes a collection of logically related pieces of data. Each piece of data in such a collection is said to be a **component**, and each component definition in a derived-type definition describes a piece of data of an intrinsic data type or of another derived type. (It is also possible in connection with pointers for a component definition to refer to the derived type of which it is a part, but discussion of this will be deferred until Chapter 11.) In Figure 5.1, the programmer has chosen the name student_type to designate a derived type with three components: name, age, and gpa. The pieces of data described by the component definitions are of types CHARACTER, INTEGER, and REAL, respectively. Now, it is important to understand that this series of statements merely constitutes a type definition—no storage has been reserved. The type definition is only a template that describes how a programmer should picture a piece of data of type student_type.

The statement

```
TYPE (student_type) :: a_student
```

declares a_student to be a scalar variable of type student_type, which implies that a_student is a composite object made up of three compo-

```
PROGRAM demo_derived_type

   ! Define a derived type named student_type.
   TYPE :: student_type
      CHARACTER(20) :: name    ! Define student_type as
      INTEGER       :: age     ! consisting of 3 components,
      REAL          :: gpa     ! each of different data type.
   END TYPE student_type

   ! Declare a variable a_student of type student_type.
   TYPE (student_type) :: a_student

   ! Assign a value to each component of a_student.
   a_student%name = "Maria Johnson"
   a_student%age  = 21
   a_student%gpa  = 3.4

   ! Display the value assigned to each component.
   PRINT "(1X, A, I3, F5.1)", a_student

END PROGRAM demo_derived_type
```

FIGURE 5.1. Program illustrating a derived type.

nents, one corresponding to name, another corresponding to age, and a third corresponding to grade point average. This declaration causes storage to be reserved for a data aggregate fitting the description set forth by the definition of student_type. In Fortran 90, a scalar data object of derived type is called a **structure**, so a_student is an example of a structure.

While the main purpose of having derived types is so that a single name such as a_student can be used to refer to a collection of data, it is still necessary to be able to refer to individual components of the collection as well. Observe in Figure 5.1 that this is done in standard Fortran 90 by specifying the variable name, followed by the percent sign (%), followed by the component name. The percent sign is called the **component selector**. Readers familiar with other computer languages and other versions of Fortran may be surprised that standard Fortran 90 does not use the period (.) in the role of component selector because it would clash with the language's use of the period in delimiting both intrinsic operators (.AND., .OR., etc.) and programmer-defined operators (a new feature to be described in Chapter 9). Incidentally, it is syntactically acceptable to surround the percent sign with blanks, but this will not be done in this tutorial because such usage is not suggestive of the relationship between the variable name and the component name and is out of step with usual practice in other languages.

Note in the PRINT statement of Figure 5.1 that using the variable name a_student by itself has the same effect as if it were coded:

```
PRINT "(1X, A, I3, F5.1)", a_student%name, &
                           a_student%age,  &
                           a_student%gpa
```

In general, if a variable or other data object of derived type appears in an I/O list of a formatted I/O statement, it is treated as if its components were individually specified, maintaining the same component order as given in the definition of the derived type. In many applications involving an external file containing character data in records of identical length, a derived type provides the best way of dealing with the file.

5.3 COMPONENTS NEED NOT BE OF DIFFERENT TYPES

Although the components of a derived type are typically of different data types, it sometimes makes good sense to define a derived type where all components are of the same type. Consider, for example, the derived type rational_type (see Figure 5.2), whose two components, num and denom, are both of type INTEGER. When executed, the program of Figure 5.2 displays

```
product = 8/35
```

Note in Figure 5.2 that it is syntactically valid to define more than one component on the same line, but this often degrades the readability of the code. Also, observe that rat_1, rat_2, and product are declared in a single statement, illustrating that more than one variable of a derived type may be declared in the same statement.

Usually, an array should be used for collections of data of the same type, and a variable of a derived type should be used for collections of data of different types. But this is not always true, and and the choice of data specifications should be made based on the clarity of the resulting code. For example, it might be clearer under some circumstances to use

```
TYPE :: point_type
   REAL :: x_coord
   REAL :: y_coord
   REAL :: z_coord
END TYPE point_type
```

```
PROGRAM demo_rational_type

    TYPE :: rational_type
        ! Components of same type may be defined on same line.
        INTEGER :: num, denom
    END TYPE rational_type

    ! Type declaration for 3 variables of same derived type:
    TYPE (rational_type) :: rat_1, rat_2, product

    rat_1%num = 4;  rat_1%denom = 7
    rat_2%num = 2;  rat_2%denom = 5

    product%num   = rat_1%num   * rat_2%num
    product%denom = rat_1%denom * rat_2%denom

    PRINT "(' product = ', I1, '/', I2)", product

END PROGRAM demo_rational_type
```

FIGURE 5.2. A derived type with components of the same type.

```
TYPE (point_type) :: point
```

rather than

```
REAL, DIMENSION(3) :: x  ! Cartesian coords of point
```

to describe a point in a three-dimensional Cartesian coordinate system.

5.4 ASSIGNMENT TO VARIABLES OF A DERIVED TYPE

The treatment of variables of a derived type differs rather dramatically from that of variables of one of the intrinsic data types, and it may not be obvious that in Fortran 90 the equal sign (=) is automatically available to assign the values of a data object of a derived type to a variable of that derived type. This is illustrated by the program of Figure 5.3, which, when executed, displays

```
10 September 1938
```

Observe in Figure 5.3 that the statement

```
date_2 = date_1
```

```
PROGRAM demo_structure_assignment

   TYPE :: date_type
      INTEGER      :: day
      CHARACTER(9) :: month
      INTEGER      :: year
   END TYPE date_type

   TYPE (date_type) :: date_1, date_2

   date_1%day   = 10
   date_1%month = "September"
   date_1%year  = 1938          .

   date_2 = date_1  ! structure-to-structure assignment

   PRINT "(I3, 1X, A, I5)", date_2

END PROGRAM demo_structure_assignment
```

FIGURE 5.3. Program illustrating structure assignment.

causes the value of each component of date_1 to be assigned to the corresponding component of date_2 and that no special action has been taken to attach this meaning to the equal sign. However, this works only for objects of the same derived type. To make this clearer, suppose the following definition and declaration were added to the program of Figure 5.3:

```
TYPE :: date
   INTEGER      :: day
   CHARACTER(9) :: month
   INTEGER      :: year
END TYPE date
TYPE (date) :: date_3
```

Then, it might be thought that since all corresponding components of the derived types date_type and date have identical names and types, the following would be valid:

```
date_3 = date_1   ! invalid
```

However, date_type and date are considered to be different derived types, and therefore date_1 and date_3 are objects of different derived types—thus, the equal sign is **not** automatically available for the invalid assignment attempted above.

Also, since the equal sign is automatically available, it might be thought that operators, such as +, *, and so forth, might be automatically available where it makes sense to operate component by component on two variables of the same derived type, but this is *not* the case. For example, it might be expected that the following would work with no special programming effort

```
TYPE :: rational_type
   INTEGER :: num, denom
END TYPE rational_type
TYPE (rational_type) :: rat_1, rat_2, product
rat_1%num = 4; rat_1%denom = 7
rat_2%num = 2; rat_2%denom = 5
product = rat_1 * rat_2  ! not automatically OK
```

But this will not automatically work, although, as will be shown in Chapter 9, there is a mechanism, known as "operator overloading," by which a programmer can attach an appropriate meaning to the asterisk (*) in the preceding code fragment. Incidentally, it should be mentioned in this connection that, unlike some languages (notably C), the equal sign is *not* considered to be an operator in Fortran.

5.5 STRUCTURE CONSTRUCTORS

As illustrated in Chapter 4, the array constructor often provides a convenient way to specify the values of the elements of an array, and somewhat analogously, Fortran 90 supports a special mechanism for specifying the values of the components of a data object of a derived type. After a derived-type definition has been established, the capability is automatically available of creating a structure of that derived type with specified component values simply by coding the derived-type name followed by a parenthesized list of component values. This is illustrated by the program of Figure 5.4, which, when executed, displays

```
2.100  10.500 Header String        73
3.000   9.000 Subheader String     76
4.000   5.080 Annotation Goes Here 88
```

Note in Figure 5.4 that the variable s_1 is initialized using the expression

```
string_type (2.1, 10.5, "Header String", 73)
```

```
PROGRAM demo_structure_constructors

   TYPE :: string_type
      REAL          :: x_loc, y_loc
      CHARACTER(20) :: text
      INTEGER       :: font
   END TYPE string_type

   ! structure constructor used to initialize a variable
   TYPE (string_type) ::                                          &
         s_1 = string_type (2.1, 10.5, "Header String", 73)

   REAL :: y = 2.0

   PRINT "(2F8.3, 1X, A, I3)", s_1

   ! structure constructor used in an executable statement
   s_1 = string_type (3, 9, "Subheader String", 76)
   PRINT "(2F8.3, 1X, A, I3)", s_1

   ! Expr list for struct constructor may contain a variable.
   s_1 =                                                          &
      string_type (4.0, 2.54 * y, "Annotation Goes Here", 88)
   PRINT "(2F8.3, 1X, A, I3)", s_1

END PROGRAM demo_structure_constructors
```

FIGURE 5.4. Program illustrating structure constructors.

This creates a structure of the type string_type and sets the component x_loc to 2.1, the component y_loc to 10.5, the component text to "Header String   " (seven blanks are padded on the right), and the component font to 73. This expression is an example of a **structure constructor**, which in general has the form

derived-type-name (expr-list)

where *derived-type-name* must have been defined earlier and *expr-list* specifies values for the components of a structure of type *derived-type-name*. The values specified in *expr-list* must agree in number and order with the components given in the definition of *derived-type-name*.

Observe in Figure 5.4 that a structure constructor can be used to initialize a variable in a declaration as well as in executable statements. Note also that, in an executable statement, the values in *expr-list* may be specified by expressions involving variables as well as constants. Finally, note that a value in *expr-list* need not agree precisely in type and type parameters with its corresponding component definition, and if it does not agree, the assignment of each component is made under the same conversion rules that apply to ordinary assignment statements.

5.6 COMPONENTS MAY BE OF DERIVED TYPES

All of the components of derived types illustrated so far have been of intrinsic data types, but Fortran 90 permits components to be of derived types as well. This is illustrated in the program of Figure 5.5, where the component address of the derived type customer_record is of the derived type address_type. When executed, the program of Figure 5.5 displays

```
Michael Wong
1234 State Street
Chicago, IL 60609
```

Observe that there are two derived types defined in Figure 5.5. The first is address_type and the second is customer_record. Type address_type is defined as having four scalar components, each of intrinsic data type CHARACTER. It is worth noting that the lengths of the four CHARACTER components of type address_type are all different.

Now focus attention on the definition of type customer_record. This derived type has two components; the first component is a scalar of type CHARACTER with length 50, and the second component is a structure of type address_type. Thus, a data object of derived type customer_record has a component named address whose data type is the derived type address_type.

Next, the variable named an_address is declared to be of the derived type address_type. Then, as described in the preceding section, a structure constructor is used in the first assignment statement to store values in each of the four components of the variable an_address.

Note that the variable named a_customer is declared to be of the derived type customer_record, and a structure constructor is used in the second assignment statement to store values in both of the components of the variable a_customer. It should be recognized that it would be possible to replace the two assignment statements of Figure 5.5 with the single assignment statement

```
a_customer = customer_record ("Michael Wong",            &
                address_type ("1234 State Street",       &
                      "Chicago", "IL", "60609"))
```

in which case the declaration of an_address would not be needed.

```
PROGRAM demo_nested_structures

  TYPE :: address_type
     CHARACTER(60) :: number_and_street
     CHARACTER(20) :: city
     CHARACTER(2)  :: state_abbreviation
     CHARACTER(5)  :: zip_code
  END TYPE address_type

  TYPE :: customer_record                   ! component types:
     CHARACTER(50)          :: customer_name ! intrinsic type
     TYPE (address_type) :: address          ! derived type
  END TYPE customer_record

  TYPE (address_type)     :: an_address
  TYPE (customer_record) :: a_customer

  an_address = address_type ("1234 State Street",       &
                             "Chicago", "IL", "60609")

  ! Structure constructor contains variable of derived type.
  a_customer = customer_record ("Michael Wong", an_address)

  PRINT "(1X, A)", a_customer%customer_name

  ! number_and_street is component of address_type, which
  ! is data type of address component of a_customer.
  PRINT "(1X, A)", a_customer%address%number_and_street

  PRINT "(1X, A)", TRIM (a_customer%address%city) // ", "   &
                   // a_customer%address%state_abbreviation &
                   // " " // a_customer%address%zip_code

END PROGRAM demo_nested_structures
```

FIGURE 5.5. A derived type with a component of another derived type.

Finally, observe that each of the three PRINT statements in Figure 5.5 produces one line of output. The first PRINT statement displays the value of a_customer%customer_name, the first component of the variable a_customer. The second PRINT statement displays the value of a_customer%address%number_and_street, the first component (named number_and_street) of the structure which is the second component (named address) of the variable a_customer. Observe here that the object a_customer%address is itself a structure, and hence to refer to one of its components, a second percent sign must be used, followed by the name of that component. The third PRINT statement uses the concatenation operator // to build an output string consisting of the values of the last three components (city, state_abbreviation, and zip_code) of the structure a_customer%address.

Incidentally, the use of the handy, new Fortran 90 standard intrinsic function TRIM is illustrated by the third PRINT statement. TRIM returns the value of its CHARACTER argument with all trailing blanks removed. Thus, in Figure 5.5, TRIM is used to avoid the 13 trailing blanks that would otherwise separate the city name "Chicago" from the following comma.

5.7 A STRUCTURE COMPONENT CAN BE AN ARRAY

A component of a structure can be an array as well as a simple (non-composite) variable or another structure. An illustration of this is given in the program of Figure 5.6. When the program of Figure 5.6 is executed, the following is displayed:

```
AB92X7R   36  45  41  48  46
```

Observe in Figure 5.6 that the array quarterly_sales is a component of the structure inv_item. Note that inv_item%quarterly_sales(1) refers to the first element in the array, inv_item%quarterly_sales(2) refers to the second element, and so on. This illustrates that, as always in Fortran, an array subscript and its enclosing parentheses immediately follow the array name. In particular, it would be an error here to code something like inv_item(1)%quarterly_sales, since inv_item is not an array and hence cannot be subscripted. However, as will be illustrated in the next section, a variable of derived type may be subscripted if the variable has been declared to be an array.

Incidentally, it should be noted that the six assignment statements in Figure 5.6 could be replaced by the single assignment statement

```
inv_item =                                          &
     inventory_rec ("AB92X7R", 36, (/ 45, 41, 48, 46 /))
```

where the right-hand side is a structure constructor. Observe that the third argument to the structure constructor is an array constructor to initialize the values of the elements of the array component quarterly_sales.

This section has illustrated that an array may be a structure component, but it should be mentioned that the Fortran 90 standard does not support the use of an allocatable array as a structure component.

```
PROGRAM demo_array_component_of_struct

  ! Define a derived type with an array component.
  TYPE :: inventory_rec
    CHARACTER(8)          :: part_number
    INTEGER               :: quantity_on_hand
    INTEGER, DIMENSION(4) :: quarterly_sales    ! Component is
                                                ! a 4-element,
                                                ! rank 1 array.

  END TYPE inventory_rec

  TYPE (inventory_rec) :: inv_item    ! Declare a scalar
                                      ! variable of type
                                      ! inventory_rec.

  inv_item%part_number       = "AB92X7R"
  inv_item%quantity_on_hand  = 36

  inv_item%quarterly_sales(1) = 45    ! Store a value in each
  inv_item%quarterly_sales(2) = 41    ! element of the array
  inv_item%quarterly_sales(3) = 48    ! component of scalar
  inv_item%quarterly_sales(4) = 46    ! variable inv_item.

  PRINT "(1X, A, 5I3)", inv_item

END PROGRAM demo_array_component_of_struct
```

FIGURE 5.6. An array that is a component of a structure.

Thus, the ALLOCATABLE attribute, which was discussed in Section 4.10, may not be specified for a component of a derived type. However, this restriction is not severe since it is possible to achieve the same effect by using pointers, as will be shown in Section 10.8.

5.8 An Element of an Array Can Be a Structure

In traditional Fortran, each element of an array must always be only a simple data object, that is, it can never be a data aggregate. However, the Fortran 90 standard permits an array element to be a structure. The program of Figure 5.7 illustrates the use of an array of structures. When the program is executed, the following is displayed:

```
PROGRAM demo_array_of_structures

   TYPE :: employee_type
      INTEGER      :: employee_number
      CHARACTER(20) :: name
      CHARACTER(15) :: job_title
      REAL         :: weekly_salary
      LOGICAL      :: is_married
   END TYPE employee_type

   ! Declare a 5-element, rank 1 array of type employee_type.
   TYPE (employee_type), DIMENSION(5) :: employee

   INTEGER :: employee_index

   employee(1) = employee_type (1111, "Karen Thorne",      &
                                "Manager",       1350.64,  &
                                                  .TRUE. )
   employee(2) = employee_type (2222, "John McIntyre",     &
                                "Engineer",      1208.37,  &
                                                  .FALSE.)
   employee(3) = employee_type (3333, "Linda Thompson",    &
                                "Secretary",      746.19,  &
                                                  .TRUE. )
   employee(4) = employee_type (4444, "George Marshall",   &
                                "Administrator", 980.46,   &
                                                  .TRUE. )
   employee(5) = employee_type (5555, "Cindy Smith",       &
                                "Receptionist",   565.07,  &
                                                  .FALSE.)

   DO employee_index = 1, 5
      IF (employee(employee_index)%weekly_salary > 900.00) &
             PRINT "(I5, 1X, 2A, F7.2, 1X, L1)",           &
                                employee(employee_index)
   END DO

END PROGRAM demo_array_of_structures
```

FIGURE 5.7. Program illustrating an array of structures.

```
1111 Karen Thorne        Manager       1350.64 T
2222 John McIntyre       Engineer      1208.37 F
4444 George Marshall     Administrator  980.46 T
```

First, note that in Figure 5.7 employee is declared to be a one-dimensional array with subscripts 1 through 5, and that each of employee(1), employee(2), employee(3), employee(4), and employee(5) is a structure of derived type employee_type. Each of the five assignment statements uses a structure constructor to store values in the components of one of the structures, each of which is an element in the array employee.

After the values are stored in the array elements, the DO construct is used to loop through the array employee. The IF statement is used to test the value of weekly_salary for each employee, and for any employee whose weekly salary exceeds $900.00, all of the information in the array about that employee is displayed. In the IF statement, note that the value of the weekly salary of each employee is referred to by the expression employee(employee_index)%weekly_salary. It is employee that is the array here, and thus the array subscript employee_index and its enclosing parentheses immediately follow the name employee. Writing employee%weekly_salary(employee_index) would be an error in Figure 5.7 since the component weekly_salary is a not an array.

It is worthwhile to think how data like that of Figure 5.7 are handled in versions of Fortran that do not support structures. The usual approach is to declare a set of separate arrays something like the following:

```
* Warning: The following declarations of parallel
*          arrays are for a version of Fortran
*          that does not support structures.
      INTEGER      employee_number(5)
      CHARACTER*20 employee_name(5)
      CHARACTER*15 employee_job_title(5)
      REAL         employee_weekly_salary(5)
      LOGICAL      employee_is_married(5)
```

The style of the declarations here is closer to previous versions of Fortran to reinforce the idea that they are not part of a Fortran 90 program (although they are all syntactically acceptable in standard Fortran 90). Arrays of this sort are called "parallel arrays." All the data items with the same subscript (say, 4) pertain to a particular employee (the fourth employee). The principal advantage in using an array of structures over using parallel arrays is that the array of structures indicates the data relationships in a clearer, more suggestive manner. Also, the array of structures approach permits the data for one logical record (here one employee) to be copied using a single structure-to-structure assignment statement, while the same operation with the parallel arrays approach typically requires a series of several scalar-to-scalar assignment statements.

5.9 A VARIABLE NAME MAY DUPLICATE A COMPONENT NAME

It should come as no surprise that there may be a component of the same name in two different derived-type definitions. Consider, for example, the following code fragment:

```
TYPE :: student_type    ! type definition for student_type
   CHARACTER(6) :: id    ! definition for component name id
            .
            .
            .
END TYPE student_type

TYPE :: class_type       ! type definition for class_type
   CHARACTER(6) :: id    ! definition for component name id
            .
            .
            .
END TYPE class_type
```

Then, suppose that variables of each of these derived types are declared:

```
TYPE (student_type) :: student
TYPE (class_type)   :: class
```

Now, in the code outside the type definitions, any reference to the component name id must be of the form student%id or class%id, and so it is not possible for ambiguity to arise.

However, it may not be quite so obvious that a variable name is permitted to duplicate a derived-type component name. Figure 5.8 presents a complete program in which the name id is used both as a component name and as the name of an ordinary, simple variable. Suppose that the program of Figure 5.8 is executed, and, at the READ, the user enters "12345" (without the quotes). Then the program displays

```
12345    89
```

In terms of Fortran 90 rules, there is no problem because any reference to the component name id outside the definition of type stock_rec is

```
PROGRAM demo_duplicate_names

   TYPE :: stock_rec
      CHARACTER(5) :: id      ! Define component named id.
      INTEGER      :: qty
   END TYPE stock_rec

   TYPE (stock_rec) :: item

   CHARACTER(5) :: id         ! Declare variable named id.

   READ *, id                 ! refers to variable

   item%id = id               ! Left side refers to component,
                              ! right side refers to variable.


   item%qty = 89

   PRINT "(1X, A, I5)", item

END PROGRAM demo_duplicate_names
```

FIGURE 5.8. Program with variable name same as component name.

prefaced by the name of a variable of type stock_rec and a percent sign (%), while any reference to the simple variable named id is not prefaced in this manner. However, it is generally recommended that the practice of giving the same name to a variable and a derived type component be avoided for reasons of readability.

Component names are so completely independent of other names in the program that it is legal even to give a name to a structure that is the same as the name of one of its components. A silly illustration of this is given in the program of Figure 5.9, which, when executed, displays

7

Except under very unusual circumstances, this practice should, of course, be avoided.

The ideas discussed in this section are related to the important notion of the **scope** of a name, that is, the part of a program within which the name has a single interpretation. As indicated by the examples in this section, the interpretation of a component name is different, depending on whether it appears inside or outside a derived-type definition. Inside a derived-type definition, a component name stands alone in a statement that is similar in form to a type declaration for a variable, while

```
PROGRAM struct_name_same_as_comp_name

    TYPE :: silly_type
        INTEGER :: silly    ! Define component named silly.
    END TYPE silly_type

    TYPE (silly_type) :: silly    ! Declare variable
                                  ! named silly.

    silly%silly = 7    ! variable name to left of %,
                       ! component name to right of %

    PRINT *, silly    ! refers to variable name

END PROGRAM struct_name_same_as_comp_name
```

FIGURE 5.9. Program with structure name same as component name.

outside a derived-type definition, a component name must be prefaced by a structure name and a percent sign.

5.10 DERIVED-TYPE DEFINITIONS AND HOST ASSOCIATION

The derived-type definition is one of the new language features that makes the issue of scope significantly more complicated in Fortran 90 than it has traditionally been in Fortran. Other such features are module subprograms (Chapter 7), internal subprograms (Chapter 8), and interface bodies (Chapter 13). To deal with matters related to scope, the Fortran 90 standard partitions a program into collections of code known as "scoping units," where a **scoping unit** is defined as one of the following:

1. A derived-type definition;

2. an interface body, excluding any derived-type definitions and interface bodies contained within it;

3. a subprogram, excluding derived-type definitions, interface bodies, and subprograms contained within it; or

4. a main program, module, or block data program unit, excluding derived-type definitions, interface bodies, and subprograms contained within it.

Furthermore, a scoping unit that immediately surrounds another scoping unit is called the **host scoping unit**.

To see how these definitions apply in a simple situation, consider the program of Figure 5.10. Any derived-type definition is a scoping unit, and so the definition of char_type is a scoping unit and is labeled "scoping unit 1" in the comments. There are no interface bodies, subprograms, modules, or block data program units in Figure 5.10, and so the main program, with the derived-type definition removed, is the only other scoping unit and is labeled "scoping unit 2." Observe that scoping unit 2 is the host scoping unit for scoping unit 1.

In the Fortran 90 standard, the rules governing the scope of names are couched in terms of scoping units. One of the most important rules is that a derived-type definition, module subprogram, or internal subprogram has access to the named entities in its host scoping unit, and

```
! Note: Scoping unit 2 is the host scoping unit for
!        scoping unit 1.  Hence, Max_len is available
!        inside the derived-type type definition by
!        host association.

PROGRAM demo_host_association              ! scoping unit 2
   INTEGER, PARAMETER :: Max_len = 132     ! scoping unit 2

   TYPE :: char_type                       ! scoping unit 1
      CHARACTER(Max_len) :: string         ! scoping unit 1
      INTEGER            :: len            ! scoping unit 1
   END TYPE char_type                      ! scoping unit 1

   TYPE (char_type), DIMENSION(100) :: s   ! scoping unit 2
   CHARACTER(Max_len) :: buffer            ! scoping unit 2
   INTEGER :: i, ios, n = 0                ! scoping unit 2
   INTRINSIC LEN_TRIM                      ! scoping unit 2
   DO                                      ! scoping unit 2
      READ (*, *, IOSTAT = ios) buffer     ! scoping unit 2
      IF (ios /= 0) EXIT                   ! scoping unit 2
      n = n + 1                            ! scoping unit 2
      s(n)%string = buffer                 ! scoping unit 2
      s(n)%len = LEN_TRIM (s(n)%string)    ! scoping unit 2
   END DO                                  ! scoping unit 2
   DO i = 1, n                             ! scoping unit 2
      PRINT *, s(i)%string(1:s(i)%len)     ! scoping unit 2
   END DO                                  ! scoping unit 2
END PROGRAM demo_host_association          ! scoping unit 2
```

FIGURE 5.10. Program illustrating scoping units and host association.

such access is said to be gained by way of **host association**. This is how, in Figure 5.10, the derived-type definition has access to the named constant Max_len. The topic of host association will arise again in Chapter 7 in connection with module subprograms and in Chapter 8 in the context of internal subprograms.

The program of Figure 5.10 is contrived to illustrate scoping units and host association and is of only academic interest. Note that s is an array of 100 elements, where each element is a structure of derived type char_type. Each element of s has two components, string and len. The program reads a sequence of character values from the terminal keyboard, storing each in the string component of the next element of s. The new standard intrinsic function LEN_TRIM is invoked to determine the length with trailing blanks trimmed of the string component of each element of s, and the result is stored in the len component. When the end of file is input, the substring consisting of the first len characters of the string component of each element of s is displayed. In the final analysis, the program of Figure 5.10 is just a convoluted way of echoing a list of user input values, but it does reveal some things worth knowing about derived types.

5.11 THE SEQUENCE STATEMENT

In traditional Fortran, programmers have used EQUIVALENCE and COMMON statements to control the physical storage of data objects. In much the same vein, Fortran 90 supports the SEQUENCE statement to provide control of the physical storage of data objects of a derived type. In fact, the Fortran 90 standard requires that if the name of a variable of a derived type appears in an EQUIVALENCE or COMMON statement, a SEQUENCE statement must be present in the definition of that derived type, but some implementations may relax this restriction.

The use of the SEQUENCE statement is illustrated by the contrived program of Figure 5.11. The Z edit descriptor in the format of the PRINT statement is the standard way in Fortran 90 to specify output in hexadecimal. The 8.8 in Z8.8 should work for the large family of implementations that store default INTEGER, default REAL, and default LOGICAL data as 32-bit quantities, but it may need to be changed for implementations outside that family. Even for those implementations within that family, the display resulting from executing this program depends on the implementation's internal representation of REAL and LOGICAL data types.

The syntax of the SEQUENCE statement is simple, consisting of the single keyword SEQUENCE. A SEQUENCE statement may appear only

```
PROGRAM demo_sequence_stmt

   TYPE :: numeric_seq_type
      SEQUENCE                   ! mandatory because of
                                 ! EQUIVALENCE below

      INTEGER :: i
      REAL    :: r
      LOGICAL :: l
   END TYPE numeric_seq_type

   TYPE (numeric_seq_type) :: a_num_seq
   INTEGER, DIMENSION(3)    :: array
   EQUIVALENCE (array, a_num_seq)

   a_num_seq = numeric_seq_type (1, 1.0, .TRUE.)

   ! Warning: The number 8 in following format
   !          may not be OK in some implementations.
   PRINT "(3(1X, Z8.8))", array

END PROGRAM demo_sequence_stmt
```

FIGURE 5.11. Program illustrating the SEQUENCE statement.

within a derived-type definition, and, if present, it must precede the component definition statement(s). If the definition of a derived type contains a SEQUENCE statement, the type is said to be a **sequence type**.

Just as the use of EQUIVALENCE and COMMON statements is discouraged in Fortran 90, use of the SEQUENCE statement is not recommended except in highly unusual circumstances. Generally speaking, the SEQUENCE statement should be avoided unless the programmer has a compelling reason to control the physical storage sequence of a derived type in a portable manner. Because application of the SEQUENCE statement is so specialized, the rather complicated details will be left to reference documents; for purposes of this tutorial, it suffices to present only the broad outline.

5.12 GENERAL SYNTAX OF A DERIVED-TYPE DEFINITION

Previous sections of this tutorial have contained several examples of derived-type definitions in rather simple programs. But most real-world programs are of sufficient complexity that a derived-type definition should usually be placed in a module, as will be discussed in Chapter

```
TYPE [[,access-spec]::] derived-type-name
          [SEQUENCE]
          [PRIVATE]
          component-definition-stmt(s)
END TYPE [derived-type-name]


Notes:
(1)   access-spec is either PRIVATE or PUBLIC.
(2)   Each component-definition-stmt has the form:

      type-spec [[,component-attr-list]::] component-decl-list

   where the only attributes permitted to appear in component-attr-list are DIMENSION and
   POINTER.
```

FIGURE 5.12. General syntax of a derived-type definition.

7. And for a derived-type definition contained in a module, one more concept must be mentioned: The programmer can specify that the derived type and/or all its components be hidden from a unit of code using the module. This capability is provided because it is not unusual that either the entire derived-type definition or the component definitions are intended only for internal use within a module. By specifying the keyword PRIVATE, the programmer can make the type definition and/or its component definitions inaccessible outside the module. A related keyword, PUBLIC, may be coded to ensure that a type definition is accessible outside a module containing it. The concept of accessibility will be discussed in further detail in Chapters 7 and 12, but for purposes of this section, it is enough to understand that the keywords PRIVATE and PUBLIC may appear in the definition of a derived type in a module.

Now that all of the concepts and terminology surrounding derived types have been presented (at least at some rudimentary level), the general syntax of a derived-type definition can be specified as in Figure 5.12. The *type-spec* in a *component-definition-stmt* must be a type specification as given in Figure 2.13 for either an intrinsic type (possibly along with its kind specification) or a derived type. An item in *component-decl-list* may be just a name or an array name followed by its dimensions in parentheses or, if *type-spec* is CHARACTER, a name followed by an asterisk (*) and a length specification.

The *component-definition-stmt* is similar in form to an ordinary type declaration of a variable, except that there can be no equal sign (=) followed by an initial value and the only attributes permitted in a *component-attr-list* are DIMENSION and POINTER. In particular, note that the standard does ***not*** permit the ALLOCATABLE attribute here. Thus, for example, the following does not conform to the standard:

```
TYPE :: var_string
   INTEGER                                   :: leng
   CHARACTER(1), DIMENSION(:), ALLOCATABLE :: strg  ! not std
END TYPE var_string
```

However, as will be discussed in Section 10.8, the desired effect can be achieved here by substituting the keyword POINTER for ALLOCATABLE.

As indicated in Figure 5.12, it is possible for one of the keywords PRIVATE or PUBLIC to appear in a TYPE statement. Note that if either of these keywords appears, it must be followed by a double colon (::), but otherwise the presence of the double colon is optional. Thus, it would be permissible to omit the double colon in all of the TYPE statements illustrated in this chapter.

It is important to understand that the keywords PRIVATE and PUBLIC are permitted only in a module. Also, if both SEQUENCE and PRIVATE statements appear, they may be in either order. And finally, the white space between the keywords END and TYPE is optional.

Fortran 90 implementations may require that the definition of a derived type precede any other appearance of the derived-type name, but once a derived-type definition has been established using the syntax just described, the programmer can declare variables, named constants, and functions of that derived type in a manner quite similar to that of declaring those entities for an intrinsic type. The only difference in terms of syntax is that kinds of intrinsic types are standard in Fortran 90 while kinds of derived types are not. Because the syntax rules governing type declaration statements for entities of a derived type are essentially the same as those for entities of an intrinsic type, the combined rules for all data types were given in Section 2.9.

5.13 SORTING AN ARRAY OF DERIVED TYPE

This section presents a program that integrates some of the ideas discussed earlier in the chapter. The program, whose listing is given in Figure 5.13, involves sorting an array of nested structures. When executed, the program alphabetizes a list of requisitioned items by description and displays the following:

```
2 Bolts              500   8.43
5 Chisel               5   9.858
3 Hammer              10  19.49
1 Nuts              1000   6.78
4 Screwdriver         30  12.855
```

```
PROGRAM sort_array_of_derived_type

   TYPE :: item_rec              ! item:
      CHARACTER(20) :: descr     ! description
      INTEGER       :: qty       ! quantity
      REAL          :: price     ! unit price
   END TYPE item_rec

   TYPE :: req_type                 ! requisition:
      INTEGER         :: req_num    ! requisition number
      TYPE (item_rec) :: item       ! item requisitioned
   END TYPE req_type

   ! Load array of structures req using an array constructor.
   ! A structure constructor is used for each element of req.
   TYPE (req_type), DIMENSION(5) :: req =                      &
    (/ req_type (1, item_rec ("Nuts",       1000,  6.78)), &
       req_type (2, item_rec ("Bolts",       500,  8.43)), &
       req_type (3, item_rec ("Hammer",       10, 19.49)), &
       req_type (4, item_rec ("Screwdriver",  30, 12.855)), &
       req_type (5, item_rec ("Chisel",        5,  9.858)) /)

   TYPE (req_type) :: temp ! for exchanging elements of req
   INTEGER :: i            ! loop index over elements in req
   LOGICAL :: no_exchange  ! true if no elements of req
                           ! found to be out of order

   ! Sort elements of req alphabetically by description.
   DO                          ! Use bubble sort.
      no_exchange = .TRUE.
      DO i = 1, SIZE (req) - 1
         IF (req(i)%item%descr > req(i+1)%item%descr) THEN
            ! Found adjacent pair of elements out of order.
            temp     = req(i)     ! Exchange
            req(i)   = req(i+1)   ! adjacent
            req(i+1) = temp       ! elements.
            no_exchange = .FALSE.
         END IF
      END DO
      IF (no_exchange) EXIT  ! Exit loop when array in order.
   END DO

   DO i = 1, SIZE (req)
      PRINT "(I3, 1X, A, I5, F6.2)", req(i)
   END DO

END PROGRAM sort_array_of_derived_type
```

FIGURE 5.13. Program that sorts an array of derived type.

Observe in the main program of Figure 5.13 that req is an array of structures of the derived type req_type. Note also that one of the components of type req_type, item, is of the derived type item_rec. Observe further that an array constructor is used to assign values to req, and that structure constructors are used to set a value for each element within the array constructor.

The program uses an elementary kind of sort, called a "bubble sort," to alphabetize by item description an array of structures of derived type req_type. The bubble sort is discussed in detail in many books, but briefly, here's how it works: Pass through the array, successively checking each pair of adjacent elements. If a pair of elements is out of order, exchange them. Pass repeatedly through the array until a complete pass is made during which no pair of elements is found to be out of order. This sorting technique may be too slow for large arrays that are badly out of sequence, but for arrays of, say, two thousand elements or so, the author has found the bubble sort adequate for many applications.

Note in the implementation of the bubble sort in Figure 5.13 that each pass through the array is controlled by a DO construct with the loop index i, which varies from 1 through SIZE (req) - 1. SIZE is the new standard Fortran 90 intrinsic function that, when given an array name as its only argument, returns the number of elements in that array, and observe that it works with derived types as well as with intrinsic types. On each pass through the array, the IF construct checks the order of adjacent elements by comparing req(i)%item%descr with req(i+1)%item%descr. If they are out of order, the elements are exchanged by using these three structure-to-structure assignment statements:

```
temp     = req(i)
req(i)   = req(i+1)
req(i+1) = temp
```

Mentally compare the clarity and convenience of this code with that which would result from using parallel arrays as would be done in versions of Fortran not supporting structures.

The LOGICAL variable no_exchange is used in Figure 5.13 to keep track of whether any adjacent pair of elements was found out of order during a particular pass through the array. When a complete pass through the array is made with no exchanges of adjacent pairs, the simple DO is exited. (Readers familiar with the Pascal REPEAT . . . UNTIL or equivalent control constructs should note how the simple DO/EXIT combination is used in this example to achieve the same result.)

CHAPTER 6

EXTERNAL SUBPROGRAMS

6.1 BACKGROUND

Most of the programs presented in this tutorial so far have consisted of only a main program, but beginning with this chapter and continuing through the three chapters following it, the focus will shift to the building blocks that are used to construct larger, more complicated programs. This chapter discusses those features of Fortran 90 subprograms that represent only rather modest extensions of the capabilities available in popular FORTRAN 77 implementations. The primary purpose of the chapter is to establish firmly the vocabulary and point of view that will provide the basis for subsequent presentation of more advanced topics. Very knowledgeable readers should be able to move quickly through this chapter, but the majority of readers can expect to encounter at least some material worthy of their consideration.

In Fortran 90, a **subroutine subprogram** is a collection of code, not in an interface block, starting with a SUBROUTINE statement and ending with its corresponding END statement. Similarly, a **function subprogram** is a collection of code, not in an interface block, starting with a FUNCTION statement and ending with its corresponding END statement. These definitions are consistent with the traditional usages of the terms. The proviso about the interface block is necessary because otherwise collections of code known as "interface bodies" would meet the definitions. Interface bodies will be the topic of Chapter 13.

Subprogram is the generic term in Fortran 90 for either a subroutine subprogram or a function subprogram. This is almost, but not quite, the same as in FORTRAN 77 because the older standard also classifies a collection of code starting with a BLOCK DATA statement and ending with its corresponding END statement as a subprogram. But the Fortran 90 standard does not consider such a collection of code to be a subprogram and designates it as a "block data program unit."

There are three categories of the Fortran 90 subprogram: internal subprogram, module subprogram, and external subprogram. The internal subprogram is a subprogram that is contained within another subprogram or a main program, and this category of subprogram will be the subject of Chapter 8. The module subprogram, which will be introduced in Chapter 7, is a subprogram contained within the program building block known as the "module." An **external subprogram**, then, is a subprogram that is not contained in another subprogram, a main program, or a module. Note that the Fortran 90 external subprogram corresponds to the FORTRAN 77 subprogram if block data collections of code are ignored.

There is a new mechanism known as the "interface body" that can be used to describe the interface with any subroutine or function defined by an external subprogram. However, the Fortran 90 standard requires the presence of an interface body only when certain new features are utilized. This chapter will be limited to those features of external subprograms that can be explained without reference to the use of interface bodies. The discussion of features where interface bodies are mandatory will be deferred until Chapter 13.

Most of the notions discussed in this chapter are present in the FORTRAN 77 standard, but the treatment here is from a Fortran 90 point of view. Particular attention is paid to the related Fortran 90 terminology, which is sometimes different from that in either the older standard or popular usage. In addition, the chapter covers the following Fortran 90 features: the INTENT attribute, automatic data objects, the RESULT option in the FUNCTION statement, and recursion. None of these features is standard in FORTRAN 77, although many implementations of the older standard have supported recursion for years. With the exception of recursion, all of the new features discussed in this chapter can be classified as minor enhancements.

6.2 ELEMENTARY ASPECTS OF SUBPROGRAMS

Figure 6.1 depicts a typical situation in Fortran where a CALL statement is employed to cause the execution of a subroutine named sub, which is defined by a subroutine subprogram. Each item in the parenthesized list in the SUBROUTINE statement is known as a dummy argument, and each item in the parenthesized list in the CALL statement is known as an actual argument. When the CALL statement is executed, we usually want to be able to think of dummy_arg_1 as taking on the current value of actual_arg_1, dummy_arg_2 as taking on the current value of actual_arg_2, and so on. The primary purpose of Figure 6.1 is to strongly make the point that the Fortran 90 standard requires that corresponding actual and dummy arguments must agree in both data type and kind. However,

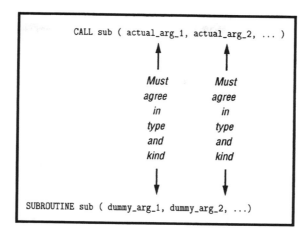

FIGURE 6.1. Corresponding actual and dummy arguments must agree in type and kind.

under some circumstances, some implementations may relax the rule regarding agreement in kind, at least for arguments of type INTEGER.

Figure 6.2a gives a main program that references an external subroutine named sub and an external function named func. The listing for the subroutine subprogram defining sub is given in Figure 6.2b, and the listing for the function subprogram defining func is given in Figure 6.2c. The main program, the subroutine subprogram, and the function

```
PROGRAM demo_external_subprograms

   IMPLICIT NONE

   REAL(KIND(0D0)) :: actual_arg_1 = 1.2345678D0
   INTEGER         :: actual_arg_2 = 1234
   CHARACTER(4)    :: actual_arg_3 = "ABCD"

   REAL(KIND(0D0)) :: func    ! type declaration for function

   ! Next statement invokes subroutine.
   CALL sub (actual_arg_1, actual_arg_2, actual_arg_3)

   PRINT "(F11.7)", 2D0 * func (0.123, 4)    ! Invoke function.

END PROGRAM demo_external_subprograms
```

FIGURE 6.2A. Main program referencing two external procedures.

```
SUBROUTINE sub (dummy_arg_1, dummy_arg_2, dummy_arg_3)

   IMPLICIT NONE

   REAL(KIND(0D0)) :: dummy_arg_1
   INTEGER         :: dummy_arg_2

   CHARACTER(*)    :: dummy_arg_3   ! * means assumed length

   PRINT "(F11.7)", dummy_arg_1
   PRINT "(I5)",    dummy_arg_2
   PRINT "(1X, A)", dummy_arg_3

END SUBROUTINE sub
```

FIGURE 6.2B. Subroutine referenced by main program of Figure 6.2a.

subprogram are shown in separate figures to emphasize that they may be compiled separately in most implementations. Note the presence of an IMPLICIT NONE statement in each of the three program units. The practice of specifying IMPLICIT NONE for each program unit of a program is highly recommended in general but will not always be followed in this tutorial, to avoid cluttering the examples.

When the CALL statement in Figure 6.2a is executed, the subroutine sub defined in Figure 6.2b is invoked. Observe that each of the three actual arguments in the CALL statement in Figure 6.2a agrees in both type and kind with its corresponding dummy argument in Figure 6.2b. However, note in Figure 6.2b that the CHARACTER variable dummy_arg_

```
FUNCTION func (dummy_arg_1, dummy_arg_2)

   IMPLICIT NONE

   REAL(KIND(0D0)) :: func    ! result variable

   REAL            :: dummy_arg_1
   INTEGER         :: dummy_arg_2

   func = dummy_arg_1 + dummy_arg_2

END FUNCTION func
```

FIGURE 6.2C. Function referenced by main program of Figure 6.2a.

3 is declared with an asterisk (*) specified for its length. This means that the length will be taken from the length of actual_arg_3, the corresponding actual argument , which is specified as 4 in Figure 6.2a. As in FORTRAN 77, a CHARACTER dummy argument with length specified by an asterisk is said to have an **assumed length**. Except for unusual situations, the author recommends using an asterisk to specify the length of all CHARACTER dummy variables.

When the PRINT statement in Figure 6.2a is executed, the function func defined in Figure 6.2c is invoked. We usually want to think of dummy_arg_1 and dummy_arg_2 in Figure 6.2c as taking on the values of their corresponding actual arguments in Figure 6.2a. Thus, we think of dummy_arg_1 as taking on the value of the literal constant 0.123 and dummy_arg_2 as taking on the value of the literal constant 4. Note that each of the two actual arguments 0.123 and 4 agrees in both type and kind with its corresponding dummy argument in Figure 6.2c. In Figure 6.2a, we want to think of the expression func (0.123, 4) as being replaced by the result of the execution of the code in Figure 6.2c. Note that the type declaration for the name func in Figure 6.2a agrees in both type and kind with the type declaration of that name in Figure 6.2c. In this connection, some readers may be surprised to see the type specified for the name func in Figure 6.2c in a type declaration statement inside the function subprogram instead of in the FUNCTION statement, but this mechanism is standard in both FORTRAN 77 and Fortran 90. An alternate way of achieving the same results would be to replace the first three statements of Figure 6.2c with the following two statements:

```
REAL(KIND(ODO)) FUNCTION func (dummy_arg_1, dummy_arg_2)
   IMPLICIT NONE
```

When the program consisting of the program units of Figures 6.2a, 6.2b, and 6.2c is executed, the following is displayed:

```
 1.2345678
1234
ABCD
 8.2460000
```

6.3 Array Arguments: A First Look

An array used as a dummy argument is known for short as a **dummy array**. Three popular ways conforming to the FORTRAN 77 standard are used to specify the bounds of a dummy array:

1. Each bound is specified by an expression containing only constants.

2. At least one bound is specified by an expression containing one or more variable names serving as dummy arguments. The FORTRAN 77 standard refers to an array with a bound specified in this manner as an "adjustable array."

3. The upper bound of the last dimension is specified by an asterisk (*). An array whose last upper bound is specified in this manner is called an **assumed-size array**.

Of course, all three of these ways of specifying the bounds of a dummy array also conform to the Fortran 90 standard.

This section will illustrate the Fortran 90 use of both the assumed-size array and the equivalent of the old adjustable array. However, the new standard abandons the term "adjustable array" and covers both (1) and (2) above as part of the more general topic of "explicit-shape arrays," about which more will be said later in this section. Also, it is recommended that the assumed-size array generally be avoided in favor of the new Fortran 90 feature known as the "assumed-shape array." But the assumed-shape array will be not be discussed until Chapter 7, and even there it will be covered only in the context of the module subprogram. Furthermore, because an interface body must be specified to use an assumed-shape array in the context of the external subprogram, full discussion of the assumed-shape array will not be completed until Chapter 13.

Figure 6.3a gives a subroutine subprogram get_stats that returns the mean and standard deviation of the values of the n elements in the one-dimensional array x. A main program that can be used to test get_stats is given in Figure 6.3b. When the main program of Figure 6.3b and the external subroutine of Figure 6.3a are compiled and the resulting object modules are linked, execution of the resulting program displays something like the following:

```
           mean =    0.324000E+01
standard deviation =    0.207364E+00
```

Look at the type declaration for the dummy argument x in Figure 6.3a:

```
REAL, DIMENSION(n) :: x
```

It is also valid in Fortran 90 to code this declaration as

```
REAL x(n)
```

Note that in this form the dummy array x looks exactly like what is known in FORTRAN 77 as an "adjustable array." However, the

```
SUBROUTINE get_stats (n, x, mean, std_dev)

   INTEGER :: n

   REAL, DIMENSION(n) :: x    ! explicit-shape dummy array

   REAL :: mean, std_dev

   mean = SUM (x) / n    ! SUM is intrinsic function that
                         ! sums elements of an array.

   std_dev = SQRT (SUM ((x - mean) ** 2) / (n - 1))

END SUBROUTINE get_stats
```

FIGURE 6.3A. Subroutine with explicit-shape dummy array.

Fortran 90 standard does not use the terminology "adjustable array" and instead considers the dummy array x of Figure 6.3a to be an example of what is known as an "explicit-shape array," a rather broad array classification that encompasses some arrays that are not dummy arguments, as well as some that are.

An **explicit-shape array** is an array whose upper bound in each of its dimensions is specified by a scalar integer expression. It turns out that any array declared in such a way that no bound is specified by either an asterisk or a colon (:) is an explicit-shape array. The Fortran 90

```
PROGRAM test_get_stats

   REAL, DIMENSION(5) ::                              &
                   sample = (/ 3.0, 3.4, 3.1, 3.5, 3.2 /)

   REAL :: avg, std_deviation

   CALL get_stats (5, sample, avg, std_deviation)

   PRINT "(A, E14.6)", "                 mean = ", avg
   PRINT "(A, E14.6)", " standard deviation = ",    &
                                          std_deviation
END PROGRAM test_get_stats
```

FIGURE 6.3B. Main program used to test subroutine of Figure 6.3a.

standard requires that the scalar integer expression specifying an upper bound for an explicit-shape array be made up of data values that are constant with only three exceptions: (1) the array is a dummy argument (as in Figure 6.3a); (2) the array is an automatic data object (see Section 6.5); or (3) the array is the result returned by a function (see Section 7.10). But in all three cases where the scalar integer expression specifying an upper bound for an explicit-shape array is permitted to depend on nonconstant data values, the array must be declared inside a subprogram and values for the nonconstant data values must be available at entry to the subprogram. Thus, what was called the "adjustable array" in FORTRAN 77 still exists in Fortran 90 as a special case of the explicit-shape array.

An alternate way to write the subroutine subprogram of Figure 6.3a is shown in Figure 6.3c. The subroutine get_stats of Figure 6.3c has a dummy argument x which is a rank 1, assumed-size array, as indicated by the asterisk in the parentheses following the keyword DIMENSION. That is to say, the upper bound of the only dimension of x may be thought of as being assumed from its corresponding actual argument, sample, in the CALL statement in the main program of Figure 6.3b. The lower bound is omitted for both x and sample, and so the lower bound defaults to 1 in both cases. In Fortran 90, as in FORTRAN 77, use of an asterisk in indicating an array bound is restricted to the

```
! Note:     The effect of this subroutine is exactly the same
!           as that of the subroutine listed in Figure 6.3a.

! Warning:  The assumed-size array is not recommended for use
!           in Fortran 90 except under unusual circumstances.

  SUBROUTINE get_stats (n, x, mean, std_dev)

     INTEGER :: n

     REAL, DIMENSION(*) :: x     ! assumed-size array

     REAL :: mean, std_dev

     ! Use of array section x(1:n) mandatory in next 2 stmts.
     mean = SUM (x(1:n)) / n
     std_dev = SQRT (SUM ((x(1:n) - mean) ** 2) / (n - 1))

  END SUBROUTINE get_stats
```

FIGURE 6.3C. Subroutine with an assumed-size array.

specification of the upper bound of the last dimension of a dummy array.

As mentioned earlier, use of the assumed-size array is not, in general, recommended in Fortran 90 since a more general capability, that of the assumed-shape array, is available. The problem with the assumed-size array is that it is considered in standard Fortran 90 to have no shape. This means that there are severe limits to the manner in which the assumed-size array name can be used without specifying any subscript or section. For example, the standard prohibits its use as an argument to any of the intrinsic functions, including any of the array functions in Appendix C which are classified as transformational. There is a way around this, however, where the intrinsic function argument can be expressed as an array section. This is the reason that in Figure 6.3c the expression

```
SUM (x(1:n))
```

is not coded simply as

```
SUM (x)
```

since SUM is a standard transformational array intrinsic function. Similarly, in Figure 6.3c, the array section x(1:n) is employed in the array expression

```
x(1:n) - mean
```

instead of simply coding

```
x - mean
```

because the latter also violates Fortran 90 rules for using an assumed-size array. In short, the benefits of the assumed-shape array and the pitfalls of using the assumed-size array favor the avoidance of the assumed-size array in all but the simplest of situations.

As discussed in the preceding section, the standard requires that corresponding dummy and actual arguments must always agree in type and kind. In addition, the author recommends that, except for unusual situations, things be arranged so that corresponding dummy and actual arguments agree in rank as well. But agreement in rank is not generally required by the Fortran 90 standard for arguments involving explicit-shape and assumed-size arrays. However, the new standard does give the following rules regarding agreement in rank:

1. If a dummy argument is scalar, its corresponding actual argument must be scalar.

2. If an actual argument is scalar, the corresponding dummy argument must be scalar, unless the actual argument is an element of an array that is not an assumed-shape array.

Of course, most implementations will have no way of detecting violations of these restrictions for external subprograms at compile time unless interface bodies (see Chapter 13) are used.

6.4   THE INTENT ATTRIBUTE

In nearly all traditional versions of Fortran, a programmer reading a subprogram written by another programmer has no way other than by reading comments or by using inference to determine whether an argument is input, output, or both. Also, when a subprogram is being written, previous compilers cannot check whether the code attempts to change the value of an argument intended only for input, say by using the name of the argument on the left side of an assignment statement. Fortran 90 addresses these problems by supporting the INTENT attribute, which is illustrated in the external subroutine subprogram change_chars of Figure 6.4a. A main program that can be used to test change_chars is listed in Figure 6.4b. When the program of Figures 6.4a and 6.4b is executed, the following is displayed:

```
SUBROUTINE change_chars (from_char, to_char,              &
                         dummy_string, number_changed)

   CHARACTER(1), INTENT (IN)     :: from_char       ! input
   CHARACTER(1), INTENT (IN)     :: to_char         ! input
   CHARACTER(*), INTENT (IN OUT) :: dummy_string    ! changed
   INTEGER,      INTENT (OUT)    :: number_changed  ! output

   INTEGER :: i    ! local

   number_changed = 0
   DO i = 1, LEN (dummy_string)
      IF (dummy_string(i:i) == from_char) THEN
         dummy_string(i:i) = to_char
         number_changed = number_changed + 1
      END IF
   END DO

END SUBROUTINE change_chars
```

FIGURE 6.4A.   Subroutine illustrating the INTENT attribute.

```
PROGRAM test_change_chars

   CHARACTER(6) :: char_string = "  1.2 "

   INTEGER      :: number_chars_changed

   PRINT "(2A)", " Before CALL, char_string = ", char_string

   CALL change_chars (" ", "0", char_string,                      &
                                 number_chars_changed)

   PRINT "(2A)", " After CALL, char_string = ", char_string
   PRINT "(A, I1)", " Number of characters changed = ",           &
                                 number_chars_changed
END PROGRAM test_change_chars
```

FIGURE 6.4B. Program used to test subroutine of Figure 6.4a.

```
Before CALL, char_string =   1.2
 After CALL, char_string = 001.20
Number of characters changed = 3
```

When the CALL statement in the main program of Figure 6.4b is executed, control is passed to the subroutine change_chars in Figure 6.4a. Subroutine change_chars examines each character in the input string dummy_string, and if a particular character in dummy_string matches a character specified by the caller in from_char, that character is changed to the character specified by the caller in to_char. In the example shown, change_chars loops through the string " 1.2 " and replaces each blank in the string with the character "0". Subroutine change_chars also passes back to its caller the number of characters that it changed in number_changed. In the example, two leading blanks and one trailing blank were changed to zeros, for a total of three characters changed.

Note in the subroutine change_chars that an INTENT attribute is specified for each of the four dummy arguments. This attribute is specified by following the keyword INTENT with a set of parentheses enclosing one of three keyword entries: IN, OUT, or IN OUT. (If preferred, the keyword pair IN OUT can be coded as the single keyword INOUT with no separation.) IN indicates that the argument value is input to the subprogram and is not to be changed by the subprogram; OUT signifies that the argument value may be undefined (that is, it may not have previously been given any value) at entry to the subprogram and is expected to be given a value during the execution of the subprogram; and

IN OUT specifies that the argument value is expected to be set at entry to the subprogram and that execution of the subprogram may change the value of that argument. In Figure 6.4a, observe that the values of from_ char and to_char are input to the subroutine, the value of number_changed is output from the subroutine, and the dummy argument dummy_string has a value at input to the subroutine that is changed in the subroutine. Of course, the INTENT attribute can be used only in declarations of dummy arguments.

6.5 AUTOMATIC DATA OBJECTS

It is commonplace for a subprogram to need a local storage area whose size varies from call to call, and traditional Fortran provides no facility for supporting this requirement. The usual way around this is for the caller of such a subprogram to declare an array of sufficient size for the subprogram to work in, and then this work array will be one of the arguments when the subprogram is called. But since dynamic storage allocation is a standard feature in Fortran 90, the old method is no longer necessary, and local storage required by a subprogram can be allocated as needed inside the subprogram. One way of accomplishing this—the allocatable array—was discussed in Section 4.10. The allocatable array gives the programmer pinpoint control over where storage is allocated and deallocated via the ALLOCATE and DEALLOCATE statements. However, Fortran 90 provides a simpler mechanism, known as the "automatic array," that will be adequate in many situations. A program illustrating the use of an automatic array is given in Figure 6.5.

The program of Figure 6.5 is made up of a main program and an external subroutine subprogram named exchange. The source code for both program units is given in a single figure to imply that they may be in the same file, but, of course, in most implementations they could be placed in separate files if desired. In either case, they will be independently compiled. The main program calls the subroutine to exchange corresponding elements of two rank 1 arrays of the same size. When the program of Figure 6.5 is executed, the following will be displayed:

```
Before exchange, a =   1.0   2.0   3.0   4.0    5.0
Before exchange, b =   6.0   7.0   8.0   9.0   10.0
 After exchange, a =   6.0   7.0   8.0   9.0   10.0
 After exchange, b =   1.0   2.0   3.0   4.0    5.0
```

Notice in Figure 6.5 that the rank 1 array temp is local to the subroutine exchange—the name temp is not in the dummy argument list—and

```
PROGRAM demo_automatic_array

   REAL, DIMENSION(5) :: a = (/ (i, i = 1,  5) /), &
                         b = (/ (i, i = 6, 10) /)

   PRINT "(A, 5F6.1)", " Before exchange, a =", a
   PRINT "(A, 5F6.1)", " Before exchange, b =", b

   CALL exchange (5, a, b)

   PRINT "(A, 5F6.1)", "  After exchange, a =", a
   PRINT "(A, 5F6.1)", "  After exchange, b =", b

END PROGRAM demo_automatic_array

      ! Exchange corresponding elements of
      ! two rank 1 arrays of size n.

SUBROUTINE exchange (n, x, y)

   INTEGER,              INTENT (IN)      :: n
   REAL, DIMENSION(n), INTENT (IN OUT)  :: x, y

   REAL, DIMENSION(n) :: temp     ! automatic array

   temp = x
   x    = y
   y    = temp

END SUBROUTINE exchange
```

FIGURE 6.5. Program illustrating the use of an automatic array.

yet the upper bound of its only dimension is not constant. This is generally not permitted in FORTRAN 77 implementations, but it is standard in Fortran 90. In fact, as discussed in Section 6.3, temp is simply another example of an explicit-shape array, as for that matter are the dummy arguments x and y of Figure 6.5. An array like temp, which is declared in a subprogram, is not a dummy argument, and whose bounds depend on nonconstant data values, is called an **automatic array**.

And just as Fortran 90 permits the bounds of local arrays in subprograms to vary from call to call, the lengths of local character strings in subprograms are allowed to vary in the same manner. An example of this is shown in the program of Figure 6.6, which is made up of a main program and an external subroutine subprogram named swap.

```
PROGRAM demo_automatic_string

   CHARACTER(5) :: s = "ABCDE", &
                   t = "FGHIJ"

   PRINT "(A, 1X, A)", " Before swap, s =", s
   PRINT "(A, 1X, A)", " Before swap, t =", t

   CALL swap (s, t)

   PRINT "(A, 1X, A)", "  After swap, s =", s
   PRINT "(A, 1X, A)", "  After swap, t =", t

END PROGRAM demo_automatic_string

! Swap 2 character strings of same length.
SUBROUTINE swap (c, d)

   CHARACTER(*), INTENT (IN OUT) :: c, d

   CHARACTER(LEN (c)) :: hold      ! automatic string

   hold = c
   c    = d
   d    = hold

END SUBROUTINE swap
```

FIGURE 6.6. Program illustrating use of an automatic character string.

The main program calls the subroutine to swap two character strings having the same declared lengths. When the program of Figure 6.6 is executed, the following is displayed:

```
Before swap, s = ABCDE
Before swap, t = FGHIJ
 After swap, s = FGHIJ
 After swap, t = ABCDE
```

Observe in the subroutine swap in Figure 6.6 that the character dummy arguments c and d are declared with an asterisk for the value of their length type parameters, which means that they take their lengths from their corresponding actual arguments, s and t, both of which have length 5. Now note that the local variable hold in the subroutine swap is declared as follows:

```
CHARACTER(LEN (c)) :: hold
```

In this declaration, LEN invokes the standard intrinsic function, which returns the length of its character string argument c. Thus, when swap is called, the local variable hold will have the same length as the dummy argument c. Hence, a character string in a subprogram whose name is not in the subprogam's dummy argument list has a nonconstant length. This is generally not permitted in FORTRAN 77, but it is standard in Fortran 90 provided that all values needed to determine the string's length are available at entry to the subprogram.

The generic term **automatic data object** is used for either an array with nonconstant bounds that is local to a subprogram or a character string of nonconstant length that is local to a subprogram. Implementations of the Fortran 90 standard typically will automatically allocate temporary storage for an automatic data object at entry to a subprogram, keep that storage allocated while the subprogram is being executed, and automatically deallocate the storage at exit from the subprogram.

6.6 THE SAVE ATTRIBUTE

The SAVE keyword is available in standard Fortran 90, and the concepts related to its use are the same as they are in standard FORTRAN 77. However, many Fortran programmers are unfamiliar with the ideas surrounding the use of the SAVE keyword, and so perhaps a brief discussion is in order even though some programmers may not require its use.

Both the FORTRAN 77 and Fortran 90 standards permit an implementation to divide local variables in subprograms into two storage classes, where the difference between the two classes is this: A variable in one of the storage classes is guaranteed to retain all its properties, including its value, after the subprogram to which it is local is exited, while a variable in the other class is not. The idea here is that since it is not necessary in most cases for the properties of a local variable in a subprogram to be retained after exit from that subprogram, the storage required to save such properties should not remain occupied by data that are no longer needed, but instead should become available for other purposes. The keyword SAVE then fits into this overall concept by providing the programmer with a mechanism for specifying in which of the two storage classes a local variable in a subprogram shall be. However, many popular implementations of FORTRAN 77 automatically save all local variables in all subprograms, and in such implementations, programmers not concerned about portability have never needed to specify the SAVE storage class.

To make these ideas less abstract, consider the program of Figure 6.7, which conforms to the Fortran 90 standard. When the program is executed, the following is displayed:

```
1
2
3
4
```

Note in the subroutine sub in Figure 6.7 that the programmer expects the local variables first_entry and counter to retain their values at each entry after the first. For the local variable counter, this is guaranteed by specifying the SAVE attribute in its declaration:

```
INTEGER, SAVE :: counter
```

As in standard FORTRAN 77, the same specifications could also be indicated in two separate statements:

```
INTEGER counter
SAVE    counter
```

If the SAVE attribute were not specified for counter, an implementation of either the FORTRAN 77 or Fortran 90 standard is not required to retain its value after sub is exited, although many implementations will do so anyway.

The situation with the local variable first_entry is different because it is given an initial value at compile time. The Fortran 90 standard specifies that all variables with initial values shall automatically acquire the SAVE attribute. Thus, in all Fortan 90 standard-conforming implementations, the value of first_entry will be retained after exit from sub, even if the programmer takes no special action.

In Figure 6.7, the initial value for first_entry is specified in a type declaration, but it could alternatively be given an initial value in a DATA statement, in which case first_entry would still be guaranteed by the Fortran 90 standard to acquire the SAVE attribute automatically. It is worth noting that the Fortran 90 rules differ subtly here from those of FORTRAN 77, since the older standard does not make it mandatory for a variable initialized in a DATA statement to acquire the SAVE attribute automatically (although, in practice, most of the popular FORTRAN 77 implementations automatically give the attribute to such a variable anyway). But observe that due to this slight difference in standards, the possibility arises that a program conforming to the FORTRAN 77 standard might behave differently when compiled by a compiler conforming to the Fortran 90 standard. Nevertheless, this sort of difference is not considered to constitute an incompatibility between the two standards—it is just that a few details that were left unspecified in the older standard are spelled out in the new.

```
PROGRAM demo_save

   INTEGER :: i

   DO i = 1, 4
      CALL sub
   END DO

END PROGRAM demo_save

SUBROUTINE sub

   LOGICAL        :: first_entry = .TRUE.  ! first_entry
                                           ! acquires SAVE
                                           ! attribute
                                           ! automatically.

   INTEGER, SAVE :: counter                ! Programmer makes
                                           ! sure counter
                                           ! retains value
                                           ! after sub is
                                           ! exited.

   IF (first_entry) THEN   ! Compiler set first_entry
                           ! before initial entry to sub.
                           ! For subsequent entries to
                           ! sub, first_entry must
                           ! retain its value from
                           ! previous entry.
      counter = 1
      first_entry = .FALSE.
   ELSE
      counter = counter + 1   ! counter must retain its
                              ! value from previous entry
                              ! to sub.
   END IF

   PRINT *, counter

END SUBROUTINE sub
```

FIGURE 6.7. Program illustrating the use of the SAVE attribute.

It is appropriate to wonder what might be different in the program of Figure 6.7 if the SAVE attribute were not specified for the variable counter in the subroutine sub. In an implementation where all local variables are automatically saved, nothing would be different, except, of course, the portability would be questionable. However, in an implementation where local variables are not automatically saved, the outcome of running the program without specifying the SAVE attribute for counter is unpredictable, depending on whether or not the storage for counter is used for some other purpose. The most likely outcomes are that the display would be the same or that values seemingly unrelated to the program being executed would be displayed.

There are some restrictions on the use of the SAVE attribute. It cannot be specified for dummy arguments or function results. Also, it cannot be specified for automatic data objects, which were described in the preceding section. Furthermore, it is permitted in Fortran 90, as it is in FORTRAN 77, to place a statement consisting solely of the keyword SAVE in a subprogram, and this is treated as though all of the allowable variables in the subprogram were listed after the keyword SAVE. Of course, the SAVE statement can still be used in Fortran 90 to save common blocks as in FORTRAN 77, but this usage will not be discussed in this tutorial.

6.7   THE RESULT OPTION IN THE FUNCTION STATEMENT

Languages such as C and Ada employ a syntax that automatically distinguishes within a function between the name of the function and the result that is to be returned when the function is invoked, but Fortran traditionally has not bothered with this distinction. However, Fortran 90 addresses this issue by providing the RESULT option in the FUNCTION statement. A virtue of the Fortran 90 approach is that it makes it possible for a function returning an array of values to invoke itself recursively with no ambiguity.

A simple example of a function subprogram illustrating the use of the RESULT option is given in Figure 6.8a. Note that the function name, max_magnitude, appears only in the FUNCTION statement and in its corresponding END statement. Now focus attention on the programmer-chosen name max_of_abs contained in parentheses following the keyword RESULT in the FUNCTION statement. The value stored in max_of_abs is the result that will be returned to the caller when the function is exited. Observe that max_of_abs is treated like a local variable inside the function.

```
! Result variable name is specified after keyword RESULT.
FUNCTION max_magnitude (val_1, val_2) RESULT (max_of_abs)

   REAL                    :: max_of_abs  ! Declare result variable.

   REAL, INTENT (IN) :: val_1, val_2

   ! Set result variable to value to be returned to caller.
   max_of_abs = MAX (ABS (val_1), ABS (val_2))

END FUNCTION max_magnitude
```

FIGURE 6.8A. Function using RESULT clause in FUNCTION statement.

Figure 6.8b lists a main program that can serve as a driver to test the function subprogram of Figure 6.8a. When the main program of Figure 6.8b is compiled and linked with the function subprogram of Figure 6.8a, execution of the resulting program will cause the following to be displayed:

   6.600

Of course, the test driver of Figure 6.8b invokes the function using the name max_magnitude and is unaware of the name max_of_abs. Notice in Figure 6.8b that the name max_magnitude is declared to be of type REAL. This is required since otherwise it would default to type INTEGER because the first letter in its name is in the range i through n. This is, of course, one of the prices to be paid for independent compilation, and it has been the source of great anguish to programmers over the years. When the main program is compiled, no information about the data type returned by the external function subprogram max_magnitude is available to the compiler except for that specified, either implicitly or

```
PROGRAM test_max_magnitude

   ! Data type of name max_magnitude must be specified.
   REAL, EXTERNAL :: max_magnitude

   PRINT "(F8.3)", 3.0 * max_magnitude (1.1, -2.2)

END PROGRAM test_max_magnitude
```

FIGURE 6.8B. Test driver for function max_magnitude.

explicitly, in the main program itself. Thus, as was the case in traditional Fortran, it is the responsibility of the Fortran 90 programmer to make sure that the type of the result returned by an external function is known by its caller.

An interesting detail in Figure 6.8b is that the attribute EXTERNAL is specified for the name max_magnitude. Here this merely specifies that max_magnitude is the name of an external procedure, and in the unlikely event that the implementation has an intrinsic procedure by that name, the existence of the intrinsic procedure would be ignored in compiling the main program of Figure 6.8b. Thus, the explicit specification of the EXTERNAL attribute is not really required here, as is true in most cases of practical interest, but its presence does serve as internal documentation and slightly improves portability since implementations are permitted to provide intrinsic procedures beyond the standard ones. Incidentally, the single Fortran 90 statement

```
REAL, EXTERNAL :: max_magnitude
```

may alternatively be coded, as is the case in FORTRAN 77, as the two statements

```
REAL      max_magnitude
EXTERNAL max_magnitude
```

Observe also in Figure 6.8a that both dummy arguments are declared to have the attribute INTENT (IN). It has long been considered poor Fortran style for a function to change the values of any of its dummy arguments. If a subprogram has any dummy argument with the attribute INTENT (OUT) or INTENT (IN OUT), good Fortran 90 style demands that the subprogram define a subroutine rather than a function.

It is true, of course, that the function subprogram given in Figure 6.8a can be written without employing the RESULT option. For example, the following is a version of max_magnitude whose behavior is identical to that of Figure 6.8a:

```
FUNCTION max_magnitude (val_1, val_2)
   REAL                :: max_magnitude  ! Declare result var.
   REAL, INTENT (IN) :: val_1, val_2
   max_magnitude = MAX (ABS (val_1), ABS (val_2))
END FUNCTION max_magnitude
```

Also, the first two statements of this version may be combined into a single statement:

```
REAL FUNCTION max_magnitude (val_1, val_2)
```

Actually, the RESULT option is never required by the Fortran 90 standard except, as explained in the next section, in connection with recursion.

However, the author recommends the use of the RESULT option for all function subprograms for reasons of clarity.

Whether or not the RESULT option appears, the variable that holds the value returned by a function is called the **result variable**. Thus, in Figure 6.8a the result variable is max_of_abs. In the other versions of the function max_magnitude described in this section, the name of the result variable is max_magnitude, the same as that of the function itself.

6.8 *RECURSION*

A subprogram that invokes itself, either directly or indirectly, is said to be **recursive**. Although several versions of Fortran have permitted recursive subprograms for some years, this is not supported by the FORTRAN 77 standard. However, the Fortran 90 standard permits any subprogram to be recursive, provided that the programmer explicitly specifies that the subprogram can be used in this manner. An example of a recursive external function subprogram is given in Figure 6.9a, and a simple test driver for it is shown in Figure 6.9b. Execution of the program made up of the function subprogram of Figure 6.9a and the

```
! Warning: The following is intended merely to illustrate
!          concepts and syntax of a recursive function
!          subprogram and is not a practical example of the
!          use of recursion.

RECURSIVE FUNCTION compute_factorial (n) RESULT (n_factorial)

   INTEGER                :: n_factorial   ! result variable
   INTEGER, INTENT (IN) :: n

   IF (n == 0) THEN
      n_factorial = 1
   ELSE
                          ! Function invokes itself.
      n_factorial = n * compute_factorial (n - 1)
   END IF

END FUNCTION compute_factorial
```

FIGURE 6.9A. A simple example of a recursive function.

```
PROGRAM test_recursive_function

    INTEGER :: compute_factorial

    PRINT *, compute_factorial (5)

END PROGRAM test_recursive_function
```

FIGURE 6.9B.   A simple test driver for the function in Figure 6.9a.

main program of Figure 6.9b computes $5! = 1 \cdot 2 \cdot 3 \cdot 4 \cdot 5$ and displays the result as

120

The function compute_factorial in Figure 6.9a is a direct translation into Fortran 90 of the mathematical definition of $n!$, read as "n factorial," as

$$n! = \begin{cases} 1 & \text{for } n = 0, \\ n(n-1)! & \text{for } n > 0, \end{cases}$$

where n is any nonnegative integer.

Observe in the body of the function subprogram compute_factorial the assignment statement

```
n_factorial = n * compute_factorial (n - 1)
```

Here, the expression

```
compute_factorial (n - 1)
```

means that the function compute_factorial is invoking itself with an actual argument of n - 1. Thus, the function subprogram compute_factorial is recursive. Note also the presence of the keyword RECURSIVE before the keyword FUNCTION in the first statement of the function compute_factorial. The Fortran 90 standard requires that the header statement of a recursive subprogram be prefixed with the keyword RECURSIVE, and even in implementations that relax this requirement, the author strongly recommends its presence for reasons of portability and readability.

Observe also in Figure 6.9a that the FUNCTION statement for compute_factorial names the result variable n_factorial in the RESULT clause. The Fortran 90 standard requires that a function that invokes itself use a RESULT clause. Then, in an executable statement, a reference to the function name is a recursive call while the result variable name is used to store the value to be returned. For example, in the statement

```
n_factorial = n * compute_factorial (n - 1)
```

n_factorial refers to the result variable and compute_factorial is a recursive function invocation.

While the external function subprogram of Figure 6.9a provides a good vehicle to illustrate the concepts and syntax considerations of Fortran 90 recursive functions, it should be mentioned that this is a hopelessly impractical example. First, observe that a better Fortran 90 implementation of the function compute_factorial would be as follows:

```
FUNCTION compute_factorial (n) RESULT (n_factorial)
   INTEGER              :: n_factorial  ! result variable
   INTEGER, INTENT (IN) :: n
   INTEGER              :: k            ! local variable
   n_factorial = 1
   DO k = 2, n
      n_factorial = k * n_factorial
   END DO
END FUNCTION compute_factorial
```

Note that this second version of the function compute_factorial is not recursive, employing iteration instead of recursion to determine the value of $n!$. The iterative version will require fewer resources in most implementations and will be easier to understand for most programmers.[1] Thus, recursion may not be a good approach for some applications, although certain rather advanced situations do arise where employing recursion will sufficiently enhance the readability of the code to make up for the execution-time inefficiencies usually associated with its use.

An even more serious objection to either version of function compute_factorial is that the range of values of n that can be handled is ridiculously limited. For example, on a typical computer with 32-bit word length, either version of compute_factorial will return incorrect results for numbers bigger than 12! because of limitations on the range of INTEGER values. There are, of course, a number of things that could be done to increase the range of factorials that could be computed, but pursuing these here would take us far afield. The important point to recognize is that while this example addresses the rather difficult problem of determining factorials in only a very limited way, it nevertheless lends some important insights into computing.

Figure 6.9a illustrates a function subprogram that invoked itself, and Fortran 90's other kind of procedure, the subroutine, can call itself as well. An example of a recursive subroutine named reverse_string is given in Figure 6.10a, which reverses the order of the characters in its argument by swapping the first and the last characters, then swapping

---

[1] Most people seem to find recursion a bit unnatural. Hence, the humorous saying, "To iterate is human; to recurse, divine."

```
! subroutine to reverse a character string in place

RECURSIVE SUBROUTINE reverse_string (char_string)

    CHARACTER(*), INTENT (IN OUT) :: char_string

    INTEGER :: str_len

    str_len = LEN (char_string)

    IF (str_len > 1) THEN
       CALL swap (char_string(1:1),                &
                  char_string(str_len:str_len))

          ! Subroutine calls itself in following statement.
          CALL reverse_string (char_string(2:str_len-1))
    END IF

END SUBROUTINE reverse_string
```

FIGURE 6.10A. A recursive subroutine.

the second and the next to last characters, and so on until the string is reversed.[2]

Note that reverse_string calls an external subroutine subprogram named swap, whose listing is given in Figure 6.10b, to perform the exchange of each pair of characters. A simple main program that tests reverse_string is shown in Figure 6.10c. When the three program units of Figures 6.10a, 6.10b, and 6.10c are compiled and linked together, execution of the resulting program causes the following to be displayed:

EDCBA   654321

A sidelight of Figure 6.10a is that when the string length str_len is 2, the expression char_string(2:str_len-1) is a zero-length string. However, this is valid in Fortran 90 and, as is usually the case, requires no special treatment.

It is interesting to note that the recursive subroutine reverse_string of Figure 6.10a could be rewritten as a nonrecursive subroutine as follows:

```
SUBROUTINE reverse_string (char_string)
    CHARACTER(*), INTENT (IN OUT) :: char_string
    INTEGER :: i, j
```

[2]This example is based on an exercise in *The C Programming Language* by B.W. Kernighan and D.M. Ritchie (Prentice-Hall, Englewood Cliffs, NJ, 1988).

```
! external subroutine that exchanges two characters

SUBROUTINE swap (char_1, char_2)

   CHARACTER(1), INTENT (IN OUT) :: char_1, char_2

   CHARACTER(1) :: temp

   temp   = char_1
   char_1 = char_2
   char_2 = temp

END SUBROUTINE swap
```

FIGURE 6.10B. External subroutine called by reverse_string.

```
      i = 1; j = LEN (char_string)
      DO
         IF (i >= j) EXIT
         CALL swap (char_string(i:i), char_string(j:j))
         i = i + 1; j = j - 1
      END DO
   END SUBROUTINE reverse_string
```

In this case, it is largely a matter of taste as to which version of reverse_ string is preferred, but it seems probable that the nonrecursive version will consume fewer computer resources and be more easily understood by most programmers working in Fortran 90.

```
PROGRAM test_reverse_string

   CHARACTER(5) :: string_1 = "ABCDE"
   CHARACTER(6) :: string_2 = "123456"

   CALL reverse_string (string_1)
   CALL reverse_string (string_2)

   PRINT "(1X, A, 2X, A)", string_1, string_2

END PROGRAM test_reverse_string
```

FIGURE 6.10C. Test driver for SUBROUTINE reverse_string.

In both subprograms given as examples of recursion in this section, it turned out to be rather easy to write equivalent nonrecursive subprograms. But it is important to understand that even though there are few, if any, simple situations where recursive subprograms are absolutely essential, there are certain rather advanced applications, such as managing a kind of data structure known as a "tree," that would be tedious without them.

Incidentally, both of the examples of recursion given in this section involved a subprogram invoking itself. This is known as "direct recursion." It is also possible for subprogram A to call subprogram B, which in turn calls subprogram A. This is an example of "indirect recursion." Fortran 90 supports indirect recursion as well as direct recursion. In the example just mentioned, the new standard requires that the RECURSIVE keyword be specified for both subprogram A and subprogram B.

6.9 SYNTAX OF *SUBROUTINE* AND *FUNCTION* STATEMENTS

The syntax of the Fortran 90 SUBROUTINE statement, which is given in Figure 6.11, is identical to that of traditional Fortran, except that the keyword SUBROUTINE may be preceded by the keyword RECURSIVE. If the subroutine is used recursively, the new standard requires the presence of the keyword RECURSIVE, and the author strongly recommends compliance for purposes of portability and readability, even in an implementation that does not enforce this requirement. An item in *arg-list* may be either a dummy argument name, as illustrated by several examples in this chapter, or an asterisk (*). The asterisk, a carryover from FORTRAN 77, is used in conjunction with a capability known as the "alternate return," which has been employed historically to handle error conditions. The subroutine is coded such that when an error condition is detected, a RETURN statement something like the following will be executed:

```
RETURN 1
```

Then, when the subroutine returns to its caller, control is transferred to a statement whose label is specified in the argument list in the CALL

[RECURSIVE] SUBROUTINE *subroutine-name* [([*arg-list*])]
where *arg* is either *dummy-arg-name* or *.

FIGURE 6.11. Syntax of the SUBROUTINE statement.

statement. However, except in Appendix F, the alternate return capability will not be discussed in this tutorial because the Fortran 90 standard has classified it as an "obsolescent feature," that is, a feature for which it is recommended that support be dropped in future revisions of the standard.

The general syntax for the Fortran 90 FUNCTION statement, which is given in Figure 6.12, is rather different from that of traditional Fortran, not only because the new keyword RECURSIVE may appear, but also because there may be a RESULT clause. As mentioned in Section 6.7, the variable that returns the value of a function is known as the "result variable." If a RESULT clause is not specified, the result variable is, as in traditional Fortran, *function-name*. But if a RESULT clause is specified, the result variable is *result-name*. Of course, *result-name* must not be the same as *function-name*. Also, if *result-name* is present, *function-name* may not appear in any specification statement in the function.

The Fortran 90 standard permits the type and type parameters of the result of a function to be specified in the FUNCTION statement as indicated by *type-spec* in Figure 6.12, where the possible entries for *type-spec* are given back in Figure 2.13 in Section 2.9. However, the author recommends that these be specified in a type declaration for the result variable in the specification part of the function subprogram. In any case, for a given function subprogram, type and type parameters of the result may not be specified both ways. If type and type parameters are not specified either way, the type will default, as in traditional Fortran, to INTEGER if the result variable name begins with one of the letters i through n, or to REAL otherwise, and the type parameters will be the corresponding default type parameters for the implementation.

If the function is used recursively, the standard demands that the keyword RECURSIVE be specified. If the function invokes itself, the standard stipulates not only that the keyword RECURSIVE be specified, but also that the RESULT clause be present. However, some people are likely to get confused about what the standard requires in this regard because

```
[prefix] FUNCTION function-name ([arg-list]) [RESULT (result-name)]
where


 ■   prefix is type-spec [RECURSIVE] or RECURSIVE [type-spec],


 ■   arg is dummy-arg-name.
```

FIGURE 6.12.   Syntax of the FUNCTION statement.

if the function is used only in indirect recursion, as opposed to direct recursion (invoking itself), the standard permits the omission of the RESULT clause.

As far as the standard is concerned, the rules governing the names of subroutines and functions are the same as for any Fortran 90 name as described in Section 2.2. In particular, the standard permits a subroutine or function name to be as long as 31 characters. However, it should be recognized that a Fortran 90 implementation may reside in a computing environment that imposes additional restrictions on names that are visible outside a compilation unit. For example, some linkers do not permit names to exceed (say) eight characters, and so there might be a requirement that the first eight characters of the name of an external subroutine or function suffice to differentiate it from other external names within the same program.

6.10   EXTERNAL SUBPROGRAMS AND SCOPE

The part of a program within which a name has a single interpretation is called the **scope** of that name. A name whose scope is an entire program is said to be **global**. A name that is not global is said to be **local** to the part of the program within which it has a single interpretation. In traditional Fortran, the basic rules governing scope are simple: External procedure names are global, and the names of scalar variables, arrays, and constants are always local to a subprogram or main program. These basic traditional rules remain useful as guiding principles, but new Fortran 90 features, such as derived types, interface bodies, internal subprograms, and modules, make the rules governing scope somewhat more complicated. Thus, before addressing the issues related to scope in Fortran 90, it seems worthwhile to take a moment to review the fundamentals.

The reader should have little difficulty understanding the program of Figure 6.13, which illustrates some of the elementary aspects of the scope of names and labels (statement numbers). When the program, which consists of a main program and the two external subroutine subprograms sub_1 and sub_2, is executed, the following is displayed:

```
Before CALL sub_1, int_var =  1
     Inside sub_1, int_var = -1
     Inside sub_1, int_var = -2
Inside sub_2 called by sub_1
  After CALL sub_1, int_var =  1
```

```
PROGRAM demo_scope
      DO 100 int_var = 1, 2
         PRINT "(A, I2)", " Before CALL sub_1, int_var = ", &
                                                  int_var
         CALL sub_1
         PRINT "(A, I2)", "  After CALL sub_1, int_var = ", &
                                                  int_var
         PRINT "(1X)"
  100 END DO
         CALL sub_2 ("main program")
END PROGRAM demo_scope

SUBROUTINE sub_1
      DO 100 int_var = -1, -2, -1
         PRINT "(A, I2)", "        Inside sub_1, int_var = ", &
                                                  int_var
  100 END DO
         CALL sub_2 ("sub_1")
END SUBROUTINE sub_1

SUBROUTINE sub_2 (caller)
   CHARACTER(*), INTENT (IN) :: caller
   PRINT "(A)", " Inside sub_2 called by " // caller
END SUBROUTINE sub_2
```

FIGURE 6.13. Program illustrating the scope of names and labels.

```
Before CALL sub_1, int_var =  2
    Inside sub_1, int_var = -1
    Inside sub_1, int_var = -2
Inside sub_2 called by sub_1
 After CALL sub_1, int_var =  2

Inside sub_2 called by main program
```

The program of Figure 6.13 is intended merely to reinforce concepts of scope that are presumably familiar to anyone having a working knowledge of traditional Fortran. For example, note that there is a variable named int_var in the main program and another with the same name in subroutine sub_1. Of course, changing the value of one of these variables has no effect on the other since they have different scopes—one int_var is local to the main program while the other is local to sub_1. Similarly, the statement label 100 appears in both the main program and the subroutine sub_1, but again there is no conflict since the use of a label in one program unit is unknown in another program unit. On the other hand, observe in Figure 6.13 that the name sub_2 is used in both the main program and the subroutine sub_1, and in both cases the name refers to the external procedure defined by the external subroutine sub_2. This is no surprise because the names of external procedures, unlike those of variables, are global in scope.

The fundamental rules of scope illustrated by the program of Figure 6.13 are largely, but not entirely, beneficial. The restricted scope of variable names and labels permits a programmer to write an external subprogram without being concerned about choosing variable names or statement labels that clash with those in another program unit. However, there are many situations where it is desirable for certain variable names to be known in more than one subprogram, and while this is not possible in traditional Fortran, the scope of variable names can be broadened in Fortran 90 by using a module. On the other side of the coin, the unrestricted scope of a subprogram name, as in traditional Fortran, is not always desirable either. But in Fortran 90, the programmer can choose to write an internal subprogram whose name is unknown outside the subprogram or main program containing it. Thus, Fortran 90 provides the programmer with greater flexibility in controlling the scope of names, but the price of this flexibility is additional complexity in the rules governing scope.

In order to deal with the more complicated set of rules related to scope, the Fortran 90 standard introduces the term "scoping unit" to refer to a part of a program containing a collection of names sharing the same scope. More formally, a **scoping unit** is defined as one of the following:

1. a derived-type definition;

2. an interface body, excluding any derived-type definitions and interface bodies contained within it;

3. a subprogram, excluding derived-type definitions, interface bodies, and subprograms contained within it; or

4. a main program, module, or block data program unit, excluding derived-type definitions, interface bodies, and subprograms contained within it.

Note that a subprogram or a main program containing no derived-type definitions, no interface bodies, and no internal subprograms constitutes a scoping unit. Thus, in Figure 6.13, each of the subroutine sub_1, the subroutine sub_2, and the main program is a scoping unit.

An important idea to be grasped here is that the Fortran 90 rules governing scope are merely generalizations of those of FORTRAN 77. In this context, it may be helpful to think of the scoping units as refinements of program units. In situations where no new Fortran 90 features are being utilized, the scoping units are identical with program units and the rules related to scope are the same as in FORTRAN 77.

6.11 TERMINOLOGY: SUBPROGRAMS AND PROCEDURES

In Fortran, the terms "subprogram" and "procedure" are so closely related that they are often not differentiated in informal discussion. However, an understanding of the difference between these two terms can be helpful in reading Fortran literature. Actually, the meanings of these terms remain basically the same in Fortran 90 as in FORTRAN 77.

The essential difference between the terms "subprogram" and "procedure" is that a subprogram is a specific collection of Fortran code, while a procedure is a sequence of actions whose execution is started in a specific way. To elaborate, a **subprogram** is either (1) a SUBROUTINE statement, its corresponding END statement, and all the statements in between, where the SUBROUTINE and END statements are not inside an interface block; or (2) a FUNCTION statement, its corresponding END statement, and all the statements in between, where the FUNCTION and END statements are not inside an interface block. On the other hand, a **procedure** is a sequence of actions started by the execution of a CALL statement (or by a special variety of assignment statement to be discussed in Chapter 9) or by a reference to a function name (or by the evaluation of a particular variety of expression to be discussed in Chapter 9). The intimate relationship between the terms "procedure" and "subprogram" arises because the sequence of actions comprising a procedure is typically thought of as being defined by the complete collection of statements within a subprogram. But this does not exhaust the possibilities since, on the one hand, a subprogram may define more than one procedure and, on the other hand, a procedure may be defined by means other than a subprogram.

For example, although subprogram execution ordinarily begins with the first executable statement after the SUBROUTINE or FUNCTION statement, both the FORTRAN 77 and Fortran 90 standards permit the programmer to specify alternate entry points by coding the keyword ENTRY. A subprogram is considered to define an additional procedure for each ENTRY statement it contains. Thus, a Fortran subprogram may define two or more procedures. An example of a function subprogram that defines three procedures is given in Section G.3 of Appendix G.

Also, for years Fortran has provided the "statement function," a single-statement procedure definition, similar in form to an assignment statement and placed in the specification part of a main program or subprogram. (For those readers not familiar with this feature, an example is given in Section G.2 of Appendix G.) The point to be understood here is that the statement function does define a procedure, but it does not meet the definition of a function subprogram since it has neither a FUNCTION statement nor an END statement.

Moreover, a procedure can be defined by some means entirely outside a Fortran programmer's control. For example, a procedure may be defined by means of another language, such as an assembly language routine or a C function. Also, a procedure may be defined as an intrinsic procedure, such as SQRT or ABS, that is built into the Fortran language. Note that these are not subprograms since no SUBROUTINE, FUNCTION, or END statements are involved, and there is typically no Fortran code at all. However, they are procedures since they are invoked either by a CALL statement or by referencing a name followed by a (possibly empty) parenthesized argument list.

It is worth mentioning that there is yet one more variety of procedure that has been around for years, namely the "dummy procedure." A dummy procedure is a dummy argument whose name corresponds to an actual argument that is a procedure name. (For those readers not familiar with this feature, an example is given in Section G.4 of Appendix G.) Such a name is a procedure name since a sequence of actions is begun by executing a CALL statement followed by the dummy argument name or by referencing the dummy argument name followed by a parenthesized argument list, but there is typically no SUBROUTINE or FUNCTION statement containing the dummy argument name—like any dummy argument name, its name is effectively replaced by the name of an actual argument at execution time.

Perhaps the trickiest thing about the terminology discussed in this section is that "procedure" is the generic term for either "subroutine" or "function," while "subprogram" is the generic term for either "subroutine subprogram" or "function subprogram." Thus, strictly speaking, "subroutine" and "subroutine subprogram" are not synonymous, although the distinction is one that we frequently do not care about. Of course, the same thing can be said for "function" and "function subprogram."

Incidentally, note that a main program is not classified as a procedure in Fortran since its execution cannot be started by any means built into the language. The execution of a Fortran main program must ordinarily be started by some action of the operating system. This classification is somewhat different from that of Pascal or C.

CHAPTER 7

INTRODUCTION TO THE MODULE

7.1 OVERVIEW OF THE MODULE

The Fortran 90 module provides the language with a flexible new category of program unit. In its simplest usage, the module is a vehicle for packaging collections of data specifications and/or sharing data between separately compiled program units. But in addition to data specifications, modules may also contain subprograms, providing capabilities somewhat similar to the *package* in Ada and the *class* in C++. The Fortran 90 module can be used to segment large, unwieldy programs into smaller, more manageable pieces, and it can be employed to package the source code for intimately related data and procedures in the same program unit, which promotes software maintainability and reusability.

An elementary use of the module is to package a collection of constants and/or definitions. This chapter will illustrate modules containing collections of related named constants and modules containing derived-type definitions. A somewhat similar use of the module is to contain the specifications for an interface block, but illustration of this is deferred until Chapter 13. In uses such as these, the module provides capabilities somewhat similar to those traditionally supplied by INCLUDE files, a widely available extension to the FORTRAN 77 standard. The Fortran 90 standard specifies a syntax for the INCLUDE line, but implementation details are permitted to vary so much that the INCLUDE mechanism should be avoided by those concerned with portability.

In addition to simply providing a convenient way of packaging collections of data specifications, a module also facilitates the sharing of data at execution time. In particular, variables declared in a module can be made available to any number of other program units, so that access to the variables in the module is shared by all the program units. In some respects, this capability is similar to that provided traditionally by common blocks, but as will be shown by the examples given later in this chapter, the approach taken by the Fortran 90 module is more intuitive, offers greater flexibility, and is less subject to error. Also, variables in a module may be given initial values, so that the old BLOCK DATA mechanism for initializing variables in a common block is not needed in Fortran 90, although it is supported for backward compatibility.

A module may contain not only data specifications, but it may contain subroutine and function subprograms as well. The module subprogram provides a mechanism for segmenting programs that is competitive with that of the traditional external subprogram. In fact, anything that can be accomplished using an external subprogram can also be accomplished with a module subprogram. Also, compilers can perform better cross-checks on interfaces for module subprograms than for external subprograms. Moreover, a module subprogram is always easy to use, while, as will be detailed in Chapter 13, the use of some external subprograms entails the added complication of supplying a block of code known as an "interface body."

Modules provide a great many new capabilities to Fortran, and this chapter will describe only their elementary aspects. Additional discussion of some of the more advanced features of modules will be given in Chapters 9 and 12.

7.2 MODULE CONTAINING RELATED NAMED CONSTANTS

One use of a module is to package a collection of related named constants, as illustrated in Figure 7.1a. It is important to understand that, in most implementations, the code of Figure 7.1a may be compiled by itself. Note that the first statement in a module consists of the

```
MODULE metric_english_conversions

    IMPLICIT NONE

    REAL, PARAMETER :: cm_in_1_ft    = 30.48006096
    REAL, PARAMETER :: ft_in_1_cm    =  0.03280833
    REAL, PARAMETER :: inches_in_1_m = 39.37000000
    REAL, PARAMETER :: lb_in_1_kg    =  2.204622341
    REAL, PARAMETER :: kg_in_1_lb    =  0.4535924277

END MODULE metric_english_conversions
```

FIGURE 7.1A. A module packaging related named constants.

keyword MODULE followed by a programmer-chosen module name. In a manner similar to other program units, an END MODULE statement delimits the end of a module.

A main program, a subprogram, another module, or other scoping unit accesses the contents of a module by the USE statement, which, in its simplest form, consists of the keyword USE followed by the name of that module as specified in its MODULE statement. This is illustrated by the main program of Figure 7.1b. A USE statement must precede any other kind of specification statement. Following the USE statement, the names in the module are known in the main program, and this mechanism of making the names available to the main program is called **use association**.

In most Fortran 90 implementations, the module of Figure 7.1a and the main program of Figure 7.1b may be in separate files, or they may be in the same file—in either case, a Fortran 90 compiler treats them as separate compilation units. However, note that in most implementations, compilation of the main program cannot be completed until after the module has been compiled. Thus, the traditional Fortran notion that program units may always be compiled completely independently of one another is not quite preserved—compilation of a program unit may have to be preceded by compilation of all modules used by that program unit.

After the two program units are compiled, the resulting object code can be linked to form an executable program. When the program units

```
PROGRAM demo_metric_english

    USE metric_english_conversions      ! gives main program
                                         ! access to all names
                                         ! in module

    IMPLICIT NONE

    PRINT "(A, E13.6)", " centimeters in 1 foot = ",          &
                                            cm_in_1_ft
    PRINT "(A, E13.6)", " feet in 1 centimeter  = ",          &
                                            ft_in_1_cm
    PRINT "(A, E13.6)", " inches in 1 meter     = ",          &
                                            inches_in_1_m
    PRINT "(A, E13.6)", " pounds in 1 kilogram  = ",          &
                                            lb_in_1_kg
    PRINT "(A, E13.6)", " kilograms in 1 pound  = ",          &
                                            kg_in_1_lb
END PROGRAM demo_metric_english
```

FIGURE 7.1B. A program unit that accesses the module of Figure 7.1a.

of Figure 7.1a and Figure 7.1b are compiled, linked, and executed, something like the following is displayed:

```
centimeters in 1 foot  =  0.304801E+02
feet in 1 centimeter   =  0.328083E-01
inches in 1 meter      =  0.393700E+02
pounds in 1 kilogram   =  0.220462E+01
kilograms in 1 pound   =  0.453592E+00
```

Many experienced programmers will immediately think of employing an INCLUDE file instead of a module in the above example program. Although not supported by the FORTRAN 77 standard, most popular implementations of Fortran have for years provided a mechanism for inserting source code from one file, known as an "INCLUDE file," into another source file. For backward compatibility, the Fortran 90 standard supports the INCLUDE line in programs, but its use is discouraged in favor of modules for reasons of portability.

While modules and INCLUDE files provide competing mechanisms for packaging collections of related specifications, there are major differences between the two mechanisms. The source code in a module is compiled by itself, while the source code in an INCLUDE file is inserted into another source file before compilation of the other source file begins. In most implementations, the source code for a module may be either in a file by itself or in a file with other program units, while the source code comprising an INCLUDE file must be in a file by itself. Perhaps most important of all, the specifications in a module are *global* to all program units that use the module, while the specifications in an INCLUDE file remain *local* to each program unit into which they are inserted.

A commonplace use of a module is to package the specifications for the KIND parameter (described in Section 2.8) for a particular Fortran 90 implementation. For example, if there were a computer called the MondoComp 7000, there might be a module something like the following:

```
MODULE mondocomp_7000_kind_parameters
    INTEGER, PARAMETER :: Single = 4,  &
                          Double = 8,  &
                          Byte   = 1,  &
                          Short  = 2,  &
                          Long   = 4
END MODULE mondocomp_7000_kind_parameters
```

Then, almost every program unit run on the MondoComp 7000 would use this module in the following manner:

```
SUBROUTINE perform_some_procedure
    USE mondocomp_7000_kind_parameters
    REAL(Double)                    :: var_1, var_2
    INTEGER(Short), DIMENSION(1000)  :: indices
    INTEGER(Byte),  DIMENSION(20000) :: dinky_numbers
                    .
                    .
                    .
```

Note that porting the above subroutine to a different make of computer, say, the CompuMix 1000, can get off to a good start by simply changing the USE statement to reference the corresponding module on the CompuMix 1000.

7.3   A Module Containing a Derived-Type Definition

Suppose that a simple main program invokes an external subprogram having a dummy argument of a derived type. As always, the corresponding actual argument in the main program must agree in data type. Now, observe that, in this situation, a requirement arises that does not exist when all of the arguments are of intrinsic types: The derived-type definition must be available both in the main program for the actual argument and in the external subprogram for the dummy argument. The best way of satisfying this requirement is to place the derived-type definition in a module and then have both the main program and the external subprogram use the module. This is illustrated by the complete program consisting of the three program units shown in Figures 7.2a, 7.2b, and 7.2c.

The program of Figures 7.2a, 7.2b, and 7.2c features a derived type named employee_type, which is defined in Figure 7.2a. Note in Figure 7.2a that the derived-type definition is placed in a module named employee_type_def, and that both the external subroutine of Figure 7.2b and the main program of Figure 7.2c access the derived-type definition by using the module. Hence, the derived-type definition is available in the subroutine of Figure 7.2b so that the dummy argument employee can be declared to be of type employee_type, and it is also available in the main program of Figure 7.2c so that the actual argument empl can be declared to be of that same derived type. When the program made up of the program units in Figures 7.2a, 7.2b, and 7.2c is executed, the following is displayed:

```
Ima Nerd              1234 T
```

```
MODULE employee_type_def

   IMPLICIT NONE

   TYPE :: employee_type
      CHARACTER(20) :: name        ! derived-
      INTEGER       :: number      !   type
      LOGICAL       :: is_married   ! definition
   END TYPE employee_type

END MODULE employee_type_def
```

FIGURE 7.2A. Module containing definition of type employee_type.

In this example, one might naively expect that instead of using a module it would be satisfactory simply to place duplicate copies of the derived-type definition for employee_type in both the main program and the external subroutine. In fact, this approach may work in some implementations of Fortran 90, but the standard specifies that identical derived-type definitions in different scoping units do not define the same data type unless they each contain a SEQUENCE statement. (The SEQUENCE statement was discussed in Section 5.11.) Hence, if a derived-type definition is duplicated in different scoping units, or if the INCLUDE mechanism is employed to insert a derived-type definition in different scoping units, conformance with the Fortran 90 standard requires that the SEQUENCE statement be present in each such definition.

```
SUBROUTINE print_struct (employee)

   USE employee_type_def    ! Access derived-type definition.

   IMPLICIT NONE

   TYPE (employee_type), INTENT (IN) :: employee  ! derived-
                                                  !   type
                                                  ! dummy arg

   PRINT "(1X, A, I5, 1X, L1)", employee

END SUBROUTINE print_struct
```

FIGURE 7.2B. External subroutine with derived-type dummy argument.

```
PROGRAM demo_derived_type_def_in_module

    USE employee_type_def    ! Access derived-type definition.

    IMPLICIT NONE

    TYPE (employee_type) :: empl      ! actual arg of
                                      ! derived type

    empl = employee_type ("Ima Nerd", 1234, .TRUE.)
    CALL print_struct (empl)

END PROGRAM demo_derived_type_def_in_module
```

FIGURE 7.2c.   Main program with actual argument of a derived type.

However, it is recommended that methods using the SEQUENCE statement be avoided in favor of the approach using a module illustrated in this section.

7.4   A MODULE MAY USE ANOTHER MODULE

Previous examples have illustrated that a module may be used by main programs and subroutine subprograms, and, of course, a module may also be used by function subprograms. But it is important to understand that a module may be used by any category of scoping unit, and in particular, a module may be used by another module. One situation in which the need for this arises is when a derived-type component is itself of a derived type. Consider, for example, the case of a derived type named triangle_type, which has three components, each of which is the Cartesian coordinates of a vertex of a triangle. Each vertex then might be modeled as a derived type named point_type, which has two components, x and y. Each of the derived types point_type and triangle_type could be placed in a module by itself, as indicated by Figures 7.3a and 7.3b. Note that the module of Figure 7.3b uses the module of Figure 7.3a.

Now consider a function subprogram that determines the perimeter of a triangle, given the coordinates of its vertices. The function calc_perim, whose listing is shown in Figure 7.3c, calculates the perimeter by determining the length of each of the three sides of a triangle and adding the lengths together. The length of each side is the distance between its

```
MODULE point_type_def

   IMPLICIT NONE

   TYPE :: point_type
      REAL :: x, y      ! Cartesian coordinates of a point
   END TYPE point_type

END MODULE point_type_def
```

FIGURE 7.3A. Module containing definition of derived-type point_type.

```
MODULE triangle_type_def

   USE point_type_def    ! Access definition of point_type.

   IMPLICIT NONE

   TYPE :: triangle_type
      TYPE (point_type) :: a, b, c  ! vertices of a triangle
   END TYPE triangle_type

END MODULE triangle_type_def
```

FIGURE 7.3B. Module that uses module of Figure 7.3a.

```
FUNCTION calc_perim (t) RESULT (perimeter)

   USE triangle_type_def

   IMPLICIT NONE

   TYPE (triangle_type), INTENT (IN) :: t
   REAL                              :: perimeter

   REAL :: dist   ! external function to find
                  ! distance between 2 points

   perimeter = dist (t%a, t%b) + dist (t%a, t%c) +          &
                                     dist (t%b, t%c)
END FUNCTION calc_perim
```

FIGURE 7.3C. External function that uses module of Figure 7.3b.

```
FUNCTION dist (pt_1, pt_2) RESULT (d)

   USE point_type_def

   IMPLICIT NONE

   TYPE (point_type), INTENT (IN) :: pt_1, pt_2
   REAL                           :: d

   d = SQRT ((pt_1%x - pt_2%x) ** 2 + (pt_1%y - pt_2%y) ** 2)

END FUNCTION dist
```

FIGURE 7.3D. External function invoked by subprogram of Figure 7.3c.

```
PROGRAM demo_nested_modules

   USE triangle_type_def

   IMPLICIT NONE

   TYPE (triangle_type) :: triangle

   REAL :: calc_perim   ! func to find perimeter of triangle

   triangle%a%x = 0.0;  triangle%a%y = 0.0
   triangle%b%x = 3.0;  triangle%b%y = 0.0
   triangle%c%x = 3.0;  triangle%c%y = 4.0

   PRINT "(F8.3)", calc_perim (triangle)

END PROGRAM demo_nested_modules
```

FIGURE 7.3E. Main program that invokes function of Figure 7.3c.

two end points, so calc_perim invokes the function dist of Figure 7.3d to determine that distance, which is computed using the usual equation:

$$d = \sqrt{(x_1 - x_2)^2 + (y_1 - y_2)^2}.$$

A main program that serves as a test driver for the function calc_perim is given in Figure 7.3e. The perimeter of the 3–4–5 right triangle whose vertices are at (0.0,0.0), (3.0,0.0), and (3.0,4.0) is calculated. When the program consisting of the code in Figures 7.3a, 7.3b, 7.3c, 7.3d, and 7.3e is executed, the following is displayed:

```
12.000
```

Note in Figure 7.3e that the main program has access to the component names x and y of Figure 7.3a, even though the module name point_type_def does not appear in a USE statement in the main program. This is, of course, because the main program uses the module triangle_type_def, which, in turn, uses the module point_type_def.

7.5 MODULES FACILITATE DATA SHARING

For years, Fortran has supported the common block as a mechanism for separately compiled program units to share data, but common blocks are easily misused, and this has resulted in many programming errors. Fortunately, the Fortran 90 module provides a better method for sharing data, making the use of common blocks unnecessary except under unusual circumstances. The complete Fortran 90 program made up of the source code in Figures 7.4a, 7.4b, and 7.4c illustrates the use of a module to facilitate sharing data between separately compiled program units.

```
PROGRAM demo_data_sharing

   USE data_to_be_shared    ! Access number_of_values
                            ! and array_of_data.

   IMPLICIT NONE

   INTEGER :: i

   number_of_values = 5    ! Store value in number_of_values.
   DO i = 1, number_of_values
      array_of_data(i) = i  ! Store values in array_of_data.
   END DO

   CALL display_data

END PROGRAM demo_data_sharing
```

FIGURE 7.4A. Main that shares data with subroutine of Figure 7.4b.

```
SUBROUTINE display_data

   USE data_to_be_shared    ! Access number_of_values
                            ! and array_of_data.

   IMPLICIT NONE

   INTEGER :: i

   DO i = 1, number_of_values    ! Fetch value from
                                 ! number_of_values.
      PRINT "(F6.1)", array_of_data(i)   ! Fetch value from
                                         ! array_of_data.
   END DO

END SUBROUTINE display_data
```

FIGURE 7.4B. Subroutine that shares data with main of Figure 7.4a.

When the source code of Figures 7.4a, 7.4b, and 7.4c is compiled, linked, and executed, the program displays

```
1.0
2.0
3.0
4.0
5.0
```

Note that the program of Figures 7.4a, 7.4b, and 7.4c consists of three program units—a main program, an external subroutine, and a module. Each of these three program units is compiled as a separate unit whether the source code for each is contained in a separate file or all three are contained in a single file.

```
MODULE data_to_be_shared

   IMPLICIT NONE

   REAL, DIMENSION(1000) :: array_of_data
   INTEGER               :: number_of_values

END MODULE data_to_be_shared
```

FIGURE 7.4C. Module used by program units of Figures 7.4a and 7.4b.

Observe that both the main program of Figure 7.4a and the external subroutine of Figure 7.4b use the module data_to_be_shared of Figure 7.4c. Thus, the main program stores values into the variable named number_of_values and the array named array_of_data, and the external subroutine display_data is able to access these values in order to display them. It is important to understand that there is only one copy of number_of_values and array_of_data, and that both the main program and the subroutine access the same copy of each variable declared in the module. Also, even though they are separately compiled, both the main program and the subroutine use the same name to access the values of a particular variable declared in the module. Hence, in effect, a module provides global scope for a variable to all program units using that module. This points up an important difference between a variable name in a module and a variable name in a COMMON statement—a variable name in a COMMON statement is local to the program unit in which that COMMON statement appears.

7.6 GLOBAL ALLOCATABLE ARRAYS

Although the author recommends always using modules for sharing data between program units, the older common block mechanism is still available and may be used to achieve the same result in most cases. However, the Fortran 90 standard imposes some restrictions on common blocks that do not apply to modules. An example of a situation where a common block cannot be used is when a program needs large global arrays whose sizes are not known until execution time. As discussed in Section 4.10, this requirement can often be met by employing allocatable arrays. But the Fortran 90 standard forbids the presence of allocatable arrays in common blocks because the length of a common block must be determined before program execution begins. On the other hand, placing allocatable arrays in a module and having any routine requiring access to the arrays use the module handles this problem quite nicely. A simple example of the approach is given by the program of Figures 7.5a, 7.5b, 7.5c, and 7.5d.

Figure 7.5a lists a module containing two allocatable arrays—a rank 1 INTEGER array named v and a rank 2 REAL array named a. The main program of Figure 7.5b and the two external subroutines of Figures 7.5c and 7.5d all use the module of Figure 7.5a. When the program is executed, the user enters an integer value at the terminal. The main program of Figure 7.5b reads the input value into the variable n and allocates storage for v and a. Then the subroutine fill_arrays of Figure 7.5c is called, and it puts values into v and a. Upon return from fill_

```
MODULE allocatable_arrays

   IMPLICIT NONE

   INTEGER, ALLOCATABLE, DIMENSION(:)   :: v
   REAL,    ALLOCATABLE, DIMENSION(:,:) :: a

END MODULE allocatable_arrays
```

FIGURE 7.5A. Module containing global allocatable arrays.

arrays, the main program calls subroutine display_arrays of Figure 7.5d, which displays the values stored in the arrays v and a and deallocates their storage. If the user enters 4 when the program is executed, the following is displayed:

```
1 101.0 102.0 103.0 104.0 105.0 106.0 107.0 108.0
2 201.0 202.0 203.0 204.0 205.0 206.0 207.0 208.0
3 301.0 302.0 303.0 304.0 305.0 306.0 307.0 308.0
4 401.0 402.0 403.0 404.0 405.0 406.0 407.0 408.0
```

```
PROGRAM demo_allocatable_arrays_in_module

   USE allocatable_arrays

   IMPLICIT NONE

   INTEGER :: n

   READ *, n
   ALLOCATE (v(n), a(n,2*n)) ! Get storage for v and a.

   CALL fill_arrays (n)  ! Store data in v and a.

   CALL display_arrays (n)  ! Display contents of v and a.

END PROGRAM demo_allocatable_arrays_in_module
```

FIGURE 7.5B. Main program that allocates storage for global arrays.

```
SUBROUTINE fill_arrays (n)

  USE allocatable_arrays

  IMPLICIT NONE

  INTEGER, INTENT (IN) :: n

  INTEGER :: i, j

  DO i = 1, n
    v(i) = i                    ! Store values in v.
    DO j = 1, 2 * n
      a(i,j) = 100 * i + j   ! Store values in a.
    END DO
  END DO

END SUBROUTINE fill_arrays
```

FIGURE 7.5C. External subroutine that stores values in global arrays.

```
SUBROUTINE display_arrays (n)

  USE allocatable_arrays

  IMPLICIT NONE

  INTEGER, INTENT (IN) :: n

  INTEGER :: i, j

  DO i = 1, n
    PRINT "(I4, 100F6.1)", v(i), (a(i,j), j = 1, 2 * n)
  END DO

  DEALLOCATE (v, a)    ! Free storage for v and a.

END SUBROUTINE display_arrays
```

FIGURE 7.5D. External subroutine displaying values in global arrays.

7.7   *THE SAVE ATTRIBUTE FOR VARIABLES IN A MODULE*

Under certain conditions, the Fortran 90 standard permits a variable in a module to become undefined upon return from a subprogram using that module. The idea is, of course, that if storage is no longer needed for a variable, then an implementation should be given the opportunity to use its storage for some other purpose. However, it should be mentioned that some implementations may make no use of this opportunity, in which case all variables in modules would retain their definition status under all conditions. Also, some implementations may offer a compiler option as to whether all variables are saved or not.

This same idea was discussed in Section 6.6 in connection with local variables in subprograms. As is the case with local variables, by specifying the SAVE attribute, a programmer can guarantee that a variable in a module will not become undefined when a subprogram is exited. Also, the Fortran 90 standard specifies that a variable in a module will not become undefined upon return from a subprogram using the module if the main program uses the module or if another subprogram using the module remains in execution. It is worth noting that this treatment of variables declared in a module is analogous to the treatment specified for variables in a named common block in the FORTRAN 77 standard.

In the example programs of Sections 7.5 and 7.6, the variables in modules are guaranteed to remain defined by virtue of the fact that, in each example program, these variables are in a module used by the main program. However, this is not always desirable, and so an alternate implementation of the example program of Section 7.6 is given in Figures 7.6a, 7.6b, 7.6c, and 7.6d. The example program presented in this section behaves exactly the same as does that of the preceding

```
MODULE saved_allocatable_arrays

  IMPLICIT NONE

  INTEGER, ALLOCATABLE, DIMENSION(:),   SAVE :: v ! Arrays
  REAL,    ALLOCATABLE, DIMENSION(:,:), SAVE :: a ! will be
                                                  ! SAVEd.

  INTEGER :: n   ! n not guaranteed to be SAVEd

END MODULE saved_allocatable_arrays
```

FIGURE 7.6A. Module containing global arrays with SAVE attribute.

```
PROGRAM demo_saved_arrays

   ! Note that main program does not
   ! use saved_allocatable_arrays.

   CALL fill_arrays

   ! v and a are guaranteed to remain defined here because
   ! of SAVE attribute when declared in module.  n is not
   ! guaranteed to be defined here (but unimportant since
   ! unused for remainder of program execution).

   CALL display_arrays

END PROGRAM demo_saved_arrays
```

FIGURE 7.6B. Main program that calls subroutines accessing global arrays.

section from a user's point of view—given the same input, the two programs produce identical output.

Note that the subroutine display_arrays of Figure 7.6d depends on the arrays v and a retaining their values after the return from subroutine

```
SUBROUTINE fill_arrays

   USE saved_allocatable_arrays    ! Access v and a.

   IMPLICIT NONE

   INTEGER :: i, j

   READ *, n                       ! Get user input.

   ALLOCATE (v(n), a(n,2*n))       ! Get storage for v and a.

   DO i = 1, n
      v(i) = i                     ! Store values in v.
      DO j = 1, 2 * n
         a(i,j) = 100 * i + j      ! Store values in a.
      END DO
   END DO

END SUBROUTINE fill_arrays
```

FIGURE 7.6C. External subroutine that stores values in global arrays.

```
SUBROUTINE display_arrays

   USE saved_allocatable_arrays   ! Access v and a.

   IMPLICIT NONE

   INTEGER :: i, j

   INTRINSIC SIZE   ! Use to get current extents of arrays.

   DO i = 1, SIZE (v)
      PRINT "(I4, 100F6.1)",                                         &
                              v(i), (a(i,j), j = 1, SIZE (a, 2))
   END DO

   DEALLOCATE (v, a)

END SUBROUTINE display_arrays
```

FIGURE 7.6D. External subroutine that displays values in global arrays.

fill_arrays of Figure 7.6c. Also, observe that the main program of Figure 7.6b does not use any module. Thus, in order to ensure that their values are retained, the SAVE attribute is specified for v and a in the module of Figure 7.6a. Note also in Figures 7.6a, 7.6b, 7.6c, and 7.6d that the value of n is not passed as an argument as it was in the program of the preceding section, but instead is a variable declared in the module. Furthermore, observe that n is not given the SAVE attribute, and so it is not guaranteed by the standard to be defined when subroutine fill_arrays is exited. This causes no problems, however, since n is not needed after the return from fill_arrays (and in fact, n could just as well have been declared as a local variable in fill_arrays). When the subroutine display_arrays of Figure 7.6d requires array extents, the new standard intrinsic function SIZE is invoked.

7.8   *INITIALIZATION MAY BE PERFORMED IN A MODULE*

To give initial values at compile time to variables in a named common block, the FORTRAN 77 standard requires that the values be specified in a special category of program unit known in the older standard as a "block data subprogram." However, some implementations do not enforce this requirement and permit named common block variables to be initialized via DATA statements in any program unit. An example of a FORTRAN 77 block data subprogram follows:

```
* Warning: FORTRAN 77 follows.
      BLOCK DATA SHARED
      REAL    X(1000)
      INTEGER NUMBER
      COMMON / BIGARR / NUMBER, X
      DATA NUMBER / 5 /
      DATA X      / 1.0, 2.0, 3.0, 4.0, 5.0, 995 * 0.0 /
      END
```

For purposes of backward compatibility, code such as the above still complies with the Fortran 90 standard. However, in Fortran 90, such a program unit is no longer considered to be a subprogram and is redesignated as a "block data program unit."

As mentioned earlier, it is recommended that the variables that would be placed in common blocks in FORTRAN 77 implementations be placed in modules in Fortran 90. In this connection, it is important to understand that initializing variables in modules at compile time is handled quite naturally and requires no special considerations on the part of the programmer. Hence, the need for the block data program unit is obviated in Fortran 90.

Figure 7.7a shows a module that serves essentially the same purpose as the block data program unit listed previously. The module is used to share data between the main program of Figure 7.7b and the external subroutine of Figure 7.7c. The main program begins by displaying the initial values of the first few elements of the array x and then calls the subroutine of Figure 7.7c. The subroutine changes some of the values of variables in the module and returns to the main program, which

```
MODULE shared_data

   IMPLICIT NONE

   INTEGER :: number_of_elements = 5

   INTEGER :: i    ! implied DO index used in initializing
                   ! last 995 elements of array x to 0.0

   REAL, DIMENSION(1000) :: x = (/ 1.0, 2.0, 3.0, 4.0, 5.0, &
                                   (0.0, i = 6, 1000) /)
END MODULE shared_data
```

FIGURE 7.7A. Module containing variables with initial values.

```
PROGRAM initializing_vars_in_module

    USE shared_data   ! Access all variables in module.

    IMPLICIT NONE

    INTEGER :: j    ! implied DO index in PRINT stmts below

    PRINT "(100F6.1)", (x(j), j = 1, number_of_elements)

    CALL change_shared_data_values

    PRINT "(100F6.1)", (x(j), j = 1, number_of_elements)

END PROGRAM initializing_vars_in_module
```

FIGURE 7.7B. Main program that uses the module of Figure 7.7a.

displays the new values stored in the first few elements of the array
x. When the program of Figures 7.7a, 7.7b, and 7.7c is executed, the
following is displayed:

```
   1.0    2.0    3.0    4.0    5.0
 -10.0  -20.0  -30.0  -40.0
```

There are some interesting sidelights to the example program
presented in this section. One of these is that an expression such as

```
995 * 0.0
```

```
SUBROUTINE change_shared_data_values

    USE shared_data

    IMPLICIT NONE

    number_of_elements = 4    ! Change value of
                              ! number_of_elements.

    ! Change values of some of the elements of x.
    x(1:4) = (/ -10.0, -20.0, -30.0, -40.0 /)

END SUBROUTINE change_shared_data_values
```

FIGURE 7.7C. Subroutine that changes variable values in module.

in a DATA statement means "repeat the value zero 995 times," while in a Fortran 90 initialization expression, it means "multiply 995 times zero." Note that in Figure 7.7a, the same result is achieved by employing a form similar to the old implied DO:

```
(0.0, i = 6, 1000)
```

Since an IMPLICIT NONE is present in the module, the variable name i must be declared, and this gives rise to a possible minor complication. As things are coded in Figure 7.7a, any module user will have access to i, as well as to the other names in the module, although it seems unlikely that such access was intended by the module author. This has the following side effect: If an attempt were made in any scoping unit that uses the module to declare a variable named i, the compiler would generate an error message. In Figure 7.7a, this side effect could have been avoided by specifying the PRIVATE attribute for i, which would mean that this variable would be unknown outside the module. This example raises the issue of dealing with name clashes, a topic that will be explored in detail in Chapter 12.

In light of the discussion in the preceding section regarding variables in modules becoming undefined under some circumstances, it should be mentioned that the Fortran 90 standard specifies that this cannot happen to the variables in the module of Figure 7.7a. The reason for this is that, as stated in Section 6.6, variables that are given initial values automatically acquire the SAVE attribute.

7.9   A MODULE MAY CONTAIN SUBPROGRAMS

Preceding sections have given examples of modules that contain data, but a Fortran 90 module can also contain subprograms. The source code for all module subprograms is placed between a CONTAINS statement and the module's END statement. The form of a module subprogram is basically the same as that of an external subprogram as described in Chapter 6. However, a subprogram in a module may be invoked only from a scoping unit that uses the module or from another subprogram contained within the same module. This is quite different from an external subprogram, which can be invoked from anywhere.

An example of a module containing three subprograms is given in Figure 7.8a. The module julian_dates is used to convert in either direction between ordinary calendar dates and Julian dates. A calendar date consists of a month, a day, and a year, while a Julian date is made up of a count of the days into the year and a year. For example, in 1995, March 3 is Julian day 62 (31 days in January, 28 days in February, plus 3 days in

```
MODULE julian_dates

   IMPLICIT NONE

   INTEGER, DIMENSION(12), PARAMETER ::                         &
      Days_per_mon_in_nonleap = (/ 31, 28, 31, 30, 31, 30,  &
                                 31, 31, 30, 31, 30, 31 /)

   ! days_per_mon will be set to number of days per month.
   INTEGER, DIMENSION(12) :: days_per_mon

CONTAINS

   ! Convert month & day to Julian day for given year.
   FUNCTION conv_to_jul (mon, day, yr) RESULT (jul_day)
      INTEGER               :: jul_day
      INTEGER, INTENT (IN) :: mon, day, yr
      days_per_mon = Days_per_mon_in_nonleap
      IF (is_leap (yr)) days_per_mon(2) = 29  ! Invoke module
                                              ! procedure.
      jul_day = SUM (days_per_mon(1:mon-1)) + day
   END FUNCTION conv_to_jul

   ! Convert Julian day in given year to month & day.
   SUBROUTINE conv_to_cal (jul_day, yr, mon, day)
      INTEGER, INTENT (IN)  :: jul_day, yr
      INTEGER, INTENT (OUT) :: mon, day
      days_per_mon = Days_per_mon_in_nonleap
      IF (is_leap (yr)) days_per_mon(2) = 29   ! Invoke module
                                              ! procedure.
      DO mon = 1, 12
         IF (jul_day <= SUM (days_per_mon(1:mon))) EXIT
      END DO
      day = jul_day - SUM (days_per_mon(1:mon-1))
   END SUBROUTINE conv_to_cal

   ! Return .TRUE. if leap year, .FALSE. if not.
   FUNCTION is_leap (yr) RESULT (its_a_leap)
      LOGICAL               :: its_a_leap
      INTEGER, INTENT (IN) :: yr
      its_a_leap = .FALSE.
      IF (MOD (yr,   4) == 0 .AND.                     &
          MOD (yr, 100) /= 0 .OR.                      &
          MOD (yr, 400) == 0      ) its_a_leap = .TRUE.
   END FUNCTION is_leap

END MODULE julian_dates
```

FIGURE 7.8A. Module containing subprograms.

March). In module julian_dates, the module function conv_to_jul returns the Julian day, given month, day, and year, while module subroutine conv_to_cal returns the month and day, given Julian day and year. The module function is_leap determines whether a given year is a leap year, and it is invoked by the other two module subprograms to establish whether February has 28 or 29 days for a given year.

An important property of a module subprogram is that it has access to the variables, constants, and definitions placed between the MOD-ULE and CONTAINS statements, and this is how the names days_per_mon and Days_per_mon_in_nonleap in Figure 7.8a can be referenced in the subprograms conv_to_jul and conv_to_cal. Both of these subprograms begin with the following executable statements:

```
days_per_mon = Days_per_mon_in_nonleap
IF (is_leap (yr)) days_per_mon(2) = 29
```

The array Days_per_mon_in_nonleap holds the number of days per month for a nonleap year. Thus, after this pair of statements is executed, the array days_per_mon will hold the number of days per month in the year yr, whether yr is a leap year or not. The PARAMETER attribute is specified for the array Days_per_mon_in_nonleap so that it is protected from change during execution.

The module function conv_to_jul determines the Julian day jul_day by using the standard intrinsic function SUM to find the total number of days in all months preceding the specified month, mon, and adds this total to day, the day in the specified month, in the statement

```
jul_day = SUM (days_per_mon(1:mon-1)) + day
```

Note that the expression days_per_mon(1:mon-1) refers to an array section of days_per_mon containing mon - 1 elements, where mon is the number of the month. Observe that for January, the value of mon is 1, and so days_per_mon(1:mon-1) refers to a zero-sized array, but this causes no difficulty since SUM returns the value zero when given a zero-sized array argument.

The module subroutine conv_to_cal determines mon, the number of the month in the year, and day, the number of the day in the month, given the Julian day jul_day and the year yr. A DO loop is used to find in which month number the Julian day falls. Determining the day of the month then is merely the reverse of the procedure described in the preceding paragraph.

The module function is_leap returns .TRUE. if the year yr is a leap year and .FALSE. if it is not. Many people seem unfamiliar with the complete rule for determining a leap year, and so here it is: A year is a leap year if it is divisible by 4, except that a year divisible by 100 is not a leap year. However, the foregoing notwithstanding, years divisible by 400 are leap years. Thus, 1904 was a leap year, 1900 was not a leap year, and 2000 will be a leap year. The module function is_leap employs the old standard intrinsic function MOD to check the divisibility of the year by 4, 100, and 400.

The main program of Figure 7.8b demonstrates the use of the module of Figure 7.8a. By using the module julian_dates, the main program is able to invoke the subprograms contained in that module. When the program consisting of the program units of Figures 7.8a and 7.8b is executed, the following is displayed:

```
Julian day for May 21, 1991, is 141
For day 231 of 1992, month = 8 day = 18
```

Thus, the program correctly determines that May 21 was day 141 of 1991 and that day 231 of 1992 was August 18. Note that 1991 was not a leap year but that 1992 was a leap year.

Observe that the main program of Figure 7.8b has access to the names Days_per_mon_in_nonleap and days_per_mon of Figure 7.8a, as well as to the name is_leap, although no use is made of of this in the example given in this section. If it were desired to hide any or all of these names from module users, this could be accomplished by specifying the PRIVATE attribute. (Restricting access to names in modules will be the subject of Chapter 12.)

By using the module julian_dates, the main program of Figure 7.8b acquires the ability to invoke subprograms contained in that module, but, of course, the main program has no access to variables local to those

```
PROGRAM demo_julian_date_procedures

   USE julian_dates    ! Access conv_to_jul, conv_to_cal.

   IMPLICIT NONE
   INTEGER :: month, day

   PRINT "(A, I3)", " Julian day for May 21, 1991, is ",  &
                    conv_to_jul (5, 21, 1991)

   CALL conv_to_cal (231, 1992, month, day)

   PRINT "(A, I1, A, I2)",                                &
                    " For day 231 of 1992, month = ",     &
                          month, " day = ", day

END PROGRAM demo_julian_date_procedures
```

FIGURE 7.8B. A main program that uses the module of Figure 7.8a.

module subprograms. Thus, names such as mon, day, and yr in Figure 7.8a are unknown in the main program because they are declared inside module subprograms. Also, a name declared inside one subprogram in a module is unknown in other subprograms within the same module. Hence, the name its_a_leap, which is declared in the function is_leap, is unknown in the subroutine conv_to_cal.

It should be mentioned that an IMPLICIT NONE statement above the CONTAINS statement in a module remains in effect throughout the module. Thus, explicit type declarations are required for all local names in each of the three subprograms in Figure 7.8a.

Observe that even though an IMPLICIT NONE statement is present in the main program in Figure 7.8b, no type declaration is given for the function conv_to_jul as would be required if it were defined by an external function subprogram instead of by a module function subprogram. Also, as will be discussed in Chapter 13, some external subprograms require the presence of interface bodies, but interface bodies are never used with module subprograms. Hence, module subprograms are, in some instances, somewhat easier for a programmer to use than external subprograms.

It should be recognized that the collection of subprograms in the module of Figure 7.8a could alternatively be provided to a user as external subprograms. In Fortran 90, it is often not so clear-cut as to whether to implement a procedure as a module subprogram or as an external subprogram. Identical program outputs can always be produced with either approach, but there may be significant differences in using and maintaining the resulting software.

7.10   THE ASSUMED-SHAPE ARRAY

Section 6.3 discussed the handling of array arguments in external subprograms as explicit-shaped arrays and as assumed-size arrays, and that discussion applies to array arguments in module subprograms as well. This section will illustrate the use of another Fortran 90 mechanism for dealing with array arguments known as the "assumed-shape array." The treament in this section will be limited to module subprograms, deferring the use of the assumed-shape array in external subprograms until Chapter 13.

A typical assumed-shape array is illustrated in the following code fragment:

```
SUBROUTINE sub (..., x, ...)
   REAL, DIMENSION(:,:), INTENT (...) :: x
```

The two colons, separated by a comma, in the parenthesis following the keyword DIMENSION indicate that x is a rank 2 array whose bounds will be determined at execution time. Now, suppose that the following code appears in a routine that calls sub:

```
REAL, DIMENSION(3:4) :: y
        .
        .
        .
CALL sub (..., y, ...)
```

Then, when sub is invoked by this CALL statement, the dummy argument x can be thought of as assuming the shape of its corresponding actual argument y, and x will be treated as a 3×4 array throughout this execution of sub.

Slightly more formally, an **assumed-shape array** is a dummy argument array that does not have the POINTER attribute whose bounds along each dimension are specified by

[*lower-bound*]:

If *lower-bound* is not specified, it defaults to 1. It is the shape, not the bounds, of an assumed-shape array that is taken from its associated actual argument, and so if the lower bound for any dimension is not the same for the dummy and actual arrays, the corresponding upper bound of the dummy array will be adjusted as necessary to force agreement in shape.

As an example of a subprogram featuring an assumed-shape array dummy argument, consider the module function det of Figure 7.9a. det returns the value of the determinant of any square rank 2 array whose size is not zero. To see how to use det, look at the main program of Figure 7.9b, which invokes det to evaluate the following determinant.

$$\begin{vmatrix} 2 & 5 & 4 & 3 \\ 3 & 2 & 5 & 1 \\ 4 & 0 & 2 & 1 \\ 3 & 0 & 3 & 2 \end{vmatrix}$$

Note in Figure 7.9a that the function det is contained in the module determinant_evaluator, and so the main program of Figure 7.9b must use the module determinant_evaluator to gain access to det. When the program is executed, the value of the preceding determinant is displayed:

```
80.0000000
```

Observe in Figure 7.9a that only the name of the array argument, a, appears in the function's argument list. Note, in particular, that the

```
MODULE determinant_evaluator

CONTAINS

  RECURSIVE FUNCTION det (a) RESULT (d)

    REAL, DIMENSION(:,:), INTENT (IN) :: a
    REAL :: d

    INTEGER :: n    ! # rows = # cols in a
    INTEGER :: i    ! index over rows in a

    REAL, DIMENSION(SIZE(a,1)-1,SIZE(a,2)-1) ::              &
                                  a_less_row_i_and_col_1
    REAL :: minor

    n = SIZE (a, 1)

    IF (n > 1) THEN
       d = 0.0
       DO i = 1, n
          a_less_row_i_and_col_1(1:i-1,1:n-1) = a(1:i-1,2:n)
          a_less_row_i_and_col_1(i:n-1,1:n-1) = a(i+1:n,2:n)
          minor = det (a_less_row_i_and_col_1)
          d = d + (-1) ** (i + 1) * a(i,1) * minor
       END DO
    ELSE
       d = a(1,1)
    END IF

  END FUNCTION det

END MODULE determinant_evaluator
```

FIGURE 7.9A. Module function with assumed-shape array argument.

number of elements along each dimension of a does not appear in the argument list. But in Fortran 90, the number of elements along each dimension of a is guaranteed to be available in det since a is an assumed-shape array. The new standard does not specify how this capability is to be implemented, but it does no harm to envision that the routine invoking det must somehow pass it a bundle of information containing at least the starting address of the actual array argument, the rank of the actual argument, and the number of elements along each dimension of the actual argument. Thus, when the main program of Figure

```
PROGRAM test_determinant_evaluator

    USE determinant_evaluator    ! Gain access to det.

    REAL, DIMENSION(4,4) :: b

    b(1,1) = 2.0; b(1,2) = 5.0; b(1,3) = 4.0; b(1,4) = 3.0
    b(2,1) = 3.0; b(2,2) = 2.0; b(2,3) = 5.0; b(2,4) = 1.0
    b(3,1) = 4.0; b(3,2) = 0.0; b(3,3) = 2.0; b(3,4) = 1.0
    b(4,1) = 3.0; b(4,2) = 0.0; b(4,3) = 3.0; b(4,4) = 2.0

    PRINT *, det (b)      ! invoke det

END PROGRAM test_determinant_evaluator
```

FIGURE 7.9B. Main program that invokes the function of Figure 7.9a.

7.9b invokes det with b as the actual argument, the function knows that there are four elements along each of the two dimensions of the array argument, and we can think of a in Figure 7.9a as assuming the 4 × 4 shape of b.

In the function subprogram det of Figure 7.9a, the value of the determinant is found using the approach known as "expansion by minors," which is discussed in many elementary mathematics textbooks. The approach is as follows: Suppose that a_{ij} is the element in the ith row and jth column of an $n \times n$ matrix A of numerical values. Assume that the determinant of A is symbolized by D_n. Then the "minor" of a_{ij} is the determinant that remains after deleting the ith row and then jth column of D_n and is designated by M_{ij}. The determinant D_n can then be expressed in terms of the minors of the elements of the jth column as

$$D_n = (-1)^{1+j}a_{1j}M_{1j} + (-1)^{2+j}a_{2j}M_{2j} + (-1)^{3+j}a_{3j}M_{3j}$$
$$+ \cdots + (-1)^{i+j}a_{ij}M_{ij} + \cdots + (-1)^{n+j}a_{nj}M_{nj}.$$

Note that each minor is itself a determinant that can in turn be expanded in terms of its minors. This suggests that recursion will be a convenient way to think about finding the value of a determinant using expansion by minors, and this is the approach taken in the function det. The method used here is always to expand a determinant about column 1. Let i range over the rows in the determinant, and for each element in column 1, form the array that remains after deleting row i and column 1 and call this array a_less_row_i_and_col_1. In order to find the value of the determinant of a_less_row_i_and_col_1 in Figure 7.9a, simply invoke det recursively:

```
minor = det (a_less_row_i_and_col_1)
```

Thus, the keyword RECURSIVE appears in the FUNCTION statement in Figure 7.9a.

The standard intrinsic function SIZE is employed in Figure 7.9a to determine the number of elements along each dimension of the input array a. The expression SIZE (a, 1) returns the number of elements along the first dimension of a, while the expression SIZE (a, 2) returns the number of elements along the second dimension of a. det assumes that these two numbers are equal and does not check this in order to keep the code simpler. Incidentally, it is permitted to invoke SIZE without the second argument, in which case it returns the total number of elements in its array argument.

At each entry, the function of Figure 7.9a needs a work array in which to store the elements of the array formed by deleting the *i*th row and first column of the input array a. The array used for this purpose is a_less_row_i_and_col_1, which is an automatic array as explained in Section 6.5. Perhaps the most difficult thing to see about the entire example is the manner in which array sections are used to load this array with the appropriate elements of the input array a by using just two assignment statements:

```
a_less_row_i_and_col_1(1:i-1,1:n-1) = a(1:i-1,2:n)
a_less_row_i_and_col_1(i:n-1,1:n-1) = a(i+1:n,2:n)
```

The first assignment statement loads the rows from a above row i, while the second loads the rows from a below row i. Observe that when i is 1 or 4, zero-sized arrays arise, but no extra code is required to handle these special cases.

In this section, the function subprogram det was implemented as a module function, but it can equally as well be implemented as an external function. However, if det had been implemented as an external function, then the example main program would be required to supply a collection of code known as an "interface body," as will be discussed in Chapter 13. The requirement for the interface body arises only because of the presence in det of an assumed-shape array argument.

7.11   FUNCTION RESULT OF DERIVED TYPE

In traditional Fortran, the result returned by a function subprogram could be only a single, noncomposite value, and, in fact, some textbooks on the language state that this is a definitive feature of a function sub-program. However, this characterization is inoperative in Fortran 90 since a function subprogram is permitted to return a structure or an array. A function subprogram that returns a structure will be illustrated in this section, and a function subprogram that returns an array of values will be given in the next.

Figure 7.10a shows a function subprogram reduce, which returns a result of derived type rat_type. The code for the function is contained in a module named reduce_rat_type, which also contains the definition for

```
MODULE reduce_rat_type

   TYPE :: rat_type                ! rational number
       INTEGER :: num, denom       ! numerator and denominator
   END TYPE rat_type

CONTAINS

   FUNCTION reduce (top, bottom) RESULT (lowest)

       TYPE (rat_type) :: lowest     ! Function result is
                                     ! of derived type.

       INTEGER, INTENT (IN) :: top, bottom

       INTEGER :: trial

       lowest = rat_type (top, bottom)
       trial = 2
       DO WHILE (trial <= lowest%num  .AND. &
                 trial <= lowest%denom)
         IF (MOD (lowest%num,   trial) == 0 .AND.    &
             MOD (lowest%denom, trial) == 0)     THEN
               lowest%num   = lowest%num   / trial
               lowest%denom = lowest%denom / trial
         ELSE
               trial = trial + 1
         END IF
       END DO

   END FUNCTION reduce

END MODULE reduce_rat_type
```

FIGURE 7.10A. Function that returns a result of a derived type.

rat_type. The purpose of the function reduce is to reduce a positive fraction to its lowest terms: For example, if 3/6 is input, a result of 1/2 is returned. Figure 7.10b gives a main program that invokes the subprogram to reduce the fraction 56/252 to lowest terms. When the program is executed, the following is displayed:

```
fraction = 2/9
```

Note in Figure 7.10a that the name lowest follows the keyword RESULT in the FUNCTION statement, and that this name is later declared to be of type rat_type in the body of the function. However, use of the RESULT option is not mandatory simply because the function returns a structure. The situation here is the same as was discussed in Section 6.2 for an external function returning an intrinsic type—if preferred, reduce could be used as both the function name and the result variable name.

Both the function and the main program have access to the derived-type definition, the function because a module subprogram always has access to the variables and definitions above the CONTAINS statement in the module and the main program because it uses the module. Also, the main program has access to the module function reduce by use association. Incidentally, note that there is no type declaration for reduce in Figure 7.10b—a routine that uses a module always knows all about the interface with any subprograms contained in that module without any special action on the part of the programmer.

Some readers might want an explanation of the method used in reduce to reduce a fraction to its lowest terms, and so here is a narrative description of this "brute force" approach: Starting with a trial divisor

```
PROGRAM demo_func_returning_struct

   USE reduce_rat_type     ! Access definition of rat_type
                           ! and module function reduce.

   IMPLICIT NONE

   TYPE (rat_type) :: reduced_fract

   reduced_fract = reduce (56, 252)    ! Invoke module func.

   PRINT "(' fraction = ', I1, '/', I1)", reduced_fract

END PROGRAM demo_func_returning_struct
```

FIGURE 7.10B. Main program invoking function of Figure 7.10b.

of 2, a check is made to see if both numerator and denominator are divisible by the trial divisor. The check is made using the old standard intrinsic function MOD, which returns the remainder of its first argument when divided by its second. If both numerator and denominator are evenly divisible, they are divided by the trial divisor, and the process is repeated for the same trial divisor; if not, the trial divisor is increased by one, and the process is repeated for the new trial divisor. The procedure of determining a trial divisor and carrying out divisions where possible is performed repeatedly. When a trial divisor larger than either the current numerator or the current denominator is reached, the fraction has been reduced to lowest terms.

Some readers will object to the method used to reduce a fraction in function reduce, noting that it typically checks trial divisors that have no chance of success. Others will complain that the method seems foreign, presumably because no use is made of either prime factors or the greatest common divisor method, which are usually taught in mathematics classes. But it is left as an exercise for such readers to improve upon the elegance, execution efficiency, and/or readability of the approach used in the function reduce.

It should be recognized that even though reduce is implemented as a module function here, it could just as well be implemented as an external function. However, if reduce is defined by an external subprogram, the definition of the derived type rat_type must be made available in both the main program and the subprogram, and the situation is basically the same as that described in Section 7.3. As in that section, the issue can be dealt with by placing the derived-type definition in a module, and then both the main program and the subprogram can use the module. As was mentioned in Section 7.3, another approach that conforms to the Fortran 90 standard is to place identical derived-type definitions, each of which contains a SEQUENCE statement, in both the main program and the subprogram, but this is not recommended.

As has always been true for an external function, the data type of its result must be known in the invoking routine. Thus, a routine that invokes an external function returning a value of derived type must provide a type declaration for that function (unless, as described in Chapter 13, an interface body is supplied).

7.12 A FUNCTION CAN RETURN AN ARRAY-VALUED RESULT

As shown in Chapter 4, many standard Fortran 90 intrinsic functions are capable of returning array-valued results, and the Fortran 90 programmer can write function subprograms that return arrays of values

as well. Thus, the old notion that a function can return only a single—
that is, to say, a scalar—value does not apply in Fortran 90. The new
capability sometimes gives the programmer a choice between writing
a subroutine, one of whose arguments returns an array of values, and
a function that returns an array-valued result. The choice should be
made based on the effect on the clarity of the code that invokes the
subroutine or function. The CALL statement required to invoke a subroutine tends to focus attention on the fact that the flow of control is
temporarily branching away from the caller, while invoking a function
by having its name appear in an expression tends to make the reader
think of that name as being replaced by the function result. One thing
to keep in mind in this connection is that Fortran function invoca-
tions are sometimes difficult to distinguish from references to array
elements. And it should always be remembered that it is considered
poor style in Fortran for a function to change the values of any of its
arguments or to perform I/O.

Examples of two very similar functions that return array-valued results are given in Figure 7.11a. The first of these, array_sin, takes as input
a rank 1 array, each element of which is an angle in degrees, and returns
a rank 1 array, each element of which is the trigonometric sine of the
corresponding element of the input array. The other function, array_cos,
is analogous to array_sin, except array_cos returns an array of values of
trigonometric cosines. Both array_sin and array_cos are implemented as
module function subprograms in the module array_trig. Note that both
functions have access to the named constant Deg_to_rad, which is the
factor for converting from degrees to radians.

Observe in the function array_sin in Figure 7.11a that the dummy
argument x is a rank 1 assumed-shape array as discussed in Section
7.10. Thus, we can think of the number of elements in x as being the
same as the number of elements in its corresponding actual argument
when array_sin is invoked. Now, note in the type declaration for the
result variable sine that its upper bound is specified as SIZE (x). SIZE
is a new intrinsic function, being used here without its optional second
argument to return the total number of elements in the assumed-shape
array x. Hence, array_sin will return a rank 1 array containing the same
number of elements as there are in the actual argument appearing in the
function invocation. In the lone executable statement in array_sin, the
scalar named constant Deg_to_rad is multiplied times the input array x,
yielding an array of angles in radians. The standard intrinsic function
SIN is then employed to find the sine of each element in the array of
angles in radians. The function array_cos in Figure 7.11a works in the
same fashion as array_sin, except the intrinsic function COS is employed
instead of SIN.

The main program of Figure 7.11b can serve as a test driver for both
functions in Figure 7.11a. When the program is executed, both array_sin

```
MODULE array_trig

   REAL, PARAMETER :: Deg_to_rad = 0.0174533

CONTAINS

   ! Function returns rank 1 array containing trigonometric
   ! sines of a rank 1 array of angles given in degrees.

   FUNCTION array_sin (x) RESULT (sine)

      REAL, DIMENSION(:), INTENT (IN) :: x  ! Dummy arg
                                            ! assumes shape
                                            ! of actual arg.

         REAL, DIMENSION(SIZE (x)) :: sine  ! Result variable
                                            ! is a rank 1
                                            ! array with same
                                            ! size as dummy arg.

      sine = SIN (Deg_to_rad * x)    ! array operations

   END FUNCTION array_sin

   ! Function returns rank 1 array containing trigonometric
   ! cosines of a rank 1 array of angles given in degrees.

   FUNCTION array_cos (x) RESULT (cosine)

      REAL, DIMENSION(:), INTENT (IN) :: x

      REAL, DIMENSION(SIZE (x)) :: cosine

      cosine = COS (Deg_to_rad * x)

   END FUNCTION array_cos

END MODULE array_trig
```

FIGURE 7.11A. Functions returning array-valued results.

and array_cos return rank 1 arrays of three elements, and the following
is displayed:

```
50.000   86.603  100.000
86.603   50.000    0.000
```

```
PROGRAM demo_function_returns_array

   USE array_trig    ! Access array_sin, array_cos, Deg_to_rad.

   REAL, DIMENSION(3) :: leg
   REAL, DIMENSION(3) :: x = (/ 30.0, 60.0, 90.0 /)

   leg = 100.0 * array_sin (x)    ! Invoke array_sin and get
                                  ! back rank 1 array of 3
                                  ! elements.
   PRINT "(3F10.3)", leg

   leg = 100.0 * array_cos (x)    ! Invoke array_cos and get
                                  ! back rank 1 array of 3
                                  ! elements.
   PRINT "(3F10.3)", leg

END PROGRAM demo_function_returns_array
```

FIGURE 7.11B.   Test driver for function of Figure 7.11a.

7.13   ELEMENTARY LANGUAGE RULES RELATED TO MODULES

The general form of a module program unit is given in Figure 7.12. Note that, in general, a module may consist of a collection of specification statements and a CONTAINS statement followed by any number of module subprograms. The CONTAINS statement consists of just the single keyword. The forms for module subprograms are the same as those

```
MODULE module-name
              [specification-part]
[CONTAINS

              module-subprogram-1
              [module-subprogram-2]
                        .

                        .

                        .

              [module-subprogram-n]]
END [MODULE [module-name]]
```

FIGURE 7.12.   General form of a module program unit.

for external subprograms, except that the keywords SUBROUTINE and FUNCTION are mandatory on END statements for module subroutine and function subprograms, respectively. As shown by several examples in this chapter, a module may contain no subprograms, in which case the standard calls for the omission of the CONTAINS statement. Also, as illustrated by the example of Section 7.10, the *specification-part* of a module may be omitted.

If *module-name* is present on the END statement indicating the end of the module, it must be the same as *module-name* in the MODULE statement. As far as the standard is concerned, the rules governing *module-name* are the same as for any Fortran 90 name. However, in most Fortran 90 implementations, some of the results of compiling a module are likely to be stored in a file whose name is somehow derived from *module-name*. Since file names may be subject to a set of rules differing from those governing Fortran 90 names, the guidelines for choosing module names may differ somewhat from implementation to implementation.

As mentioned in Section 5.10, any subprogram, excluding derived-type definitions, interface bodies, and subprograms contained within it, is a scoping unit. Also, a module, excluding derived-type definitions, interface bodies, and subprograms contained within it, is a scoping unit. Now, for simplicity, consider the case of a module where no derived-type definitions, interface bodies, or internal subprograms are present. Then each module subprogram is a scoping unit, and the code in the module that remains when its subprograms are removed is a scoping unit. The scoping unit formed by removing the subprograms is said to be the **host scoping unit** for each of the module subprogram scoping units, and each module subprogram has access to the names in the *specification-part* of the module by the process known as **host association**. Of course, one module subprogram has no access to those names local to another module subprogram. However, a module subprogram may invoke a procedure defined by another module subprogram contained in the same module.

By default, a module user has access to the names in the *specification-part* of the module by the process known as **use association**, although this access can be blocked by specification of the PRIVATE attribute, as will be discussed in Chapter 12. Also, a module user may invoke any procedure defined by a module subprogram in the module unless access to it is blocked by the PRIVATE attribute. Of course, a module user has no access to those names local to a subprogram contained in a module.

There are some additional rules related to the use of modules, most of which will be discussed in Chapters 9 and 12.

CHAPTER 8

INTERNAL SUBPROGRAMS

8.1 OVERVIEW OF INTERNAL SUBPROGRAMS

Generally speaking, module subprograms and external subprograms provide adequate facilities for partitioning programs. However, for a subprogram that is so specialized that it is referenced in only a single routine, it is sometimes convenient to employ Fortran 90's third category of subprogram, the "internal subprogram." The internal subprogram can be an effective mechanism for avoiding repetitive segments of code and awkward control structures involving GO TO statements.

An **internal subprogram** is a subprogram that is contained within an external subprogram, a module subprogram, or a main program. A subprogram or main program containing an internal subprogram is said to be the **host** of the internal subprogram. Fortran 90 rules do not permit an internal subprogram to be invoked from outside its host, and it follows from this that general-purpose subprograms should be implemented as either module or external subprograms rather than as internal subprograms. In the opinion of the author, it usually makes good sense to keep internal subprograms short, say up to 20 lines or so of code.

The standard Fortran 90 internal subprogram is slightly different from the internal subprogram provided as an extension in some implementations of FORTRAN 77. In Fortran 90, the statement keyword CONTAINS is coded to separate the body of a subprogram or main program from any internal subprograms it may contain. A host always knows all about the interface with any subprogram that it contains, so a type declaration is never required in the host for an internal function subprogram. Also, an interface body, which is sometimes required for an external subprogram, is never supplied for an internal subprogram.

The issue of the scope of names is treated in a manner rather similar to other languages, such as Pascal, permitting the nesting of routines: The internal subprogram can access host variables, host derived-type definitions, and so on, but the host does not have access to the local entities of any subprogram that it contains. However, unlike many other languages permitting the nesting of routines, the Fortran 90 standard prohibits an internal subprogram from containing an internal subprogram itself. Of course, some implementations of Fortran 90 support the nesting of internal subprograms, but, as always, the author advises against capricious use of nonstandard features.

Essentially all of the nontraditional features available with module and external subprograms can be used with internal subprograms as well. For example, internal subprograms may be recursive. Also, the result of an internal function subprogram may be a structure, an array, or a pointer. Furthermore, it is permissible for an internal subprogram to have optional arguments and to be invoked using the argument keyword mechanism, although such usage would be unusual in practice.

This chapter will present a variety of examples of internal subprograms. The Fortran 90 internal subprogram, like many of the new language features, serves chiefly as a tool that can be used to enhance program readability. In this connection, it is recommended that use of the old statement function be avoided in most cases in favor of the internal function subprogram.

8.2   EXAMPLE OF AN INTERNAL SUBROUTINE

As a first example of an internal subprogram, consider the external subroutine print_page_header of Figure 8.1a, which contains one internal subroutine. The CONTAINS statement, which consists of the single new keyword, indicates the presence of one or more internal subprograms to follow, and the internal subprogram(s) must be the only code between the CONTAINS statement and the END statement marking the end of the host. Note in Figure 8.1a that the internal subroutine, which is named print_line_centered, is delimited by its own SUBROUTINE and END SUBROUTINE statements. Observe also that the internal subroutine is invoked three times in the host by the usual mechanism of issuing a CALL.

The internal subroutine print_line_centered employs two standard intrinsic functions. The first is LEN, a mainstay in standard FORTRAN 77, which returns the length of the character string dummy argument text. The second is the new intrinsic function REPEAT, which is used in Figure 8.1a to create a blank character string of the length needed to center the following text on a line that is 80 characters wide. In general, the expres-

```
SUBROUTINE print_page_header      ! Begin external subroutine.

   ! Invoke internal sub in each of next 3 statements.
   CALL print_line_centered ("Twelfth Armored Division")
   CALL print_line_centered ("Daily Flypaper Report")
   CALL print_line_centered ("May 3, 1992")

CONTAINS   ! indicates internal subprogram(s) follow

   SUBROUTINE print_line_centered (text)   ! Begin internal
                                            ! subroutine.
      CHARACTER(*), INTENT (IN) :: text

      INTEGER, PARAMETER :: Line_length = 80
      INTEGER            :: leading_blanks

      leading_blanks = (Line_length - LEN (text)) / 2
      PRINT "(A)", REPEAT (" ", leading_blanks) // text

   END SUBROUTINE print_line_centered     ! End internal sub.

END SUBROUTINE print_page_header          ! End external sub.
```

FIGURE 8.1A. External subroutine containing one internal subroutine.

sion REPEAT (STRING, NCOPIES) consists of a concatenated character string made up of NCOPIES of STRING.

Figure 8.1b gives a simple test driver for the external subroutine of Figure 8.1a. When the program consisting of the main program of Figure 8.1b and the external subroutine of Figure 8.1a is executed, the following is displayed:

```
Twelfth Armored Division
   Daily Flypaper Report
      May 3, 1992
```

```
PROGRAM test_print_page_header

   CALL print_page_header   ! Invoke external subroutine.

END PROGRAM test_print_page_header
```

FIGURE 8.1B. Test driver that calls subroutine of Figure 8.1a.

8.3 Example of an Internal Function

An internal subprogram may be a function subprogram as well as a subroutine subprogram. Figure 8.2a gives an external function vowel_count, which contains one internal function subprogram. As required by the Fortran 90 standard, the internal function is placed between the END statement of its host and the CONTAINS statement. The form of an internal function is basically the same as that of an external function.

Note in Figure 8.2a that although the internal function is_vowel returns a result of type LOGICAL, the host has no type declaration for the name is_vowel as would be required for an external function in traditional Fortran. But this is, of course, to be expected: Since an internal

```
FUNCTION vowel_count (string) RESULT (count)    ! Begin ex-
                                                ! ternal func.

   INTEGER                    :: count
   CHARACTER(*), INTENT (IN) :: string

   INTEGER :: i

   count = 0
   DO i = 1, LEN (string)
      ! Invoke internal func is_vowel in next statement.
      IF (is_vowel (string(i:i))) count = count + 1
   END DO

CONTAINS    ! indicates internal subprogram(s) follow

   FUNCTION is_vowel (char) RESULT (vowel)      ! Begin in-
                                                ! ternal func.

      LOGICAL                    :: vowel
      CHARACTER(1), INTENT (IN) :: char

      IF (INDEX ("aAeEiIoOuU", char) /= 0) THEN
         vowel = .TRUE.
      ELSE
         vowel = .FALSE.
      END IF

   END FUNCTION is_vowel                        ! End internal func.

END FUNCTION vowel_count                        ! End external func.
```

FIGURE 8.2A. An external function containing one internal function.

```
PROGRAM test_vowel_count

    CHARACTER(*), PARAMETER ::                              &
        Sentence = "Fortran 90 was developed jointly " //  &
                   "by the X3 technical subcommittee " //  &
                   "X3J3 and IEC/ISO JTC1/SC22/WG5."

    INTEGER :: vowel_count    ! type decl for external func

    PRINT *, vowel_count (Sentence)   ! Invoke external func.

END PROGRAM vowel_count
```

FIGURE 8.2B. Test driver that invokes function of Figure 8.2a.

subprogram is compiled with the collection of code that invokes it, the compiler always knows all the details of the interface without special action by the programmer.

In Figure 8.2a, the external function vowel_count determines the number of vowels in its dummy argument string. In the body of vowel_count there is a loop over the characters in string, inside of which the internal function is_vowel is invoked for each character. The internal function uses the old standard intrinsic function INDEX to determine if that character is in the list of upper- and lowercase vowels. If the character is in the vowel list, is_vowel returns .TRUE. and the host increments count.

Figure 8.2b gives a main program to serve as a test driver for the external function of Figure 8.2a. The main program invokes the external function vowel_count with the named constant Sentence as an argument. Because Sentence has the PARAMETER attribute, it is acceptable in Fortran 90, as it is in standard FORTRAN 77, to specify its length with an asterisk (*) and let the compiler count the number of characters in the string following the equal sign (=). When the program consisting of the main program of Figure 8.2b and the external function of Figure 8.2a is executed, the vowels in the named constant Sentence of Figure 8.2b are counted, and the following is displayed:

23

8.4 EXAMPLE OF A HOST CONTAINING FOUR INTERNAL SUBPROGRAMS

In previous examples, the host contained only a single internal subprogram. But it is permissible for a host to contain any number of internal subprograms, and, of course, the host may invoke any of its internal subprograms. As always, an internal subprogram may not be invoked from outside its host, but it should be recognized that this does not prevent an internal subprogram from invoking one of its host's other internal subprograms. This is illustrated in Figure 8.3.

Figure 8.3 is a complete program whose only program unit is a main program. However, the main program contains four internal subprograms—two subroutines and two functions. Note that the only statement in the body of the main program is a CALL statement, which invokes the internal subroutine display_binomial_coeffs. In turn, this subroutine calls the internal subroutine get_user_input. Also, in the PRINT statement, display_binomial_coeffs invokes the internal function binomial_coeff. The function binomial_coeff then invokes the internal function fact three times. Thus, while the names of the internal subprograms are unknown outside the main program, they are known everywhere inside the main program, even below the CONTAINS statement.

Observe in Figure 8.3 that a variable named n occurs in each of the four internal subprograms and a variable named k occurs in three of the four. But the fact that a variable name is duplicated inside two or more internal subprograms causes no problems. Each of these names is local to the internal subprogram in which it appears and is unknown outside that internal subprogram.

The program of Figure 8.3 reads a positive integer value n and displays the binomial coefficients $_nC_k$ for $k = 0, 1, \ldots, n$, where

$$_nC_k = \frac{n!}{k!(n-k)!}$$

For example, if a value of 4 is input for n, the program displays

0	1
1	4
2	6
3	4
4	1

Perhaps a couple of additional comments are in order regarding the program of Figure 8.3. Observe that the internal function fact returns a REAL value, so the range of values it can handle is fairly large. However, the precision of the result returned by fact will be rather limited on most computers. Also, the division in internal function binomial_coeff causes further loss of precision. The use in binomial_coeff of the intrinsic function NINT (standard in both FORTRAN 77 and Fortran 90) to round results to the nearest integer compensates for these difficulties for small n (say, n less than 20 or so for a computer with 32-bit word length), but the precision of the output for large n is suspect.

```
PROGRAM one_internal_may_invoke_another

   CALL display_binomial_coeffs    ! Invoke internal sub.

CONTAINS          ! Four internal subprograms follow.

   SUBROUTINE display_binomial_coeffs
      INTEGER :: n, k
      CALL get_user_input (n)       ! Invoke internal sub.
      DO k = 0, n
         ! Next stmt invokes internal func binomial_coeff.
         PRINT "(2I10)", k, binomial_coeff (n, k)
      END DO
   END SUBROUTINE display_binomial_coeffs

   SUBROUTINE get_user_input (n)
      INTEGER, INTENT (OUT) :: n
      PRINT "(A)", " Input a value for n:"
      READ *, n
   END SUBROUTINE get_user_input

   FUNCTION binomial_coeff (n, k) RESULT (bin_coeff)
      INTEGER            :: bin_coeff
      INTEGER, INTENT (IN) :: n, k
      INTRINSIC NINT
      ! Next stmt invokes internal function fact 3 times.
      bin_coeff =                                        &
             NINT (fact (n) / (fact (k) * fact (n - k)))
   END FUNCTION binomial_coeff

   FUNCTION fact (n) RESULT (n_fact)
      REAL               :: n_fact
      INTEGER, INTENT (IN) :: n
      INTEGER :: k
      n_fact = 1
      DO k = 2, n
         n_fact = k * n_fact
      END DO
   END FUNCTION fact

END PROGRAM one_internal_may_invoke_another
```

FIGURE 8.3. Internal procedures invoked by internal procedures.

The example of this section illustrates that it is permissible for an internal subprogram to be contained within a main program, but it seems to the author that this capability will not often be utilized in large, team-written programs, where the main program usually plays the role of an executive.

8.5   THE SCOPE OF VARIABLE NAMES

The Fortran 90 rules applying to the scope of variables in internal subprograms are similar to those governing variables in nested procedures in Pascal. A variable declared within an internal subprogram can never be accessed outside that internal subprogram. If the name of a variable appearing outside an internal subprogram duplicates that of a variable declared within the internal subprogram, the names represent separate, unrelated variables. But if the name of a variable is used inside an internal subprogram within which no type declaration is given for that name and if the name duplicates that of a variable appearing above the preceding CONTAINS statement, the names refer to the same variable. In connection with this last case, it should be mentioned that the process by which an internal subprogram accesses a variable in its host is known as **host association**.

The program of Figure 8.4, which consists of a main program containing the internal subroutine sub, illustrates the rules given in the preceding paragraph. When the program is executed, the following is displayed:

```
In host, v1 =  1, v2 =  2
In sub,  v1 =  2, v2 = 21, v3 = 31
In host, v1 =  3, v2 =  3
In sub,  v1 =  4, v2 = 22, v3 = 32
```

The name v1 in Figure 8.4 is not declared within the internal subroutine, so v1 refers to the same variable both above and below the CONTAINS statement. On the other hand, the name v2 is declared within the internal subroutine, so v2 refers to one variable when used above the CONTAINS statement and another when used below the CONTAINS statement. Finally, the declaration of the name v3 within the internal subroutine means that it is inaccessible outside sub. This implies that as the code of Figure 8.4 stands, it would be illegal to place a statement such as

```
PRINT *, v3
```

```
PROGRAM demo_scope_of_var_names

  IMPLICIT NONE   ! in effect both above and below CONTAINS

  INTEGER :: v1 = 1  ! v1, v2 accessible above CONTAINS and
  INTEGER :: v2 = 2  ! also, except where in conflict with
                     ! local variable names, below CONTAINS

  PRINT "(2(A, I2))", " In host, v1 = ", v1, ", v2 = ", v2

  CALL sub

  v1 = v1 + 1
  v2 = v2 + 1   ! this v2 **NOT** same as v2 inside sub

  PRINT "(2(A, I2))", " In host, v1 = ", v1, ", v2 = ", v2

  CALL sub

CONTAINS

  SUBROUTINE sub

    INTEGER :: v2 = 20  ! v2, v3 are local
    INTEGER :: v3 = 30  ! to this subroutine

    v1 = v1 + 1   ! access v1 by host association
    v2 = v2 + 1   ! refers to v2 local to sub
    v3 = v3 + 1

    PRINT "(3(A, I2))", " In sub,  v1 = ", v1, &
                          ", v2 = ", v2, &
                          ", v3 = ", v3
  END SUBROUTINE sub

END PROGRAM demo_scope_of_var_names
```

FIGURE 8.4. Program illustrating the scope of variable names.

above the CONTAINS statement.

The presence of the IMPLICIT NONE statement in Figure 8.4 forces the explicit declaration of the data types of all variables used in the internal subroutine as well as in the host. An IMPLICIT statement in a subprogram or main program remains in effect below any CONTAINS statement that may be present.

8.6   *THE SCOPE OF STATEMENT LABELS*

As indicated in the preceding section, a variable name declared inside an internal subprogram may duplicate a name appearing in the body of the host, and the compiler treats such identifiers as two separate, unrelated names. It is no surprise then that when the same statement number appears as a label in both an internal subprogram and the body of its host, the compiler treats the duplicate statement numbers as two separate, unrelated labels. This is illustrated by the program of Figure 8.5.

In Figure 8.5, an internal subroutine named find_avg is contained in a main program. The label 100 near the top of the program is unrelated to the label 100 near the bottom because the 100 at the top is in the body of the host while the 100 at the bottom is inside an internal subprogram. For the same reason, the label 200 in the PRINT and FORMAT statements is unrelated to the label 200 in the GO TO and CONTINUE statements.

The internal subroutine find_avg determines the average of the elements in a rank 1 REAL array. The subroutine checks for input of a zero-sized array and sets the dummy argument error to .TRUE. if this condition arises. In Figure 8.5, the second CALL deliberately generates a zero-sized array by specifying the array section x(2:1) as an actual argument. When executed, the program displays

```
   3.000
Can't find average for zero-sized array.
```

As indicated in the preceding section, an internal subprogram has access to a variable appearing in the body of its host, provided that the internal subprogram does not declare any variable with the same name. It is perhaps natural then to think that the treatment of statement labels would be analogous, but this is not the case. That is, some readers might expect that (say) inside an internal subroutine, the number 100 in code such as

```
WRITE (*, 100) x, y
```

might refer to the label of a FORMAT statement up in the body of the host, outside the internal subroutine, but this is ***not*** permitted by the Fortran 90 standard. The standard requires that a labeled statement be in the same scoping unit as any statement referring to that label. Note that an implication of this restriction is that it is not permitted in standard Fortran 90 to use a GO TO statement to jump out of an internal subprogram into its host as is possible in some FORTRAN 77 implementations enhanced to support internal subprograms.

```
PROGRAM demo_scope_of_labels

      REAL, DIMENSION(5) :: x
      REAL    :: avg
      INTEGER :: i
      LOGICAL :: error

      DO 100 i = 1, 5          ! refers to label in body
         x(i) = i
  100 END DO

      CALL find_avg (x, avg, error)
      PRINT "(F8.3)", avg

      CALL find_avg (x(2:1), avg, error)

      IF (error) PRINT 200    ! refers to label in body

  200 FORMAT (" Can't find average for zero-sized array.")

CONTAINS

   SUBROUTINE find_avg (x, avg, error)

         REAL, DIMENSION(:), INTENT (IN)  :: x
         REAL,               INTENT (OUT) :: avg
         LOGICAL,            INTENT (OUT) :: error

         REAL    :: total
         INTEGER :: i

         IF (SIZE (x) == 0) GO TO 200    ! refers to label
                                         ! in sub

         total = 0.0
         DO 100 i = 1, SIZE (x)          ! refers to label
                                         ! in sub

            total = total + x(i)
     100 END DO
         avg = total / SIZE (x)
         error = .FALSE.
         RETURN

     200 CONTINUE
         avg = 0.0
         error = .TRUE.
   END SUBROUTINE find_avg

END PROGRAM demo_scope_of_labels
```

FIGURE 8.5. Host and internal subprogram may have duplicate labels.

8.7   AN INTERNAL FUNCTION WHOSE RESULT IS OF A DERIVED TYPE

For an external subprogram having an argument of a derived type, the programmer must take steps, as discussed in Section 7.3, to assure that the derived-type definition is available in both the code that invokes the subprogram and the subprogram itself. As mentioned near the end of Section 7.11, the same is true for an external function subprogram whose result is of a derived type. But the situation for an internal subprogram with an argument of a derived type or an internal function whose result is a structure is somewhat easier to handle. For such an internal subprogram, the programmer needs only to assure that the derived-type definition is available in the host, because an internal subprogram automatically has access to its host's entities. In this respect, the internal subprogram is rather like the module subprogram, described in Section 7.11.

Figure 8.6a gives an example of an internal function find_top_gpa whose argument student_list is of derived type student_type. In addition, note that the result variable top_student in find_top_gpa is also of derived type student_type. Now observe in Figure 8.6a that the host of find_top_gpa is the external subroutine get_top_student, and that the only appearance of the derived-type definition for student_type is in the body of the host. It is unnecessary to repeat the derived-type definition inside find_top_gpa, because the internal function automatically has access to it. Also, note that the keyword SEQUENCE need not be part of the derived-type definition, as discussed in Sections 7.3 and 7.11.

It should be noted in Figure 8.6a that the dummy argument student_list in the function find_top_gpa is not only of a derived type, but it is also an assumed-shape array, as described in Section 7.10. If find_top_gpa were an external subprogram, an interface body would be required, as discussed in Chapter 13, but an interface body is not used here because find_top_gpa is internal. Observe that the standard intrinsic function SIZE is employed in find_top_gpa to determine the number of elements in the dummy array student_list.

Figure 8.6b gives a main program that can be used as a test driver for the external subroutine of Figure 8.6a. When the program is executed, the main program of Figure 8.6b calls the external subroutine get_top_student of Figure 8.6a. An array of structures of derived type student_type is initialized in get_top_student by using an array constructor, each element of which is a structure constructor. The internal function find_top_gpa is then invoked, and it runs through the array and finds the student having the highest grade point average (GPA). The result returned by find_top_gpa is a copy of an element in the array student_list, so find_top_gpa returns a structure. Thus, the statement

```
SUBROUTINE get_top_student (student_name, student_number,   &
                                                   top_gpa)

   CHARACTER(*), INTENT (OUT) :: student_name
   INTEGER,      INTENT (OUT) :: student_number
   REAL,         INTENT (OUT) :: top_gpa

   TYPE :: student_type          ! only derived-type definition
      CHARACTER(20) :: name
      INTEGER       :: number
      REAL          :: gpa
   END TYPE student_type

   TYPE (student_type), DIMENSION(4) :: student_list =      &
             (/ student_type ("Ray Johnson",  1111, 2.3),  &
                student_type ("George Stern", 2222, 3.4),   &
                student_type ("Maria Garcia", 3333, 3.7),   &
                student_type ("Sammy Wo",     4444, 3.2) /)

   TYPE (student_type) :: top_student

   ! Invoke internal func find_top_gpa in next stmt.
   top_student = find_top_gpa (student_list)

   student_name   = top_student%name
   student_number = top_student%number
   top_gpa        = top_student%gpa

CONTAINS

   FUNCTION find_top_gpa (student_list) RESULT (top_student)

     ! Internal has access to derived-type def'n in host.

     ! Function returns a result of derived type.
      TYPE (student_type) :: top_student

     ! dummy arg of derived type (also assumed-shape array)
      TYPE (student_type), DIMENSION(:), INTENT (IN) ::    &
                                            student_list

      INTEGER :: i

      top_student = student_list(1)
      DO i = 2, SIZE (student_list)
         IF (student_list(i)%gpa > student_list(i-1)%gpa)   &
                           top_student = student_list(i)
      END DO
   END FUNCTION find_top_gpa
END SUBROUTINE get_top_student
```

FIGURE 8.6A. An internal function whose result is of a derived type.

```
PROGRAM internal_and_derived_type

    CHARACTER(20) :: student_name
    INTEGER       :: student_number
    REAL          :: top_gpa

    CALL get_top_student (student_name, student_number,     &
                                                  top_gpa)
    PRINT "(A, F3.1, A)", " Top GPA of ", top_gpa,          &
                                           " is held by:"
    PRINT "(I5, 2X, A)", student_number, student_name

END PROGRAM internal_and_derived_type
```

FIGURE 8.6B. Test driver that calls subroutine of Figure 8.6a.

```
top_student = find_top_gpa (student_list)
```

in Figure 8.6a performs a structure-to-structure assignment. Each component of top_student is then assigned to a simple, nonaggregate variable, and these values are passed back to the main program of Figure 8.6b, which displays the following:

```
Top GPA of 3.7 is held by:
3333  Maria Garcia
```

8.8 AN INTERNAL FUNCTION WHOSE RESULT IS AN ARRAY

As discussed in Section 7.12, a Fortran 90 function can return an array of values. In that section, an example of a module function whose result is array-valued was given, but an internal function can return an array-valued result as well. An external function is also capable of returning an array-valued result, but, as will be discussed in Chapter 13, a special block of code known as an "interface body" must be supplied to specify fully the external subprogram's interface. However, an interface body is never used with an internal subprogram because it is compiled along with its host, rather than being compiled independently as external subprograms are.

Figure 8.7a gives a main program containing an internal function named sort that returns an array of values. The function sort performs a bubble sort, as described in Section 5.13, to order an array of INTEGER values, which is input as the only argument. Note that the dummy

```fortran
PROGRAM demo_array_valued_internal_func

   INTEGER, PARAMETER       :: Cnt = 5
   INTEGER, DIMENSION(Cnt) :: unordered = (/ 3, 5, 1, 4, 2 /)
   INTEGER, DIMENSION(Cnt) :: ordered
   INTEGER                  :: i

   ! Next stmt invokes array-valued internal function sort.
   ordered = sort (unordered)  ! array assignment

   DO i = 1, Cnt
      PRINT *, ordered(i)
   END DO

CONTAINS

   FUNCTION sort (source) RESULT (target)
      INTEGER, DIMENSION(:), INTENT (IN) :: source
      INTEGER, DIMENSION(SIZE (source))  :: target ! Result
                                                   ! is array.

      LOGICAL :: no_exchange
      INTEGER :: i

      target = source    ! array assignment

      DO
         no_exchange = .TRUE.
         DO i = 1, SIZE (target) - 1
            IF (target(i) > target(i+1)) THEN

                ! Next stmt invokes external subroutine.
                CALL exchange (target(i), target(i+1))

                no_exchange = .FALSE.
            END IF
         END DO
         IF (no_exchange) EXIT
      END DO

   END FUNCTION sort

END PROGRAM demo_array_valued_internal_func
```

FIGURE 8.7A. An internal function whose result is an array.

```
! Interchange two scalar INTEGER values.

SUBROUTINE exchange (x, y)

   INTEGER, INTENT (IN OUT) :: x, y
   INTEGER :: temp

   temp = x;   x = y;   y = temp

END SUBROUTINE exchange
```

FIGURE 8.7B. Subroutine called by internal function of Figure 8.7a.

argument source is an assumed-shape array, as discussed in Section 7.10.

A noteworthy feature of sort in Figure 8.7a is that it does not disturb the elements of source. Instead, the elements of source are copied to the variable named target by an array assignment:

```
target = source
```

Then, all of the reordering of elements takes place in the array target. Note in the RESULT clause of Figure 8.7a that target is the result variable of the function sort, and that since the upper bound for target is specified to be SIZE (source), target will have the same number of elements as the actual argument associated with source when sort is invoked.

A sidelight of Figure 8.7a is that the internal subprogram sort calls an external subroutine named exchange to swap elements in the array target. A listing of exchange is given in Figure 8.7b.

When the program made up of the main program of Figure 8.7a and the external subroutine of Figure 8.7b is executed, the following is displayed:

1
2
3
4
5

It is instructive to consider whether it would be better to implement sort as a subroutine with two arguments (an input source array and an output target array) rather than as a function, as is illustrated in Figure 8.7a. If it is desired that the name sort be available for use in array expressions, the function implementation would be preferable; otherwise, the procedure should be coded as a subroutine so that attention will be drawn to its invocation by a CALL statement.

8.9 An Internal Subprogram May Be Recursive

Recursion was discussed in Section 6.8 in connection with external sub-programs and arose again in Section 7.10 in the context of a module subprogram, but it may not be obvious that recursive internal subprograms are also standard in Fortran 90. However, as is the case for the other varieties of subprogram, the standard requires that the keyword RECURSIVE be specified in the SUBROUTINE or FUNCTION statement serving as the header for an internal subprogram that is used recursively. An example of a recursive subroutine named print_int, which is contained in a main program, is given in Figure 8.8.

The program of Figure 8.8 produces a table of powers of 2 for integer exponents in the range 0 through 15. The internal subroutine print_int is used to display a nonnegative integer value in the minimum possible

```
PROGRAM demo_recursive_internal_sub

   INTEGER :: n

   DO n = 0, 15
      WRITE (*, "(A)", ADVANCE="NO") " 2 to the power "
      CALL print_int (n)
      WRITE (*, "(A)", ADVANCE="NO") " is "
      CALL print_int (2 ** n)
      WRITE (*, "()", ADVANCE="YES")
   END DO

CONTAINS

   RECURSIVE SUBROUTINE print_int (int)      ! keyword
                                             ! RECURSIVE
                                             ! mandatory

      INTEGER, INTENT (IN) :: int

      IF (int >= 10) CALL print_int (int / 10)   ! Sub calls
                                                 ! itself.

      WRITE (*, "(I1)", ADVANCE="NO") MOD (int, 10)

   END SUBROUTINE print_int

END PROGRAM demo_recursive_internal_sub
```

FIGURE 8.8. Example of a recursive internal subroutine.

space. Observe in Figure 8.8 that print_int is recursive since it calls itself, and as required by the Fortran 90 standard, the keyword RECURSIVE is specified at the beginning of the SUBROUTINE statement.

The program of Figure 8.8 exploits a new feature of Fortran 90 known as "nonadvancing I/O." Traditionally in Fortran, an end-of-record indication (simply a code for line feed in many implementations) is automatically output when a WRITE statement is executed. But in Fortran 90, the entry ADVANCE="NO" may be placed in the I/O control specification list of a WRITE statement to specify that output of the end-of-record indicator is to be suppressed. In Figure 8.8, the feature is used to create a single line of output using several WRITE statements.

When the program of Figure 8.8 is executed, the following is displayed:

```
2 to the power 0 is 1
2 to the power 1 is 2
2 to the power 2 is 4
2 to the power 3 is 8
2 to the power 4 is 16
2 to the power 5 is 32
2 to the power 6 is 64
2 to the power 7 is 128
2 to the power 8 is 256
2 to the power 9 is 512
2 to the power 10 is 1024
2 to the power 11 is 2048
2 to the power 12 is 4096
2 to the power 13 is 8192
2 to the power 14 is 16384
2 to the power 15 is 32768
```

Since many are unfamiliar with recursion, perhaps a brief explanation of the internal subroutine print_int is in order. The subroutine displays one digit of its integer argument each time it is called. The ideas involved are easier to understand by focusing on a specific example, so suppose that the value of the argument originally input to print_int is 123. Since the value of its argument int is greater than 10, the subroutine divides 123 by 10, and calls itself with an argument value of 12. At this entry, the value of int is 12, which is greater than 10, so the subroutine again divides the value of its argument by 10, and calls itself with an argument of 1. At this entry, the input argument value is less than 10, so this time the CALL is not performed. The WRITE statement in print_int is now executed. The old intrinsic function MOD is used to find the remainder of the value of int, which is 1 at this entry, divided by 10. The subroutine then displays that remainder, which is 1, and returns to its caller. The caller was the print_int that received an argument value of 12, so at this entry the remainder of 12 divided by 10 is found. The value of that remainder, which is 2, is now displayed and control is returned to the caller. That caller was the print_int that received the argument value of 123, so the value of the remainder of 123 divided by 10, which is 3, is now displayed, and control will be returned to the original caller.

8.10 A MODULE SUBPROGRAM MAY CONTAIN INTERNAL SUBPROGRAMS

Both a module subprogram and an internal subprogram must be preceded by a CONTAINS statement, and the rules governing scope are quite similar for both. However, there are some important differences between these two categories of subprograms. One of these differences is that a module subprogram, like an external subprogram, may contain one or more internal subprograms, whereas an internal subprogram may not contain any internal subprogram. The module of Figure 8.9a contains a module subprogram named reduce, which, in turn, contains an internal subprogram named find_gcd.

The module rational_numbers of Figure 8.9a contains the definition of a derived type named rat_type, which consists of two INTEGER components, num and denom. Each data value of type rat_type represents a rational number. The module contains two module subprograms: mult, which multiplies one rational number times another, and reduce, which reduces a rational number to its lowest terms. That is to say, reduce transforms 2/4 into 1/2, 6/9 into 2/3, and so on.

To reduce a rational number to its lowest terms, reduce divides both numerator and denominator by their greatest common divisor (GCD), where the GCD of two integers is the largest integer that divides into both of them with no remainder. The GCD is determined by the internal function subprogram find_gcd, which is based on the property that the GCD of two integers, m and n, is the same as the GCD of n and m modulo n, provided that n is not zero.[1] Thus, find_gcd is a Fortran 90 way of expressing the following mathematical equation:

$$\gcd(m,n) = \begin{cases} m & \text{for } n = 0, \\ \gcd(n, m \bmod n) & \text{for } n > 0. \end{cases}$$

[1]Based on an example in *Pascal User Manual and Report* by K. Jensen and N. Wirth (Springer-Verlag, New York, 1974).

```
MODULE rational_numbers

  TYPE :: rat_type              ! Define a derived
      INTEGER :: num, denom     ! type describing a
  END TYPE rat_type             ! rational number.

CONTAINS         ! Module subprograms follow.

  ! Return product of two rational numbers.
  FUNCTION mult (rat_1, rat_2) RESULT (product)

     TYPE (rat_type)                :: product
     TYPE (rat_type), INTENT (IN) :: rat_1, rat_2

     product = rat_type (rat_1%num  * rat_2%num,    &
                         rat_1%denom * rat_2%denom)
  END FUNCTION mult

  ! Reduce rational number to lowest terms.
  FUNCTION reduce (rat) RESULT (reduced)

     TYPE (rat_type)               :: reduced
     TYPE (rat_type), INTENT (IN) :: rat
     INTEGER :: gcd

     gcd = find_gcd (rat%num, rat%denom)   ! Invoke
                                           ! internal func.

     reduced = rat_type (rat%num / gcd, rat%denom / gcd)

     CONTAINS        ! internal subprogram follows

        ! Find greatest common divisor of two integers.
        RECURSIVE FUNCTION find_gcd (m, n) RESULT (gcd)

           INTEGER               :: gcd
           INTEGER, INTENT (IN) :: m, n

           IF (n == 0) THEN
              gcd = m
           ELSE
              gcd = find_gcd (n, MOD (m, n))   ! Func invokes
                                               ! itself.

           END IF

        END FUNCTION find_gcd

  END FUNCTION reduce
END MODULE rational_numbers
```

FIGURE 8.9A. Module subprogram containing an internal subprogram.

Hence, the internal function find_gcd invokes itself, and so the key-word RECURSIVE appears in its FUNCTION statement as required by the Fortran 90 standard.

Figure 8.9b gives a main program that uses the module of Figure 8.9a. By using the module rational_numbers, the main program accesses the derived-type definition for rat_type, as well as the module procedures mult and reduce. In Figure 8.9b, two variables, rat_1 and rat_2, are declared to be of type rat_type, and structure constructors are employed to give them initial values. Then the module function mult is invoked to multiply rat_1 times rat_2, and the resulting product is the argument of the module function reduce. When the program units of Figure 8.9a and 8.9b are executed, the following is displayed

    1/6

It is worthwhile to work through the steps leading to this display. The module function mult first multiplies 6/7 times 7/36 and returns the product 42/252. The module function reduce then invokes the internal function find_gcd, which determines that the greatest common divisor of 42 and 252 is 42. Finally, the numerator and denominator of 42/252 are both divided by 42 to yield the result returned by reduce.

Note in the example given in this section that the module is made up of a derived-type definition and module subprograms that perform manipulations on data of that derived type. This turns out to be a par-ticularly important way of structuring a module, and in practice, many modules containing subprograms can be expected to fall into this cat-egory. In many cases, such a module will contain several subprograms to manipulate derived-type data, even though the example of Figure 8.9a was limited to only two module subprograms for tutorial purposes.

```
PROGRAM demo_rational_numbers

    USE rational_numbers   ! Access rat_type, mult, reduce.

    ! Declare and initialize variables of type rat_type:
    TYPE (rat_type) :: rat_1 = rat_type (6,  7),  &
                       rat_2 = rat_type (7, 36)

    ! Following stmt invokes module functions mult & reduce.
    PRINT "(I2, '/', I1)", reduce (mult (rat_1, rat_2))

END PROGRAM demo_rational_numbers
```

FIGURE 8.9B. Main program that uses module of Figure 8.9a.

Obviously, the utility of the module rational_numbers would be greatly enhanced by the inclusion of additional module procedures to divide, add, and subtract rational numbers. Also, it would be desirable to indicate multiplication of a pair of rational numbers by an asterisk (*), addition by a plus sign (+), and so on, as is done for the intrinsic numerical data types. This capability is supported in Fortran 90, but discussion of this topic will be deferred until Chapter 9.

8.11   INTERNAL SUBPROGRAMS AND SCOPING UNITS

Recall that a program consists of a set of nonoverlapping collections of code known as "scoping units," where a **scoping unit** is defined to be any one of the following:

1. a derived-type definition;

2. an interface body, excluding any derived-type definitions and interface bodies contained within it;

3. a subprogram, excluding derived-type definitions, interface bodies, and subprograms contained within it; or

4. a program unit, excluding derived-type definitions, interface bodies, and subprograms contained within it.

Now that several examples of internal subprograms have been presented, it is worthwhile to break down into its scoping units a program containing an internal subprogram, and this is done in Figure 8.10. The program of Figure 8.10 consists of three program units—a main program, a module named rat_type_conversions, and an external subroutine named display. Observe that the comments indicate the scoping units obtained by applying the preceding definition.

Any derived-type definition is a scoping unit; thus, the only derived-type definition in Figure 8.10, the definition for rat_type in the specification part of the module rat_type_conversions, is designated as "scoping unit 1." There are no interface bodies in Figure 8.10, so these play no role in this example. Any subprogram that contains no derived-type definition, no interface body, and no internal subprogram is a scoping unit, and so the subroutine subprogram display is designated as "scoping unit 2." The internal subroutine conv_to_decimal contains no derived-type definition, no interface body, and, of course, no internal subprogram, so it is marked as "scoping unit 3." The module subroutine subprogram conv_to_fract contains no derived-type definitions or interface bodies,

```
MODULE rat_type_conversions              ! scoping unit 6

   TYPE :: rat_type                      ! scoping unit 1
      INTEGER :: num, denom              ! scoping unit 1
   END TYPE rat_type                     ! scoping unit 1

CONTAINS                                 ! scoping unit 6

   SUBROUTINE conv_to_fract (num, denom) ! scoping unit 4
      INTEGER, INTENT (IN) :: num, denom ! scoping unit 4
      TYPE (rat_type) :: fract           ! scoping unit 4
      fract%num   = num                  ! scoping unit 4
      fract%denom = denom                ! scoping unit 4
      CALL conv_to_decimal               ! scoping unit 4
   CONTAINS                              ! scoping unit 4

      SUBROUTINE conv_to_decimal         ! scoping unit 3
         REAL :: dec_val                 ! scoping unit 3
         dec_val =                     & ! scoping unit 3
             fract%num / REAL (fract%denom) ! scoping unit 3
         CALL display (dec_val)          ! scoping unit 3
      END SUBROUTINE conv_to_decimal     ! scoping unit 3

   END SUBROUTINE conv_to_fract          ! scoping unit 4

END MODULE rat_type_conversions          ! scoping unit 6

PROGRAM demo_scoping_units               ! scoping unit 5
   USE rat_type_conversions              ! scoping unit 5
   INTEGER :: num, denom                 ! scoping unit 5
   num = 3;  denom = 5                   ! scoping unit 5
   CALL conv_to_fract (num, denom)       ! scoping unit 5
END PROGRAM demo_scoping_units           ! scoping unit 5

SUBROUTINE display (real_val)            ! scoping unit 2
   REAL, INTENT (IN) :: real_val         ! scoping unit 2
   PRINT "(F8.3)", real_val              ! scoping unit 2
END SUBROUTINE display                   ! scoping unit 2
```

FIGURE 8.10. A program broken down into its scoping units.

so the portion left when its only internal subprogram (conv_to_decimal) is removed constitutes a scoping unit, which is identified as "scoping unit 4." The main program of Figure 8.10 contains neither derived-type definitions, nor interface bodies, nor internal subprograms, so the main program is designated as "scoping unit 5." Finally, the module rat_

```
subroutine-stmt
           [specification-part]
           [execution-part]
END SUBROUTINE [subroutine-name]
```

FIGURE 8.11A. General form of an internal subroutine subprogram.

type_conversions contains no interface bodies, so when its only derived-type definition (for rat_type) and its only module subprogram (conv_to_fract) are removed, the remainder constitutes a scoping unit, and this is designated as "scoping unit 6."

When the program of Figure 8.10 is executed, the following is displayed:

```
0.600
```

8.12 LANGUAGE RULES RELATED TO INTERNAL SUBPROGRAMS

The general form for an internal subroutine subprogram is given in Figure 8.11a. The header statement *subroutine-stmt* features the keyword SUBROUTINE and was described in Section 6.9. The *subroutine-name* on the END SUBROUTINE statement is optional, but if present it must match the name of the subroutine as given in *subroutine-stmt*. Note in Figure 8.11a that the Fortran 90 standard requires that the keyword SUBROUTINE be specified on the END statement for an internal subroutine.

The general form for an internal function subprogram is given in Figure 8.11b, and the related rules parallel those for an internal subroutine subprogram. The header statement *function-stmt* features the keyword FUNCTION and was also described in Section 6.9. The *function-name* on the END FUNCTION statement is optional, but if present it must match the

```
function-stmt
           [specification-part]
           [execution-part]
END FUNCTION [function-name]
```

FIGURE 8.11B. General form of an internal function subprogram.

name of the function as given in *function-stmt*. Observe in Figure 8.11b that the Fortran 90 standard requires that the keyword FUNCTION be specified on the END statement for an internal function.

There are a couple of restrictions on internal subprograms that do not apply to external subprograms. Neither an internal subroutine subprogram nor an internal function subprogram is permitted to contain an ENTRY statement. Also, neither is permitted to contain a CONTAINS statement, which is to say that an internal subprogram may not contain an internal subprogram. Thus, in standard Fortran 90, subprograms may be nested to only one level.

The general form of an external subroutine subprogram is given in Figure 8.12a, and the general form of an external function subprogram is given in Figure 8.12b. Either an external subroutine subprogram or an external function subprogram may optionally contain any number of internal subprograms, where an internal subprogram is either an internal subroutine or an internal function, as specified in Figures 8.11a and 8.11b. Note that the keyword SUBROUTINE is not mandatory on the END statement for an external subroutine subprogram, and the keyword FUNCTION is not compulsory on the END statement for an external function subprogram.

The general form of a module subroutine subprogram is given in Figure 8.13a, and the general form of a module function subprogram is given in Figure 8.13b. The only difference between the form of a module subprogram and its corresponding category of external subprogram is that the standard requires the presence of either the keyword SUBROUTINE or the keyword FUNCTION, whichever is applicable, in the END statement of a module subprogram, while this requirement is relaxed for an external subprogram. Relaxation of this requirement for external

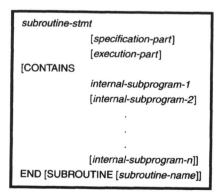

FIGURE 8.12A. General form of an external subroutine subprogram.

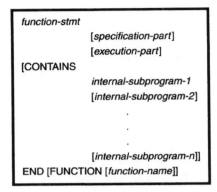

```
function-stmt
          [specification-part]
          [execution-part]
[CONTAINS
          internal-subprogram-1
          [internal-subprogram-2]
                    .
                    .
                    .
          [internal-subprogram-n]]
END [FUNCTION [function-name]]
```

FIGURE 8.12B. General form of an external function subprogram.

subprograms provides backward compatibility with previous versions of Fortran.

The general form of a standard Fortran 90 main program was given earlier in Section 2.4 and is repeated in Figure 8.14. A main program may optionally contain any number of internal subprograms. The PRO-GRAM statement is optional, but if present *program-name* must not be the same as the name of another program unit, an external procedure, a common block, or any local variable in the main program. If *program-name* appears on the END statement, the PROGRAM statement must be present and *program-name* must agree on the two statements. Traditional Fortran prohibited the appearance of a RETURN statement in a main program, and Fortran 90 maintains that prohibition. As has been tra-

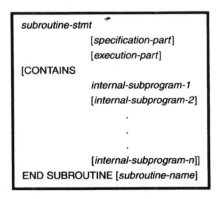

```
subroutine-stmt
          [specification-part]
          [execution-part]
[CONTAINS
          internal-subprogram-1
          [internal-subprogram-2]
                    .
                    .
                    .
          [internal-subprogram-n]]
END SUBROUTINE [subroutine-name]
```

FIGURE 8.13A. General form of a module subroutine subprogram.

```
function-stmt
                [specification-part]
                [execution-part]
[CONTAINS
                internal-subprogram-1
                [internal-subprogram-2]
                         .
                         .
                         .
                [internal-subprogram-n]]
END FUNCTION [function-name]
```

FIGURE 8.13B. General form of a module function subprogram.

```
[PROGRAM program-name]
                [specification-part]
                [execution-part]
[CONTAINS
                internal-subprogram-1
                [internal-subprogram-2]
                         .
                         .
                         .
                [internal-subprogram-n]]
END [PROGRAM [program-name]]
```

FIGURE 8.14. General form of a main program.

ditional, a STOP statement may be used to terminate execution in a main program or anywhere else in a program.

CHAPTER 9

OVERLOADING AND DEFINED OPERATIONS

9.1 INTRODUCTION TO GENERIC IDENTIFIERS

Fortran 90 permits a programmer to arrange things so that the same name can be used to invoke different procedures, the meaning of an intrinsic operator can be extended so that it has programmer-defined meaning(s) in addition to its intrinsic meanings, and the meaning of the equal sign (=) can also be extended so that it has programmer-defined meaning(s) in addition to its intrinsic meanings. There are similar capabilities in Ada and C++, and the term "overloading" is frequently used in discussing such capabilities. But in addition to supporting the overloading of intrinsic operators, Fortran 90 permits the programmer to define new operators, a capability not currently available in other popular languages. The remainder of this section will introduce overloading and programmer-defined operators as implemented in Fortran 90, and the rest of the chapter will discuss the details.

For some time, Fortran has provided the capability of invoking any one of a family of intrinsic functions by referencing the name of the family. For example, standard-conforming FORTRAN 77 implementations are required to provide the intrinsic function IABS to find the absolute value of an argument of type INTEGER, the intrinsic function DABS to find the absolute value of an argument of type DOUBLE PRECISION, and the intrinsic function CABS to find the absolute value of an argument of type COMPLEX. However, a programmer is permitted to use the name ABS to find the absolute value of an argument of any numerical data type, and the compiler must infer from the type of the argument which intrinsic procedure is to be invoked. Thus, ABS is the generic name for a family of intrinsic procedures that determine absolute value, and IABS, DABS, and CABS are the specific names of some of the members of the family.

In Fortran 90, the capability of using generic names is extended to procedures written by application programmers. For example, suppose a programmer writes a function subprogram alog2 that finds the base 2 logarithm of a scalar argument of type default REAL and another function subprogram dlog2 that finds the base 2 logarithm of a scalar argument whose type is specified as DOUBLE PRECISION. Then it is possible to arrange things so that the following code

```
y = log2 (x)    ! log2 is a generic name.
```

causes alog2 to be invoked if x is a default REAL scalar and dlog2 to be invoked if x is a DOUBLE PRECISION scalar. As will be illustrated later in this chapter, a collection of code known as an "interface block" provides the mechanism whereby the name log2 is specified to be a generic name for the specific names alog2 and dlog2.

In addition to permitting generic names, Fortran 90 allows application programmers to define new meanings for intrinsic operators in much the same way that operators can be overloaded in C++ and Ada. The main idea here is as follows: Suppose, for example, that a programmer defines a derived type to represent rational numbers:

```
TYPE :: rational_type
    INTEGER :: numerator
    INTEGER :: denominator
END TYPE rational_type
```

Then, if variables rat_a and rat_b are of type rational_type, it would be desirable to be able to code expressions such as the following:

```
rat_a + rat_b
rat_a + 1
    2 + rat_b
```

Fortran 90 permits the programmer to extend the meaning of the plus sign so that such expressions have their intuitive interpretations. As will be shown, the mechanism for accomplishing this is to employ an interface block to associate the plus sign with a collection of function subprograms, each of which contains statements defining how the addition is to be carried out for a particular pairing of data types to be added.

Not only does Fortran 90 permit the overloading of intrinsic operators, but the programmer is also allowed to specify new operators, a capability not supported by either Ada or C++. In Fortran 90, a programmer-defined operator is symbolized by a programmer-chosen sequence of letters delimited by periods. Hence, as will be illustrated later, the programmer can set things up in such a way that an expression such as

```
.uppercase. string
```

causes a programmer-defined operator indicated by .uppercase. to be applied to a variable named string.

Although the Fortran standards do not consider the equal sign (=) to be an operator, the meaning of the equal sign can be extended by the programmer so that assignments that are not intrinsically available in Fortran 90 can be made. The mechanism for accomplishing this is quite similar to that for overloading an operator, except that the programmer defines the extended meanings of the overloaded equal sign by writing subroutines, while functions are written to define the meanings of overloaded operators. The treatment of the overloaded equal sign in Fortran 90 is somewhat analogous to that of Ada.

It should be mentioned that the Fortran 90 standard avoids the use of the term "overloading," and instead, a name, an operator, or an equal sign used in any of the ways described in the preceding discussion is referred to as a "generic identifier." In terms of mechanics, a generic identifier always appears in an INTERFACE statement, a new variety of statement that indicates the beginning of an interface block. The interface block is used to associate the generic identifier with functions or subroutines, which may be either module subprograms or external subprograms. Only the approach using module subprograms will be dealt with in this chapter; the technique using external subprograms will be outlined in Chapter 13. Incidentally, while an interface block must be employed in specifying overloading and programmer-defined operations, there are, as will be detailed in Chapter 13, other uses for interface blocks as well.

Since some people seem to become overly enamored with overloading, perhaps a word of caution is in order. Properly used, generic identifiers can make Fortran 90 programs easier to develop and maintain, but early experience in C++ indicated that overloaded operators sometimes had the opposite effect. Generic identifiers should be employed only in those situations where their meaning within the context of the program can be intuitively understood by those familiar with the application. In this connection, the author recommends that programmer-defined operations and programmer-defined assignments be used only in situations involving at least one data object of some derived type.

9.2 A PROGRAMMER-DEFINED GENERIC NAME

Suppose that an engineering application requires a family of functions that find the sines of angles given in degrees, where each function returns a result of the same type, kind, and rank as its argument. Figure

```
MODULE generic_sin_in_deg

        ! Interface block associates generic name
        ! sin_in_deg with four specific names.

   INTERFACE sin_in_deg
      MODULE PROCEDURE sin_in_deg_for_real_scalar, &
                       sin_in_deg_for_real_rank1,  &
                       sin_in_deg_for_dble_scalar, &
                       sin_in_deg_for_dble_rank1
   END INTERFACE

   INTEGER, PARAMETER :: Dble = KIND (0D0)
   REAL, PARAMETER :: Deg_to_rad_real = 0.1745329E-1
   REAL(Dble), PARAMETER ::                                        &
                    Deg_to_rad_dble = 0.17453292519943D-1
CONTAINS

   ! Find sine of scalar of type default REAL.

   FUNCTION sin_in_deg_for_real_scalar (x) RESULT (sine)
      REAL, INTENT (IN) :: x
      REAL            :: sine
      sine = SIN (Deg_to_rad_real * x)
   END FUNCTION sin_in_deg_for_real_scalar

   ! Find sine of rank 1 array of type default REAL.

   FUNCTION sin_in_deg_for_real_rank1 (x) RESULT (sine)
      REAL, DIMENSION(:), INTENT (IN) :: x
      REAL, DIMENSION(SIZE (x))       :: sine
      sine = SIN (Deg_to_rad_real * x)
   END FUNCTION sin_in_deg_for_real_rank1

   ! Find sine of scalar of type double precision REAL.

   FUNCTION sin_in_deg_for_dble_scalar (x) RESULT (sine)
      REAL(Dble), INTENT (IN) :: x
      REAL(Dble)              :: sine
      sine = SIN (Deg_to_rad_dble * x)
   END FUNCTION sin_in_deg_for_dble_scalar

   ! Find sine of rank 1 array of type double precision REAL.

   FUNCTION sin_in_deg_for_dble_rank1 (x) RESULT (sine)
      REAL(Dble), DIMENSION(:), INTENT (IN) :: x
      REAL(Dble), DIMENSION(SIZE (x))       :: sine
      sine = SIN (Deg_to_rad_dble * x)
   END FUNCTION sin_in_deg_for_dble_rank1
END MODULE generic_sin_in_deg
```

FIGURE 9.1A. A generic name for a family of module procedures.

9.1a gives a module containing four functions in this family, where the argument properties are as follows: REAL scalar, rank 1 REAL array, DOUBLE PRECISION scalar, and rank 1 DOUBLE PRECISION array. The specific names for these four functions are as follows:

```
sin_in_deg_for_real_scalar
sin_in_deg_for_real_rank1
sin_in_deg_for_dble_scalar
sin_in_deg_for_dble_rank1
```

Because of the interface block, users of this module need not employ any of these specific names:

```
INTERFACE sin_in_deg
    MODULE PROCEDURE sin_in_deg_for_real_scalar, &
                     sin_in_deg_for_real_rank1,  &
                     sin_in_deg_for_dble_scalar, &
                     sin_in_deg_for_dble_rank1
END INTERFACE
```

The INTERFACE statement indicates that any reference by a module user to the name sin_in_deg is to be taken as a reference to one of the four functions named in the MODULE PROCEDURE statement. When the name sin_in_deg appears, the parenthesized actual argument following that name must match the dummy argument of exactly one of the four functions in type, kind, and rank. The compiler will treat the reference to sin_in_deg as a reference to the function with the matching argument.

Figure 9.1b lists a main program that uses the module of Figure 9.1a. The generic name sin_in_deg appears four times in the main program, and each time a different module function is invoked. In the initial appearance of the name sin_in_deg, the argument is 30.0, a scalar of default REAL type, so the function sin_in_deg_for_real_scalar is invoked. The second appearance of sin_in_deg has the array constructor

```
(/ 30.0, 60.0, 90.0 /)
```

as its argument, so the argument is a rank 1 array containing three elements, each of default REAL type, and the specific function named sin_in_deg_for_real_rank1 is invoked. In the third appearance of the name sin_in_deg, the argument is 30D0, a scalar of the kind of REAL equivalent to DOUBLE PRECISION, so the function sin_in_deg_for_dble_scalar is invoked. The final appearance of sin_in_deg has the array constructor

```
(/ 30D0, 60D0 /)
```

as its argument, so the argument is a rank 1 array containing two elements, each of type double precision REAL, and the specific function sin_in_deg_for_dble_rank1 is invoked. When the program consisting of the

```
PROGRAM demo_generic_name

  USE generic_sin_in_deg

  REAL                          :: sine_of_real_scalar
  REAL,            DIMENSION(3) :: sine_of_real_array
  REAL(KIND (0D0))              :: sine_of_dble_scalar
  REAL(KIND (0D0)), DIMENSION(2) :: sine_of_dble_array

  ! Invoke sin_in_deg_for_real_scalar.
  sine_of_real_scalar = sin_in_deg (30.0)
  PRINT "(E20.12)", sine_of_real_scalar

  ! Invoke sin_in_deg_for_real_rank1.
  sine_of_real_array = sin_in_deg ( (/ 30.0, 60.0, 90.0 /) )
  PRINT "(3E20.12)", sine_of_real_array

  ! Invoke sin_in_deg_for_dble_scalar.
  sine_of_dble_scalar = sin_in_deg (30D0)
  PRINT "(E20.12)", sine_of_dble_scalar

  ! Invoke sin_in_deg_for_dble_rank1.
  sine_of_dble_array = sin_in_deg ( (/ 30D0, 60D0 /) )
  PRINT "(2E20.12)", sine_of_dble_array

END PROGRAM demo_generic_name
```

FIGURE 9.1B. A main program that uses the module of Figure 9.1a.

main program of Figure 9.1b and the module of Figure 9.1a is executed, the resulting display will vary somewhat from implementation to implementation, but will be something like the following:

```
0.499999970198E+00
0.499999970198E+00   0.866025388241E+00   0.100000000000E+01
0.500000000000E+00
0.500000000000E+00   0.866025403784E+00
```

The use of the double-precision kind of REAL only slightly improves the precision of the results in this example.

An interesting sidelight in Figure 9.1a is that two of the functions, sin_in_deg_for_real_rank1 and sin_in_deg_for_dble_rank1, return array results. Note that the standard intrinsic function SIZE is invoked in both functions in the specification of the result variable. This is done so that the array returned by the function has the same number of elements as are in the actual argument when the function is invoked.

It should always be remembered that anything that can be accomplished using module subprograms can also be accomplished using external subprograms. Thus, external functions could have been employed instead of module functions in the overloading example given in this section; this alternate approach will be illustrated in Section 13.11.

Incidentally, a user of module generic_sin_in_deg can invoke any one of the four functions in Figure 9.1a either by its specific name or by the generic name sin_in_deg. However, the PRIVATE statement, which will be discussed in Chapter 12, could be employed in the module to prevent a module user from accessing any or all of the specific names or the generic name or any combination of them.

9.3 INTRINSIC OPERATORS

This section will consider some of the fundamental notions surrounding the use of intrinsic operators. Except for straightforward extensions, intrinsic operations in Fortran 90 are the same as in FORTRAN 77. The primary purpose of this section is merely to set the stage for the detailed discussion of programmer-defined operations that will follow.

Consider the following Fortran expression:

```
2 * y
```

The asterisk (*) here is called an **operator**, and 2 and y are called **operands**. Some intrinsic Fortran operators, such as *, /, +, −, ** and //, are symbolized by nonalphanumeric characters, while others, such as .AND., .OR., and .NOT., are made up of letters between two periods. In the Fortran 90 free source form, an operator may not contain embedded blanks. Also, for an implementation supporting lowercase letters in the source, letters in an operator may be in any combination of upper and lower case. However, in this tutorial, letters in intrinsic operators will always appear in upper case to indicate that they are not chosen by the programmer.

Any operator can be classified as either a **binary operator** or a **unary operator**, depending on whether it has two operands or one operand. Most Fortran intrinsic operators can be used only as binary operators, but one, .NOT., is always a unary operator. The characters + and − can be used in Fortran to symbolize either binary or unary operators, and the context must be considered to determine which usage is intended. The Fortran use of the symbols + and − is, of course, consistent with their usage in everyday mathematics.

Each intrinsic operator has certain predefined meanings, but these predefined meanings are couched in terms of the operands' being restricted to specified intrinsic data types. For example, the operator // has a predefined meaning only for operands of type CHARACTER, while the operator .AND. has a predefined meaning only for operands of type LOGICAL. Similarly, the operator * has predefined meanings only for operands of some numerical data type, where the numerical data types are INTEGER, REAL (including DOUBLE PRECISION), and COMPLEX.

Table 9.1 gives a summary of all Fortran 90 standard intrinsic operators. All of the intrinsic operators listed in the left column are also standard in FORTRAN 77, except for ==, /=, <, <=, >, and >=. However, the six new intrinsic operators are merely synonyms for the old operators .EQ., .NE., .LT., .LE., .GT., and .GE., respectively. Basically, the usage of Fortran 90 intrinsic operators is carried over from FORTRAN 77, except that in Fortran 90, operands are generally permitted to be arrays as well as scalars. Also, for the operators **, *, /, binary +, and binary −, the FORTRAN 77 standard does not permit one operand to be COMPLEX if the other is DOUBLE PRECISION, but the Fortran 90 standard relaxes this restriction.

Conceptually, intrinsic operations in Fortran 90 remain fundamentally unchanged from those of FORTRAN 77, but a thorough understanding of intrinsic operations is prerequisite to the discussion of programmer-defined operations. In this connection, there is insight to be gained by recognizing that it would be possible to write Fortran programs without ever using any operators at all. Suppose, for example, that there were a family of functions with generic name plus that could return the sum of any two numeric values. Then the expression

```
plus (1, 2.3)
```

would accomplish the same result as

```
1 + 2.3
```

The idea of actually writing Fortran code that always uses functions instead of operators is, of course, outrageous sacrilege: one of the definitive features of the language—indeed, the feature from which the name of the language is derived—is that mathematical formulas can be expressed in source code in a manner that closely resembles the way they are written in ordinary mathematics. But the important idea to be grasped here is that it is often possible to achieve the same results using either functions or operators, and the choice between these competing mechanisms should be governed by which yields the more expressive source code.

TABLE 9.1   The Fortran 90 standard intrinsic operators.

Intrinsic operator	Usage in expression	Type(s) of operand(s) or intrinsic meaning	Interpretation of expression when operator used with intrinsic meaning
**	$x_1 ** x_2$	Both numeric	Result of raising x_1 to the power x_2
*	$x_1 * x_2$	Both numeric	Product of x_1 and x_2
/	x_1 / x_2	Both numeric	Quotient of x_1 divided by x_2
Unary +	$+x_2$	Numeric	Same as x_2
Unary −	$-x_2$	Numeric	Negation of x_2
Binary +	$x_1 + x_2$	Both numeric	Sum of x_1 and x_2
Binary −	$x_1 - x_2$	Both numeric	Result of subtracting x_2 from x_1
//	$x_1 // x_2$	Both character	Concatenation of x_1 with x_2
.EQ.	x_1 .EQ. x_2	Both numeric or both character	True if x_1 is equal to x_2
==	$x_1 == x_2$	Both numeric or both character	True if x_1 is equal to x_2
.NE.	x_1 .NE. x_2	Both numeric or both character	True if x_1 is not equal to x_2
/=	$x_1 /= x_2$	Both numeric or both character	True if x_1 is not equal to x_2
.LT.	x_1 .LT. x_2	Both noncomplex numeric or both character	True if x_1 is less than x_2
<	$x_1 < x_2$	Both noncomplex numeric or both character	True if x_1 is less than x_2
.LE.	x_1 .LE. x_2	Both noncomplex numeric or both character	True if x_1 is less than or equal to x_2
<=	$x_1 <= x_2$	Both noncomplex numeric or both character	True if x_1 is less than or equal to x_2
.GT.	x_1 .GT. x_2	Both noncomplex numeric or both character	True if x_1 is greater than x_2
>	$x_1 > x_2$	Both noncomplex numeric or both character	True if x_1 is greater than x_2
.GE.	x_1 .GE. x_2	Both noncomplex numeric or both character	True if x_1 is greater than or equal to x_2
>=	$x_1 >= x_2$	Both noncomplex numeric or both character	True if x_1 is greater than or equal to x_2
.NOT.	.NOT. x_2	Logical	True if x_2 is false
.AND.	x_1 .AND. x_2	Both logical	True if x_1 and x_2 are both true
.OR.	x_1 .OR. x_2	Both logical	True if x_1 and/or x_2 is true
.EQV.	x_1 .EQV. x_2	Both logical	True if both x_1 and x_2 are true or both are false
.NEQV.	x_1 .NEQV. x_2	Both logical	True if exactly one of x_1 or x_2 is true

9.4   A FIRST EXAMPLE OF OPERATOR OVERLOADING

Intrinsic operators, such as +, *, and //, have certain predefined meanings, but as discussed in the preceding section, these predefined meanings are applicable only for certain intrinsic data types. For example, + and * have predefined meanings only for INTEGER, REAL, and COMPLEX data types, and // has a predefined meaning only for data objects of CHARACTER type. The Fortran 90 programmer can define one or more new meanings for such an operator, in which case the operator retains its predefined meaning(s) as well and is said to be **overloaded**. For example, Fortran 90 language rules permit a programmer to define a new meaning for the plus sign (+) such that when it appears between two scalar values of type CHARACTER, the values are concatenated. The new meaning would then make it possible to code expressions as in the following:

```
CHARACTER(13) :: s
s = "Hello, " + "World"  ! this use of + not recommended
```

In addition to its programmer-defined meaning of character concatenation, the intrinsic meanings of the plus sign would still be available, and expressions such as 2.3 + 4.5 would have their usual interpretation. In a given expression containing the plus sign, the compiler would select which meaning was intended based on the type(s), kind(s), and rank(s) of the data object(s) with which the operator was juxtaposed. Of course, attaching the meaning given above to the plus sign would be silly since this would duplicate the meaning of the intrinsic concatenation operator //.

Two examples of the operator overloading mechanism are presented in the module of Figure 9.2a, where a derived type named rat_type is defined. The idea, of course, is that data objects of type rat_type represent rational numbers, and it is desirable to be able to code expressions like

```
rat_1 * (rat_2 + rat_3)
```

where rat_1, rat_2, and rat_3 are of type rat_type. The module function add_rats in Figure 9.2a returns a value of type rat_type that is the sum of the input arguments rat_1 and rat_2. The interface block

```
INTERFACE OPERATOR (+)
   MODULE PROCEDURE add_rats
END INTERFACE
```

indicates that when the operator + appears, module function add_rats is to be invoked, provided that there is a data object of type rat_type to the immediate left of the plus sign and another to the immediate right. The

```
MODULE rational_numbers

   TYPE :: rat_type
      INTEGER :: num, denom
   END TYPE rat_type

   INTERFACE OPERATOR (+)              ! Invoke add_rats when +
      MODULE PROCEDURE add_rats        ! appears surrounded by
   END INTERFACE                       ! objects of type rat_type.

   INTERFACE OPERATOR (*)              ! Invoke mult_rats when *
      MODULE PROCEDURE mult_rats       ! appears surrounded by
   END INTERFACE                       ! objects of type rat_type.

CONTAINS

   ! Add two data objects of type rat_type.

   FUNCTION add_rats (rat_1, rat_2) RESULT (sum)
      TYPE (rat_type)           :: sum
      TYPE (rat_type), INTENT (IN) :: rat_1, rat_2

      ! The + and *'s below refer to intrinsic operators.
      sum = rat_type (rat_1%num   * rat_2%denom +   &
                      rat_1%denom * rat_2%num,       &
                      rat_1%denom * rat_2%denom)
   END FUNCTION add_rats

   ! Multiply two data objects of type rat_type.

   FUNCTION mult_rats (rat_1, rat_2) RESULT (product)
      TYPE (rat_type)           :: product
      TYPE (rat_type), INTENT (IN) :: rat_1, rat_2

      ! The *'s below refer to the intrinsic operator.
      product = rat_type (rat_1%num   * rat_2%num,   &
                          rat_1%denom * rat_2%denom)
   END FUNCTION mult_rats

END MODULE rational_numbers
```

FIGURE 9.2A. Two examples of the operator overloading mechanism.

module function mult_rats and the operator * are treated in an analogous fashion.

Figure 9.2b gives a main program that uses the module of Figure 9.2a. Structure constructors are employed to initialize the variables rat_1 and rat_2 to represent the rational numbers 2/3 and 4/5, respectively. The appearance of the plus sign between rat_1 and rat_2 causes the module function add_rats to be invoked. Similarly, the appearance of the asterisk (*) between rat_1 and rat_2 causes the module function mult_rats to be invoked. In the final PRINT statement, the plus sign and the asterisk have their intrinsic meanings since the data objects surrounding the operators are of intrinsic numerical types. When the program consisting of the main program of Figure 9.2b and the module of Figure 9.2a is executed, the following is displayed:

```
22/15
 8/15
 9
```

Note in Figure 9.2a that an interface block for an overloaded operator is quite similar to that for a generic name, as illustrated in

```
PROGRAM overloading_operators

  USE rational_numbers

  TYPE (rat_type) :: rat_1 = rat_type (2, 3),  &
                     rat_2 = rat_type (4, 5)

  TYPE (rat_type) :: result

  result = rat_1 + rat_2   ! Invoke module proc add_rats
                           ! to add 2/3 to 4/5.
  PRINT "(I3, '/', I2)", result

  result = rat_1 * rat_2   ! Invoke module proc mult_rats
                           ! to multiply 2/3 times 4/5.
  PRINT "(I3, '/', I2)", result

  PRINT "(I3)", (1 + 2) * 3   ! + and * also retain their
                              ! usual intrinsic meanings.

END PROGRAM overloading_operators
```

FIGURE 9.2B. Main program using the module of Figure 9.2a.

Section 9.2. The only difference is that for overloading an operator, the keyword OPERATOR, followed by the operator enclosed in parentheses, appears in the INTERFACE statement. A procedure to be invoked when a programmer-defined operation is specified may be implemented as either a module procedure or as an external procedure. However, if an external procedure is to be invoked by an operator, the interface block for that operator must contain an interface body for the procedure rather than specifying the procedure name in a MODULE PROCEDURE statement as illustrated in this section. Interface bodies will be discussed in Chapter 13.

9.5 DEFINED OPERATIONS ARE NOT AUTOMATICALLY COMMUTATIVE

The preceding section illustrated the basic Fortran 90 mechanism for specifying a programmer-defined operation, which is to employ an interface block to identify the operator with a function subprogram that will carry out the operation. So suppose that this mechanism is used to give the asterisk (*) in the expression

```
var_1 * var_2
```

the meaning defined by a function named mult. Then that expression can be considered a synonym for the function reference

```
mult (var_1, var_2)
```

Therefore, the Fortran 90 rules governing agreement of actual and dummy arguments dictate that var_1 must agree in type, kind, and rank with the first dummy argument of mult, and var_2 must agree with the second. Now if var_1 and var_2 are both of the same type, kind, and rank, as was the case in the preceding section, then it is sufficient to identify the operator with only one function. However, if var_1 and var_2 are of (say) different data types, then it is usually necessary to identify the operator with two procedures—one to be invoked if the expression

```
var_1 * var_2
```

occurred and the other to be invoked if the expression

```
var_2 * var_1
```

appeared.

The module of Figure 9.3a illustrates overloading the asterisk to indicate multiplication between a data object of default INTEGER type

```
MODULE rat_nums

   TYPE :: rat_type
      INTEGER :: num, denom
   END TYPE rat_type

   INTERFACE OPERATOR (*)
      MODULE PROCEDURE rat_times_int, &   ! Associate * with
                       int_times_rat      ! module funcs below.
   END INTERFACE

CONTAINS

   ! Multiply rational times INTEGER.

   FUNCTION rat_times_int (rat, int) RESULT (product)
      TYPE (rat_type)               :: product
      TYPE (rat_type), INTENT (IN) :: rat
      INTEGER,         INTENT (IN) :: int
      product = rat_type (rat%num * int, rat%denom)
   END FUNCTION rat_times_int

   ! Multiply INTEGER times rational.

   FUNCTION int_times_rat (int, rat) RESULT (product)
      TYPE (rat_type)               :: product
      INTEGER,         INTENT (IN) :: int
      TYPE (rat_type), INTENT (IN) :: rat
      product = rat_type (int * rat%num, rat%denom)
   END FUNCTION int_times_rat

END MODULE rat_nums
```

FIGURE 9.3A. Operator overloading when operands are of different types.

and a data object of derived type rat_type, which represents rational numbers, as discussed in the preceding section. The module contains two function subprograms, rat_times_int and int_times_rat. The function rat_times_int defines the meaning of the asterisk when the data object to the left of the operator is a scalar of type rat_type and the data object to the right is a scalar of the default kind of intrinsic type IN-TEGER; the function int_times_rat defines the meaning when the order is reversed. Note that the MODULE PROCEDURE statement associates both of these functions with the asterisk, and, of course, the intrinsic

```
PROGRAM operands_of_different_types

    USE rat_nums

    TYPE (rat_type) :: product

    product = rat_type (3, 5) * 2   ! Invoke func rat_times_int.
    PRINT "(I2, '/', I1)", product

    product = 3 * rat_type (1, 7)   ! Invoke func int_times_rat.
    PRINT "(I2, '/', I1)", product

END PROGRAM operands_of_different_types
```

FIGURE 9.3B. Main program using the module of Figure 9.3a.

meanings of the asterisk remain available as well. When the asterisk appears in an expression, the compiler will select the appropriate meaning based on the type, kind, and rank of the data objects surrounding the asterisk.

Figure 9.3b gives a main program that uses the module of Figure 9.3a. For the first asterisk in Figure 9.3b, the module function rat_times_int is invoked; and for the second, int_times_rat is invoked. When the program made up of the main program of Figure 9.3b and the module of Figure 9.3a is executed, the following is displayed:

```
6/5
3/7
```

9.6 OVERLOADING A RELATIONAL OPERATOR

In most of the popular languages, all operators are symbolized by nonalphanumeric characters. In Fortran, however, some intrinsic operators, such as +, *, and //, are symbolized by nonalphanumeric characters, while others, such as .AND., .OR., and .EQV., are symbolized by a sequence of letters between periods. Traditionally, the relational operators fall into the latter category, but Fortran 90 standardizes support of equivalent nonalphanumeric character forms for relational operators. Hence, as discussed in Section 3.2, .EQ. and ==

are aliased, .LT. and < are aliased, and so on. In Fortran 90, the intrinsic operators symbolized by a sequence of letters between periods can be overloaded using the same mechanism illustrated in the preceding two sections for operators symbolized by nonalphanumeric characters.

The module of Figure 9.4a illustrates overloading the relational operator .EQ. so that it can be used to test whether two data objects of derived type rat_type are equal. As in the preceding two sections, rat_type represents rational numbers, so the operator .EQ. should determine not only that identical rational numbers are equal, but also that, for example, 1/2 and 2/4 are equal. Observe in Figure 9.4a that the interface block associates the operator .EQ. with the module function is_equal_to. The function is_equal_to invokes the module function reduce to reduce each rational number to lowest terms. Note that the values of the arguments are unchanged by the processing in the function is_equal_to. If, after being reduced to lowest terms, the input rational numbers have identical numerators and identical denominators, the result .TRUE. is returned; otherwise, .FALSE. is returned. The module function reduce is basically the same as was described in Section 7.12, except that here the function find_gcd, whose listing is given in Figure 9.4b, is implemented as an external function for variety of illustration.

Figure 9.4c gives a main program that uses the module of Figure 9.4a. The first IF statement uses the operator .EQ. to test whether 2/4 is equal to 3/6. The second IF statement uses the operator == to test whether 2/4 is equal to 4/6. It is important to understand that .EQ. and == do *not* symbolize distinct operations but rather are alternative ways of symbolizing the same operation. Thus, the result of using the module of Figure 9.4a will be the same whether .EQ. or == appears in the parentheses following the keyword OPERATOR. When the program consisting of the main program of Figure 9.4c, the module of Figure 9.4a, and the external function of Figure 9.4b is executed, the following is displayed:

```
2/4 equals 3/6
2/4 does not equal 4/6
```

For those readers familiar with Ada, this example illustrates some differences between that language and Fortran 90. The capability of testing for the equality of objects is automatically available in Ada (except for limited private types) without any special action by the programmer, but note that there is no analogous capability in Fortran 90. Also, in Ada, whenever a test for equality is available, the corresponding test for inequality is automatically available. However, in Fortran 90, defining a meaning for the operator == (or its alias, .EQ.) implies nothing about the operator /= (or its alias, .NE.).

```
MODULE rat_numbers

  TYPE :: rat_type
     INTEGER :: num, denom
  END TYPE rat_type

  INTERFACE OPERATOR (.EQ.)              ! Associate .EQ. and ==
     MODULE PROCEDURE is_equal_to        ! with func is_equal_to.
  END INTERFACE

CONTAINS

  ! Return .TRUE. if 2 rationals equal; else return .FALSE.

  FUNCTION is_equal_to (rat_1, rat_2) RESULT (equal)
     LOGICAL                     :: equal
     TYPE (rat_type), INTENT (IN) :: rat_1, rat_2
     TYPE (rat_type) :: temp_1, temp_2

     temp_1 = reduce (rat_1)  ! Reduce rat_1 to lowest terms.
     temp_2 = reduce (rat_2)  ! Reduce rat_2 to lowest terms.

     ! Numerators & denoms identical for reduced rationals?
     equal = (temp_1%num   == temp_2%num)   .AND.  &
             (temp_1%denom == temp_2%denom)
  END FUNCTION is_equal_to

  ! Return rational number reduced to lowest terms.

  FUNCTION reduce (rat) RESULT (reduced)
     TYPE (rat_type)                :: reduced
     TYPE (rat_type), INTENT (IN) :: rat
     INTEGER :: gcd        ! greatest common divisor
     INTEGER :: find_gcd  ! external func to determine GCD

     gcd = find_gcd (rat%num, rat%denom)   ! Invoke external
                                           ! function.

     reduced = rat_type (rat%num / gcd, rat%denom / gcd)
  END FUNCTION reduce

END MODULE rat_numbers
```

FIGURE 9.4A. Overloading operator .EQ. to test rationals for equality.

```
! Find greatest common divisor of two integers.

RECURSIVE FUNCTION find_gcd (m, n) RESULT (gcd)

   INTEGER             :: gcd
   INTEGER, INTENT (IN) :: m, n

   IF (n == 0) THEN
      gcd = m
   ELSE
      gcd = find_gcd (n, MOD (m, n))
   END IF

END FUNCTION find_gcd
```

FIGURE 9.4B.   External function to find greatest common divisor.

```
PROGRAM overloading_relational_operator

   USE rat_numbers

   TYPE (rat_type) :: rat_1 = rat_type (2, 4),  &
                      rat_2 = rat_type (3, 6)

   IF (rat_1 .EQ. rat_2) THEN           ! Invoke is_equal_to.
      PRINT "(A)", " 2/4 equals 3/6"
   END IF

   IF (rat_1 == rat_type (4, 6)) THEN   ! Invoke is_equal_to.
      ! Do nothing if equal.
   ELSE
      PRINT "(A)", " 2/4 does not equal 4/6"
   END IF

END PROGRAM overloading_relational_operator
```

FIGURE 9.4C.   Main program using the module of Figure 9.4a.

9.7   PROGRAMMER-DEFINED OPERATORS

Examples in the preceding three sections have illustrated how a programmer can extend the meanings of intrinsic operators, such as * and .EQ., so that they can be used in ways other than those built into the language, but Fortran 90 also permits programmers to create entirely new operators. However, special characters may not be employed in symbolizing programmer-defined operators, but rather the programmer must choose a sequence of 1 to 31 letters, which are placed between periods to symbolize the operator. For example, if set is a variable of a derived type set_of_chars, then it might be desirable to define an operator .in. so that statements such as the following could be used in a program:

```
IF ("A" .in. set) THEN
```

The Fortran 90 standard permits only letters to appear between the periods in a programmer-defined operator, and even underscores and digits are prohibited.

As illustrated in Figure 9.5a, the mechanism for specifying a programmer-defined operator is the same as that for overloading an intrinsic operator. The interface block associates the defined operator symbolized by .invert. with the module function invert_rat, which returns the reciprocal of a rational number. As in the three preceding sections, rational numbers are again represented by the derived type rat_type.

```
MODULE rational_numbs

   TYPE :: rat_type
      INTEGER :: num, denom
   END TYPE rat_type

   INTERFACE OPERATOR (.invert.)     ! operator .invert. to
      MODULE PROCEDURE invert_rat    ! invoke func invert_rat
   END INTERFACE

CONTAINS

   ! Return the reciprocal of a rational number.

   FUNCTION invert_rat (rat) RESULT (reciprocal)
      TYPE (rat_type)             :: reciprocal
      TYPE (rat_type), INTENT (IN) :: rat

      reciprocal = rat_type (rat%denom, rat%num)
   END FUNCTION invert_rat

END MODULE rational_numbs
```

FIGURE 9.5A. Module illustrating programmer-defined operator.

```
PROGRAM new_programmer_defined_operator

  USE rational_numbs

  TYPE (rat_type) :: rat = rat_type (2, 5)    ! Set rat = 2/5.

  PRINT "(I2, '/', I1)", .invert. rat   ! Ref to .invert.
                                        ! invokes invert_rat
                                        ! with rat as arg.


END PROGRAM new_programmer_defined_operator
```

FIGURE 9.5B. Main program using the module of Figure 9.5a.

The main program of Figure 9.5b illustrates the use of the new operator .invert. by applying it to the rational number 2/5. When the program consisting of the main program of Figure 9.5b and the module of Figure 9.5a is executed, the following is displayed:

5/2

Observe that the example of this section features a unary operator, which is an operator that takes only one operand, as opposed to a binary operator, which is an operator that takes two operands. A programmer is permitted to define a new operator to be unary, binary, or either. If such an operator may be either unary or binary, the compiler will determine, based on context, which usage is intended for each appearance of the operator. This treatment parallels that of intrinsic operators, where .NOT. is an example of an operator that is always unary, the asterisk (*) is an example of an operator that is always binary, and the minus sign (-) is an example of an operator that may be either unary or binary.

Incidentally, note that .invert. has only one meaning in this example, and so the terms "overloading" and "generic" are not particularly descriptive here. Nevertheless, for tutorial purposes, this sort of programmer-defined operator is grouped with generic identifiers since the underlying interface block mechanism is the same.

9.8 PRECEDENCE OF OPERATORS

Operator precedence in Fortran 90 remains unchanged from FORTRAN 77 except for minor extensions to accommodate programmer-defined operators. Basically, the standard built-in operators in

Fortran 90 are identical with those of FORTRAN 77, and their precedence remains the same. And even when a Fortran 90 programmer defines an extended meaning for an intrinsic operator as described earlier in the chapter, the precedence of its extended meaning is the same as for its intrinsic meaning. Thus, in an expression such as a + b * c, the * will be applied before the +, even if the operator symbols + and * have programmer-defined meanings.

The precedence of all Fortran 90 operators is given in Figure 9.6. The list of operators is the same as in FORTRAN 77, except for the addition of the synonyms for the relational operators as described in Section 3.2, the programmer-defined unary operators, and the programmer-defined binary operators. The new synonyms for the relational operators have no effect on the precedence of operators, while the programmer-defined unary operators are given the highest precedence and the programmer-defined binary operators are given the lowest. A programmer-defined operator consists of 1 to 31 programmer-chosen letters between periods such that the programmer-defined operator looks like neither .TRUE. nor .FALSE. and does not duplicate any of the intrinsic operators given in Table 9.1.

Examples of two programmer-defined operators, .minus. and .tothepower., are given in the module of Figure 9.7a, along with a programmer-defined extended meaning for the * operator. All of the programmer-defined operations given in Figure 9.7a are performed on a derived type named rat_type, which represents rational numbers. The programmer-defined operator .minus. can be used to take the negative of a variable of type rat_type; the overloaded * can be used to find the product of two variables of type rat_type; and the programmer-defined operator .tothepower. can be used to raise a variable of type rat_type to an INTEGER power.

```
programmer-defined unary operator
              **
             *, /
        unary +, unary −
        binary +, binary −
.EQ., ==, .NE., /=, .LT., <, .LE., <=, .GT., >, .GE., >=
           we.NOT.
            .AND.
             .OR.
        .EQV., .NEQV.
programmer-defined binary operator
```

FIGURE 9.6. Precedence of operators, ordered from highest to lowest.

```
MODULE rational_numbers

  TYPE :: rat_type
     INTEGER :: num, denom      ! represents a rational number
  END TYPE rat_type

  INTERFACE OPERATOR (.minus.)        ! Take the negative of
     MODULE PROCEDURE unary_minus     ! a rational number.
  END INTERFACE

  INTERFACE OPERATOR (*)              ! Find the product of
     MODULE PROCEDURE mult            ! two rational numbers.
  END INTERFACE

  INTERFACE OPERATOR (.tothepower.)   ! Raise a rational
     MODULE PROCEDURE exponentiate    ! number to an
  END INTERFACE                       ! integer power.

CONTAINS

  FUNCTION unary_minus (rat) RESULT (negative)
     TYPE (rat_type)              :: negative
     TYPE (rat_type), INTENT (IN) :: rat

     negative = rat_type (-rat%num, rat%denom)
  END FUNCTION unary_minus

  FUNCTION mult (rat_1, rat_2) RESULT (product)
     TYPE (rat_type)              :: product
     TYPE (rat_type), INTENT (IN) :: rat_1, rat_2

     product = rat_type (rat_1%num  * rat_2%num,    &
                         rat_1%denom * rat_2%denom)
  END FUNCTION mult

  FUNCTION exponentiate (rat, n) RESULT (nth_power)
     TYPE (rat_type)              :: nth_power
     TYPE (rat_type), INTENT (IN) :: rat
     INTEGER,         INTENT (IN) :: n

     nth_power = rat_type (rat%num ** n, rat%denom ** n)
  END FUNCTION exponentiate

END MODULE rational_numbers
```

FIGURE 9.7A. Module with programmer-defined operations.

Since the module function named unary_minus has only one dummy argument, .minus. is a unary operator. Similarly, since the module functions mult and exponentiate have two dummy arguments, * and .tothepower. are binary operators.

The main program of Figure 9.7b illustrates the use of the programmer-defined operations given in the module of Figure 9.7a. Note that the type declaration statement in Figure 9.7b initializes rat_1 to the representation of $-1/3$ and rat_2 to the representation of 2/3. When the assignment statement is executed, the operations are performed in the order specified by Figure 9.6. Since the programmer-defined operator .minus. is a unary operator, it will be applied first to rat_1, yielding a result representing 1/3. The overloaded operator * will be applied next, multiplying the negative of rat_1 times rat_2, that is, finding the product of $-(-1/3)$ times 2/3, which is 2/9. The programmer-defined operator .tothepower. is a binary operator, so it will be applied last, raising 2/9 to the power 2, yielding a final result of 4/81. Hence, when the PRINT statement in Figure 9.7b is executed, the following will be displayed:

```
4    81
```

In addition to illustrating the precedence of operators in Fortran 90, the example presented in this section also demonstrates why caution must be exercised when using programmer-defined operations. The manner in which the operators .minus. and .tothepower. are defined in Figure 9.7a is confusing since any sane programmer would want

```
PROGRAM demo_precedence_of_operators

   USE rational_numbers    ! Access definition of rat_type
                           ! and programmer-defined operations.

   TYPE (rat_type) ::: rat_1 = rat_type (-1, 3),  &
                       rat_2 = rat_type ( 2, 3),  &
                       rat_3

   rat_3 = .minus. rat_1 * rat_2 .tothepower. 2    ! Invoke
                                                   ! all 3
                                                   ! funcs in
                                                   ! module.

   PRINT "(2I5)", rat_3

END PROGRAM demo_precedence_of_operators
```

FIGURE 9.7B. Main program demonstrating programmer-defined operations.

an exponentiation operation to have higher precedence than a nega-
tion operation. Of course, parentheses can be employed in expressions
containing programmer-defined operators to force operations to be performed in an order different from that specified by Figure 9.6. For
example, the assignment statement in Figure 9.7b could be recoded
as follows:

```
rat_3 = .minus. (rat_1 * (rat_2 .tothepower. 2))
```

Execution of this assignment statement causes rat_3 to represent the
rational number 4/27 as one would intuitively expect that it should.

The principal problem in the example program of this section is that
the author of the module of Figure 9.7a unwisely chose to create new
operators instead of extending the meaning of intrinsic operators. If
the author simply overloads the operators – and ** appropriately, rather
than defining new operators .minus. and .tothepower., the precedence of
operators would be exactly as one would intuitively expect. Also, in this
example, the symbols – and ** are more suggestive of the action that
will be performed than are .minus. and .tothepower., respectively.

9.9 DEFINED ASSIGNMENT: OVERLOADING THE EQUAL SIGN

Traditionally, the data types of the quantities on either side of the equal
sign (=) in an assignment statement must be both numeric, both CHAR-
ACTER, or both LOGICAL. This idea is extended in Fortran 90 so that
assignment is automatically available when the quantities on both sides
of an equal sign are of the same derived type. However, there are oc-
casions when it is desirable to be able to code assignment statements
where the quantities on opposite sides of the equal sign are of fundamentally different data types. For example, suppose that rational
numbers are represented by a derived type rat_type as in the four preceding sections. Then if x is a variable of type REAL, it might be desirable
to write statements such as

```
x = rat_type (3, 5) ! Convert from rat_type to REAL.
```

and have x take on the value 0.6. Fortran 90 provides a mechanism that
permits a programmer to define such assignments by overloading the
equal sign.

Figure 9.8a gives a module that illustrates extending the meaning of
the equal sign to permit assigning values of a derived type named point_
type to a rank 1 array variable of type REAL, and vice versa. Since the
equal sign is not considered to be an operator in Fortran, the operator
overloading mechanism illustrated in preceding sections is not used;

```
MODULE struct_array_assignments

   TYPE :: point_type
      REAL :: x1, x2, x3
   END TYPE point_type

   INTERFACE ASSIGNMENT (=)                     ! Associate equal
      MODULE PROCEDURE struct_to_array, &       ! sign with procs
                       array_to_struct          ! struct_to_array,
   END INTERFACE                                ! array_to_struct.

CONTAINS

   ! Convert data from structure of type point_type
   !              to size 3 REAL array of rank 1.

   SUBROUTINE struct_to_array (x, point)

      TYPE (point_type),  INTENT (IN)  :: point
      REAL, DIMENSION(3), INTENT (OUT) :: x

      x(1) = point%x1
      x(2) = point%x2
      x(3) = point%x3

   END SUBROUTINE struct_to_array

   ! Convert data from size 3 REAL array of rank 1
   !              to structure of type point_type.

   SUBROUTINE array_to_struct (point, x)

      REAL, DIMENSION(3), INTENT (IN)  :: x
      TYPE (point_type),  INTENT (OUT) :: point

      point%x1 = x(1)
      point%x2 = x(2)
      point%x3 = x(3)

   END SUBROUTINE array_to_struct

END MODULE struct_array_assignments
```

FIGURE 9.8A. Module illustrating overloading the equal sign.

instead, a different, although analogous, mechanism is employed. The keyword ASSIGNMENT followed by the parenthesized equal sign in the INTERFACE statement indicates that the procedures named in the MODULE PROCEDURE statement, struct_to_array and array_to_struct, are to be invoked when the equal sign appears in contexts that can be inferred from the declarations of the dummy arguments for those procedures. Observe that the procedures that define the extended meanings of the equal sign are subroutines rather than functions, as were used to define the extended meanings of overloaded operators. A defined assignment subroutine must always have two dummy arguments, the first of which must specify the type, kind, and rank of a variable permitted to appear on the left-hand side of the overloaded equal sign, and the second of which must specify these properties for the data object permitted to appear on the right-hand side.

The module of Figure 9.8a contains the definition of the derived type point_type, which has three REAL scalar components named x1, x2, and x3. A structure of type point_type can be used to hold the Cartesian coordinates of a point in three-dimensional space. Sometimes, however, it might also be convenient to store such coordinates in a rank 1 REAL array having three elements. The module subroutine struct_to_array is invoked to convert a point stored as a structure of type point_type to its equivalent array representation. Conversely, the module subroutine array_to_struct is invoked to convert a point stored as a size 3 REAL array of rank 1 to its equivalent representation as a structure of type point_type.

The main program of Figure 9.8b illustrates both uses of the overloaded equal sign defined in Figure 9.8a, as well as one of its intrinsic uses. In the first assignment statement in the main program, a structure constructor is employed to store values in the variable point, illustrating that the intrinsic meanings of the overloaded equal sign are still available. The second appearance of the equal sign in Figure 9.8b causes the module subroutine struct_to_array to be invoked, which stores the values 1.0, 2.0, and 3.0 in the three elements of the array x. In the third assignment statement in the main program, the product of the scalar constant 2.0 times each element of the array x is stored in a temporary size 3 REAL array of rank 1, and the equal sign causes the module subroutine array_to_struct to be invoked, which copies each element of the temporary array to the corresponding component of the structure point. When the program made up of the main program of Figure 9.8b and the module of Figure 9.8a is executed, the following is displayed:

```
1.0   2.0   3.0
2.0   4.0   6.0
```

The author recommends overloading the equal sign only when the quantity on at least one side of the equal sign is of a derived type. However, the Fortran 90 standard permits overloading the equal sign when

```
PROGRAM demo_defined_assignment

    USE struct_array_assignments   ! Access meanings of =
                                    ! defined in module.

    TYPE (point_type)  :: point
    REAL, DIMENSION(3) :: x

    point = point_type (1.0, 2.0, 3.0)  ! intrinsic assignment

    x = point           ! assignment defined by struct_to_array

    PRINT "(3F5.1)", x

    point = 2.0 * x   ! assignment defined by array_to_struct

    PRINT "(3F5.1)", point

END PROGRAM demo_defined_assignment
```

FIGURE 9.8B. Main program using the module of Figure 9.8a.

the quantities on both sides are of intrinsic types, provided that the defined assignment does not conflict with any of the valid intrinsic assignments. For example, language rules permit defining an assignment that legalizes code such as the following:

```
CHARACTER(20) :: number
number = 12.34              ! Convert REAL to CHARACTER.
```

This is not recommended in general because most people find it too unexpected. Instead, achieving the same result with code such as

```
CALL real_to_char (number, 12.34)
```

is recommended.

9.10 RULES APPLYING TO GENERIC IDENTIFIERS

Figure 9.9 gives the general form of the Fortran 90 interface block. A scoping unit may contain any number of interface blocks, and other nonexecutable statements may be placed between interface blocks. In the examples of interface blocks given in this chapter, there are no

```
INTERFACE [generic-spec]
              [interface-body-1]
              [interface-body-2]
                        .
                        .
                        .
              [interface-body-m]
              [MODULE PROCEDURE proc-name-list-1]
              [MODULE PROCEDURE proc-name-list-2]
                        .
                        .
                        .
              [MODULE PROCEDURE proc-name-list-n]
END INTERFACE

where generic-spec is generic-name
              or OPERATOR (operator-token)
              or ASSIGNMENT (=)
```

FIGURE 9.9. General form of the interface block.

interface bodies and *generic-spec* is always present. Chapter 13 discusses
interface bodies and interface blocks where *generic-spec* is not present.
Interface bodies are used only for external or dummy procedures and
are never used for internal or module procedures.

Preceding sections of this chapter give examples of all three forms
of *generic-spec* and several examples of MODULE PROCEDURE statements.
A MODULE PROCEDURE statement is allowed in an interface block only
when *generic-spec* is present. If *generic-spec* is present, an interface block
may contain a mix of interface bodies and MODULE PROCEDURE statements. The names listed in a MODULE PROCEDURE statement must be
those of accessible procedures contained in a module.

If *generic-spec* is *generic-name*, then all procedures whose specific
names are given inside the interface block must be subroutines or all
must be functions. It is permitted for *generic-name* to be the same as
the name of an intrinsic procedure, provided that all references to the
name are unambiguous.

If *generic-spec* is OPERATOR (*operator-token*), then all procedures must
be functions having either one or two dummy arguments specified with
INTENT (IN). If *operator-token* is one of the intrinsic operators listed in the
left column of Table 9.1, the number of function arguments must be
consistent with intrinsic uses of that operator. Extending the meaning
of one form of a relational operator (say, >=) automatically defines both

forms (>= and .GE.). If *operator-token* is not an intrinsic operator, then it must consist of 1 to 31 letters between periods, and neither .TRUE. nor .FALSE. is permitted to play this role. The precedence of operators in Fortran 90 remains unchanged from FORTRAN 77, except that if *operator-token* is programmer-defined, it has the highest possible precedence if it has one operand and the lowest possible precedence if it has two operands. If *operator-token* is an intrinsic operator, the precedence of its extended meaning is the same as for its intrinsic meaning.

If *generic-spec* is ASSIGNMENT (=), then all procedures must be subroutines having two dummy arguments. The first dummy argument must be specified INTENT (OUT) or INTENT (IN OUT). The second dummy argument must be specified INTENT (IN). The programmer is not permitted to redefine or overload the intrinsic meaning of the equal sign when the quantities on both sides of the equal sign are both numeric, both CHARACTER, or both LOGICAL. However, if the quantities on both sides of the equal sign are of the same derived type, the standard permits the programmer to specify a subroutine that redefines the meaning of the equal sign.

For procedures with the same *generic-spec*, argument lists must differ sufficiently for any invocation to be unambiguous, irrespective of whether the procedure is invoked using the traditional positional correspondence or the new argument keyword mechanism, which will be discussed in Section 13.9. In most instances of practical interest, references to such procedures can be resolved by noting that corresponding arguments differ in type, kind, or rank. It seems unlikely that programmers will have much difficulty observing this rule in practice as long as they do not have two such procedures whose argument lists are identical except that the arguments are in a different order.

One might expect that if *generic-spec* is present in an INTERFACE statement, then the same *generic-spec* could be specified on the corresponding END INTERFACE statement for purposes of readability. But as indicated in Figure 9.9, this is not supported by the Fortran 90 standard, although some implementations may provide this capability as an extension.

CHAPTER 10

POINTERS TO ARRAYS

10.1 *INTRODUCTION TO FORTRAN 90 POINTERS*

The notion of pointers has been around computing from very early times, but traditionally their availability in Fortran has been rare so, presumably, many readers are not familiar with them. Conceptually, a pointer is a variable that does not itself contain data of interest but rather holds some sort of description of a storage location that does. In its simplest form, such a description might consist of only the starting address of the storage location containing the data of interest, but in more sophisticated realizations of the concept, additional information about the storage location, such as its size, the type and organization of data stored there, and so forth, will be embodied in the description.

As put forth in the new standard, the Fortran 90 pointer bears some resemblance to pointers in assembly languages, Pascal, and C, as well as to Ada access variables and C++ references. There also are some similarities between pointers in Fortran 90 and pointers in the few FORTRAN 77 implementations (notably Cray) that offer them. But in spite of the fact that the Fortran 90 pointer shares some characteristics in common with pointers existing elsewhere in the software universe, there are enough elementary differences that even a widely experienced programmer can expect to expend considerable time in mastering their use.

A limitation of an ordinary, nonpointer variable is that it has a fixed association with a specific data object. This limitation is not shared by a pointer variable, however. A programmer can dynamically change the association of a pointer during execution so that at one time it is associated with (that is, points to) one data object and later it is associated with another. In Fortran 90, pointers are used for such things as linked lists, variable-length character strings, and functions having a result whose size is determined within the function. The unwary should be forewarned, however, that while the increased flexibility provided by pointers puts great power in the hands of the programmer, the price to be paid for this is increased complexity. It is important that pointers be used with discipline, because when used improperly, they are often the source of baffling execution-time behavior.[1]

In Fortran 90, in order to use a variable as a pointer, the POINTER attribute must be explicitly specified. A representative declaration of a Fortran 90 pointer is

```
REAL(2), DIMENSION(:), POINTER :: p
```

This specifies that p is a pointer that is capable of pointing to any rank 1 array of type REAL with kind type parameter 2. The programmer may cause p to hold the description of one such array at one time during execution, and later the programmer may cause the description held by p to change to that of another such array. However, Fortran 90 pointers are permitted to point only to a data object of a particular type, type parameter, and rank. Thus, p can never hold the description of a rank 2 array or a scalar. (Recall that a scalar has rank 0.) Also, p may not point to a data object of type INTEGER or to a derived type or even to a data object of type REAL whose kind type parameter is not 2.

In Fortran 90, the target of a pointer may be either a nameless storage area created by executing an ALLOCATE statement or a storage area associated with a name declared by the programmer. In this respect, the Fortran 90 pointer differs from the Pascal pointer and the Ada access variable, which are permitted to point only to dynamically allocated storage. In this connection, however, it should be mentioned that the Fortran 90 standard imposes the nonintuitive requirement that the programmer must specify the TARGET attribute when declaring a name that may be the target of a pointer. This will be illustrated in several examples in the remaining sections of this chapter.

C programmers should probably be forewarned that the Fortran 90 pointer is far less flexible than the C pointer. Fortran 90 provides no mechanism for indicating that a pointer to one data type is to be treated as if it were a pointer to another data type, and Fortran 90 does not support a generic pointer type like the pointer to void. Also, there is no pointer arithmetic in Fortran 90 as there is in C.

The Fortran 90 standard permits the programmer to declare a pointer to a data object of any type and rank. In practice, however, pointers are nearly always intended to point to data aggregates (structures or arrays). Except for tutorial examples, it is seldom worth the trouble to employ a pointer to a simple, noncomposite value. This chapter will focus on pointers to arrays of intrinsic data types. Pointers to

---

[1]Dealing with execution time problems caused by errant pointers can lead to the state of melancholy expressed in the song lyric: "I've got those segmentation violation, core dumped blues."

structures, which provide the underlying mechanism for linked lists, will be covered in the following chapter.

10.2 *POINTER ASSIGNMENT*

In production Fortran 90 programs, pointers are nearly always intended to be capable of pointing to a composite data object, that is, an array or a structure. However, to establish some fundamental notions, this section will present two examples featuring pointers to simple, nonaggregate variables. After this section, nearly all examples of pointers will involve either arrays or structures.

Consider the example program of Figure 10.1. Note that the keyword POINTER appears in the declaration of the programmer-chosen name ptr_to_int. In Fortran 90, a variable that serves as a pointer must always be specified to have the POINTER attribute. The presence of the keyword INTEGER in the declaration of ptr_to_int, along with the absence of either kind type parameter or array extent list, means that ptr_to_int can point to storage areas intended to hold scalar INTEGER values of the default kind.

```
PROGRAM demo_ptr_assignment

    INTEGER, POINTER :: ptr_to_int    ! ptr_to_int may alias
                                      ! any storage area
                                      ! intended to hold a
                                      ! scalar INTEGER value
                                      ! of default kind.

    INTEGER, TARGET  :: n             ! n may be aliased.

    n = 1

    ! Pointer assignment statement follows:
    ptr_to_int => n    ! Make ptr_to_int an alias for n.

    PRINT "(3I5)", n, ptr_to_int, ptr_to_int + 2

END PROGRAM demo_ptr_assignment
```

FIGURE 10.1. POINTER and TARGET attributes, pointer assignment.

Now turn attention to the declaration of n in Figure 10.1. The variable n is simply an ordinary, nonpointer variable, except that we would like to use the pointer variable ptr_to_int to point to n. Any variable that is to be pointed to by a pointer variable must have the same type, type parameters, and rank as the pointer variable, and the Fortran 90 standard also requires that in order to be pointed to, a variable must be given the TARGET attribute. The standard requires that the TARGET attribute be specified only for purposes of code optimization by the compiler.

With the variables ptr_to_int and n declared as described above, the statement

```
ptr_to_int => n
```

causes a description of n, probably including its address, to be stored in ptr_to_int, and ptr_to_int is said to point to n. After this statement is executed, ptr_to_int is an alias for n, and the programmer can use these two names interchangeably. When the program of Figure 10.1 is executed, the following is displayed:

```
1     1     3
```

Note that when the PRINT statement is executed, references to ptr_to_int are treated the same as if they were references to n.

The statement in Figure 10.1 where ptr_to_int becomes an alias for n is an example of a **pointer assignment statement**, which has the following general form:

pointer-name => target

Both *pointer-name* and *target* must agree in type, type parameters, and rank. If *target* is not a pointer, then it must have the TARGET attribute. The pointer assignment symbol is entered by immediately following the equal sign (=) with the greater than sign (>) with no intervening white space. Note that in Fortran 90, no special dereferencing symbols, such as ^ in Pascal or * in C, are employed.

The major capability a pointer offers is to provide the programmer with the means to associate a name with different data objects at different times during the execution of a program. A simple illustration of this capability is given in Figure 10.2. Note in Figure 10.2 that a pointer named ptr_to_real, which is capable of pointing to scalar REAL values of default kind, is declared. Observe also that two possible targets, named x and y, are declared. Then x is set to 1.0, and a pointer assignment statement is executed, which causes ptr_to_real to point to x. After the first PRINT statement is executed, a second pointer assignment statement changes the description stored in ptr_to_real so that it now points to y. Observe that at the moment when the second pointer assignment statement is executed, y has never been given a value, which implies, according to both the FORTRAN 77 and Fortran 90 standards,

```
PROGRAM demo_change_ptr_association

    REAL, POINTER :: ptr_to_real

    REAL, TARGET  :: x, y

    x = 1.0

    ptr_to_real => x    ! Make ptr_to_real an alias for x.

    PRINT "(2F8.2)", x, ptr_to_real

    ptr_to_real => y    ! Change ptr_to_real to alias y.

    y = 500.0

    PRINT "(3F8.2)", x, y, ptr_to_real

END PROGRAM demo_change_ptr_association
```

FIGURE 10.2. A pointer's association may be dynamically changed.

that it is not guaranteed to have any particular value. Nevertheless, ptr_to_real is aliased to y by the second pointer assignment statement, even though ptr_to_real is pointing to a storage location that is not guaranteed to hold any meaningful value. Then, in the next statement, y is set to 500.0.

When the program of Figure 10.2 is executed, the following is displayed:

```
1.00    1.00
1.00  500.00  500.00
```

As indicated by the display, ptr_to_real is an alias for x when the first PRINT statement is executed and an alias for y when the second PRINT statement is executed. Of course, associating ptr_to_real with y breaks the association between ptr_to_real and x, but observe that this has no effect on x itself.

10.3 POINTER TO A DECLARED ARRAY

The preceding section illustrated pointers to simple, noncomposite values, but, in practice, pointers are almost always intended to point to

```
PROGRAM demo_ptr_to_declared_arrays

    REAL, DIMENSION(:,:), POINTER :: p    ! ptr to a REAL
                                          ! array of rank 2


    REAL, DIMENSION(2,2), TARGET  :: a
    REAL, DIMENSION(4,3), TARGET  :: b


    INTEGER :: i, j

    a(1,1) = 1.0;   a(1,2) = 3.0
    a(2,1) = 2.0;   a(2,2) = 4.0


    p => a              ! p points to a 2 x 2 array.

    PRINT "(2F8.3)", p(1,1), p(1,2)
    PRINT "(2F8.3)", p(2,1), p(2,2)


    PRINT "(1X)"


    p => b              ! p points to a 4 x 3 array.

    b(1,1) = -1.0;  b(1,2) = -5.0;  b(1,3) =  -9.0
    b(2,1) = -2.0;  b(2,2) = -6.0;  b(2,3) = -10.0
    b(3,1) = -3.0;  b(3,2) = -7.0;  b(3,3) = -11.0
    b(4,1) = -4.0;  b(4,2) = -8.0;  b(4,3) = -12.0


    DO i = 1, SIZE (p, 1)
        PRINT "(3F8.3)", (p(i,j), j = 1, SIZE (p, 2))
    END DO

END PROGRAM demo_ptr_to_declared_arrays
```

FIGURE 10.3.   Pointer that points to rank 2 REAL arrays.

arrays or structures. Figure 10.3 gives an example of an array pointer named p. Note that p can serve as a pointer to any rank 2 array of REAL values of default kind. When the POINTER attribute is specified for an array, the extent of each dimension must be specified by a colon (:). The colon indicates that the range of subscripts that can be used for each dimension of the array pointer will be determined during execution. In fact, the valid subscripts for a given array pointer may fall into one range at one time and another range at another time.

In addition to the declaration of the array pointer p, the program of Figure 10.3 contains declarations for a and b, which are both rank 2 REAL arrays that may be targets of a pointer. Now, observe that p serves

as a pointer to arrays having different shapes: First p points to the
2 × 2 array a, and then later to the 4 × 3 array b. Consider the pointer
assignment statement

```
p => a
```

After the execution of this statement, note that p is an alias for a and
p(1,1) is an alias for a(1,1), p(1,2) is an alias for a(1,2), and so on. Later,
the pointer assignment statement

```
p => b
```

breaks the association of p with a, and p becomes an alias for b. Observe that no difficulties are raised by the fact that the values of b are
undefined (according to the Fortran 90 standard) at the time that p is
associated with it.

When the program of Figure 10.3 is executed, the following is
displayed:

```
1.000    3.000
2.000    4.000


-1.000   -5.000   -9.000
-2.000   -6.000  -10.000
-3.000   -7.000  -11.000
-4.000   -8.000  -12.000
```

Note in Figure 10.3 that the valid subscript range of each dimension
of the pointer p is determined by the extent along the corresponding
dimension of its current target. For example, when p is pointing to a,
both the first and the second subscripts range from 1 through 2 since a
is 2 × 2, but when p is pointing to b, the first subscript for p ranges from
1 through 4 while the second ranges from 1 through 3. Observe in Figure
10.3 that the standard intrinsic function SIZE is used to determine the
extents along each dimension of the current target of the pointer p.

10.4 An Array Section May Be the Target of a Pointer

Under Fortran 90 rules, a section of an array having the TARGET attribute will automatically acquire that attribute. Thus, a pointer may
point to a section of a declared array for which the TARGET attribute is
specified. This is illustrated by the program of Figure 10.4, which, when
executed, displays the following:

```
1    22.0
2    33.0
3    44.0
```

```
PROGRAM demo_ptr_to_array_section

   REAL, DIMENSION(5), TARGET ::                              &
                   a = (/ 11.0, 22.0, 33.0, 44.0, 55.0 /)

   REAL, DIMENSION(:), POINTER :: p    ! ptr to a REAL
                                       ! array of rank 1

   INTEGER :: i

   p => a(2:4)        ! p points to an array section
                      ! where stride defaults to 1.

   DO i = 1, SIZE (p)
      PRINT "(I4, F6.1)", i, p(i)
   END DO

   PRINT "(1X)"

   p => a(1:5:2)    ! p points to an array section
                    ! where stride is different from 1.

   DO i = 1, SIZE (p)
      PRINT "(I4, F6.1)", i, p(i)
   END DO

END PROGRAM demo_ptr_to_array_section
```

FIGURE 10.4.   Pointer that points to array sections.

```
1    11.0
2    33.0
3    55.0
```

Note that the first pointer assignment statement in Figure 10.4 causes p to point to the array section a(2:4), which is an array consisting of three elements whose values are the same as those of a(2), a(3), and a(4). Thus, p can be thought of as an alias for a(2:4), but observe in the above display that the range of subscripts that can be used with p are not 2 through 4, but instead start with 1 and extend through 3, the number of elements in its target. Hence, p(1) is an alias for a(2), p(2) is an alias for a(3), and p(3) is an alias for a(4).

The second pointer assignment statement in Figure 10.4 causes p to point to the array section a(1:5:2), which is an array consisting of three elements whose values are the same as those of a(1), a(3), and a(5). Thus, it is permissible for an array section specified by the subscript triplet mechanism where the stride is not unity to be the target of a pointer. But note in the output displayed by the program that the valid subscripts for p are 1 through 3 when its target is a(1:5:2), and that p(1) is an alias for a(1), p(2) is an alias for a(3), and p(3) is an alias for a(5).

Observe that the second pointer assignment of Figure 10.4 illustrates that the elements in the target of an array pointer are not required to be contiguous. However, the Fortran 90 standard does not permit an array section specified using the vector subscript mechanism to be used as the target of a pointer. (Vector subscripts were discussed in Section 4.6.)

10.5 POINTER ASSOCIATION STATUS

In Fortran 90, a pointer that is pointing to a target is said to be **associated**. We think of a pointer that is associated as holding a valid description of a storage area that contains some data of interest. However, there are stages in program execution where a pointer is not pointing to any target, and this leads to the notion of **pointer association status**.

In reality, the characterization of a pointer as a variable holding the description of a storage area needs some refinement. It will serve us better to think of a pointer as a variable that is *capable* of holding such a description but does not necessarily do so. Actually, the contents of a pointer's description are unpredictable until the programmer takes some action to put something into that description. In much the same way that it is the programmer's responsibility that an ordinary variable hold meaningful values, it is the programmer's responsibility to make sure that the descriptions contained by a pointer variable are meaningful. Before the programmer puts something meaningful into a pointer's description, that pointer is said to have an **undefined** pointer association status. A pointer whose association status is undefined can be thought of as containing an unpredictable address and therefore pointing wildly.

As illustrated in previous sections, one of the ways that a programmer can be sure that a pointer's association status is defined is to associate the pointer with a target by executing a pointer assignment statement. However, as will be shown in subsequent sections, it is sometimes convenient to set the description held by a pointer so as to indicate in a verifiable manner that the pointer is not currently pointing to anything. It probably does no great harm to think that part of the description held by a pointer is the address of the target, and that setting that address to zero is the mechanism employed to indicate that the pointer currently has no target. However, this mental model cannot necessarily be taken as a literal explanation, since the Fortran 90 standard leaves such implementation details unspecified.

In Pascal and Ada, the reserved words NIL and NULL can be used, respectively, on the right-hand side of an assignment statement to set a pointer not to point to any target; in C, it is conventional to use the symbolic constant NULL in the same manner. But in Fortran 90, a special statement is ordinarily used to cause the description held by one or more pointers to be set to indicate that the pointer(s) is/are not pointing at any target. The form of this special statement is

```
NULLIFY (pointer-name-list)
```

For example, if p_1 and p_2 are pointers, then

```
NULLIFY (p_1, p_2)
```

causes the descriptions held by p_1 and p_2 to be set so that the programmer can test that they are not currently associated with any target. A pointer that is set not to point to any target is said to be **disassociated**.

The standard intrinsic function ASSOCIATED is provided to determine whether a pointer is associated or disassociated. However, when a program begins execution, the Fortran 90 standard permits the description held by a pointer variable to be unpredictable; in this situation, the pointer is neither associated nor disassociated, and, as mentioned earlier, its association status is said to be "undefined." It is the programmer's responsibility to be sure that a pointer whose association status is undefined is not referenced inappropriately. In particular, it is an error to use a pointer whose association status is undefined as an argument of the ASSOCIATED intrinsic function.

The example program of Figure 10.5 illustrates some of the ideas revolving around pointer association status. The pointer association status of the pointer p starts out undefined, and then the pointer assignment statement associates p with the array x. Then the NULLIFY statement causes p to become disassociated, but this, of course, has no effect on x. Note that the intrinsic function ASSOCIATED returns .TRUE. if p is associated and .FALSE. if p is disassociated. The pointer association status of the argument of ASSOCIATED must not be undefined.

When the program of Figure 10.5 is executed, the following is displayed:

```
The pointer association status of p starts out undefined.
p is currently associated.
p =    1  2  3  4
p is currently disassociated.
x =    1  2  3  4
```

```
PROGRAM demo_ptr_association_status

   INTEGER, DIMENSION(:), POINTER :: p

   INTEGER, DIMENSION(4), TARGET  :: x = (/ 1, 2, 3, 4 /)

   INTRINSIC ASSOCIATED

   PRINT "(A)", " The pointer association status" //  &
               " of p starts out undefined."

   p => x         ! Associate p with x.

   IF (ASSOCIATED (p)) THEN
      PRINT "(A)", " p is currently associated."
      PRINT "(A, 4I3)", " p = ", p
   ELSE
      PRINT "(A)", " p is currently disassociated."
   END IF

   NULLIFY (p)    ! Disassociate p.

   IF (ASSOCIATED (p)) THEN
      PRINT "(A)", " p is currently associated."
   ELSE
      PRINT "(A)", " p is currently disassociated."
   END IF

   PRINT "(A, 4I3)", " x = ", x

END PROGRAM demo_ptr_association_status
```

FIGURE 10.5. Program that illustrates pointer association status.

One must not grow so befuddled as to think that the existence of an undefined target means that the pointer association status of any pointer is undefined. A pointer may be associated with a target whether the target is defined or undefined, and both cases were illustrated in both Figures 10.2 and 10.3. And, by definition, a pointer that is associated does not have an undefined pointer association status.

10.6 DYNAMICALLY ALLOCATED TARGETS

Previous examples have illustrated associating a pointer with a target that is a declared array. However, Fortran 90 also permits the programmer dynamically to create nameless arrays that are pointer targets. The mechanism for accomplishing this is the ALLOCATE statement, which in this usage plays a role that is rather similar to the NEW statement in Pascal and Ada and the malloc() function in C.

An example program that illustrates some of the ideas involved is given in Figure 10.6. Note that two pointers, p_1 and p_2, are declared, and each is capable of pointing to any rank 1 array of type REAL. Now examine the first executable statement in Figure 10.6:

```
ALLOCATE (p_1(5))
```

This allocates storage for a nameless array of five elements. The type and type parameters are the same as those declared for p_1. When the storage for the array is allocated, a description of the array (probably including the the starting address of its storage area) is placed in p_1,

```
PROGRAM demo_allocating_target

   REAL, DIMENSION(:), POINTER :: p_1, p_2

   REAL, DIMENSION(4), TARGET ::                              &
                       x = (/ -1.0, -2.0, -3.0, -4.0 /)

   INTEGER :: i

   ALLOCATE (p_1(5))     ! Allocate storage for nameless array
                         ! of 5 elements and point p_1 to it.

   DO i = 1, 5
      p_1(i) = i         ! Store values in allocated array.
   END DO

   p_2 => p_1            ! Point p_2 to same target that p_1
                         ! points to, which is allocated array.

   p_1 => x              ! Point p_1 to x.

   PRINT "(A, 4F6.2)", " p_1 = ", p_1    ! Display values in x.

   PRINT "(A, 5F6.2)", " p_2 = ", p_2    ! Display values in
                                         ! allocated array.

   DEALLOCATE (p_2)      ! Deallocate storage for nameless
                         ! array and disassociate p_2.

END PROGRAM demo_allocating_target
```

FIGURE 10.6. Program that allocates a target.

and p_1 is said to be associated with (that is, point to) the array. While p_1 remains associated with the array, its elements can be referred to as p_1(1), p_1(2), . . ., p_1(5). This is exploited in the DO loop to store values into the nameless array.

After the END DO comes the pointer assignment statement:

```
p_2 => p_1
```

This is the first example in this tutorial where a pointer appears on both sides of a pointer assignment statement. The meaning of this statement is, "Cause p_2 to hold the same description as p_1." Thus, if p_1 points to a target, p_2 will point to the same target. If p_1 is disassociated, then p_2 will be disassociated. If the association status of p_1 is undefined, then that of p_2 will be undefined. In the program of Figure 10.6, p_1 is pointing to the nameless array created by the ALLOCATE statement, so after the execution of the first pointer assignment statement, p_2 points to that same array.

Now look at the second pointer assignment statement:

```
p_1 => x
```

The array x is a declared target, so this is similar to the pointer assignment statements illustrated in previous sections of this chapter. The association between p_1 and the nameless array is broken, and p_1 becomes an alias for x.

When the PRINT statements of Figure 10.6 are executed, the following is displayed:

```
p_1 =  -1.00 -2.00 -3.00 -4.00
p_2 =   1.00  2.00  3.00  4.00  5.00
```

At the moment that the PRINT statements are executed, p_1 is pointing to x, while p_2 is pointing to the nameless array created by the ALLOCATE statement.

Finally, the DEALLOCATE statement of Figure 10.6 deallocates the storage for the current target of p_2, which is the nameless array created earlier by the ALLOCATE statement. Also, the DEALLOCATE statement disassociates p_2, that is, the description held by p_2 is set in some manner that indicates that it does not point to anything.

Note in Figure 10.6 that, although the ALLOCATE statement associates the pointer p_1 with the array that is created, p_1 is not a permanent name for the array. Only two statements beyond the ALLOCATE statement, the association between p_1 and that array is broken when p_1 is made to point to x by a pointer assignment statement. Also, observe that if the statement

```
p_2 => p_1
```

were omitted, the array created by the ALLOCATE statement would become inaccessible. When using a dynamically allocated target, it is the responsibility of the programmer to assure that at least one pointer is associated with the target throughout the time period that access to the target is required.

Also, note in Figure 10.6 that the name p_2 appears in the DEAL-LOCATE statement that deallocates the storage for the array that was originally associated with p_1 by the ALLOCATE statement. Suppose that the statement

```
p_1 => x
```

were omitted. Then, both p_1 and p_2 would point to the array created by the ALLOCATE statement up until the DEALLOCATE statement is executed. After the DEALLOCATE statement is executed, p_1 would still hold the now-useless address of the deallocated target. The pointer p_1 would be an example of what is known as a "dangling pointer."

In light of the fact that pointers may appear on both sides of a pointer assignment statement, it is appropriate to wonder what meaning might be attached to an (ordinary) assignment statement such as

```
ptr_2 = ptr_1    ! suspicious?
```

where ptr_1 and ptr_2 are both pointers. The answer is that this indicates that the value of the target of ptr_1 is to be assigned to the target of ptr_2, and so attempting such an assignment is an error unless both ptr_1 and ptr_2 are associated with targets and the targets are such that it is permissible to assign one to the other under the rules for ordinary assignment. In practice, it is often undesirable for pointers to be on both sides of an equal sign (=), and such code should be viewed with suspicion.

This section has illustrated the use of the ALLOCATE statement to create a target for a pointer. Recall from Section 4.10 that the ALLOCATE statement may also be used to create an array with the ALLOCATABLE attribute. In some situations, allocatable arrays and pointers to arrays provide competing mechanisms, but pointers to arrays offer much greater flexibility. However, if the capabilities offered by allocatable arrays are sufficient to meet a particular requirement, they are to be preferred in order to avoid the complexities surrounding the use of pointers. It should be mentioned that the POINTER and ALLOCATABLE attributes may not both be specified for the same name.

10.7 SWAPPING POINTERS INSTEAD OF SWAPPING ARRAYS

A commonplace requirement in computing is to exchange two sets of data values. Sorting and iterative algorithms are examples of applications where a large number of such exchanges may be required. When the sets of data values are large, rather than swapping the data themselves, the code for exchanging pointers to the data may be more efficient and easier to understand. This section presents a simple example where pointers to arrays are swapped.

The program of Figure 10.7 declares three array pointers named a, b, and temp. Array sizes for two arrays are then read from user input at the terminal, and the ALLOCATE statement attempts to allocate storage for two nameless arrays. If the allocation is successful, the pointer a is associated with one of the arrays and b will point to the other. If the ALLOCATE statement is unsuccessful, alloc_stat will be nonzero, an error message will be printed, and the STOP statement will cause execution to cease. After the ALLOCATE statement is successfully executed, DO loops are used to store positive values in the target of a and negative values in the target of b. Then the values of the first few elements of the targets of a and b are displayed.

Next in Figure 10.7, the addresses held by a and b are swapped, so that a comes out pointing to what was originally the target of b and b emerges pointing to what was originally the target of a. Note that the arrays themselves are not swapped—only the pointers to the arrays are exchanged. As is usually the case for exchanges in computing, a third variable, temp, is needed to effect the swap.

If the user at the terminal enters

```
3   4
```

when the program of Figure 10.7 is executed, the following is displayed:

```
Before swap:
a =    1.00   2.00   3.00
b =   -1.00  -2.00  -3.00  -4.00

After swap:
a =   -1.00  -2.00  -3.00  -4.00
b =    1.00   2.00   3.00
```

The DEALLOCATE statement of Figure 10.7 deallocates the storage originally created by the ALLOCATE statement, and it also disassociates the pointers a and b. This leaves temp as a dangling pointer, pointing to the deallocated storage area that was the target of b just prior to the execution of the DEALLOCATE statement. The contents of a deallocated storage area may be undefined, but the fact that temp is pointing to such an area is of only academic interest since temp is not used after the swap is completed.

```
PROGRAM demo_swapping_pointers

   REAL, DIMENSION(:), POINTER :: a, b, temp

   INTEGER :: m, n, alloc_stat, i

   INTRINSIC MIN, SIZE

   READ *, m, n
   ALLOCATE (a(m), b(n), STAT = alloc_stat)  ! Allocate tar-
                                             ! gets for a & b.

   IF (alloc_stat /= 0) THEN
      PRINT *, "ALLOCATE failed."
      STOP
   END IF

   DO i = 1, m
      a(i) = i       ! Store positive values in target of a.
   END DO

   DO i = 1, n
      b(i) = -i      ! Store negative values in target of b.
   END DO

   PRINT "(A)", " Before swap:"
   PRINT "(A, 5F6.2)", " a = ",                             &
                       (a(i), i = 1, MIN (5, SIZE (a)))
   PRINT "(A, 5F6.2)", " b = ",                             &
                       (b(i), i = 1, MIN (5, SIZE (b)))

   temp => a;   a => b;   b => temp    ! Swap a and b.

   PRINT "(/A)", " After swap:"
   PRINT "(A, 5F6.2)", " a = ",                             &
                       (a(i), i = 1, MIN (5, SIZE (a)))
   PRINT "(A, 5F6.2)", " b = ",                             &
                       (b(i), i = 1, MIN (5, SIZE (b)))

   DEALLOCATE (a, b)    ! Deallocate targets for a and b.

END PROGRAM demo_swapping_pointers
```

FIGURE 10.7. Program that exchanges pointers to arrays.

10.8 ARRAY POINTER AS A COMPONENT OF A DERIVED TYPE

A collection of data where each record consumes the same amount of storage can usually be stored and manipulated quite nicely in an array. But handling a collection of data where the amount of storage consumed by each record varies widely may present special problems, particularly in the case where only a few of the records consume much more storage than the rest. One approach to dealing with such a collection of data in Fortran 90 is to define a derived type consisting of two components: One component holds the starting address of a storage area containing one record of the data collection, and the other component contains the size of that storage area. The storage area for each record of the data collection is dynamically allocated to be the minimal size needed to contain it. Hence, storage is conserved at the expense of software complexity and, probably, execution efficiency. However, such an approach often makes it possible to provide users with software that can handle records of any length likely to arise in practice.

An example of a program dealing with records of varying length is given in Figure 10.8. Admittedly, the example is somewhat simplified, but it still serves to illustrate many of the ideas surrounding this rather important topic. The program stores and displays up to 1,000 notes, where each note is a string of text of not more that 10,000 characters. For each note, the program allocates just enough storage to store its text minus any trailing blanks that may be present. Presumably, nearly all notes will consist of far fewer than 10,000 characters.

The key to handling the variable-length notes in the program of Figure 10.8 lies in the definition of the derived type note_type, which has a component text that is a pointer to a CHARACTER array with each element containing only one character and a component length that is an INTEGER variable used to store the number of elements in the CHARACTER array. The 1,000-element array note of type note_type is declared, and each element is capable of containing a pointer to a storage location of the text for one note and the number of characters stored at that location. The storage for the text of each note is dynamically allocated after a determination is made of how much storage is needed.

In the program of Figure 10.8, the user inputs the text of each note at the terminal, but this is merely a simplification of the input mechanism in order to move on to the main ideas involved. Each input record is read into the CHARACTER variable named buffer, which is 10,000 bytes long, even though a terminal cannot ordinarily support such long records. In a more realistic setting, the user might be presented with a scrolling window on the computer screen, and everything input into one window might be treated as a single note. The important thing is that all of the text for one note is stored into buffer, with blanks padded

```
PROGRAM array_ptr_as_derived_type_comp

   TYPE :: note_type
      CHARACTER(1), DIMENSION(:), POINTER :: text
      INTEGER                             :: length
   END TYPE note_type

   INTEGER, PARAMETER :: Max_notes        = 1000, &
                         Max_chars_in_note = 10000

   TYPE (note_type), DIMENSION(Max_notes) :: note

   CHARACTER(Max_chars_in_note) :: buffer

   INTEGER :: io_stat, note_count = 0, trimmed_len, char, n

   ! Read and store notes until end of file.
   DO
      READ (*, "(A)", IOSTAT = io_stat) buffer  ! Read 1 note.
      IF (io_stat < 0) EXIT
      trimmed_len = LEN_TRIM (buffer)
      note_count = note_count + 1
      note(note_count)%length = trimmed_len   ! Store length.

      ! Get storage for text of 1 note.
      ALLOCATE (note(note_count)%text(trimmed_len))

      ! Store text for 1 note.
      DO char = 1, trimmed_len
         note(note_count)%text(char) = buffer(char:char)
      END DO
   END DO

   ! Display all notes stored earlier.
   DO n = 1, note_count
      trimmed_len = note(n)%length

      ! Copy text to output buffer.
      DO char = 1, trimmed_len
         buffer(char:char) = note(n)%text(char)
      END DO

      PRINT *, buffer(1:trimmed_len)   ! Display 1 note.

      DEALLOCATE (note(n)%text)   ! Free storage for 1 note.
   END DO

END PROGRAM array_ptr_as_derived_type_comp
```

FIGURE 10.8. An array pointer that is a component of a derived type.

to the right. In Figure 10.8, after each input record is read into buffer, the length of the text string with trailing blanks trimmed off is determined by using the new standard intrinsic function LEN_TRIM.

A count of the number of notes input is kept in the variable named note_count, and the notes are stored in consecutive elements of the array note. As the text for each note is input, its trimmed length is stored in note(note_count)%length. Next, the ALLOCATE statement is used to allocate storage for an array of sufficient size to contain the text with trailing blanks trimmed, and the pointer note(note_count)%text is associated with that array. Finally, the input text is copied, one character at a time, from buffer into the array created by the ALLOCATE statement. In the example program, the user inputs the end-of-file indicator to signal that the input of notes is complete.

Before exiting, the program of Figure 10.8 displays the text of all the notes that were input earlier, simply as an indication that the notes were stored properly. For example, suppose that the following notes are input:

```
Wash car.
Get baby-sitter for Saturday night.
Buy birthday present for Billy.
Do laundry!
```

The program output will merely look like a copy of the input. Observe that after the text of each note is displayed, the DEALLOCATE statement is used to free its storage.

A common mistake by newcomers to Fortran 90 is to think that allocatable arrays could be employed in place of the pointers used in Figure 10.8. The difficulty with this idea is that Fortran 90 rules do not allow the ALLOCATABLE attribute to be specified for a derived-type component. In fact, the only attributes permitted for a derived-type component are those specified for text in Figure 10.8, namely the DIMENSION and POINTER attributes.

10.9 ACHIEVING THE EFFECT OF AN ARRAY OF POINTERS

There are times when it would be convenient to use an array of pointers, but this is not supported directly by Fortran 90. For example, if it is desired to have an array of 1000 elements, each of which is a pointer to a storage area capable of containing a CHARACTER value of length 132, it might seem natural to make the following declaration:

```
CHARACTER(132), DIMENSION(1000), POINTER :: ptr    ! error
```

The 1000 in parentheses following the keyword DIMENSION is not permitted here since the Fortran 90 standard requires that the subscript range for a pointer to an array be specified only by a colon (:) in its declaration, indicating that determination of the bounds will be deferred until execution time. However, this restriction can be worked around by defining a derived type having a single component which is a pointer, and then declaring an array of that derived type. This achieves the effect of an array of pointers, although references to elements of the array are a bit awkward.

The program of Figure 10.9 illustrates the idea described in the preceding paragraph. A derived type named info_ptr_type is defined which

```
PROGRAM demo_array_of_ptrs_workaround

   TYPE :: info_ptr_type
      CHARACTER(132), POINTER :: ptr
   END TYPE info_ptr_type

   TYPE (info_ptr_type), DIMENSION(1000) :: info

   CHARACTER(132) :: buffer
   INTEGER :: io_stat, n = 0, i

   ! Read and store lines of input until end of file.
   DO
      PRINT "(A)", " Enter some text info (EOF to quit):"
      READ (*, "(A)", IOSTAT = io_stat) buffer
      IF (io_stat < 0) EXIT

      n = n + 1                    ! Count lines of input.

      ALLOCATE (info(n)%ptr)    ! Get storage for 1 line.

      info(n)%ptr = buffer      ! Store line in storage gotten.
   END DO

   ! Display input lines stored and free storage.
   DO i = 1, n
      PRINT "(1X, A)", TRIM (info(i)%ptr)    ! Display 1 line.

      DEALLOCATE (info(i)%ptr)    ! Free storage for 1 line.
   END DO

END PROGRAM demo_array_of_ptrs_workaround
```

FIGURE 10.9. Array of derived type whose only component is a pointer.

contains only one component, a pointer to a CHARACTER value of length 132. Then an array named info of 1000 elements of type info_ptr_type is declared. Bear in mind that an element of info cannot hold 132 characters—it can contain only a description of a storage location capable of holding 132 characters. Such storage locations will be dynamically allocated as needed, and their descriptions will be placed in info.

Could decide on map level & new level refinement?

The program of Figure 10.9 prompts the user repeatedly for a line of input until an end-of-file indication is input. Each time a fresh line is read into buffer, the variable n is incremented. Sufficient storage to hold 132 characters is created by the statement

```
ALLOCATE (info(n)%ptr)
```

Also, the ALLOCATE statement associates the pointer info(n)%ptr with the storage that is created. The ordinary assignment statement

```
info(n)%ptr = buffer
```

stores the contents of buffer into the target of the pointer info(n)%ptr, which is the storage just created by the ALLOCATE statement.

After all input lines are read, the program of Figure 10.9 loops over the descriptions stored in the array info and displays each pointer's target. The program simply displays whatever was entered earlier in response to the prompts. Because there is a possibility of trailing blanks wrapping around to the line below, the new standard intrinsic function TRIM is applied to each target for the cosmetic purpose of trimming its trailing blanks before display.

10.10   *A DUMMY ARGUMENT MAY HAVE THE POINTER ATTRIBUTE*

Fortran 90 permits pointers to be used as subprogram arguments, but some special rules apply. Any category of subprogram—external, module, or internal—may have a dummy pointer argument, but an interface body as described in Chapter 13 must be supplied to use an external subprogram with this sort of argument. Of course, an interface body is never provided for either a module or internal subprogram. A dummy pointer argument will be illustrated in this section in a module subprogram.

Figure 10.10a gives an example of a module subroutine named get_data with two dummy arguments, one of which has the POINTER attribute. The first dummy argument, x, is a pointer to a rank 1 array

```
MODULE store_data_in_array

  IMPLICIT NONE

CONTAINS

  SUBROUTINE get_data (x, alloc_stat)

    REAL, DIMENSION(:), POINTER :: x    ! pointer dummy arg
                                        ! (INTENT not
                                        ! permitted)


    INTEGER, INTENT (OUT) :: alloc_stat

    INTEGER :: i, n

    READ *, n
    ALLOCATE (x(n), STAT = alloc_stat)   ! Allocate target
                                         ! array and store
                                         ! its description
                                         ! in x.

    IF (alloc_stat == 0) THEN
      DO i = 1, n
         x(i) = i   ! Store values in array pointed to by x.
      END DO

      ! Return description of target array to caller.

    END IF

  END SUBROUTINE get_data

END MODULE store_data_in_array
```

FIGURE 10.10A. Module subprogram with a pointer dummy argument.

of REAL values of the default kind. The second dummy argument, al-loc_stat, is an ordinary variable of type INTEGER. Note in Figure 10.10a that while INTENT (OUT) is specified for alloc_stat, there is no INTENT at-tribute specified for x. The INTENT attribute for x is omitted because the Fortran 90 standard prohibits an INTENT specification for a dummy argument from having the POINTER attribute. The reason for this rule is that the standard provides no mechanism to distinguish whether an INTENT attribute of IN, OUT, or IN OUT for a pointer refers to the pointer association or to the target. Thus, for a pointer dummy argument, the compiler is unable to check whether values are input, output, or both, and there is no way for a programmer to indicate its intent to other persons reading the code.

In Figure 10.10a, the subroutine get_data reads an INTEGER value n input by the user, creates a nameless rank 1 REAL array of n elements, and loads the array elements with the values 1.0, 2.0, and so on, up through the value REAL (n). If the ALLOCATE statement is successful, a description of the array created is returned to the caller, and the extents of that array can be thought of as being part of this description. In addition to returning the description contained in x, get_stat returns the value of alloc_stat, which is zero for a successful allocation. If the ALLOCATE statement fails, the association status of the pointer x remains undefined, and the value of alloc_stat will be an implementation-dependent, positive value.

Some readers might think that it would be possible to use an allocatable array in the subroutine of Figure 10.10a instead of the pointer. However, the Fortran 90 standard forbids the specification of the ALLOCATABLE attribute for a dummy argument. Recall that Section 10.8 gave another example of a situation in which the ALLOCATABLE attribute is not permitted, and a third example will be presented in Section 10.12.

Figure 10.10b gives a main program that calls the subroutine of Figure 10.10a. The main program gains access to the module subroutine get_data by using the module that contains it. The new standard requires that if a dummy argument has the POINTER attribute, then its corresponding actual argument must also be a pointer. Note in Figure 10.10b that the POINTER attribute is specified for y, the actual argument corresponding to the pointer dummy argument x in Figure 10.10a.

If the ALLOCATE statement of Figure 10.10a is successful, alloc_stat is zero and the description of the array created is held by the pointer y in Figure 10.10b upon return from the call to get_data. The DO loop of Figure 10.10b then displays the value of each element of that array. If the user inputs the value 5 at the terminal when the complete program consisting of the main program of Figure 10.10b and the module of Figure 10.10a is executed, the following is displayed:

```
1.000
2.000
3.000
4.000
5.000
```

Observe in Figure 10.10b that the standard intrinsic function SIZE is applied to the actual argument y to determine the number of elements in the array pointed to by x in Figure 10.10a. This works because the description of the target array held by the actual argument y in the

```
PROGRAM demo_ptr_dummy_arg

   USE store_data_in_array    ! Access get_data.

   IMPLICIT NONE

   REAL, DIMENSION(:), POINTER :: y    ! Actual arg corre-
                                       ! sponding to POINTER
                                       ! dummy arg must have
                                       ! POINTER attribute.
   INTEGER :: i, alloc_stat

   CALL get_data (y, alloc_stat)   ! Call sub having
                                   ! ptr dummy arg.

   IF (alloc_stat == 0) THEN

      ! y points to target array allocated in get_data.

      DO i = 1, SIZE (y)      ! y also holds extents of target.
         PRINT "(F8.3)", y(i)
      END DO

      DEALLOCATE (y)    ! Free storage allocated in get_data.

   ELSE
      PRINT *, "Error in attempting to allocate storage."
   END IF

END PROGRAM demo_ptr_dummy_arg
```

FIGURE 10.10B. Main program that calls subroutine of Figure 10.10a.

main program is the same as that held by the dummy argument x in the module subroutine. Finally, note in Figure 10.10b that the storage allocated in the subroutine is freed by the DEALLOCATE statement in the main program.

10.11 A DUMMY ARGUMENT MAY HAVE THE TARGET ATTRIBUTE

It sometimes happens that a pointer in a subprogram points to a variable serving as a dummy argument, in which case conformance with

the Fortran 90 standard requires that the TARGET attribute be specified for the dummy argument. An example of such a subprogram is the
module subroutine display_array_with_bigger_sum of Figure 10.11a. Two
rank 1 arrays, x1 and x2, with sizes n1 and n2, respectively, are input
to the subroutine. The sum of the elements is determined for each array, using the standard intrinsic function SUM. The values are displayed
for the array whose elements have the larger sum. To avoid two separate display loops, it is convenient to alias a pointer p to whichever of
the two arrays has the bigger sum of its elements. Since p will point
to one of x1 or x2, it is necessary to specify the TARGET attribute for

```
MODULE find_sum_and_display_array

CONTAINS

   SUBROUTINE display_array_with_bigger_sum (n1, x1, n2, x2)

      ! Declarations for dummy args with TARGET attribute:
      REAL, DIMENSION(n1), TARGET, INTENT (IN) :: x1
      REAL, DIMENSION(n2), TARGET, INTENT (IN) :: x2

      INTEGER, INTENT (IN) :: n1, n2

      REAL, DIMENSION(:), POINTER :: p    ! local ptr
      INTEGER :: i

      IF (SUM (x1) > SUM (x2)) THEN

         p => x1    ! Make p point to 1st TARGET dummy arg.

      ELSE

         p => x2    ! Make p point to 2nd TARGET dummy arg.

      END IF

      DO i = 1, SIZE (p)          ! p is an alias for
         PRINT "(F8.3)", p(i)     ! one of x1 or x2.
      END DO

   END SUBROUTINE display_array_with_bigger_sum

END MODULE find_sum_and_display_array
```

FIGURE 10.11A. Subprogram with TARGET dummy argument.

```
PROGRAM demo_target_dummy_args

    USE find_sum_and_display_array

    REAL, DIMENSION(4) :: y1 = (/ 6.0, 7.0, 8.0, 9.0 /)
    REAL, DIMENSION(5) :: y2 = (/ 1.0, 2.0, 3.0, 4.0, 5.0 /)

    ! Call subroutine having dummy arg with TARGET attribute.
    CALL display_array_with_bigger_sum (4, y1, 5, y2)

END PROGRAM demo_target_dummy_args
```

FIGURE 10.11B.   Main program that calls subroutine of Figure 10.11a.

these arrays, both of which are dummy arguments. Observe in Figure 10.11a that the INTENT attribute is specified for both x1 and x2, and so the rule, mentioned in the preceding section, of not specifying an intent for pointer dummy arguments does not apply to target dummy arguments.

Figure 10.11b gives a main program that calls the module subroutine of Figure 10.11a. In order to be able to access the subroutine, the main program uses the module containing it. Two rank 1 arrays, y1 and y2, of sizes 4 and 5, respectively, are passed to the subroutine. The fact that a dummy argument has the TARGET attribute imposes no special requirements on its corresponding actual argument.

ie. you don't have to start off calling it a target.

When the complete program consisting of the main program of Figure 10.11b and the module of Figure 10.11a is executed, the following is displayed:

```
6.000
7.000
8.000
9.000
```

This section illustrates a module subprogram having a dummy argument with the TARGET attribute, but such a dummy argument may appear in an internal or external subprogram as well. However, the Fortran 90 standard makes the use of an interface body mandatory for an external subprogram having a dummy argument with the TARGET attribute. But in some implementations, enforcement of this requirement may be relaxed, at least for some compiler options.

10.12 *A FUNCTION MAY RETURN A RESULT THAT IS A POINTER*

In Fortran 90, a function may return a result that is a pointer, and this is illustrated in the program of Figure 10.12 by the internal function named char_1_array. The pointer returned by char_1_array points to a nameless rank 1 array for which storage is dynamically allocated. Each element of the nameless array is of type CHARACTER and has length 1.

The internal function char_1_array in Figure 10.12 employs the new standard intrinsic function LEN_TRIM to determine what the length of the input argument string would be if its trailing blanks were trimmed off. Next, it uses the ALLOCATE statement to create storage for a nameless array capable of holding CHARACTER(1) values. The DO loop inside the internal function then copies the input string, minus any trailing blanks, into the newly created storage area.

In the body of the main program in Figure 10.12, internal function char_1_array is invoked in the pointer assignment statement

```
ptr => char_1_array ("ABCD      ")
```

Here the argument to char_1_array consists of four nonblank characters followed by several trailing blanks, so the variable trimmed_len in the internal function is assigned the value of 4. Thus, a nameless array of four elements is created by the ALLOCATE statement, and a description of that array is placed in p, the result variable in char_1_array. Hence, execution of the pointer assignment statement causes that description to be copied to ptr, so ptr then points to the storage area that was dynamically allocated in the function.

When the DO loop in the body of the main program in Figure 10.12 is executed, the characters stored in the target of ptr are displayed as follows:

```
1 A
2 B
3 C
4 D
```

Some readers might think that an allocatable array could be used in this example in place of the pointer to the dynamically allocated storage. However, this is not the case since the Fortran 90 standard does not permit the ALLOCATABLE attribute to be specified for a function result variable.

This section illustrates an internal function whose result is a pointer, but the result of a module or external function can be a pointer as well. Of course, if such a function were in a module, it could only be invoked in a routine having access to the module (or from another

```
PROGRAM demo_ptr_func_result

   CHARACTER(1), DIMENSION(:), POINTER :: ptr

   INTEGER :: i

   ptr => char_1_array ("ABCD       ")  ! Invoke internal func
                                        ! char_1_array and
                                        ! store description
                                        ! returned in ptr.

   DO i = 1, SIZE (ptr)   ! Display chars contained in
      PRINT *, i, ptr(i)  ! storage allocated in func.
   END DO

CONTAINS

   FUNCTION char_1_array (string) RESULT (p)

      CHARACTER(1), DIMENSION(:), POINTER :: p  ! Func result
                                                ! is a ptr.

      CHARACTER(*), INTENT (IN) :: string

      INTEGER :: trimmed_len
      INTEGER :: j

      trimmed_len = LEN_TRIM (string)  ! Find length of input
                                       ! arg with trailing
                                       ! blanks trimmed off.

      ALLOCATE (p(trimmed_len))   ! Create nameless array &
                                  ! associate p with it.

      DO j = 1, trimmed_len  ! Copy chars from input arg to
         p(j) = string(j:j)  ! nameless array just created.
      END DO

   END FUNCTION char_1_array

END PROGRAM demo_ptr_func_result
```

FIGURE 10.12. Example of internal function returning a pointer result.

subprogram contained within the same module). Also, if a function returning a pointer result is defined by an external function subprogram, the Fortran 90 standard requires an invoking routine to supply an interface body.

CHAPTER 11

POINTERS TO STRUCTURES

11.1 INTRODUCTION TO POINTERS TO STRUCTURES

Chapter 10 gave several examples of pointers to variables of intrinsic types, and this chapter will discuss pointers to variables of derived types. A representative example of a declaration of a pointer to a structure is

```
TYPE (employee_type), POINTER :: ptr
```

This specifies that ptr is a pointer that is capable of pointing to any scalar variable of type employee_type. However, ptr can never point to a variable of another derived type, and of course, it cannot point to a variable of any intrinsic type. Furthermore, ptr can never point to any array, not even to an array of type employee_type. This is because a Fortran 90 pointer is permitted to point only to a data object of a particular rank, and ptr can point only to a data object of rank 0 (that is, to a scalar) as indicated by the absence of array extent specifications in its declaration.

As is the case for a pointer to a variable of an intrinsic type, the target of a pointer to a variable of a derived type may be either a storage area associated with a name declared by the programmer or a nameless storage area created by executing an ALLOCATE statement. The Fortran 90 standard requirement that the TARGET attribute must be specified for a variable name that is pointed to applies to a variable of a derived type as well as to a variable of an intrinsic type. The use of the ALLOCATE statement for variables of derived types is the same as for variables of intrinsic types. For example, if ptr is declared as above, then executing the statement

```
ALLOCATE (ptr)
```

dynamically creates a nameless storage area that is capable of containing the values of a structure of type employee_type, and ptr holds a description of that storage area. The nature and content of that description are not dictated by the Fortran 90 standard, but it probably does no harm to think of the description as including the starting address of the storage area, its size, the data types and type parameters of the structure components that can be stored there, and so on.

Although on the surface there is not much difference between a pointer to a variable of a derived type and a pointer to a variable of an intrinsic type, there is a special feature of the former that provides the Fortran 90 programmer with the capability of constructing and manipulating linked lists, such as queues and stacks, as well as trees. This special feature is that a derived type may be defined with a component that is a pointer to a variable of the derived type being defined. For example:

```
TYPE :: empl_node_type
    CHARACTER(40)                          :: empl_name
    INTEGER                                :: empl_number
    REAL                                   :: salary
    TYPE (empl_node_type), POINTER :: next_empl
END TYPE  empl_node_type
```

Note that derived type empl_node_type is defined as having a component next_empl, which is a pointer to a variable of type empl_node_type. The big idea here, which is depicted conceptually in Figure 11.1, is a familiar one to readers who know C, Pascal, or Ada, but it may seem foreign to those readers lacking background in a language supporting both structures and pointers. The approach is to allocate storage dynamically as the need arises for a nameless structure that will contain the data for one employee. Each box in Figure 11.1 represents a nameless structure of type empl_node_type. The pointer component of each structure, indicated below the dashed line in each box, is utilized to hold the description of the storage area of the next structure in the sequence as indicated by the arrows. Thus, part of each structure is used to point to the next structure in the sequence. Observe that it is possible for the programmer to retrieve information about a particular employee by beginning at the first nameless structure, whose description is symbol-

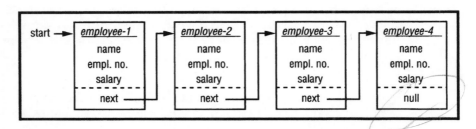

FIGURE 11.1.   Conceptual view of a linked list of four employee records.

ized by the word start in Figure 11.1, and using the sequence of pointers to traverse the list. The word null is used in Figure 11.1 to indicate which structure is last in the sequence. However, it should be mentioned that neither the word start nor the word null has special meaning in standard Fortran 90—their use in Figure 11.1 is intended merely to help the reader grasp the concepts more readily.

The linked list of employee records depicted in Figure 11.1 is an elementary example of how structures and pointers can be employed to create linked data structures. A linked data structure is a collection of individual elements, each of which is a nameless storage area that is dynamically allocated. The dynamically allocated storage areas are linked to one another by pointers, which are contained within the storage areas themselves. There is no single variable name that refers to the entire linked data structure—each element is processed individually. An important property of a linked data structure is that the number of elements may vary as program execution progresses. The number of elements in such a data structure is limited only by the amount of computer storage available. Another characteristic of linked data structures is that it is relatively easy and efficient to insert or remove elements anywhere in the data structure. Thus, linked data structures provide the Fortran 90 programmer with enormous flexibility, but the price of this flexibility is program complexity. Hence, linked data structures should be avoided except for those situations in which simpler data structures, such as arrays, are inadequate.

The topic of data structures is large and complex, and the material in this chapter is no more that an introductory description of how selected data structures might be implemented in Fortran 90. Short examples will be given which present some of the aspects of the linear linked lists known as "queues" and "stacks." Also, an example of a two-dimensional data structure called the "binary tree" will be presented. For those readers whose applications do not require the use of the rather sophisticated capabilities provided by linked data structures, it is perhaps sufficient to recognize that Fortran 90's ability to deal with such data structures compares favorably with that of most other competitive languages.

11.2 POINTER TO A DECLARED STRUCTURE

As with any Fortran 90 pointer, a pointer to a structure may point either to a storage area associated with a name declared by the programmer or to a nameless storage area created by the execution of an ALLOCATE statement. This section will present a program that illustrates the use of a pointer to a declared structure. The more important case of pointers

to nameless dynamically allocated structures will then be discussed for
the remainder of the chapter.

As with the intrinsic types, the Fortran 90 standard requires that
if a structure that is pointed to is any part of a declared data object,
then the TARGET attribute must be specified for that data object. This
is illustrated by the program of Figure 11.2, where two structures, msr_1
and msr_2, are declared to be of the derived type measurement_type. It is
desired that msr_1 and msr_2 be targets of a pointer, and so the TARGET
attribute is specified for both names. Also, the variable ptr is declared
as a pointer to any storage area, whether declared or dynamically al-

```
PROGRAM struct_ptr_to_declared_target

   TYPE :: measurement_type
      INTEGER :: sensor_id
      REAL    :: voltage
   END TYPE measurement_type

   TYPE (measurement_type), TARGET  :: msr_1, msr_2
   TYPE (measurement_type), POINTER :: ptr

   msr_1 = measurement_type (123, 4.5)

   ptr => msr_1    ! Make ptr an alias for msr_1.

   PRINT "(A, I3, A, F3.1)",                                    &
                     " msr_1%sensor_id = ", msr_1%sensor_id, &
                     " msr_1%voltage = ",   msr_1%voltage

   PRINT "(A, I3, A, F3.1)",                                    &
                     "   ptr%sensor_id = ",   ptr%sensor_id, &
                     "   ptr%voltage = ",     ptr%voltage

   PRINT "(' msr_1 = ', 10X, I3, 17X, F3.1)", msr_1
   PRINT "('   ptr = ', 10X, I3, 17X, F3.1)",   ptr

   ptr => msr_2    ! Change ptr to alias msr_2.

   msr_2 = measurement_type (678, 9.0)

   PRINT "(/'   ptr = ', 10X, I3, 17X, F3.1)", ptr

END PROGRAM struct_ptr_to_declared_target
```

FIGURE 11.2. Program illustrating a pointer to declared structures.

located, set up to contain values of a structure of type measurement_ type.

In Figure 11.2, both components of the structure named msr_1 are assigned values using a structure constructor. Next, the pointer assignment statement

```
ptr => msr_1
```

causes ptr to hold the description of msr_1, and ptr is said to point to msr_1, that is, ptr is associated with msr_1. Then, the first four PRINT statements are executed. Next, the pointer assignment statement

```
ptr => msr_2
```

breaks the association between ptr and msr_1 and associates ptr with msr_2. Observe that the fact that the value of msr_2 is undefined at the moment it appears on the right-hand side of the pointer assignment statement causes no problems. The declared structure msr_2 is assigned a value using a structure constructor in the following statement, and ptr is no longer pointing to a storage area whose contents are unpredictable. Finally, the fifth and last PRINT statement is executed.

When the program of Figure 11.2 is executed, the following is displayed:

```
msr_1%sensor_id = 123 msr_1%voltage = 4.5
   ptr%sensor_id = 123    ptr%voltage = 4.5
msr_1 =            123               4.5
  ptr =            123               4.5

  ptr =            678               9.0
```

The display shows that ptr is treated as an alias for msr_1 when the second and fourth PRINT statements are executed and as an alias for msr_2 when the final PRINT statement is executed.

11.3 POINTER TO A DYNAMICALLY ALLOCATED STRUCTURE

Although a Fortran 90 pointer may point to a declared structure as shown in the preceding section, it is more common in practice that a target structure be a nameless storage area created by an ALLOCATE statement. In general, the considerations surrounding the dynamic allocation of structures are the same as those discussed for the dynamic allocation of arrays in Section 10.6. This section will discuss some of the elementary aspects of pointers to dynamically allocated structures, and the remainder of the chapter will show how these ideas are used in constructing and manipulating linked data structures.

The program of Figure 11.3 illustrates some of the fundamentals of using pointers to dynamically allocated structures. Note that two pointers, ptr_1 and ptr_2, are declared, and each is capable of pointing to a structure of derived type part_type. Now, when the statement

```
PROGRAM struct_ptr_to_allocated_target

   TYPE :: part_type
      CHARACTER(10) :: description
      INTEGER       :: part_number
   END TYPE part_type

   TYPE (part_type), POINTER :: ptr_1, ptr_2

   ALLOCATE (ptr_1)    ! Create storage for structure of type
                       ! part_type and associate ptr_1 with it.

   ptr_1%description = "gizmo"    ! Store values in
   ptr_1%part_number = 1234       ! structure just created.

   PRINT "(2A, I6)", " ptr_1 = ", ptr_1    ! Display values
                                           ! stored in struc-
                                           ! ture just created.

   ptr_2 => ptr_1    ! Associate ptr_2 with ptr_1's target,
                     ! which is created structure.

   NULLIFY (ptr_1)    ! Disassociate ptr_1.

   IF (.NOT. ASSOCIATED (ptr_1)) THEN
      PRINT "(A)", " ptr_1 is disassociated."
   END IF

   PRINT "(2A, I6)", " ptr_2 = ", ptr_2    ! Display values
                                           ! stored in struc-
                                           ! ture created.

   DEALLOCATE (ptr_2)    ! Free storage for created structure
                         ! and disassociate ptr_2.

END PROGRAM struct_ptr_to_allocated_target
```

FIGURE 11.3. Program illustrating pointers to an allocated structure.

```
ALLOCATE (ptr_1)
```

is executed, a nameless storage area will be created which is capable of containing values for one structure of type part_type, and ptr_1 will hold the description of that storage area. The values in the newly allocated structure may be undefined according to the Fortran 90 standard, although some implementations may supply default values, such as zeros. In the program of Figure 11.3, values are stored in the dynamically allocated structure by the assignment statements

```
ptr_1%description = "gizmo"
ptr_1%part_number = 1234
```

Observe that the effect of these two statements could be achieved by the single statement

```
ptr_1 = part_type ("gizmo", 1234)
```

The pointer assignment statement

```
ptr_2 => ptr_1
```

causes ptr_2 to hold the same description as ptr_1. Thus, if ptr_1 points to a target, ptr_2 will point to that target; if ptr_1 is disassociated, then ptr_2 will be disassociated; and if the association status of ptr_1 is undefined, the association status of ptr_2 will be undefined. In the program of Figure 11.3, ptr_1 is associated with the nameless structure created by the ALLOCATE statement, so the pointer assignment statement associates ptr_2 with that same target. Thus, immediately after the execution of the pointer assignment statement, the programmer could refer to the nameless structure by either of the names ptr_1 or ptr_2.

The statement

```
NULLIFY (ptr_1)
```

causes ptr_1 to hold a description indicating that it has no current target, and ptr_1 is said to be disassociated. But even though ptr_1 is not pointing to any target, its association status is defined and may be tested using the intrinsic function ASSOCIATED as is done in Figure 11.3. Of course, disassociating the pointer ptr_1 from the dynamically allocated structure has no effect on the structure itself, and it also has no effect on the association of ptr_2 with the structure.

When the program of Figure 11.3 is executed, the following is displayed:

```
ptr_1 = gizmo        1234
ptr_1 is disassociated.
ptr_2 = gizmo        1234
```

Observe that between the ALLOCATE and NULLIFY statements, ptr_1 may be treated as if it were the name of the structure, and between the pointer assignment statement and the DEALLOCATE statement, ptr_2 may be treated as if it were the name of the structure. The DEALLOCATE statement not only frees the storage for the dynamically allocated structure, but it also causes ptr_2 to be disassociated.

When working with code that uses pointers to dynamically allocated targets, it is important to recognize that the programmer must be able to identify which pointers are associated with which targets at any given moment during program execution. Observe that a pointer can become associated with a dynamically allocated target only through the execution of either an ALLOCATE or a pointer assignment statement, and a pointer can become disassociated only through the execution of either a DEALLOCATE or a NULLIFY statement. Much of the difficulty that programmers have in correctly using pointers revolves around the following human failing: Since a dynamically allocated storage area can be accessed only by using the name of some pointer, it is all too easy to confuse a pointer, which is only a description of a target, with the nameless storage area that constitutes the target itself.

11.4 INTRODUCTION TO THE QUEUE

Pointers to dynamically allocated structures provide the programmer with almost unlimited flexibility in creating data structures. The simplest and most important examples of such data structures are known as "linked lists." A **linked list** is an ordered collection of data objects, each of the same type, but not necessarily stored contiguously. Each data object in a linked list is called a **node**, and a node consists of two parts: One part is some data of interest (or perhaps a pointer to some data of interest) and the other part, in the most elementary case, is a pointer to the next node in the list. This section will introduce a particular form of linked list known as the **queue**, in which new nodes are added only to the end of the list while old nodes are deleted only from the beginning of the list. In this section, a short main program in which an example queue is constructed will be presented. The following section will continue the discussion of queues, showing how the various queue manipulations may be broken out into external subprograms.

A familiar situation in the real world involving a queue is a ticket line at a movie theater. People join the queue at the back, buy tickets at the front, and exit the queue. Tickets are sold on a first come, first served basis. A queue in the software world is rather similar, if somewhat idealized. Data items are placed at the rear of the queue to await processing. If the queue is not empty, the item at the front of the queue is processed and removed from the queue. Thus, items are removed from a queue in the same order in which they were added, so a queue operates on a first-in-first-out (FIFO) basis.

Figure 11.4 gives a conceptual representation of a queue consisting of four nodes. Each node is made up of two parts: a data object of interest and a pointer to the next node in the queue. Of course, there is no successor to the last node at the rear of the queue, so what would otherwise be its pointer to the next node is disassociated to indicate end of queue. A pointer front is used to keep track of the location of the first node in the queue. For example, when *node-1* in Figure 11.4 is removed, front will be changed to point to *node-2*. Also, a pointer rear is used to keep track of the location of the last node in the queue. For example, when another node is added after *node-4* in Figure 11.4, rear will be changed to point to the location of the added node. Observe that when the queue consists of only a single node, both pointers front and rear must point to the same node. Also, the queue may be empty, and a sensible way of treating this situation is to disassociate the pointers front and rear.

Figure 11.5 gives the listing for a Fortran 90 program that constructs a queue as a linked list along the lines discussed in the preceding paragraph. The user at the terminal inputs a sequence of character values, one line at a time. Each line of input is limited to 20 characters or less. The end of the sequence is indicated by inputting end of file. The program of Figure 11.5 dynamically allocates one node for each line of user input and stores that input employing the scheme depicted in Figure 11.4. The queue starts out empty, and for each line of input, a new node is added at the end of the queue. After the user inputs an end-of-file indicator, the program of Figure 11.5 demonstrates that the queue has been correctly constructed by traversing the queue from front to rear, displaying the data stored at each node. The output of the program simply repeats the list of data values previously entered by the user. For simplicity, the program of Figure 11.5 does not remove any nodes from the queue—illustration of this operation will be deferred until the next section.

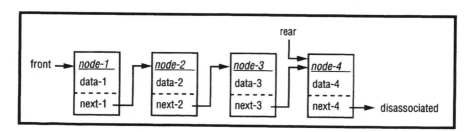

FIGURE 11.4. Conceptual view of a queue consisting of four nodes.

```
PROGRAM demo_queue
   TYPE :: node_type
      CHARACTER(20)                :: data
      TYPE (node_type), POINTER :: next    ! ptr to next
                                           ! node in queue
   END TYPE node_type
   TYPE (node_type), POINTER :: front, rear  ! ptrs to first
                                             ! and last nodes
                                             ! in queue
   TYPE (node_type), POINTER :: node_ptr   ! ptr to arbitrary
                                           ! node in queue
   CHARACTER(20) :: buffer
   INTEGER :: io_stat

   NULLIFY (front, rear)   ! Set indicators for queue empty.

   ! Read data input at terminal & store in FIFO linked list.
   DO
      READ (*, "(A)", IOSTAT = io_stat) buffer
      IF (io_stat < 0) EXIT
      ! Test whether queue is currently empty or not.
      IF (.NOT. ASSOCIATED (front)) THEN
         ! Queue is empty -- this will be only node in queue.
         ALLOCATE (front)   ! Create storage for only node
                            ! & cause front to point to it.
         rear => front  ! Cause rear to point to only node.
      ELSE
         ! Queue not empty -- this will be the new last node.
         ALLOCATE (rear%next)  ! Create storage for new last
                               ! node & cause old last node's
                               ! next to point to it.
         rear => rear%next   ! Cause rear to point
                             ! to new last node.
      END IF
      rear%data = buffer     ! Store data in last node.
      NULLIFY (rear%next)    ! Set indicator that this
                             ! is last node in queue.
   END DO

   ! Traverse queue, displaying data at each node.
   node_ptr => front    ! Make node_ptr point to first node.
   DO WHILE (ASSOCIATED (node_ptr))
      PRINT *, node_ptr%data
      node_ptr => node_ptr%next   ! Make node_ptr
                                  ! point to next node.
   END DO
END PROGRAM demo_queue
```

FIGURE 11.5. Program illustrating a queue constructed as a linked list.

Pay particular attention in Figure 11.5 to the definition of the derived type node_type, which has two components, data and next. Observe that the component next is a pointer to a structure of type node_type, so the derived-type definition contains a component definition, which in turn references the derived-type definition. This will no doubt seem strange to those readers unaccustomed to recursive definitions, but it is the usual idiom for dealing with linked data structures. In concept, the Fortran 90 approach here is the same as that used in C, Pascal, Ada, and other popular languages. In any event, note that the definition of node_type in Figure 11.5 corresponds to the conceptual representation of Figure 11.4, where a component of each node is a pointer to another node.

Observe in Figure 11.5 that front and rear are declared as pointers to structures of type node_type, and these pointers are used to keep track of the first and last nodes, respectively, in the queue. In the first executable statement of the program, front and rear are disassociated using the NULLIFY statement to indicate that the queue is empty. Actually, it turns out that the code will still work if the pointer association status of rear is left undefined at this stage of the program. However, as the code of Figure 11.5 is written, it is crucial that front be disassociated before its first use as the argument of the intrinsic function ASSOCIATED.

The queue is built up during execution of the first DO construct in Figure 11.5. After each value is read into the CHARACTER variable buffer, a nameless structure of type node_type to hold that value is created using one of the two ALLOCATE statements. In the IF construct, the two statements above the ELSE statement are executed if this will be the first node added to the queue, while the two statements below the ELSE are executed for each of the remaining nodes. In dealing with a linked list, there are often special considerations surrounding the cases where the list consists of one or zero nodes.

When a queue is not empty and a new node is added, only the end of the queue needs to be updated—the front is unaffected. For a new arrival joining a nonempty queue, the pointer portion of the old last node must point to the new node that is created to accommodate the new arrival, and this is reflected in Figure 11.5 by the ALLOCATE statement following the ELSE. Also, the pointer rear must point to the newly created node as well, and this is handled by the pointer assignment statement:

```
rear => rear%next
```

On the other hand, when the first node is added to a previously empty queue, the front pointer must point to that node, and this is accomplished in Figure 11.5 by the ALLOCATE statement appearing before the ELSE statement. Also, after the first node is added and before a second node is added, the queue will consist of only one node, and so the pointer rear must also point to that node. In Figure 11.5, this is handled by the pointer assignment statement

```
rear => front
```

For any new last node added to the queue, whether the only node or not, the newly arrived data in buffer must be placed in the data portion of the node. This is accomplished in Figure 11.5 with the ordinary assignment statement

```
rear%data = buffer
```

Also, the pointer portion of any new last node, whether the only node or not, must be disassociated to indicate that the node has no successor. This is done in Figure 11.5 by the statement

```
NULLIFY (rear%data)
```

To demonstrate that the queue has been correctly constructed, the program of Figure 11.5 employs the DO WHILE construct to display the sequence of data values stored in the nodes. The variable node_ptr is used to point to each node in the queue in order, starting with the first node and sequentially stepping to the next node until the data portion of the last node has been displayed. The last node in the queue is distinguished by the property that its next pointer is disassociated.

Incidentally, observe that only the first and last elements in a queue are readily accessible; there is no easy way to access an arbitrary element. For example, if required to retrieve (say) the fifth data value in a queue, the only way to do this is to start at the front and move from node to node until the fifth node is reached. Contrast this with retrieving the fifth element of an array a, where all that is required is to reference a(5).

11.5 QUEUE OPERATIONS BROKEN OUT INTO SUBPROGRAMS

The preceding section discussed the main ideas surrounding the implementation of a queue as a linked list, and a simple main program was presented that illustrated how to add nodes to the end of a queue. In addition to the appending of nodes, there are a variety of other operations that may be performed on a queue, including removing nodes from the front of a queue and counting the number of elements in a queue. Also, it is usually desirable to isolate each queue operation in a subprogram and to provide the user with an interface that makes the collection of definitions and subprograms dealing with queues easy to use. This section will illustrate how queue operations can be broken out into external subprograms.[1]

The derived-type definition for node_type will be the same as it was in Figure 11.5, but since node_type will be needed in several different scoping units, its definition will be placed in a module as was recommended in Section 7.3. The module containing the definition of node_type is listed in Figure 11.6a. Also, to allow for the possibility that the user of the queue procedures might need to maintain more than one queue at the same time, a derived type queue_type will be defined. Then for each desired queue, the user will declare a variable of type queue_type. Now a queue is fully characterized by a description of each node, together with pointers to the front and rear nodes, and so the derived-type definition queue_type in Figure 11.6b suffices. Note in Figure 11.6b that the definition of queue_type is placed in a module that uses the module of Figure 11.6a to access the definition of node_type.

With the type definitions of Figures 11.6a and 11.6b established, a user who needs two queues can declare them simply by coding something like

```
TYPE (queue_type) :: q_1, q_2
```

However, to ensure that each queue starts off with a verifiable status of empty, the user will be required to initialize each queue before attempting any other operations on that queue. A subroutine init_queue will be provided for this purpose. For example, to initialize queues q_1 and q_2, the user will code

```
MODULE node_type_def

   IMPLICIT NONE

   TYPE :: node_type
      CHARACTER(20)                  :: data
      TYPE (node_type), POINTER  :: next    ! ptr to successor
                                            ! node in queue
   END TYPE node_type

END MODULE node_type_def
```

FIGURE 11.6A. Module containing definition of derived type node_type.

---

[1] The queue implementation presented in this section and the stack implementation given in the next section are influenced by *Data Structures: An Advanced Approach Using C* by J. Esakov and T. Weiss (Prentice Hall, Englewood Cliffs, NJ, 1989).

```
MODULE queue_type_def

   USE node_type_def        ! Access definition of node_type.

   IMPLICIT NONE

   TYPE :: queue_type
      TYPE (node_type), POINTER :: front    ! ptr to 1st node
      TYPE (node_type), POINTER :: rear     ! ptr to last node
   END TYPE queue_type

END MODULE queue_type_def
```

FIGURE 11.6B. Module containing definition of type queue_type.

```
CALL init_queue (q_1)
CALL init_queue (q_2)
```

After a queue is initialized, the user will then be able to store the data in a variable named buffer in a new node at the end of queue q_1 simply by coding something like

```
CALL put_in_rear (q_1, buffer)
```

Similarly, the user can store the data in buffer in a new node at the end of queue q_2 by coding

```
CALL put_in_rear (q_2, buffer)
```

Of course, a detailed knowledge of how the queue procedures are implemented will not be required in order to use them; the only thing that a user will have to know is how to interface with the procedures.

The listing for the subroutine init_queue, which must be called to initialize a new queue, is shown in Figure 11.6c. All init_queue does is to disassociate the pointers to the front and rear of the queue. The only reason that the subroutine is needed is to guarantee that the association status of each of these pointers is defined so that they can safely be used as arguments of the intrinsic function ASSOCIATED in other queue procedures.

Figure 11.6d gives the listing for the subroutine put_in_rear, which creates a new node at the rear of a queue and stores data in that node. The logic employed in put_in_rear is that described in Section 11.4 for constructing a queue, and the code in Figure 11.6d parallels that inside the first DO construct of Figure 11.5. As before, the first node added to an empty queue is treated differently from any other node added to a queue. Note that before calling put_in_rear to insert the first node in a

```
SUBROUTINE init_queue (q)

   USE queue_type_def

   IMPLICIT NONE

   TYPE (queue_type), INTENT (OUT) :: q

   NULLIFY (q%front, q%rear)    ! Disassociate pointers to
                                ! front and rear of queue.

END SUBROUTINE init_queue
```

FIGURE 11.6c. Subroutine to initialize a queue.

```
SUBROUTINE put_in_rear (q, buffer)

   USE queue_type_def

   IMPLICIT NONE

   TYPE (queue_type), INTENT (IN OUT) :: q
   CHARACTER(*),       INTENT (IN)     :: buffer

   IF (.NOT. ASSOCIATED (q%front)) THEN

      ALLOCATE (q%front)        ! This is 1st node in queue.
      q%rear => q%front

   ELSE

      ALLOCATE (q%rear%next)    ! new last node in queue
      q%rear => q%rear%next

   END IF

   q%rear%data = buffer        ! Store data in this node.

   NULLIFY (q%rear%next)        ! This node has no successor.

END SUBROUTINE put_in_rear
```

FIGURE 11.6d. Subroutine to append a node to a queue.

new queue, the user must call the subroutine init_queue of Figure 11.6c; otherwise the test in Figure 11.6d of whether or not the pointer q%front is associated is unreliable according to the Fortran 90 standard.

At various times during the execution of a program, a user might want to know the number of elements currently in a queue. The function subprogram count_elements of Figure 11.6e can be invoked to provide this information. The function determines the length of the queue by starting at the front and progressing to the rear, counting each node visited along the way. The logic in Figure 11.6e parallels that of the display loop in Figure 11.5, except that the variable count is incremented each time through the loop in the function count_elements, instead of executing a PRINT statement as is done in Figure 11.5.

Another operation that a user would certainly desire, but which was not illustrated in Section 11.4, is to delete the node at the front of a queue. The subroutine take_from_front in Figure 11.6f performs this operation. The data value stored in the first node in the queue is returned to the caller in the CHARACTER variable buffer and the storage for that node is freed. Also, q%front, the pointer to the front of the queue, is up-

```
FUNCTION count_elements (q) RESULT (count)

   USE queue_type_def

   IMPLICIT NONE

   INTEGER :: count    ! result variable

   TYPE (queue_type), INTENT (IN) :: q

   TYPE (node_type), POINTER :: node_ptr    ! pointer to
                                            ! arbitrary node

   count = 0                      ! Init node count.
   node_ptr => q%front            ! Start at front.

   ! Traverse the list.
   DO WHILE (ASSOCIATED (node_ptr))
      count = count + 1           ! Increment node count.
      node_ptr => node_ptr%next   ! Move to next node.
   END DO

END FUNCTION count_elements
```

FIGURE 11.6E. Function to count the number of elements in a queue.

dated to point to whatever the pointer portion of the first node in the queue points to before that node is deallocated. Thus, q%front will be moved back one node if the queue had two or more nodes at entry to take_from_front, and q%front will be disassociated if the queue had only one node at entry to the subroutine. In order to update q%front, care must be taken to save the pointer portion of the first node in the queue before that node is deallocated, and this is accomplished in Figure 11.6f by the pointer assignment statement

```
temp => q%front%next
```

Observe that the subroutine take_from_front of Figure 11.6f assumes that the queue is not empty. Thus, it is the responsibility of the caller to make sure that there is at least one element in the queue before calling take_from_front. One way of doing this would be to check the return of the function subprogram count_elements of Figure 11.6e against zero, but this will be rather inefficient if there are many elements in the queue. A more direct approach is the function subprogram is_empty of Figure

```
! Warning:  This subroutine assumes that queue is not empty.

SUBROUTINE take_from_front (q, buffer)

   USE queue_type_def

   IMPLICIT NONE

   TYPE (queue_type), INTENT (IN OUT) :: q
   CHARACTER(*),      INTENT (OUT)    :: buffer

   TYPE (node_type), POINTER :: temp   ! place to temporarily
                                       ! save address of
                                       ! successor to
                                       ! first node

   buffer = q%front%data    ! Return data value to caller.

   temp => q%front%next     ! Save address of second node.

   DEALLOCATE (q%front)     ! Free storage for first node.

   q%front => temp          ! Advance front of queue.

END SUBROUTINE take_from_front
```

FIGURE 11.6F. Subroutine to delete front node from a queue.

```
FUNCTION is_empty (q) RESULT (empty)

   USE queue_type_def

   IMPLICIT NONE

   LOGICAL :: empty    ! result variable

   TYPE (queue_type), INTENT (IN) :: q

   empty = .NOT. ASSOCIATED (q%front)    ! Return .TRUE. if
                                          ! q%front is
                                          ! disassociated.

END FUNCTION is_empty
```

FIGURE 11.6G. Function that determines if a queue is empty.

11.6g, which returns .TRUE. if the queue is currently empty and .FALSE. if it is not. The function is_empty merely determines whether q%front, which points to the beginning of the queue q, is associated or disassociated.

In order to make the collection of definitions and subprograms easier to use, the module queue_interface of Figure 11.6h is provided. The user of the module gains access to the definitions of both queue_type and node_type, and type declarations are provided for the external functions of Figures 11.6e and 11.6g. Actually, instead of the two type declarations, it would be better to supply interface bodies for each of the external subprograms given in Figures 11.6c through 11.6g, as discussed in Chapter 13, but this is not mandatory. The inclusion of the

```
MODULE queue_interface

   USE queue_type_def    ! Access definitions for
                         ! queue_type and node_type.

   IMPLICIT NONE

   INTEGER, EXTERNAL :: count_elements  ! type decl for func

   LOGICAL, EXTERNAL :: is_empty        ! type decl for func

END MODULE queue_interface
```

FIGURE 11.6H. Derived-type definitions and function type declarations for queue procedures.

interface bodies would permit the compiler to cross-check each invocation of a queue procedure by a module user, thus reducing the risk of improper use.

The main program of Figure 11.6i provides a simple test driver for the code of Figures 11.6a through 11.6h. Note that the user of the queue procedures need not be aware of most of the details of their

```fortran
PROGRAM demo_queue_procedures

    USE queue_interface

    IMPLICIT NONE

    TYPE (queue_type) :: queue_1
    CHARACTER(20) :: buffer
    INTEGER :: io_stat

    CALL init_queue (queue_1)    ! Create a new queue.

    ! Get data from user and append each item to end of queue.
    DO
        PRINT "(A)", " Enter data (EOF to quit):"
        READ (*, "(A)", IOSTAT = io_stat) buffer    ! Get data.
        IF (io_stat < 0) EXIT
        CALL put_in_rear (queue_1, buffer)    ! Append to end
                                              ! of queue_1.
    END DO

    ! Display number of elements currently in queue_1.
    PRINT "(/A, I6)", " Number of elements in queue = ",      &
                              count_elements (queue_1)

    ! Display data values in order read.
    DO
        IF (is_empty (queue_1)) EXIT                ! Quit when
                                                    ! queue_1 empty.

        CALL take_from_front (queue_1, buffer)  ! Get 1st data
                                                ! val & delete
                                                ! 1st node.
        PRINT "(1X, A)", buffer
    END DO

END PROGRAM demo_queue_procedures
```

FIGURE 11.6I. Test driver for code of Figures 11.6a through 11.6h.

implementation. In Figure 11.6i, a variable named queue_1 of type
queue_type is declared, and all manipulations are performed on this variable by invoking subprograms. First, the queue is created by calling init_
queue, and then data is stored in the queue by repeated calls to put_in_
rear. Next, count_elements is invoked, and the program displays the number of elements that have been put in the queue. Finally, take_from_front
is called repeatedly to return the data stored in the node at the front
of the queue and to deallocate the storage for that node. The function
subprogram is_empty is used to determine when all elements have been
removed from the queue. Observe that at no time is the user of the
queue procedures concerned with pointers.

For purposes of illustration, the queue-handling procedures shown
in this section are implemented as external subprograms. But always
bear in mind that a module combining derived-type definitions with
subprograms defining procedures operating on data of those derived
types is an extremely attractive design approach. Instead of external
subprograms, it would probably be preferable to implement the subprograms of Figures 11.6c through 11.6g as module subprograms, as
discussed in Chapter 7, bundling them in a single module with the
derived-type definitions of Figures 11.6a and 11.6b. However, either alternative will work, and there are no hard and fast rules for choosing
between them.

11.6 STACKS AS LINKED LISTS

The queue, which was discussed in the preceding two sections, is a
linked list that works on the first-in-first-out (FIFO) principle. This section will focus on the **stack**, which is a linked list that works on the
last-in-first-out (LIFO) principle. Thus, the stack may be viewed as the
dual of the queue.

Just as it is helpful in thinking about queues to envision a movie
theater ticket line, in grasping the concept of a stack it is helpful to
think of a pile of plates at the beginning of a food line at a cafeteria or
buffet. Food service workers add a plate to the pile by putting it on top
of those already there, and customers take a plate from the pile only
from the top. In some cafeterias, there is a spring underneath the stack
of plates that keeps the top plate in the stack at a level that is convenient
for the customers.

In the software world, a stack is made up of a collection of nodes,
where each node consists of (1) some data of interest and (2) a pointer
to its predecessor node. A conceptual representation of a stack with
three nodes is shown in Figure 11.7, where node-1 started the stack, then

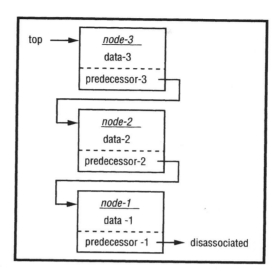

FIGURE 11.7. Conceptual view of a stack consisting of three nodes.

node-2 was added to the stack, and the most recent addition to the stack was *node-3*. A pointer top always points to the node most recently added to the stack, and each node contains a pointer to the node below. The bottom node is distinguished by the fact that it contains a disassociated pointer, indicating that there are no nodes below it in the stack. There are only two permissible operations that can change a stack, and both affect only the top node: The operation **push** adds a new node at the top of the stack, and the operation **pop** removes the top node from the stack. If a push were performed on the stack of Figure 11.7, *node-4* would be added above *node-3*, predecessor-4 would point to *node-3*, and top would point to *node-4*. If a pop were performed on the stack of Figure 11.7, *node-3* would be removed, and *top* would point to *node-2*. Observe that the last node to be pushed onto the stack is always the first to be removed.

In the preceding section, a collection of modules and external subprograms dealing with queues was illustrated, and this section will present a similar collection of modules and subprograms for handling stacks. The definition of the derived type node_type to be used for a stack is placed in a module node_type_def, which is listed in Figure 11.8a. Note in Figure 11.7 that a stack is fully characterized by the definition of its nodes, together with a pointer to the top of the stack. Thus, the definition of type stack_type given in the module stack_type_def in Figure 11.8b adequately describes a stack, even though stack_type has only the single component top. An alternative approach would be to omit the derived

```
MODULE node_type_def

   INTEGER, PARAMETER :: Data_len = 80

   TYPE :: node_type
      CHARACTER(Data_len)          :: data
      TYPE (node_type), POINTER  :: predecessor    ! ptr to
                                                    ! node
                                                    ! below

   END TYPE node_type

END MODULE node_type_def
```

FIGURE 11.8A. Module containing definition of node_type for stack.

type stack_type altogether and instruct the user of the stack procedures
to declare a stack along the following lines:

```
TYPE (node_type), POINTER :: stack    ! awkward for user
```

However, it is more natural for a user to declare a stack by coding
something like

```
TYPE (stack_type) :: stack
```
then at the top level you don't need to bother with pointers

Hence, the implementation of a stack presented here will make use of
the module of Figure 11.8b.

As was the case for the queue procedures given in the preceding
section, the user of the stack procedures will be required to initialize a
stack before attempting any other operations on it. The subroutine init_
stack of Figure 11.8c is provided for this purpose. The only action performed by init_stack is to disassociate the pointer to the top of the stack

```
MODULE stack_type_def

   USE node_type_def     ! Access definition of node_type.

   TYPE :: stack_type
      TYPE (node_type), POINTER :: top    ! ptr to top node
                                          ! in stack
   END TYPE stack_type

END MODULE stack_type_def
```

FIGURE 11.8B. Module containing definition of derived type stack_type.

```
SUBROUTINE init_stack (s)

   USE stack_type_def

   TYPE (stack_type), INTENT (OUT) :: s

   NULLIFY (s%top)    ! Disassociate pointer to top of stack.

END SUBROUTINE init_stack
```

FIGURE 11.8C. Subroutine to initialize a stack.

so that it can be safely used as an argument of the intrinsic function
ASSOCIATED in other stack procedures.

Figure 11.8d gives the listing for the subroutine push, which creates a
new node at the top of a stack and stores data in that node. The
pointer portion of the new node must point to the old top node, and
s%top, the pointer to the top of the stack, must be changed to point to
the new node. This is handled in Figure 11.8d by temporarily associating a pointer temp with the storage for the new node. Note that in the
statement

```
SUBROUTINE push (s, buffer)

   USE stack_type_def

   TYPE (stack_type), INTENT (IN OUT) :: s
   CHARACTER(*),        INTENT (IN)     :: buffer

   TYPE (node_type), POINTER :: temp    ! ptr to new node

   ALLOCATE (temp)                 ! Create storage for new node.

   temp%data = buffer              ! Store data in new node.

   temp%predecessor => s%top    ! Make old top node
                                ! predecessor of new node.

   s%top => temp                ! Make new node top of stack.

END SUBROUTINE push
```

FIGURE 11.8D. Subroutine to push a new node onto the top of a stack.

```
temp%predecessor => s%top
```

s%top still points to the old top of the stack, that is, the top of the stack before the new node is pushed onto it. But when the new node is pushed onto the stack by the statement

```
s%top => temp
```

s%top is changed to point to the new node, which is now at the top of the stack. Care must be taken here not to change s%top before its previous association has been saved. Observe that, unlike the situation for a queue, the first node to be added to a stack is treated the same as any other node.

Subroutine pop, whose listing is given in Figure 11.8e, retrieves the data from the top node of the stack and deletes the top node. The pointer temp is used to save the address of the node that is at the top of the stack at entry to the subroutine. The pointer to the top of the stack, s%top, is changed to point to the node below the node that is at the top at entry. Then the storage for the node at the top at entry is deallocated. Incidentally, some readers might think that, instead of coding pop as a subroutine, it would be a good idea to code it as a function with result variable buffer. This would be permitted by Fortran 90 language rules,

```
! Warning: This subroutine assumes that stack is not empty.

SUBROUTINE pop (s, buffer)

   USE stack_type_def

   TYPE (stack_type), INTENT (IN OUT) :: s
   CHARACTER(*),      INTENT (OUT)    :: buffer

   TYPE (node_type), POINTER :: temp    ! ptr to node to
                                        ! be deleted

   temp => s%top               ! Save address of top node.

   buffer = temp%data          ! Retrieve data from top node.

   s%top => temp%predecessor   ! Move down ptr to top of stack.

   DEALLOCATE (temp)           ! Free storage for old top node.

END SUBROUTINE pop
```

FIGURE 11.8e. Subroutine to pop the top node off a stack.

```
FUNCTION is_empty (s) RESULT (empty)

  USE stack_type_def

  LOGICAL :: empty    ! result variable

  TYPE (stack_type), INTENT (IN) :: s

  empty = .NOT. ASSOCIATED (s%top)    ! Return .TRUE. if
                                      ! s%top is
                                      ! disassociated.
END FUNCTION is_empty
```

FIGURE 11.8F. Function subprogram that determines if a stack is empty.

but note that the value of the argument s will be changed during execution of the function, and this has long been considered poor Fortran style.

Observe that the subroutine pop of Figure 11.8e assumes that the stack is not empty. In order to permit the user to check for an empty stack, the function subprogram is_empty of Figure 11.8f is provided. The function is_empty merely checks whether s%top, which points to the top of the stack s, is associated or disassociated, and returns the value .TRUE. if s%top is disassociated.

The module stack_interface of Figure 11.8g is provided to make the collection of stack-handling definitions and subprograms easier to use. The module stack_interface uses the module stack_type_def of Figure 11.8b, so the user of stack_interface has access to the type definition for stack_type. Since the module stack_type_def uses the module node_type_def of Figure 11.8a, the user of stack_interface will also have access to the type definition for node_type, as well as the named constant Data_

```
MODULE stack_interface

  USE stack_type_def    ! Access definitions for
                        ! stack_type & node_type.

  LOGICAL, EXTERNAL :: is_empty    ! type decl for func

END MODULE stack_interface
```

FIGURE 11.8G. Derived-type definitions and function type declaration for stack procedures.

len. Also, the module stack_interface of Figure 11.8g contains a type declaration for the external function is_empty. It would provide an element of safety if, instead of the type declaration for is_empty, interface bodies for all of the subprograms of Figures 11.8c through 11.8f were provided in Figure 11.8g, but for simplicity this is not done here.

Figure 11.8h gives a main program that serves as a simple test driver for the code of Figures 11.8a through 11.8g. A variable named stack_1 of type stack_type is declared, and all operations are performed on this variable by invoking the stack-handling procedures. The stack named stack_1 is created by the call to subroutine init_stack of Figure 11.8c, and data are stored in it by repeated calls to the subroutine push of Figure 11.8d. The subroutine pop of Figure 11.8e is called to retrieve the data from each node in stack_1 and to deallocate the storage. The function

```
PROGRAM demo_stack_procedures

    USE stack_interface

    TYPE (stack_type) :: stack_1
    CHARACTER(Data_len) :: buffer
    INTEGER :: io_stat

    CALL init_stack (stack_1)    ! Create a new stack.

    ! Get data from user and push each item onto top of stack.
    DO
        PRINT "(A)", " Enter data (EOF to quit):"
        READ (*, "(A)", IOSTAT = io_stat) buffer    ! Get data.
        IF (io_stat < 0) EXIT
        CALL push (stack_1, buffer)  ! Push onto top of stack_1.
    END DO

    ! Display data values in reverse of order read.
    PRINT "(/A)", " Data entered (in reverse order):"
    DO
        IF (is_empty (stack_1)) EXIT  ! Quit when stack_1 empty.

        CALL pop (stack_1, buffer)    ! Get top data value and
                                      ! delete top node.
        PRINT "(1X, A)", TRIM (buffer)
    END DO

END PROGRAM demo_stack_procedures
```

FIGURE 11.8H. Test driver for code of Figures 11.8a through 11.8g.

subprogram is_empty of Figure 11.8f is used to determine when all nodes have been deleted from stack_1. The final DO construct of Figure 11.8h displays the list of values entered earlier, but the order of the output is the reverse of that of the input.

This section introduced the notion of the stack and illustrated the implementation of the stack-handling procedures as external sub-programs. However, a somewhat better implementation would be to package push, pop, and the other routines along with the definitions of stack_type and node_type in a module.

11.7 BINARY TREES

The three previous sections have illustrated data structures made up of a collection of nodes, where each node consisted of some data of interest and a pointer to one other node. It is possible to construct more complicated data structures by having each node contain pointers to two or more other nodes. The two-dimensional linked structures known as "trees" make up an important family of data structures that can be constructed in this manner. Examples of trees that are familiar to most people include family trees and organizational charts. Of course, these abstract representations are upside down relative to the tall, woody plants for which they are named.

This section will focus attention on the simple, but important, category of tree known as the **binary tree**. Figure 11.9 gives a conceptual representation of a typical binary tree. Each node of a bi-nary tree consists of some data of interest plus two pointers, labeled left and right in Figure 11.9, each capable of pointing at another node. The top node will always be the first node added to the binary tree, and it is called the **root**. Each node added to the tree after the root node must be added below an existing node, so there can only be pointers downward from each node. Each node may point to zero, one, or two other nodes. In Figure 11.9, the symbol • indicates a pointer, and a disassociated pointer is represented by the symbol • with no line coming out of it. The root node has the special property that no other node is permitted to point to it. Each node other than the root node must be pointed to by exactly one other node. If node A points to node B, then node B is said to be the **child** of node A.

A little thought reveals that the set of all nodes to the left of any given node in the tree can itself be considered as a tree, and such a tree is called the left **subtree** of the given node. Similarly, the nodes to the right of a given node form a right subtree. Using the notion of subtrees, an order can be imposed on a binary tree by requiring that the data

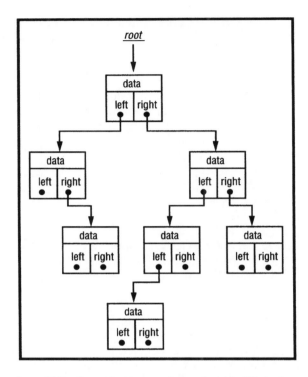

FIGURE 11.9. Conceptual representation of a typical binary tree.

value at each node be greater than all data values in its left subtree and less than or equal to all data values in its right subtree. An important property of a binary tree is that it is rather easy to add a new node in such a way that the order is preserved.

Now suppose that it is desired to have an alphabetized list of all words in a large document. It would be possible, of course, to read all the words into a big array and then sort the array. However, an alternative approach is to read through the document, storing each word in a node in a binary tree. Storage for each node can be dynamically allocated, and new nodes can be added to the binary tree in such a way that the list is always in alphabetical order, thus avoiding the sort required for an array. This section will show how to use a binary tree to alphabetize a list.

Here is a method for constructing a binary tree of alphabetized words from a list of words in arbitrary order: Place the first word in the list at the root node. For each new word in the list after the first, start at the root node and compare the new word with the tree word stored there. If

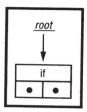

FIGURE 11.10A. Binary tree containing first word in list.

the new word is less than the tree word, consider the left child to be the root node of a new tree and repeat the comparison process; otherwise, consider the right child to be the root node of a new tree and repeat the comparison process. Repeat this procedure until a node having no child in the required direction is encountered. Then create a child in that direction and store the new word in it.

To illustrate the method described in the preceding paragraph, consider its application to the list of words in the following proverb:

If wishes were horses, then beggars would ride.

Figures 11.10a through 11.10h show the build-up of the binary tree as each new node is added. The first word encountered, "if," is stored in the root node as shown in Figure 11.10a. The second word, "wishes," is greater than "if," so it is stored in the right child of the root node as illustrated in Figure 11.10b. The third word, "were," is greater than "if," so its right child, which contains the word "wishes," is considered to be the root node of a new tree. The word "were" is less than the word "wishes," so a left child is created and "were" is stored there as shown in Figure 11.10c. The fourth word, "horses," is less than "if," so it is

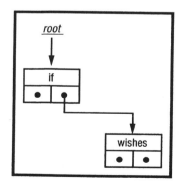

FIGURE 11.10B. Binary tree containing first two words in list.

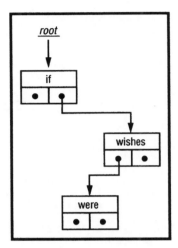

FIGURE 11.10c.   Binary tree containing first three words in list.

stored in the left child of the root node as shown in Figure 11.10d. The fifth word in the proverb, "then," is greater than "if," so the move is to the right child to compare "then" with "wishes." The new word "then" is less than "wishes," so we move to the left child and compare "then" with "were." Since "then" is less than "were," a left child is created and "then" is stored there as illustrated in Figure 11.10e. The sixth word,

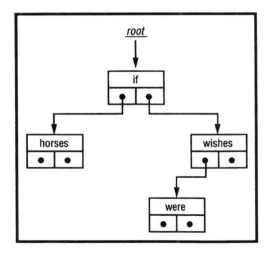

FIGURE 11.10d.   Binary tree containing first four words in list.

"beggars," is less than "if," so the move is to the left child, where it is determined that "beggars" is less than "horses." Thus, "beggars" is stored in a new left child as shown in Figure 11.10f. The seventh word in the list, "would," is found to be greater than "if" and also greater than "wishes," so a new right child is created and "would" is stored there as shown in Figure 11.10g. The final word in the list, "ride," is greater than "if" but less than "wishes," so we move to the left child below "wishes." The new word "ride" is less than "were" and it is also less than "then," so "ride" is stored in a new left child as illustrated in Figure 11.10h.

The foregoing description of binary trees provides sufficient background to write a rather short Fortran 90 program that will store a sequence of words in alphabetical order. The underlying code needed for dealing with a binary tree of CHARACTER data is given in the module of Figure 11.11a. Note that a derived type named node_type is defined in the module, and that its definition agrees with the conceptual representation of nodes given in Figure 11.9. The module of Figure 11.11a also contains a subroutine to add a node to a binary tree and another to display in order the data stored in a binary tree. However, before attempting any other tree operation, the pointer to the root node must be disassociated to indicate that the tree is empty. This can be done by calling the module subroutine init_tree of Figure 11.11a, in which no

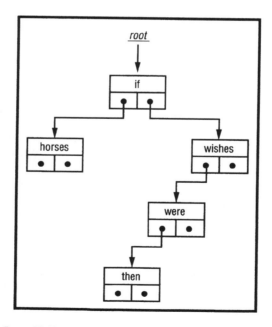

FIGURE 11.10E.   Binary tree containing first five words in list.

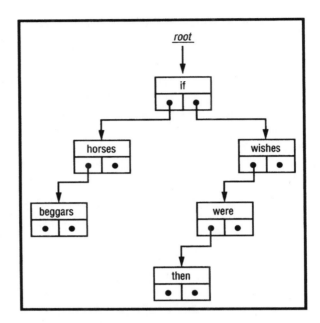

Figure 11.10F. Binary tree containing first six words in list.

INTENT is indicated for the dummy argument root. Recall from Section 10.10 that Fortran 90 rules do not permit the INTENT attribute to be specified for a dummy argument with the POINTER attribute.

Now focus attention on the subroutine add_node in Figure 11.11a, which adds a new node to a binary tree. Subroutine add_node starts at the root node of the tree pointed to by root and adds a node to the tree containing the CHARACTER value stored in buff. If the tree is empty when add_node is called, then the pointer argument root should have been disassociated by an earlier call to init_tree, and add_node will create the root node for the tree. If root is not disassociated, add_node compares the value in buff against the data stored in the root node to determine whether the new value should be stored in the left subtree or the right subtree. If the new value should be stored in the left subtree, add_node calls itself, treating the left subtree as a tree whose root node is the node pointed to by root%left; if the new value should be stored in the right subtree, add_node calls itself, treating the right subtree as a tree whose root node is the node pointed to by root%right. Hence, add_node is a recursive subroutine, and the Fortran 90 standard requires that the keyword RECURSIVE be specified in the SUBROUTINE statement as shown in Figure 11.11a.

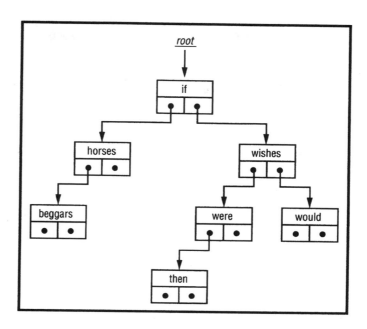

FIGURE 11.10G. Binary tree containing first seven words in list.

The subroutine display_tree of Figure 11.11a is used to display the data stored in a binary tree. For the ordered binary tree of words illustrated in Figure 11.10h, display_tree will display the words in alphabetical order. At each node, display_tree displays the words contained in the node's left subtree, then the word contained in the node, and then the words contained in the node's right subtree. Since display_tree calls itself, the keyword RECURSIVE is specified in the SUBROUTINE statement. The subroutine display_tree stops calling itself when, for some entry, an empty subtree is encountered.

A main program that serves as a test driver for the module of Figure 11.11a is given in Figure 11.11b. The main program uses the module tree_interface of Figure 11.11a to access the definition of node_type and the module procedures init_tree, add_node, and display_tree. A variable tree is declared as a pointer to a structure of type node_type, and all tree operations are performed on this variable. First, the tree is initialized by calling module subroutine init_tree. Next, the user inputs a list of words at the terminal, one word per line. The program calls module subroutine add_node to store each word in a node in the ordered binary tree. After all words have been read and stored, the module subroutine display_tree is called to display the list of words in alphabetical order.

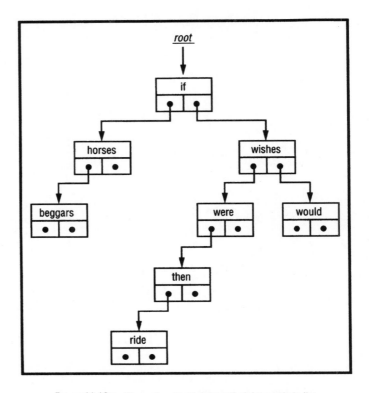

FIGURE 11.10H.   Binary tree containing all eight words in list.

To pursue the example presented in Figure 11.10h, suppose the list of words entered is as follows:

```
if
wishes
were
horses
then
beggars
would
ride
```

The output of the program made up of the program units of Figures 11.11a and 11.11b will be

```
In alphabetical order, words entered were:
                 beggars
                 horses
```

```
MODULE tree_interface
  INTEGER, PARAMETER :: Data_len = 60
  TYPE :: node_type
    CHARACTER(Data_len)       :: data
    TYPE (node_type), POINTER :: left    ! ptr to left child
    TYPE (node_type), POINTER :: right   ! ptr to right child
  END TYPE node_type
CONTAINS
  SUBROUTINE init_tree (root)
    TYPE (node_type), POINTER :: root    ! ptr to root of tree

    NULLIFY (root)  ! Disassociate ptr to root node of tree.
  END SUBROUTINE init_tree

  RECURSIVE SUBROUTINE add_node (root, buff)
    TYPE (node_type), POINTER :: root
    CHARACTER(*), INTENT (IN) :: buff

    ! Check for empty tree/subtree.
    IF (.NOT. ASSOCIATED (root)) THEN
      ! tree/subtree empty
      ! Make this the root node for tree/subtree.
      ALLOCATE (root)
      root%data = buff
      NULLIFY (root%left, root%right)
    ELSE IF (buff < root%data) THEN
      ! tree/subtree not empty
      ! Add node to left subtree of this tree/subtree.
      CALL add_node (root%left, buff)
    ELSE
      ! tree/subtree not empty
      ! Add node to right subtree of this tree/subtree.
      CALL add_node (root%right, buff)
    END IF
  END SUBROUTINE add_node

  RECURSIVE SUBROUTINE display_tree (root)
    TYPE (node_type), POINTER :: root

    ! Check for empty tree/subtree.
    IF (ASSOCIATED (root)) THEN
      ! Tree/subtree is not empty.
      CALL display_tree (root%left)    ! Display left subtree.
      PRINT "(17X, A)",                &  ! Display root node of
                  TRIM (root%data)     ! this tree/subtree.
      CALL display_tree (root%right)   ! Display right subtree.
    END IF
  END SUBROUTINE display_tree
END MODULE tree_interface
```

FIGURE 11.11A. Module for dealing with a tree of CHARACTER data.

```
PROGRAM demo_tree

    USE tree_interface   ! Access definition of node_type,
                          ! Data_len, & tree-handling procedures.

    TYPE (node_type), POINTER :: tree
    CHARACTER(Data_len)       :: buffer

    INTEGER :: io_stat

    CALL init_tree (tree)   ! Initialize the tree.

    PRINT "(A)", " Enter words (EOF to quit):"
    DO
        READ (*, "(A)", IOSTAT = io_stat) buffer  ! Read 1 word.
        IF (io_stat < 0) EXIT
        CALL add_node (tree, buffer)  ! Store word read in tree.
    END DO

    PRINT "(/A)",                                              &
                " In alphabetical order, words entered were:"
    CALL display_tree (tree)    ! Display words stored in tree.

END PROGRAM demo_tree
```

FIGURE 11.11B.   Test driver for code of Figure 11.11a.

```
if
ride
then
were
wishes
would
```

In both subroutines add_node and display_tree of Figure 11.11a, a nonempty binary tree is viewed as consisting of a root node, a left subtree, and a right subtree. But since a subtree is defined in terms of a tree, this is a recursive characterization. Hence, it is natural that add_node and display_tree are recursive subroutines. In general, many of the most practical uses of recursive subprograms arise in connection with data structures, such as trees, that are defined recursively. But it would be a mistake to believe that routines to handle such applications cannot be written without using recursion. Indeed, since most machine languages do not support recursion, compilers usually translate recursive code into nonrecursive code by using stacks to achieve the same results.

However, in dealing with recursive data structures, such as trees, non-recursive routines are usually even more difficult to understand than recursive ones.

In the example of this section, the tree-handling procedures were implemented as module subroutines, but it would not be difficult to implement them as external subroutines. If this approach were taken, however, it would be mandatory to supply an interface body for each of the subroutines init_tree, add_node, and display_tree since each has a dummy argument that is a pointer. Interface bodies will be discussed in Chapter 13.

CHAPTER 12

ACCESSIBILITY OF IDENTIFIERS IN A MODULE

12.1 *OVERVIEW OF MODULE ACCESS*

Traditionally, names in one Fortran program unit have been unknown in other program units, but, as discussed in Chapter 7, the module changes this. If no special action is taken, a module user has access to the names in the specification part of the module, where the specification part consists of the portion of the module remaining after any subprograms it contains (along with any **CONTAINS** statement that may be present) are removed. Also, a module user has access to the names of the procedures defined by module subprograms unless special action is taken. While the capability of sharing names in modules is a major improvement to the language, it also opens the door to the possibility of name clashes arising in ways not historically encountered by Fortran programmers. For example, when programmers are working in teams, software development may be slowed because module authors and module users have chosen names that conflict. Also, a programmer may wish to use a module in an existing program, where the module is supplied only in the form of object code by an outside organization, but accessible names in the module may duplicate names with different meanings already in the program.

While the discussion in the preceding paragraph was couched in terms of name conflicts, a slight additional complexity comes about because of the existence in Fortran 90 of programmer-defined operations and overloaded equal signs. As discussed in Chapter 9, operator tokens (such as +, .AND., etc.) used with programmer-defined meanings; the equal sign (=) used with programmer-defined meanings; and programmer-defined generic names are referred to collectively as "generic identifiers" in the new standard. The same accessibility issues that must be considered for names also arise in the context of generic identifiers for operator tokens and equal signs, and the same mechanisms are employed in dealing with these issues. Hence, the word "identifier" is used in this chapter to refer to either a name or a generic identifier that is symbolized by an operator token or an equal sign.

When writing a module that is expected to be used by others, the module author has the responsibility of organizing the code in the module so as to minimize the chances of name clashes ever arising. The principal mechanisms available to a module author for accomplishing this are the statement keywords PRIVATE and PUBLIC, which are permitted to appear only in the specification part of a module. The first few sections of this chapter will be devoted to a discussion of the use of these two keywords in controlling the accessibility to module users of identifiers in a module. The use of these keywords in Fortran 90 is related conceptually to that of the keywords private and public in C++, as well as to that of the reserved word PRIVATE in Ada, but the usage in Fortran 90 is not quite the same as in the other languages.

A module author need be concerned about the accessibility of only the identifiers in the specification part plus the names of any procedures that are defined in the module, since identifiers local to module subprograms are not accessible to users anyway. The Fortran 90 standard supports two statement keywords that can be used in specifying whether identifiers in modules are accessible to users or not: PRIVATE can be specified to make identifiers inaccessible outside a module, while PUBLIC can be specified to make identifiers accessible to module users. In terms of syntax, there are two slightly different ways of specifying identifier accessibility. One of these ways is to specify the PRIVATE or PUBLIC attribute in a type declaration, which can be used to specify the accessibility of an entity such as a variable name or a named constant outside the module in which it is declared. The second way is the PRIVATE statement or the PUBLIC statement, which can be employed to specify the accessibility to module users of any category of identifier, whether it has a type declaration or not.

As is so often true in Fortran 90, the treatment of derived-type definitions merits special consideration, and the new standard addresses this by supporting three levels of accessibility for a derived-type definition in a module:

1. the entire derived-type definition is accessible to module users; or

2. the entire derived-type definition is inaccessible; or

3. the name of the derived-type is accessible, but its component definitions are inaccessible.

The latter mechanism is particularly associated with modules that contain a derived-type definition along with a collection of module subprograms that manipulate data of that derived type. This category of module provides the basis for the Fortran 90 implementation of the software concept known as the "abstract data type," which has been found in other languages to make it easier for programmers to deal with application-specific data types.

But even if module authors live up to their responsibility of not cluttering the name space of module users, it is unavoidable that module users must sometimes take special action to relieve name conflicts. In many cases a module user can deal with name clashes by simply employing a text editor to change those names that are in conflict, but to deal with those situations where this is undesirable or impossible, Fortran 90 provides special forms of the USE statement. These special forms involve a rename capability, which can be utilized to specify local aliases for names appearing in the module, and an ONLY option, which can be used to limit access only to specified identifiers in the module. Details of restricting module access by means of the USE statement will be given in the last three sections of the chapter.

12.2 USING *PRIVATE* TO MAKE NAMES INACCESSIBLE

It is the duty of module authors to write their modules so as to minimize the likelihood of name clashes ever occurring. One of the ways that a module author can meet this obligation is to specify the PRIVATE keyword for names not intended to be accessible to module users. Such names will remain accessible throughout the module itself, but they will be inaccessible to module users.

The keyword PRIVATE is permitted to appear only within a module; moreover, its appearance is further limited to the specification part of a module, that is, the part of a module that remains when any subprograms it contains, along with any CONTAINS statement that may be present, are removed. By default, a module user has access to the names in the specification part of a module by use association, as described in Chapter 7, but the keyword PRIVATE can be used to block that access. Furthermore, if a module author takes no special action, a module user also has access to the names of functions and subroutines contained in the module, but the keyword PRIVATE can be employed to block this access as well.

Figure 12.1a gives a module that illustrates the use of the keyword PRIVATE to make names inaccessible to module users. Note that the named constants Upper_case and Lower_case and the variables i, n, and c are made inaccessible to module users by specifying the attribute PRIVATE in their type declarations. The names of the subroutines

```
MODULE uniform_case

  IMPLICIT NONE

  CHARACTER(26), PARAMETER, PRIVATE ::                          &
                Upper_case = "ABCDEFGHIJKLMNOPQRSTUVWXYZ", &
                Lower_case = "abcdefghijklmnopqrstuvwxyz"

  INTEGER, PRIVATE :: i       ! handy loop index
  INTEGER, PRIVATE :: n       ! handy temp integer var
  CHARACTER(1), PRIVATE :: c  ! handy temp character var

  PRIVATE :: upper, lower   ! module subroutines below

CONTAINS

  SUBROUTINE make_upper_case (string)
    CHARACTER(*), INTENT (IN OUT) :: string

    DO i = 1, LEN (string)
       c = string(i:i)
       IF (c >= "a" .AND. c <= "z") CALL upper (string(i:i))
    END DO
  END SUBROUTINE make_upper_case

  SUBROUTINE make_lower_case (string)
    CHARACTER(*), INTENT (IN OUT) :: string

    DO i = 1, LEN (string)
       c = string(i:i)
       IF (c >= "A" .AND. c <= "Z") CALL lower (string(i:i))
    END DO
  END SUBROUTINE make_lower_case

  SUBROUTINE upper (char)
    CHARACTER(1), INTENT (IN OUT) :: char

    n = INDEX (Lower_case, char)
    char = Upper_case(n:n)
  END SUBROUTINE upper

  SUBROUTINE lower (char)
    CHARACTER(1), INTENT (IN OUT) :: char

    n = INDEX (Upper_case, char)
    char = Lower_case(n:n)
  END SUBROUTINE lower

END MODULE uniform_case
```

FIGURE 12.1A. Module illustrating use of keyword PRIVATE.

lower and upper are also made inaccessible to users, but by a PRIVATE statement:

```
PRIVATE :: upper, lower
```

If preferred, the named constants and variables could have been made inaccessible by a PRIVATE statement instead of by the PRIVATE attribute in their type declarations. But since type declarations for module subprograms do not appear in the specification part of the module—not even for module function subprograms—the PRIVATE statement is the only mechanism provided for specifying that a module subprogram is inaccessible.

Observe in Figure 12.1a that the names i and c appear in both subroutines make_upper_case and make_lower_case. The two subroutines still have access to these variable names by host association, even though both names have the PRIVATE attribute. The names i and c are inaccessible only to module users—specifying them as PRIVATE has no effect inside the module itself. In a similar vein, note that module subroutine

```
PROGRAM demo_private

   USE uniform_case   ! Access make_upper_case
                      ! and make_lower_case.

   IMPLICIT NONE

   INTEGER :: i   ! not same var as i in module
                  ! since i in module is PRIVATE

   CHARACTER(7) :: lower, upper   ! no clash with names of
                                  ! subs since these names in
                                  ! module are PRIVATE

   lower = "Ab - yZ"
   CALL make_lower_case (lower)    ! Call module subroutine.

   upper = "Ab - yZ"
   CALL make_upper_case (upper)    ! Call module subroutine.

   DO i = 1, 7
      PRINT *, lower(i:i) // " " // upper(i:i)
   END DO

END PROGRAM demo_private
```

FIGURE 12.1B. Main program using module of Figure 12.1a.

make_upper_case is able to call module subroutine upper, but a module user will not be able to do so since upper is specified as PRIVATE. Since, as always, local names in module subprograms are inaccessible to module users, it turns out that the only two names in the module of Figure 12.1a that are available to users are those of the subroutines make_upper_case and make_lower_case.

Figure 12.1b gives a main program that uses the module of Figure 12.1a. Note that the names i, lower, and upper in the main program duplicate names appearing in the module. However, there is no need for the writer of the main program to take action of any kind since the author of the module has employed the PRIVATE specification to avoid cluttering the user's name space.

The main program of Figure 12.1b calls the accessible module subroutines of Figure 12.1a to first make a string all lower case and then to make the same string all upper case. When the program is executed, the following is displayed:

```
a A
b B
- -
y Y
z Z
```

12.3 USING PUBLIC TO MAKE NAMES ACCESSIBLE

As illustrated in the preceding section, the PRIVATE statement can be employed to make specific names inaccessible to module users. Similarly, Fortran 90 provides the PUBLIC statement for the purpose of specifying names that are accessible to module users. The principal use of the PUBLIC statement is to permit module users to access names whose accessibility would otherwise default to PRIVATE. It is perhaps not immediately obvious why such a capability is highly desirable, and this section will be devoted to an exploration of this topic.

The preceding section illustrated that the PRIVATE statement can be used to specify a list of names that are inaccessible, but it is also valid to omit the list, in which case the optional double colon (::) must be omitted as well. The PRIVATE statement consisting only of the lone keyword is equivalent to a PRIVATE statement listing every name that could legally appear in such a list. If such a PRIVATE statement is present, all names in the module are inaccessible by default, but this can be overridden by using the PUBLIC statement to specify a list of names that are to be accessible.

Figure 12.2 illustrates the use of PRIVATE and PUBLIC statements along the lines described in the preceding paragraph. From a user's point of view, the behavior of the module of Figure 12.2 is exactly the same as that of the module of Figure 12.1a. The absence of any list in the initial PRIVATE statement in Figure 12.2 has the effect of specifying that all of the names in the specification part, along with the names of all module subprograms, are inaccessible to module users unless explicitly specified elsewhere as PUBLIC. The PUBLIC statement in Figure 12.2 then specifies make_upper_case and make_lower_case as accessible to module users.

The modules of Figure 12.1a and Figure 12.2 illustrate competing approaches to achieving the same result. In Figure 12.1a, the names in the module are accessible to module users by default, and the keyword PRIVATE is employed to specify those names that are to be inaccessible. In Figure 12.2, the PRIVATE statement with no list is used to make the names inaccessible by default, and the keyword PUBLIC is employed to specify those names that are to be accessible. Both approaches will always work, and the choice between them should ordinarily be based on the readability of the resulting source code. In most cases, the approach of Figure 12.2 can be expected to yield code that is easier to understand and easier to maintain.

This section illustrated the use of the PUBLIC statement to specify names in a module that are to be accessible to module users. The PUBLIC statement can be used for the names of module subprograms, variable names, named constants, or any other category of name that can be exported to a module user. But for a name appearing in a type declaration, such as a declared variable or a named constant, an alternative way of indicating that the name is to be accessible to module users is to specify the keyword PUBLIC in its attribute list. The use of the PUBLIC attribute is analogous to that of the PRIVATE attribute, as illustrated in Section 12.2.

12.4 A DERIVED TYPE MAY BE ENTIRELY INACCESSIBLE

As shown by examples in Chapters 7 and 9, a derived-type definition in the specification part of a module is, by default, accessible to a user of that module. However, such a derived-type definition can be hidden from module users, as illustrated in Figure 12.3a. Focus attention on the statement

```
TYPE, PRIVATE :: card_type
```

```
! This module behaves the same as the module of Figure 12.1a.

MODULE uniform_case

  IMPLICIT NONE

  PRIVATE   ! everything PRIVATE unless explicitly made PUBLIC

  PUBLIC :: make_upper_case, make_lower_case

  CHARACTER(26), PARAMETER ::                               &
               Upper_case = "ABCDEFGHIJKLMNOPQRSTUVWXYZ", &
               Lower_case = "abcdefghijklmnopqrstuvwxyz"

  INTEGER :: i        ! handy loop index
  INTEGER :: n        ! handy temp integer var
  CHARACTER(1) :: c   ! handy temp character var

CONTAINS

  SUBROUTINE make_upper_case (string)
    CHARACTER(*), INTENT (IN OUT) :: string
    DO i = 1, LEN (string)
       c = string(i:i)
       IF (c >= "a" .AND. c <= "z") CALL upper (string(i:i))
    END DO
  END SUBROUTINE make_upper_case

  SUBROUTINE make_lower_case (string)
    CHARACTER(*), INTENT (IN OUT) :: string
    DO i = 1, LEN (string)
       c = string(i:i)
       IF (c >= "A" .AND. c <= "Z") CALL lower (string(i:i))
    END DO
  END SUBROUTINE make_lower_case

  SUBROUTINE upper (char)
    CHARACTER(1), INTENT (IN OUT) :: char
    n = INDEX (Lower_case, char)
    char = Upper_case(n:n)
  END SUBROUTINE upper

  SUBROUTINE lower (char)
    CHARACTER(1), INTENT (IN OUT) :: char
    n = INDEX (Upper_case, char)
    char = Lower_case(n:n)
  END SUBROUTINE lower

END MODULE uniform_case
```

FIGURE 12.2. Module Illustrating PUBLIC statement.

```
MODULE poker_deck

   TYPE, PRIVATE :: card_type          ! This derived-type
      CHARACTER(5) :: denomination      ! definition is not
      CHARACTER(8) :: suit              ! accessible to users
   END TYPE card_type                  ! of this module.

   TYPE (card_type), PRIVATE :: card   ! mandatory that this
                                       ! variable be PRIVATE
                                       ! since its type is
                                       ! PRIVATE

   CHARACTER(5), DIMENSION(13), PARAMETER, PRIVATE ::       &
      Denomination =                                        &
           (/ "Ace  ", "King ", "Queen", "Jack ", "Ten  ", &
              "Nine ", "Eight", "Seven", "Six  ",          &
              "Five ", "Four ", "Three", "Two  "       /)

   CHARACTER(8), DIMENSION(4), PARAMETER, PRIVATE ::        &
      Suit =                                                &
        (/ "Spades  ", "Hearts  ", "Diamonds", "Clubs   " /)

   INTEGER, EXTERNAL, PRIVATE :: random_int  ! external func
                                             ! invoked by
                                             ! draw_from_deck

CONTAINS

   ! Draw a card at random from a 52-card poker deck.
   SUBROUTINE draw_from_deck (playing_card)

      CHARACTER(17), INTENT (OUT) :: playing_card

      card%denomination = Denomination(random_int (13))
      card%suit = Suit(random_int (4))

      WRITE (playing_card, "(A)") TRIM (card%denomination) &
                            // " of " // card%suit
   END SUBROUTINE draw_from_deck

END MODULE poker_deck
```

FIGURE 12.3A. Module containing a PRIVATE type.

The presence of the keyword PRIVATE in this statement makes card_type inaccessible to users of the module, so there is no way for a user to reference either the name of this derived type or those of its components.

Next, observe in Figure 12.3a that the variable name card is made inaccessible to module users by the specification of the PRIVATE attribute in its type declaration:

```
TYPE (card_type), PRIVATE :: card
```

The Fortran 90 standard requires that an entity whose type is PRIVATE must also be PRIVATE, so the PRIVATE specification for card is mandatory. Actually, nothing could be done with such an entity outside the module anyway. While inaccessible outside the module, the structure card is, of course, available inside the module, and note that it is referenced in module subroutine draw_from_deck.

A call to the subroutine draw_from_deck in Figure 12.3a simulates drawing a single playing card from a 52-card poker deck. When the subroutine is called, it simulates the draw of a card by selecting an element from the named array constant Denomination and an element from the named array constant Suit. The blank padding in the specification of these two array constants in Figure 12.3a is required by the Fortran 90 standard, but some implementations may relax this requirement.

After the selection of elements from Denomination and Suit in Figure 12.3a, the results are transferred to the CHARACTER dummy argument playing_card by using an internal WRITE, a carryover from FORTRAN 77. The new intrinsic function TRIM is employed to get rid of any trailing blanks that may be present in the denomination.

The random selection of elements from each of the arrays Denomination and Suit is done in the subroutine of Figure 12.3a by invoking an external function named random_int, which is given in Figure 12.3b. This function returns a random integer in the range 1 through n, where n is its only argument. random_int computes its result from the value returned by a call to the new standard intrinsic subroutine RANDOM_NUMBER, which yields a random REAL value between 0.0 and 1.0.

The main program of Figure 12.3c uses the module of 12.3a, and thereby gains access to the module subroutine draw_from_deck. When the program consisting of the program units of Figures 12.3a, 12.3b, and 12.3c is executed, the resulting display will vary from implementation to implementation, and perhaps even from run to run for a given implementation, but sample output will look something the following:

```
Jack of Hearts
```

A noteworthy sidelight in the module of Figure 12.3a is the type declaration for the function of Figure 12.3b:

```
FUNCTION random_int (n) RESULT (ran_no)

   INTEGER                 :: ran_no
   INTEGER, INTENT (IN) :: n

   INTRINSIC RANDOM_NUMBER   ! new standard intrinsic sub

   REAL :: number_between_0_and_1

   CALL RANDOM_NUMBER (number_between_0_and_1)

   ran_no = number_between_0_and_1 * n + 1

END FUNCTION random_int
```

FIGURE 12.3B. Function invoked in module of Figure 12.3a.

```
INTEGER, EXTERNAL, PRIVATE :: random_int
```

In spite of the specification of the PRIVATE attribute here, the external procedure random_int can still be invoked from anywhere in the program, as has always been true in Fortran. The effect of the PRIVATE attribute is not to hide the name of the external function random_int from the module user, but rather to hide this type declaration from the user. Thus, the main program of Figure 12.3c is not prevented from invoking the function of Figure 12.3b, although a type declaration (or an interface

```
PROGRAM draw_a_card_from_a_poker_deck

   USE poker_deck

   IMPLICIT NONE

   CHARACTER(17) :: card_drawn

   CALL draw_from_deck (card_drawn)   ! Call subroutine
                                      ! in module.
   PRINT *, card_drawn

END PROGRAM draw_a_card_from_a_poker_deck
```

FIGURE 12.3C. A main program that uses the module of Figure 12.3a.

body as described in Chapter 13) for random_int will be required in Figure 12.3c because of the presence of the IMPLICIT NONE statement.

Observe that the alternative approach to handling accessibility specifications that was illustrated in Section 12.3 could be used to advantage in the module of Figure 12.3a. If the keyword PRIVATE was removed everywhere in Figure 12.3a and instead the statements

```
PRIVATE
PUBLIC :: draw_from_deck
```

were placed in the specification part, the code would be easier to understand and the accessibility would be unchanged.

12.5 A PUBLIC DERIVED TYPE WITH INACCESSIBLE COMPONENTS

In the preceding examples, a derived-type definition has been either entirely PUBLIC or entirely PRIVATE, but there is a third alternative: The name of the derived type may be PUBLIC, but its components may be PRIVATE. This level of accessibility is supported primarily to improve software maintainability in environments where programmers write modules for use over time by others. The idea is to permit the definition of a derived type in a module to be such that module users are allowed to declare and manipulate variables of the derived type but are prevented from writing code relying on any particular definition of its components. Then, if the component definitions need to be changed, the chances are improved that only the module containing the definition for the derived type will need to be changed, while the source code in program units using the module remains unaffected.

The mechanism given in the Fortran 90 standard for making the components of a derived type inaccessible is quite simple: A PRIVATE statement with no list of names is placed inside the derived-type definition, but preceding the component definitions. Observe that this mechanism does not permit some components of a derived type to be PUBLIC while others are PRIVATE—all components must have the same accessibility.

The module of Figure 12.4a illustrates a derived type whose components are PRIVATE, and Figures 12.4b and 12.4c give the source code for program units that use the module. The module of Figure 12.4a begins to provide its users with the capability of handling variable-length character strings. The main idea is to store each character string in such a way that there will be no trailing blanks. Each variable-length string will be represented as a structure of the derived type var_string_

```
MODULE var_len_string

   TYPE, PUBLIC :: var_string_type

      PRIVATE    ! User has no access to component names
                 ! and may not use structure constructor
                 ! for this derived type.

      INTEGER                           :: len
      CHARACTER(1), DIMENSION(:), POINTER :: val
   END TYPE var_string_type

   INTEGER, PRIVATE :: i   ! handy loop index

CONTAINS
   ! Given character string, return variable length string.
   FUNCTION set_var_string (c) RESULT (s)
      TYPE (var_string_type)    :: s
      CHARACTER(*), INTENT (IN) :: c
      s%len = LEN_TRIM (c)
      ALLOCATE (s%val(s%len))
      DO i = 1, s%len
         s%val(i) = c(i:i)
      END DO
   END FUNCTION set_var_string

   ! Given variable length string, return character string.
   SUBROUTINE get_var_string (s, c)
      TYPE (var_string_type), INTENT (IN)  :: s
      CHARACTER(*),           INTENT (OUT) :: c
      DO i = 1, MIN (s%len, LEN (c))
         c(i:i) = s%val(i)
      END DO
      c(i:) = " "  ! pad blanks on right
   END SUBROUTINE get_var_string

   ! Determine if one var length string > another.
   FUNCTION is_gt (s_1, s_2) RESULT (gt)
      LOGICAL :: gt
      TYPE (var_string_type), INTENT (IN) :: s_1, s_2
      DO i = 1, MIN (s_1%len, s_2%len)
         IF (s_1%val(i) >  s_2%val(i)) THEN
            gt = .TRUE. ; RETURN
         ELSE IF (s_1%val(i) <  s_2%val(i)) THEN
            gt = .FALSE.; RETURN
         END IF
      END DO
      gt = (s_1%len > s_2%len)
   END FUNCTION is_gt
END MODULE var_len_string
```

FIGURE 12.4A. A derived type whose components are PRIVATE.

```
PROGRAM demo_var_len_string

    USE var_len_string

    TYPE (var_string_type), DIMENSION(1000) :: name

    CHARACTER(133) :: buffer
    INTEGER :: count = 0
    INTEGER :: io_stat, i

    DO
        READ (*, "(A)", IOSTAT = io_stat) buffer
        IF (io_stat < 0) EXIT
        count = count + 1
        name(count) = set_var_string (buffer)
    END DO

    CALL sort_array_of_var_string (count, name)

    DO i = 1, count
        CALL get_var_string (name(i), buffer)
        PRINT "(1X, A)", TRIM (buffer)
    END DO

END PROGRAM demo_var_len_string
```

FIGURE 12.4B. A main program that uses the module of Figure 12.4a.

type, which has two components: len, which is the number of characters in the string with all trailing blanks removed, and val, which is a
pointer to a dynamically allocated array where each element holds one
character. The idea here is the same as that discussed in Section 10.8.

The main program of Figure 12.4b reads and stores up to 1000 names.
Each name is first read into the variable named buffer, which is of intrinsic type CHARACTER. Then, module function set_var_string is used to
move the name into an element of the array name, where it is stored
with the trailing blanks trimmed. The variable count keeps track of the
number of names stored in the array. When all the names to be input
have been read and stored, the array name and the count of the number
of names stored in it are passed to the external subroutine sort_array_
of_var_string of Figure 12.4c, where the array is sorted into alphabetical
order. The sort is a simple bubble sort as was described in Section 5.13,
and the only unusual feature of sort_array_of_var_string is that the module function is_gt is used to determine whether one element in name is
greater than another. Upon return from the call to sort_array_of_var_string,

```
SUBROUTINE sort_array_of_var_string (n, s)

   USE var_len_string

   INTEGER,                        INTENT (IN)     :: n
   TYPE (var_string_type), DIMENSION(n),                    &
                                   INTENT (IN OUT) :: s


   LOGICAL :: no_exchange
   INTEGER :: i

   TYPE (var_string_type) :: temp

   DO
      no_exchange = .TRUE.
      DO i = 1, n - 1
         IF (is_gt (s(i), s(i+1))) THEN

            temp   = s(i)      ! Pointer assignment
            s(i)   = s(i+1)    ! is performed for
            s(i+1) = temp      ! component val.

            no_exchange = .FALSE.
         END IF
      END DO
      IF (no_exchange) EXIT
   END DO

END SUBROUTINE sort_array_of_var_string
```

FIGURE 12.4c. External subroutine that uses module of Figure 12.4a.

the main program loops through the alphabetized array of names, displaying each name. Before it is displayed, the name in each element of the array name is moved to the CHARACTER variable named buffer using the module subroutine get_var_string since no way is provided for directly displaying a structure of the derived type var_string_type.

   The most important thing to note about the program of Figures 12.4a, 12.4b, and 12.4c is the keyword PRIVATE in the definition of the derived type var_string_type in Figure 12.4a. The placement of the keyword PRIVATE on a line by itself above the definitions of the components indicates that neither component selection nor structure constructors are available for the derived type var_string_type to a user of the module. The advantage to having the module hide the component names from a user in this fashion is that the module implementation can easily be changed without affecting the code in programs using the module. The disadvantage is that the module must provide appropriate subprograms for module users to give values to variables of the derived type and to obtain the information they need about variables of the derived type.

In Figure 12.4a, the module function set_var_string is provided for users to give values to a variable of type var_string_type, and the module subroutine get_var_string is supplied for users to retrieve the characters in a variable length string. However, suppose that it is necessary to obtain the number of characters in element i of the array name in the main program of Figure 12.4b. Observe that the programmer could not obtain the name length by coding something like:

```
name_length = name(i)%len ! won't work
```

The expression name(i)%len cannot be used outside the module, because the component name len is PRIVATE to the module and hidden from module users. The way around this difficulty is to provide in the module of Figure 12.4a another module function such as the following:

```
FUNCTION get_length (s) RESULT (num_chars)
   INTEGER :: num_chars
   TYPE (var_string_type), INTENT (IN) :: s
   num_chars = s%len
END FUNCTION get_length
```

With the function get_length in the module of Figure 12.4a, the main program of Figure 12.4b could obtain the required length by coding a statement such as

```
name_length = get_length (name(i))
```

In addition to the function get_length shown in the preceding paragraph and the module function is_gt of Figure 12.4a, it would be desirable to include several additional procedures in the module var_len_string. Among these would be procedures to determine whether a pair of variable-length strings were exactly equal, whether one was strictly less than the other, whether one was less than or equal to the other, and so on. Also, it would be handy to have a module procedure that would concatenate two variable-length strings.

Of course, the statement

```
IF (is_gt (s(i), s(i+1))) THEN
```

in Figure 12.4c is a rather awkward way to test whether s(i) is greater than s(i+1). It would be better to place the interface block

```
INTERFACE OPERATOR (>)
   MODULE PROCEDURE is_gt
END INTERFACE
```

in the specification part of the module of Figure 12.4a, as discussed in Chapter 9. Then the above IF statement could be coded in the natural way:

```
IF (s(i) > s(i+1)) THEN
```

When the meaning of the symbol > is extended in this way, additional functions should be added to the module of Figure 12.4a to associate similarly natural meanings with <, ==, <=, >=, /=, etc. Also, it would be advantageous to associate the symbol // with a module function that concatenates variable-length strings.

A noteworthy sidelight to the example program of this section arises in the structure-to-structure assignment statements of Figure 12.4c. In that figure, consider the statement

```
temp = s(i)    ! structure-to-structure assignment
```

where each of temp and s(i) is a structure of type var_string_type. Observe in the definition of var_string_type in Figure 12.4a that the component val is a pointer, while the component len is not. The two components are treated differently when the above assignment statement is executed: corresponding pointer components are assigned using pointer assignment, while corresponding nonpointer components are assigned using ordinary assignment. Thus, the above assignment statement achieves the same effect as the following two statements:

```
temp%len =  s(i)%len   ! ordinary assignment
temp%val => s(i)%val   ! pointer  assignment
```

Before leaving this example, it should be mentioned that the variable-string length module discussed in this section is only of academic interest because a standard module to handle variable-length strings has already been developed. Similarly, there is a standard module for dealing with matrix operations. Before developing a general-purpose module, one should always first check around to determine if such a module already exists.

12.6 GENERIC IDENTIFIERS ARE NOT AUTOMATICALLY ACCESSIBLE

Accessibility is usually thought of in terms of names, but it is possible for operators, such as +, .AND., //, and so on, to be either PRIVATE or PUBLIC, and this is true for the equal sign (=) as well. Of course, the possibility of an operator or an equal sign being inaccessible arises only in the context of such an identifier having a programmer-defined meaning, as discussed in Chapter 9. As has always been true, operators and equal signs used with their intrinsic meanings are globally accessible at all times in a Fortran program.

Figure 12.5a gives an example of a situation where a module author must deal with the accessibility of programmer-defined meanings for the asterisk (*) operator and the equal sign. The PRIVATE statement in Figure 12.5a is not inside a derived-type definition and has no access list, which means that all of the entities in the module for which accessibility could legally be specified will default to PRIVATE if no further action is taken. This default applies to the names of module subprograms contained within the module, as well as to the names of variables, named constants, derived types, and the like in the specification part of the module, and it also applies to any generic identifier whose interface block is contained in the specification part of the module. Thus, in Figure 12.5a, the asterisk with the meaning defined by the module procedure mult_rats and the equal sign with the meaning defined by the module procedure rat_to_real will be inaccessible to module users unless further action is taken. This is the reason for the presence of the statement

```
PUBLIC :: OPERATOR (*), ASSIGNMENT (=)
```

in Figure 12.5a. This statement makes the generic identifiers * and = accessible to module users by overriding the default established by the PRIVATE statement.

The main program of Figure 12.5b uses the module of Figure 12.5a to gain access to the derived-type definition for rat_type, as well as to the special meanings defined in the module for the generic identifiers * and =. When the expression

```
fract_1 * fract_2
```

is evaluated in Figure 12.5b, the function mult_rats in Figure 12.5a is invoked. The result returned by mult_rats is then assigned in Figure 12.5b to the variable dec_num by invoking the subroutine rat_to_real in Figure 12.5a. When the PRINT statement in Figure 12.5b is executed, the output will look something like the following:

```
0.533
```

It is worth noting that even though the main program of Figure 12.5b can cause mult_rats and rat_to_real to be invoked by means of the asterisk and the equal sign, respectively, it is not possible to invoke either of these procedures in the main program by referencing its name. The reason for this is that the accessibility of the names mult_rats and rat_to_real defaults to PRIVATE in Figure 12.5a, even though the generic identifiers associated with them are PUBLIC.

A final thing to note about the module given in Figure 12.5a is that the components of the derived type rat_type are accessible to module users.

```
MODULE rational_numbers

  PRIVATE  ! everything PRIVATE unless explicitly made PUBLIC

  ! Permit user to access * and = as defined in module.
  PUBLIC :: OPERATOR (*), ASSIGNMENT (=)

  PUBLIC :: rat_type   ! Permit user to access rat_type.

  TYPE :: rat_type      ! Since rat_type is PUBLIC and there
     INTEGER :: num      ! is no PRIVATE statement inside
     INTEGER :: denom    ! this derived-type definition, user
  END TYPE rat_type      ! can access its component names and
                         ! employ its structure constructor.

  INTERFACE OPERATOR (*)
     MODULE PROCEDURE mult_rats
  END INTERFACE

  INTERFACE ASSIGNMENT (=)
     MODULE PROCEDURE rat_to_real
  END INTERFACE

CONTAINS

  FUNCTION mult_rats (rat_1, rat_2) RESULT (product)
     TYPE (rat_type)              :: product
     TYPE (rat_type), INTENT (IN) :: rat_1, rat_2

     product = rat_type (rat_1%num   * rat_2%num,     &
                         rat_1%denom * rat_2%denom)
  END FUNCTION mult_rats

  SUBROUTINE rat_to_real (real_num, rat)
     REAL,            INTENT (OUT) :: real_num
     TYPE (rat_type), INTENT (IN)  :: rat

     real_num = rat%num / REAL (rat%denom)
  END SUBROUTINE rat_to_real

END MODULE rational_numbers
```

FIGURE 12.5A. Generic specifiers in an accessibility list.

```
PROGRAM demo_public_generic_identifiers

    USE rational_numbers   ! Access rat_type, *, and =.

    TYPE (rat_type) :: fract_1 = rat_type (2, 3), &
                       fract_2 = rat_type (4, 5)

    REAL :: dec_num

    dec_num = fract_1 * fract_2   ! meanings of * and =
                                  ! defined in module

    PRINT "(F8.3)", dec_num

END PROGRAM demo_public_generic_identifiers
```

FIGURE 12.5B.   Main program using the module of Figure 12.5a.

The applicable rule here is that the components of a PUBLIC derived type are also PUBLIC unless a PRIVATE statement with omitted access list appears *inside* the derived-type definition. There is a PRIVATE statement with no access list in Figure 12.5a, but it appears outside any derived-type definition, and thus has no effect on the components of a PUBLIC derived type, such as rat_type. If desired, the component names num and denom in Figure 12.5a could be made inaccessible to module users by placing a PRIVATE statement with no access list immediately before the component definitions, but this would also mean that users could not employ a structure constructor for rat_type as is done in the main program of Figure 12.5b. In fact, if the components of rat_type are specified as PRIVATE and no other code is added to Figure 12.5a, there will be no way at all for a module user to store values in a structure of type rat_type. But this capability can be easily provided by placing in the module of Figure 12.5a an additional subprogram that takes two integer values as input and returns a structure of type rat_type where the value of the component num is equal to one of the input values and the value of the component denom is equal to the other.

12.7 RULES FOR ACCESSIBILITY STATEMENTS

The general form of the PRIVATE statement is given in Figure 12.6. The PRIVATE statement may appear only in the specification part of

```
PRIVATE [[::] access-id-list]
```

FIGURE 12.6. General form of the PRIVATE statement.

a module. Observe that the double colon is never required in a PRIVATE statement. The programmer may specify in *access-id-list* one or more names or access identifiers, separated by commas, that are to be inaccessible to module users. Entries in *access-id-list* may be variables, named constants, subroutine names, function names, and derived-type names, but they may also be namelist group names (Section 14.10), generic names (Section 9.2), and other generic specifiers, such as OPERATOR (+) and ASSIGNMENT (=), as discussed in Sections 9.4 through 9.9.

Observe in Figure 12.6 that *access-id-list* may be omitted in the PRIVATE statement, in which case the double colon (::) must not be present. If this form of the PRIVATE statement appears outside any derived-type definition, the default accessibility for the module is PRIVATE; otherwise the default accessibility for the module is PUBLIC. When this form of the PRIVATE statement appears inside the definition of a derived type whose name is PUBLIC, module users are precluded from taking any action requiring knowledge of the components. Not only does this make the component names inaccessible, but it also prevents module users from employing structure constructors of the type since such use requires knowledge of the number, order, and data types of the components.

In addition to the PRIVATE statement, Fortran 90 also provides the PUBLIC statement for use in controlling accessibility to names in modules. The effect on accessibility of the keyword PUBLIC is, of course, the exact opposite of that of the keyword PRIVATE. The usage of the PUBLIC statement parallels that of the PRIVATE statement with the exception that the PUBLIC statement may not appear inside a derived-type definition. The PUBLIC statement with *access-id-list* omitted is permitted to appear in a module outside any derived-type definition to confirm the default accessibility.

The general form of the PUBLIC statement is identical to that shown in Figure 12.6, except, of course, the keyword PUBLIC is substituted for the keyword PRIVATE. In fact, even though this tutorial treats the PRIVATE statement and the PUBLIC statement as if they were separate kinds of statements, the Fortran 90 standard combines their discussion under the single heading "accessibility statements." Except for PRIVATE statements appearing inside derived-type definitions, a module may have only one accessibility statement with omitted *access-id-list*.

12.8   The Rename Capability in the USE Statement

When a program unit uses two or more modules, it is quite possible that the same name may appear in more than one of the modules. If the modules are used by other programs, it may be undesirable to change them. Moreover, it may be that the modules were written elsewhere and thus only their object code is available. Thus, it sometimes becomes necessary for the user of two or more modules to resolve the ambiguity that arises when the same name appears in more than one of the modules. How this can be handled is illustrated in the main program of Figure 12.7a, which uses the modules of Figures 12.7b and 12.7c.

When the three program units of Figures 12.7a, 12.7b, and 12.7c are compiled, linked, and executed, the program displays

```
1111
AAAA
2222
BBBB
4444
EEEE
```

```
PROGRAM demo_rename_capability

    USE module_1

    USE module_2, Name_x => Name_a, Name_y => Name_b   ! rename

    PRINT "(I5)",      Name_a    ! Name_a in module_1

    PRINT "(1X, A)", Name_x      ! Local alias for
                                 ! Name_a in module_2

    PRINT "(I5)",      Name_b    ! Name_b in module_1

    PRINT "(1X, A)", Name_y      ! Local alias for
                                 ! Name_b in module_2

    PRINT "(I5)",      Name_d    ! Name_d in module_1

    PRINT "(1X, A)", Name_e      ! Name_e in module_2

END PROGRAM demo_rename_capability
```

Figure 12.7a.   Program unit using modules of Figures 12.7b and 12.7c.

```
MODULE module_1

    INTEGER, PARAMETER ::                 &    ! module_2 also
                      Name_a = 1111, &         ! declares names
                      Name_b = 2222, &         ! Name_a, Name_b,
                      Name_c = 3333, &         ! and Name_c.
                      Name_d = 4444            ! no clash for
                                               ! Name_d

END MODULE module_1
```

FIGURE 12.7B. First module used by program unit of Figure 12.7a.

Note in Figures 12.7b and 12.7c that Name_a, Name_b, and Name_c appear in both modules. Assume that the main program of Figure 12.7a needs to access Name_a and Name_b in both modules, but that there is no requirement to access Name_c in either module. The ambiguity in the names Name_a and Name_b is resolved in the second USE statement of Figure 12.7a:

```
USE module_2, Name_x => Name_a, Name_y => Name_b
```

This renames Name_a and Name_b in module_2 to Name_x and Name_y, respectively, as far as references in the main program are concerned. Thus, the name Name_x is a local alias in the main program for the name Name_a in module_2, and Name_y is a local alias in the main program for Name_b in module_2. Hence, the name clashes are resolved, and the names Name_a and Name_b in the main program are those of module_1. The aliasing symbol => is entered by typing an equal sign followed by a greater than sign with no intervening blank. This is the same symbol as is used in the pointer assignment statement described in Chapter 10.

Observe that although the name Name_c also appears in both modules, the main program takes no special action with regard to Name_c.

```
MODULE module_2

    CHARACTER(4), PARAMETER ::             &    ! module_1 also
                     Name_a = "AAAA", &         ! declares names
                     Name_b = "BBBB", &         ! Name_a, Name_b,
                     Name_c = "CCCC", &         ! and Name_c.
                     Name_e = "EEEE"            ! no clash for
                                                ! Name_e
END MODULE module_2
```

FIGURE 12.7C. Second module used by program unit of Figure 12.7a.

```
PROGRAM demo_only_option

   ! The following statement permits access to only the names
   ! Read, Insert, and Update in module db_access_codes.
   ! Also, Insert is renamed so that its local name is Add.

   USE db_access_codes, ONLY: Read, Add => Insert, Update

   INTEGER :: delete = 5  ! local name only;  does not clash
                          ! with name Delete in module
                          ! because of ONLY option above

   PRINT "(I4)", Read     ! refers to Read in module

   PRINT "(I4)", Add      ! Add is an alias for
                          ! Insert in module.

   PRINT "(I4)", Update   ! refers to Update in module

   PRINT "(I4)", delete   ! refers to local variable name

END PROGRAM demo_only_option
```

FIGURE 12.8A.   Illustration of the ONLY option of the USE statement.

This causes no difficulties because Name_c is not referenced in the main program. A name clash is permitted if the name is not referenced in the scoping unit (main program, subprogram, module, etc.) using the module where the name appears.

In the foregoing discussion it was assumed that the renaming capability described in this section would be used to resolve a name clash between modules, but it is also valid to employ this sort of aliasing to resolve a name clash between a local entity and an entity in a module. However, this practice is generally not recommended. In most such cases, it is preferable to utilize a text editor to change the local name in the scoping unit that uses the module.

12.9   *THE ONLY OPTION OF THE USE STATEMENT*

In previous examples, a program unit that uses a module has had access to all of the PUBLIC names in the module. However, for cases where it is desired that the user limit access to only a subset of the PUBLIC names

```
MODULE db_access_codes

    INTEGER, PARAMETER :: Read   = 1, &
                          Insert = 2, &
                          Update = 3, &
                          Delete = 4

END MODULE db_access_codes
```

FIGURE 12.8B.   Module used by program unit of Figure 12.8a.

in a module, the USE statement provides the ONLY option. The ONLY option is illustrated in the main program of Figure 12.8a, which uses the module of Figure 12.8b.

When the two program units of Figures 12.8a and 12.8b are compiled, linked, and executed, the program displays

```
1
2
3
5
```

To employ the ONLY option of the USE statement, the module name is followed with a comma, the keyword ONLY, a colon (:), and a list of the identifiers in the module to which the scoping unit using the module is to have access. Note that the main program of Figure 12.8a has access only to the names Read, Insert, and Update in the module. Also, note that renames, as discussed in the preceding section, are also permitted in the list following the keyword ONLY. Thus, in Figure 12.8a, the main program refers to the module name Insert by the local name Add. Observe that because the module name Delete is not listed following the keyword ONLY, the main program does not have access to it. Hence, there is no clash with the local name delete in the main program.

12.10   RULES APPLICABLE TO THE USE STATEMENT

The USE statement, whose syntax is given in Figure 12.9, is employed to gain access to PUBLIC entities in a module. A main program, subprogram, module, or other scoping unit may contain any number of USE statements, but all USE statements must precede any other specification statements or executable statements. As indicated in Figure

```
┌─────────────────────────────────────────────────────────┐
│  USE module-name [, rename-list]                          │
│                                                           │
│           where each entry in rename-list has the form:   │
│                    local-name => use-name                 │
│                                                           │
│                            or                             │
│                                                           │
│  USE module-name, ONLY: [only-list]                       │
│                                                           │
│           where each entry in only-list has the form:     │
│                   [local-name =>] use-name                │
│                            or                             │
│                         access-id                         │
└─────────────────────────────────────────────────────────┘
```

FIGURE 12.9.   General forms of the USE statement.

12.9, there are two forms of the USE statement, depending on whether or not the keyword ONLY is specified.

Consider first the form of the USE statement that does not feature the ONLY option. For this form, the scoping unit containing the USE statement has access to all generic identifiers in *module-name* which are not PRIVATE, as well as to all names in *module-name* which are not PRIVATE and which do not appear as a *use-name* in *rename-list*. If a name in *module-name* appears as a *use-name* in *rename-list*, such a name is accessible to the scoping unit by its corresponding *local-name*. Of course, each *use-name* must be a name in *module-name* and must not be PRIVATE.

Now turn attention to the form of the USE statement in which the keyword ONLY is present. For this form, the scoping unit containing the USE statement has access only to those identifiers appearing in *only-list*. The only names that are accessible are those names in *module-name* that appear in *only-list* without a preceding *local-name*. If a name appears in *only-list* with a preceding *local-name*, it is accessible to the scoping unit by that *local-name*. As before, each *use-name* must be in *module-name* and must not have the PRIVATE attribute.

When *module-name* contains programmer-defined meanings for operators and equal signs that are PUBLIC, these will not be accessible when the ONLY keyword is present unless specified as an *access-id* in *only-list*. Such operators and equal signs are specified in *only-list* in the same way that they are specified in accessibility statements, as described in Section 12.7. For example, consider the following USE statement:

```
USE sparse_matrix_module, ONLY: sparse_matrix_type,          &
                          OPERATOR (*), ASSIGNMENT (=)
```

Only three identifiers in sparse_matrix_module are accessible in the scoping unit containing this USE statement: the name sparse_matrix_type, the asterisk (*) with the meanings defined for it in the module, and the equal sign (=) with the meanings defined for it in the module. Note that even though a name in a module can be remapped to a different local name using the rename capability, there is no way to remap an operator token or the equal sign to a different local identifier.

Observe in Figure 12.9 that it is syntactically valid to code a USE statement such as the following:

```
USE some_module, ONLY:
```

The empty *only-list* here implies that the scoping unit containing this USE statement has access to no names in the module named some_module. Nevertheless, there is a valid reason for employing this form of the USE statement, and it goes back to the discussion in Section 7.8 of saving shared data in a module. For example, when the above USE statement is placed in a subprogram, its presence ensures that the variables in the module named some_module will be available for as long as statements in that subprogram are being executed. Hence, even though the subprogram containing the USE statement does not access any variable in some_module, the presence of the USE statement guarantees that for as long as any procedure defined in that subprogram remains in execution, other subprograms that are lower in the program hierarchy will be able to communicate with one another through some_module.

A module may contain any number of USE statements that reference other modules. However, it is forbidden for a module to reference itself indirectly. For example, if Module A references Module B, then Module B is not permitted to reference Module A.

The Fortran 90 standard permits more than one USE statement for the same module to be present in the same scoping unit, but this practice is strongly discouraged. When such USE statements are not identical, the standard specifies detailed rules for determining accessibility, but these will not be given in this tutorial. The interested reader is referred to appropriate reference documents.

CHAPTER 13

INTERFACE BODIES

13.1 GENERAL REMARKS ABOUT THE INTERFACE BODY

Although the presence in Fortran 90 of the module subprogram, the internal subprogram, and a greatly expanded collection of intrinsic procedures should reduce the heavy reliance on external procedures that has characterized Fortran in the past, the external subprogram can still be expected to continue to play an important role. But the interface between a routine and an external procedure that it invokes was too simple in traditional Fortran to accommodate many of the capabilities desired for Fortran 90. In order for the new features to be employed with external procedures, as well as with module and internal procedures, the Fortran 90 standard introduces a mechanism known as the "interface body."

An interface body permits the programmer explicitly to specify every detail of the interface with an external procedure—for example, whether it is invoked as a subroutine or a function; the number, order, and data types of its arguments; and, if it is invoked as a function, the data type of the result returned. An interface body may be supplied for any external procedure, but in simple cases, such as those encountered in FORTRAN 77, it is not mandatory, so that backward compatibility is maintained. However, some of the new language features require that interface properties be explicitly specified for certain uses of external procedures.

The interface body is the Fortran 90 mechanism used to address several issues surrounding the use of external procedures, including the following:

(1) In other languages featuring independently compiled routines, experience has shown that it is beneficial to the software process to provide separate interface specifications for external routines. This permits compilers to make more checks and heightens programmer awareness of interfacing.

(2) It is useful for an array argument to carry its extents along with its beginning storage location (as described in Section 7.10), functions to be able to return an array of values (as discussed in Section 7.12), and arguments and function results to be pointers (as covered in Sections 10.10 and 10.12).

(3) It is convenient to allow procedures to be invoked in new ways. For example, as detailed in Chapter 9, a programmer may associate subprograms with symbols like the plus sign (+) or the equal sign (=), and the appearance of one of these symbols in certain contexts will cause the code in an associated subprogram to be executed.

The situations in which interface bodies are employed will be explored in the remaining sections of this chapter, along with the rules governing their use.

This chapter will illustrate the use of interface bodies with external procedures, which accounts for nearly all uses of this mechanism in practice. Interface bodies can also be used with dummy procedures, and an example of this is given in Section G.4 of Appendix G. Always bear in mind that interface bodies are never used with internal procedures, module procedures, intrinsic procedures, or statement functions.

An interface body is always placed inside an interface block—a collection of code starting with the keyword INTERFACE and ending with the keywords END INTERFACE—which was described in Section 9.10. Several examples of interface blocks were given in Chapter 9, but they contained only MODULE PROCEDURE statements. This chapter will focus attention on interface blocks that contain interface bodies.

13.2   ELEMENTARY ASPECTS OF INTERFACE BODIES

In order to give an elementary example of the use of interface bodies, this section will present a program consisting of a main program that invokes two external procedures, one a subroutine and the other a function. The source code for the subroutine, which is named sort, is given in Figure 13.1a. The subroutine uses a bubble sort, which was described back in Section 5.13, to order a rank 1 array of REALs from low to high. All of the features exhibited by the subroutine sort have been discussed previously.

In addition to the external subroutine of Figure 13.1a, the example program of this section also invokes the external function median of

```
SUBROUTINE sort (n, x)

   IMPLICIT NONE

   INTEGER,                  INTENT (IN)     :: n
   REAL, DIMENSION(n), INTENT (IN OUT) :: x

   ! Data specifications for local variables follow.
   LOGICAL :: no_exchange
   INTEGER :: i
   REAL    :: temp

   ! Executable statements follow.
   DO
      no_exchange = .TRUE.
      DO i = 1, n - 1
         IF (x(i) > x(i+1)) THEN
            temp    = x(i)
            x(i)    = x(i+1)
            x(i+1) = temp
            no_exchange = .FALSE.
         END IF
      END DO
      IF (no_exchange) EXIT
   END DO

END SUBROUTINE sort
```

FIGURE 13.1A. Subroutine that sorts an array of reals.

Figure 13.1b. The function median determines the median of the REAL values in a sorted array of rank 1. In statistics, if a set of sample observations is ordered from smallest to largest, the median is defined as the middle observation if the number of observations is odd, and as the number halfway between the two middle observations if the number of observations is even. The standard intrinsic function MOD is employed to determine if the number of observations is odd or even since Fortran 90 provides no standard intrinsic procedure that is the direct counterpart of Pascal's ODD.

The main program of Figure 13.1c invokes both the external subroutine sort of Figure 13.1a and the external function median of Figure 13.1b. Now, an interface body can always be constructed for an external subprogram by stripping from a copy of that subprogram those parts that are not relevant to the interface. Note in Figure 13.1c that the interface body for the subroutine sort is an exact copy of the subroutine as

```
FUNCTION median (n, x) RESULT (median_val)

   IMPLICIT NONE

   REAL                                  :: median_val
   INTEGER,              INTENT (IN) :: n
   REAL, DIMENSION(n), INTENT (IN) :: x

   INTRINSIC MOD    ! old standard intrinsic function

   ! Executable statements follow.
   IF (MOD (n, 2) /= 0) THEN
      median_val = x(n/2+1)
   ELSE
      median_val = (x(n/2) + x(n/2+1)) / 2.0
   END IF

END FUNCTION median
```

FIGURE 13.1B.   Function subprogram to determine median.

given in Figure 13.1a, except that all of the executable statements have been removed, as have all of the specifications that deal with anything other than the dummy arguments. Observe also in Figure 13.1c that the interface body for function median is an exact copy of the function as given in Figure 13.1b, except that all of the executable statements have been removed. Also, all specifications in median dealing with anything other than the dummy arguments and the result variable have been removed in the interface body of Figure 13.1c, although this turns out to be only the INTRINSIC statement. Furthermore, note in Figure 13.1c that an interface body looks like a subprogram with no executable statements. Therefore, some indication must be given that such a collection of code does not constitute a subprogram, but instead is only an interface specification. This is accomplished by placing the interface body inside a block of code known as an "interface block," which starts with the keyword INTERFACE and ends with the keywords END INTERFACE, as is done in Figure 13.1c.

It is always legal to construct an interface body mechanically by simply stripping from a copy of the corresponding subprogram those parts that are not relevant to the interface. A variable name used inside an interface body may duplicate a variable name used outside, and the two names will be completely independent because an interface body is completely insulated from the data environment of its host.

```
PROGRAM demo_interface_bodies

   IMPLICIT NONE

   ! Interface block containing 2 interface bodies follows.
   INTERFACE

      ! interface body for external subroutine sort:
      SUBROUTINE sort (n, x)
         IMPLICIT NONE
         INTEGER,              INTENT (IN)     :: n
         REAL, DIMENSION(n), INTENT (IN OUT) :: x
      END SUBROUTINE sort

      ! interface body for external function median:
      FUNCTION median (n, x) RESULT (median_val)
         IMPLICIT NONE
         REAL                            :: median_val
         INTEGER,          INTENT (IN) :: n
         REAL, DIMENSION(n), INTENT (IN) :: x
      END FUNCTION median

   END INTERFACE

   REAL, DIMENSION(5) :: x = (/ 4.4, 3.3, 1.1, 5.5, 2.2 /)

   CALL sort (5, x)    ! Invoke subroutine sort.

   PRINT "(F8.3)", median (5, x)    ! Invoke function median.

END PROGRAM demo_interface_bodies
```

FIGURE 13.1C. Program illustrating interface bodies.

Observe in Figure 13.1c that an IMPLICIT NONE statement is present inside each of the interface bodies. In addition, there is another IM-PLICIT NONE immediately following the PROGRAM statement. The first IMPLICIT NONE in Figure 13.1c forces the declaration of all variables in the main program appearing outside of any interface body. However, this statement has no effect on the interface bodies. Thus, to force the declaration of all variables within an interface body, it is necessary to place an IMPLICIT NONE inside that interface body, as in Figure 13.1c. The author recommends putting an IMPLICIT NONE inside each interface body in a production program, although this practice will not always be followed in this tutorial in the interest of presenting uncluttered examples.

When the program consisting of the program units of Figures 13.1a, 13.1b, and 13.1c is executed, the following is displayed:

```
3.300
```

While it is always legal to construct an interface body by duplicating statements in the subprogram, this is not required—it is permissible to give the interface information in an interface body by a different combination of specifications. This is illustrated in Figure 13.1d, which presents a main program whose behavior is identical to that of Figure 13.1c. The only difference between the two main programs is that the information concerning interfacing with sort and median is given in a slightly different, but equivalent, manner. Note that it is not necessary for argument names or the function result name in an interface body to match the names in its corresponding subprogram—it is only the positional correspondence of these names that matters. Also, the version in Figure 13.1d illustrates that it is not required to place all of the interface bodies in a single interface block—there may be any number of interface blocks, each containing any number of interface bodies.

In the examples given in this section, the interface blocks (that is, those sections of code starting with an INTERFACE statement and ending with an END INTERFACE statement) are not required. Here, the programs could be made to yield exactly the same results with the interface blocks removed, but it would still be necessary to specify the data type of the result returned by the external function in some manner such as

```
REAL :: median
```

Even though the interface bodies are not required, they serve as good internal documentation when a listing of the main program is being examined without the listings of subroutine sort and function median close at hand. Also, if an attempt were made during program development to use sort or median improperly in the main program, the interface bodies enable the compiler to detect most such attempts and issue a message.

13.3   PLACING AN INTERFACE BLOCK IN A MODULE

In the software development process, it is commonplace for one programmer to develop subprograms that are used by other programmers. In this situation, execution-time errors occur all too frequently because an external procedure is referenced in some manner that it is not designed to handle. However, through the use of interface bodies, many

```
! Note:   This main program is equivalent to that of Figure
!         13.1c.  The difference is that the interface bodies
!         for two external procedures give the same
!         information using slightly different specifications.

PROGRAM demo_alt_interface_bodies

    IMPLICIT NONE

    ! Interface block containing one interface body follows.
    INTERFACE

        ! interface body for external function median:
        REAL FUNCTION median (points, sample)
            INTEGER, INTENT (IN) :: points
            REAL,    INTENT (IN) :: sample(points)
        END FUNCTION median

    END INTERFACE

    REAL, DIMENSION(5) :: x = (/ 4.4, 3.3, 1.1, 5.5, 2.2 /)

    ! Interface block containing a 2nd interface body follows.
    INTERFACE

        ! interface body for external subroutine sort:
        SUBROUTINE sort (num_elts, vector)
            INTEGER, INTENT (IN)     :: num_elts
            REAL,    INTENT (IN OUT) :: vector(num_elts)
        END SUBROUTINE sort

    END INTERFACE

    CALL sort (5, x)    ! Invoke subroutine sort.

    PRINT "(F8.3)", median (5, x)    ! Invoke function median.

END PROGRAM demo_alt_interface_bodies
```

FIGURE 13.1D. Program with alternate specification of interface bodies.

of these errors can be detected at compile time, when they are easier
to deal with.

Figure 13.2a gives the source code for a small library of trigonometric
functions that accept arguments in degrees instead of in radians as do
the standard intrinsic trigonometric functions. Note that there are

```
! trig functions for use with angles in degrees

FUNCTION sin_in_deg (x) RESULT (sin_val)

    REAL                :: sin_val
    REAL, INTENT (IN) :: x

    sin_val = SIN (0.0174533 * x)

END FUNCTION sin_in_deg

FUNCTION cos_in_deg (x) RESULT (cos_val)

    REAL                :: cos_val
    REAL, INTENT (IN) :: x

    cos_val = COS (0.0174533 * x)

END FUNCTION cos_in_deg

FUNCTION tan_in_deg (x) RESULT (tan_val)

    REAL                :: tan_val
    REAL, INTENT (IN) :: x

    tan_val = TAN (0.0174533 * x)

END FUNCTION tan_in_deg
```

FIGURE 13.2A. A small library of related external subprograms.

three subprograms: sin_in_deg, cos_in_deg, and tan_in_deg. Typically, object modules for these functions will be placed in a library, and users will be required to link with that library. Observe that if an IMPLICIT NONE statement is in effect where any of these three functions is referenced, either an appropriate type declaration or interface body must be provided for the function. Also, note that each of these functions is intended to be referenced with only a single scalar argument of the default kind of type REAL, and if a user references one of the functions with some argument mismatch, some type of execution-time error may occur.

However, all of the issues discussed in the preceding paragraph can be dealt with rather nicely if the library containing the object modules for the functions of Figure 13.2a also contains the object module of a

```
MODULE trig_in_degrees_interface

    INTERFACE    ! interface bodies for 3 external procedures

        FUNCTION sin_in_deg (x) RESULT (sin_val)
            REAL                :: sin_val
            REAL, INTENT (IN) :: x
        END FUNCTION sin_in_deg

        FUNCTION cos_in_deg (x) RESULT (cos_val)
            REAL                :: cos_val
            REAL, INTENT (IN) :: x
        END FUNCTION cos_in_deg

        FUNCTION tan_in_deg (x) RESULT (tan_val)
            REAL                :: tan_val
            REAL, INTENT (IN) :: x
        END FUNCTION tan_in_deg

    END INTERFACE

END trig_in_degrees_interface
```

FIGURE 13.2B.   Interface bodies for functions of Figure 13.2a.

Fortran 90 module program unit such as that of Figure 13.2b. The interface bodies of Figure 13.2b can then be accessed by using the trig_in_degrees_interface module, and the compiler will be able to check the user's function references against the interface bodies. Hence, most attempts to use the subprograms in a manner that is not consistent with their design will be detected at compile time.

Figure 13.2c gives a simple example of a main program that uses the module of Figure 13.2b and references sin_in_deg and tan_in_deg. When the program is executed, the following is displayed:

```
0.50000
0.57735
```

Observe that type declarations are not given for sin_in_deg and tan_in_deg in Figure 13.2c because interface bodies describing these functions are accessed by use association. Also, note that the fact that the function cos_in_deg is not referenced in Figure 13.2c causes no problems, even though the module of Figure 13.2b contains an interface body for this function.

```
PROGRAM demo_interface_bodies_in_module

    USE trig_in_degrees_interface    ! Access interface bodies.

    IMPLICIT NONE

    PRINT "(F8.5)", sin_in_deg (30.0)    ! Invoke external
    PRINT "(F8.5)", tan_in_deg (30.0)    ! functions.

END PROGRAM demo_interface_bodies_in_module
```

FIGURE 13.2c.   Test driver that uses the module of Figure 13.2b.

13.4   VARIABLE NAMES OF A DERIVED TYPE IN AN INTERFACE BODY

The Fortran 90 standard specifies that, except for globally available names such as the names of external procedures, names outside an interface body are unknown inside the interface body. The intention is to give an interface body a high degree of independence so that a programmer can construct an interface body without giving any thought as to whether names inside the interface body duplicate names used elsewhere. However, a rather undesirable implication of this rule is that special treatment may be required when constructing an interface body for a subprogram with a dummy argument of a derived type because the derived-type definition must be available inside the interface body. The same problem exists for the interface body for a function whose result is a structure. The situation is quite similar to that of making a derived-type definition available to independently compiled program units, as was discussed in Section 7.3. As was described in that section, the preferred way of dealing with this kind of situation is to place the derived-type definition in a module and then use the module in any scoping unit where the definition is needed.

Figure 13.3a gives a module containing the definition of a derived type named rat_type. Figure 13.3b lists a function named rat_to_real, whose dummy argument rat is of type rat_type. Observe that the function uses the module of Figure 13.3a to access the definition of rat_type. Finally, the main program of Figure 13.3c invokes the external function of Figure 13.3b. Although Fortran 90 rules do not require that an interface block for rat_to_real be supplied in this situation, note that one is present in Figure 13.3c. When the program is executed, the rational

```
MODULE rat_type_def

    TYPE :: rat_type
       INTEGER :: num
       INTEGER :: denom
    END TYPE rat_type

END MODULE rat_type_def
```

FIGURE 13.3A. Module containing definition of derived type rat_type.

number 3/5 is converted to its decimal equivalent, and the following is displayed:

```
0.60
```

The important thing to note in Figure 13.3c is that identical USE statements appear in two places—at the top of the main program and at the top of the interface body for the function rat_to_real. The first USE statement makes the definition of rat_type generally available in the main program. But according to the Fortran 90 standard, an interface body has no access to any names outside itself. Therefore, conformance to the standard requires the presence of the second USE statement to make the definition of rat_type accessible inside the interface body, although some implementations may not enforce this rule.

Incidentally, recall from Section 7.3 that the module is used here for the derived-type definition because the standard does not permit simply

```
FUNCTION rat_to_real (rat) RESULT (decimal)

   USE rat_type_def    ! Access definition of rat_type.

   REAL :: decimal    ! result variable

   TYPE (rat_type), INTENT (IN) :: rat    ! dummy argument

   INTRINSIC REAL    ! old intrinsic func converts int to real

   decimal = REAL (rat%num) / REAL (rat%denom)

END FUNCTION rat_to_real
```

FIGURE 13.3B. External function with dummy argument of derived type.

```
PROGRAM demo_structure_arg

   USE rat_type_def    ! provides access to definition
                       ! of rat_type outside interface body


   INTERFACE
      FUNCTION rat_to_real (rat) RESULT (decimal)

         USE rat_type_def   ! provides access to definition of
                            ! rat_type inside interface body

         REAL                         :: decimal
         TYPE (rat_type), INTENT (IN) :: rat
      END FUNCTION rat_to_real
   END INTERFACE

   TYPE (rat_type) :: rational = rat_type (3, 5)
   REAL            :: dec_equiv

   dec_equiv = rat_to_real (rational)   ! Invoke external func.

   PRINT "(F7.2)", dec_equiv

END PROGRAM demo_structure_arg
```

FIGURE 13.3C. Interface body containing name of a derived type.

repeating the code for the definition (unless the SEQUENCE statement, discussed in Section 5.11, is present). Also, while the example in this section is for a procedure with a dummy argument of a derived type, the situation is similar for a function that returns a value of a derived type.

13.5   WHEN AN INTERFACE BODY IS MANDATORY

The circumstances surrounding the use of interface bodies are sufficiently complex that confusion is bound to arise sometimes. The confusion is likely to be compounded by the fact that it is possible for an interface body to be used for a particular external procedure in one part of the program but not in another part of the same program. Furthermore, a programmer may be in the position of trying to use (say) a procedure in a library and being unaware of whether an interface body is required or not. In light of these difficulties, it seems worthwhile to enumerate the conditions under which an interface body is mandatory. In all situations other than those listed in this section, use of an interface body is optional.

First, interface bodies are used only with external and dummy procedures; they are never used with internal procedures, module procedures, intrinsic procedures, or statement functions. Second, although it is always a good idea to use an interface body for external or dummy procedures, in many situations of practical interest, an interface body is not compulsory. The following is a complete list of the circumstances under which the Fortran 90 standard requires that an interface body be specified for an external or dummy procedure:

(1) When the external or dummy procedure fits one or more of the following categories:

    (a) It has a dummy argument that is an assumed-shape array, that is, an array whose rank is specified but whose extents along each dimension are taken from its corresponding actual argument. (This will be illustrated in Section 13.6. A related example was presented using a module procedure in Section 7.10.)

    (b) It is a function returning a result that is an array of values. (An example of this will be given in Section 13.7. A related example was presented using a module procedure in Section 7.12.)

    (c) It is a function returning a result of type CHARACTER whose length is specified neither by a constant nor by an asterisk (*). (This will be illustrated in Section 13.8.)

    (d) It has a dummy argument with the OPTIONAL attribute, that is, it has a dummy argument that is permitted to be omitted when the procedure is invoked. (An example of this will be given in Section 13.10.)

    (e) It has a dummy argument with the POINTER attribute. (This will not be illustrated for an external procedure, but a related example involving a module procedure was given in Section 10.10.)

    (f) It has a dummy argument with the TARGET attribute. (This will not be illustrated for an external procedure, but a related example involving a module procedure was given in Section 10.11.)

(g) It is a function whose result variable has the **POINTER** attribute. (This will not be illustrated for an external function, but a related example involving an internal function was given in Section 10.12.)

(2) When the external or dummy procedure is invoked using one of the following mechanisms:

(a) The actual argument list contains an "argument keyword," that is, a dummy argument name followed by an equal sign (=) and an actual argument name. Fortran 90 permits actual and dummy argument correspondence to be set up using argument keywords as an alternate to the traditional positional correspondence. (This will be illustrated in Section 13.9.)

(b) A procedure is invoked by a generic name. (An example of this employing external procedures will be shown in Section 13.11. A related example was presented using module procedures in Section 9.2.)

(c) An operator, such as +, .AND., or .xor., having a programmer-defined meaning appears in an expression. (This will not be illustrated for external functions, but related examples involving module functions were given in Sections 9.4 through 9.8.)

(d) The equal sign (=) is used with a programmer-defined meaning. (This will not be illustrated for external subroutines, but a related example involving a module subroutine was given in Section 9.9.)

Again, an interface body may be used for any external or dummy procedure, and the author recommends this practice. However, the Fortran 90 standard requires the use of an interface body only for an external or dummy procedure having one of the characteristics listed in (1) or when an external or dummy procedure is invoked using one of the mechanisms listed in (2).

The terminology **explicit interface** is sometimes employed in connection with the above set of rules, as in the statement, "The interface must be explicit in order to use an assumed-shape array." If a procedure interface is not explicit, it is said to be an **implicit interface**. The most important thing to understand about this terminology is that the interface for an external procedure is said to be *explicit* if an appropriate interface body is supplied (or accessible), and conversely, the interface for an external procedure is said to be *implicit* if there is no such interface body. However, it is worth knowing that in addition to classifying the interfaces for external procedures as being either explicit or implicit, the Fortran 90 standard enumerates all possible varieties of procedure interfaces and states for each whether it is classified as explicit or implicit. But the standard offers no rationale for the classification scheme employed, and the precise manner in which the standard uses the terms "explicit interface" and "implicit interface" is probably not entirely intuitive to most application programmers. For purposes of this tutorial, it is perhaps most helpful to view this terminology from the standpoint of backward compatibility: Interfaces for procedure usages exhibiting new Fortran 90 features are classified as explicit, while the interfaces for simpler FORTRAN 77-style procedure usages are characterized as implicit.

According to the Fortran 90 standard, there are only two situations, both carried over from FORTRAN 77, in which a procedure interface is implicit: (1) an external or dummy procedure is invoked where no interface body is supplied or accessible, or (2) during any invocation of a statement function. Under all other circumstances, procedure interfaces in Fortran 90 are considered to be explicit. In particular, the interface is explicit when an external or dummy procedure is invoked where an interface body for that procedure is supplied or accessible. Observe that this procedure usage involves a new feature, namely the interface body. Also—and this seems to surprise many people— the interface for any module procedure or any internal procedure is considered to be explicit, but note that the module procedure and the internal procedure are new features. Furthermore, a recursive subroutine or a recursive function having a RESULT clause is considered to have an explicit interface within the subprogram that defines it, and recall that neither recursion nor the RESULT clause is supported by standard FORTRAN 77. Finally, the interface for any intrinsic procedure is always considered to be explicit, even for intrinsic functions whose names are carried over from FORTRAN 77. This last characterization may be surprising at first, but bear in mind that Fortran 90 intrinsic functions have capabilities beyond those of their FORTRAN 77 namesakes: For example, they can return array results.

13.6   EXTERNAL SUBPROGRAM WITH ASSUMED-SHAPE ARGUMENT

The traditional ways of dealing with a dummy argument array in an external subprogram were discussed in Section 6.3. One of those ways is to use the assumed-size array, and the other involves using the explicit-shape array. But as discussed in Section 7.10 in the context of module subprograms, a dummy argument in Fortran 90 may also be an assumed-shape array. In order to facilitate comparison of the various approaches to handling dummy argument arrays in external subprograms, this section will begin by presenting an alternate version of the example of Section 6.3; here the use of an assumed-shape array will be illustrated. As in Section 6.3, the example consists of an external subroutine subprogram get_stats, which returns the mean and the standard deviation of the elements of a rank 1 REAL array, and a main program to serve as a test driver for get_stats.

As defined in Section 7.10, an **assumed-shape array** is a dummy argument array that takes its shape from the corresponding actual array argument. In Figure 13.4a, the subroutine get_stats exhibits a dummy argument x that is an assumed-shape array. In the declaration of x, note that there is a colon (:) in the parentheses following the keyword DIMENSION. The fact that there is only one colon indicates that x is a rank 1 array. Since there is no expression to the left of the colon, the lower bound for the subscript of x defaults to 1, and since there is no expression to the right of the colon, the upper bound for the subscript of x will be determined from the corresponding actual argument array when get_stats is called.

Observe in Figure 13.4a that there is no variable in the get_stats argument list for the user to input the number of elements in the actual argument array, as would typically be the case in FORTRAN 77. Instead, when the number of elements in the actual argument array is needed in Figure 13.4a, it is determined by invoking the new standard intrinsic function SIZE. Thus, it is not enough to pass only the starting address of the argument array to get_stats—the size must be passed as well. In order for the compiler to get ready to pass the additional information,

```
SUBROUTINE get_stats (x, mean, std_dev)

   REAL, DIMENSION(:), INTENT (IN)  :: x    ! assumed-shape
                                            ! array

   REAL,                INTENT (OUT) :: mean, std_dev

   mean = SUM (x) / SIZE (x)

   std_dev = SQRT (SUM ((x - mean) ** 2) / (SIZE (x) - 1))

END SUBROUTINE get_stats
```

FIGURE 13.4A. Subroutine with an assumed-shape array.

the Fortran 90 standard requires that the caller must provide an interface body if get_stats is used as an external subroutine. An example of a main program that invokes get_stats is given in Figure 13.4b. As in Section 6.3, the program displays the following when executed:

```
          mean =   0.324000E+01
standard deviation =   0.207364E+00
```

As a second example of an assumed-shape array, consider the problem of finding the transpose of a matrix, that is, of interchanging the rows and columns of a two-dimensional array. Before beginning, however, it should be mentioned that this example is only for tutorial purposes. If the need arises to transpose a matrix in a production program, use of the new Fortran 90 standard intrinsic function TRANSPOSE is recommended.

```
PROGRAM test_get_stats

    INTERFACE

        ! Interface body for get_stats is mandatory because
        ! dummy argument x is an assumed-shape array.

        SUBROUTINE get_stats (x, mean, std_dev)
            REAL, DIMENSION(:), INTENT (IN)   :: x
            REAL,               INTENT (OUT) :: mean, std_dev
        END SUBROUTINE get_stats

    END INTERFACE

    REAL, DIMENSION(5) ::                                      &
                    sample = (/ 3.0, 3.4, 3.1, 3.5, 3.2 /)

    REAL :: avg, std_deviation

    ! Invoke external subroutine.
    CALL get_stats (sample, avg, std_deviation)

    PRINT "(A, E14.6)", "                       mean = ", avg

    PRINT "(A, E14.6)", " standard deviation = ",            &
                                            std_deviation

END PROGRAM test_get_stats
```

FIGURE 13.4B. Main program used to test subroutine of Figure 13.4a.

```
                    ! Find the transpose of a matrix.

         SUBROUTINE mat_transp (a, a_transp)

             REAL, DIMENSION(:,:),                      & ! assumed-
                               INTENT (IN)  :: a          ! shape

             REAL, DIMENSION(SIZE (a, 2),SIZE (a, 1)),  & ! explicit-
                               INTENT (OUT) :: a_transp   ! shape

             INTEGER :: k

             DO k = 1, SIZE (a, 1)
                a_transp(:,k) = a(k,:)
             END DO

         END SUBROUTINE mat_transp
```

FIGURE 13.5A.   Subprogram with a rank 2 assumed-shape array.

Consider the external subroutine mat_transp of Figure 13.5a, whose dummy argument a is an assumed-shape array. The two colons separated by a comma in the parentheses following the keyword DIMENSION indicate that a is a rank 2 array. The extents along each dimension of a will be taken from the corresponding dimension of the associated rank 2 actual argument array when mat_transp is called.

The extents for the dummy argument array a_transp in Figure 13.5a are also determined when mat_transp is called, but they are not taken from the corresponding actual argument. Rather, the extents for a_transp are determined by using the standard intrinsic function SIZE on the dummy array a. Thus, a_transp is actually an explicit-shape array.

In Figure 13.4a, SIZE is invoked with only one argument, an array name, and it returns the total number of elements in that array. However, SIZE may also be invoked with a second argument, specifying the dimension of the array along which the number of elements is to be determined. In Figure 13.5a, SIZE (a, 1) determines the extent of a along its first dimension, while SIZE (a, 2) determines the extent of a along its second dimension.

The main program of Figure 13.5b serves as a test driver for the external subroutine mat_transp of Figure 13.5a. Note that the interface body in Figure 13.5b is mandatory because mat_transp has a dummy argument that is an assumed-shape array. When the CALL in Figure 13.5b is executed, the dummy argument a in Figure 13.5a will assume the shape of the actual argument b of Figure 13.5b, which is 3 × 2. The

```
PROGRAM test_mat_transp

   INTERFACE

      ! Interface body is mandatory for mat_transp
      ! because a is an assumed-shape dummy argument.

      SUBROUTINE mat_transp (a, a_transp)
         REAL, DIMENSION(:,:),        INTENT (IN)  :: a
         REAL, DIMENSION(SIZE (a, 2),SIZE (a, 1)),            &
                                      INTENT (OUT) :: a_transp
      END SUBROUTINE mat_transp

   END INTERFACE

   REAL, DIMENSION(3,2) :: b
   REAL, DIMENSION(2,3) :: b_transp
   INTEGER              :: i

   b(1,1) = 1.0;  b(1,2) = 4.0
   b(2,1) = 2.0;  b(2,2) = 5.0
   b(3,1) = 3.0;  b(3,2) = 6.0

   CALL mat_transp (b, b_transp)    ! Invoke external sub.

   DO i = 1, SIZE (b_transp, 1)
      PRINT "(3F5.1)", b_transp(i,:)
   END DO

END PROGRAM test_mat_transp
```

FIGURE 13.5B. Main program used to test subroutine of Figure 13.5a.

shape of dummy argument a_transp will then be determined from a to be 2×3.

When the program consisting of the main program of Figure 13.5b and the subroutine of Figure 13.5a is executed, the following is displayed:

```
1.0  2.0  3.0
4.0  5.0  6.0
```

It is important not to confuse the assumed-shape array described in this section with the allocatable array, which was discussed back in Section 4.10. The similarity between the two is that the colon is used in the declaration of both. However, an assumed-shape array appears only as a dummy argument, and a dummy argument is not permitted to have the ALLOCATABLE attribute, which is the hallmark of the allocatable array. Also, another use of the colon in an array declaration occurs for pointers, as was discussed in Chapter 10. However, a variable with the POINTER attribute is never regarded as being an assumed-shape array, even if it is used as a dummy argument.

13.7 External Function Returning Array of Values as Result

Section 7.12 illustrated that a module function can return an array-valued result, and the same capability is available with an external function. This section will give a simple example involving the invocation of an external function that returns an array of values.

An example of an array-valued function named log_to_arb_base is shown in Figure 13.6a, which takes as input a REAL rank 1 array x and a REAL scalar a and returns a rank 1 array, each element of which is the logarithm to the base a of the corresponding element of the input

```
! function that returns rank 1 array containing logarithms
! to an arbitrary base of a rank 1 array of input values

FUNCTION log_to_arb_base (x, a) RESULT (log_x_to_base_a)

   REAL, DIMENSION(:), INTENT (IN) :: x   ! Dummy arg assumes
                                          ! size of actual arg.

   REAL, INTENT (IN) :: a   ! scalar arbitrary base for logs

   REAL, DIMENSION(SIZE (x)) :: log_x_to_base_a   ! Result var
                                                  ! is a rank
                                                  ! 1 array
                                                  ! with same
                                                  ! size as
                                                  ! dummy arg.

   log_x_to_base_a = LOG (x) / LOG (a)   ! array operations

END FUNCTION log_to_arb_base
```

Figure 13.6a. Function returning an array of values as a result.

array. Note in Figure 13.6a that the dummy argument x is an assumed-shape array, as was discussed in the preceding section. The upper bound of the result variable log_x_to_base_a is then determined from x by using the standard intrinsic function SIZE. For a function returning an array-valued result, the specifications for the result variable must be given within the body of the function since an open parenthesis following the function name in a FUNCTION statement indicates the beginning of the argument list, even when the argument list is empty.

As discussed in elementary algebra books, the logarithm of a value x to an arbitrary base a can be found by exploiting the following relationship:

$$\log_a x = \frac{\log_b x}{\log_b a}.$$

For manual computations, b is usually chosen to be either 10 (common logarithms) or e (natural logarithms). This method is used in the lone executable statement in log_to_arb_base, where the intrinsic function LOG is used to find the natural logarithm of each element of the input array x and of the input scalar a. The scalar value LOG (a) is then divided

```
PROGRAM test_log_to_arb_base

   INTERFACE

      ! Interface body is mandatory for log_to_arb_base
      ! because result variable is an array.

      FUNCTION log_to_arb_base (x, a) RESULT (log_x_to_base_a)
         REAL, DIMENSION(:), INTENT (IN) :: x
         REAL, INTENT (IN) :: a
         REAL, DIMENSION(SIZE (x)) :: log_x_to_base_a
      END FUNCTION log_to_arb_base

   END INTERFACE

   ! Invoke external function log_to_arb_base.
   PRINT "(3F7.3)",                                          &
              log_to_arb_base ( (/ 10.0, 100.0, 0.1 /), 10.0)

END PROGRAM test_log_to_arb_base
```

FIGURE 13.6B. Test driver for function of Figure 13.6a.

into each element of the array returned by LOG (x) to yield the array-valued result log_x_to_base_a.

Figure 13.6b gives a main program that can serve as a test driver for the function of Figure 13.6a. As was mentioned in Section 13.5, an interface body must be used for log_to_arb_base if it is invoked as an external function since it returns an array-valued result. Also, because log_to_arb_base has a dummy argument that is an assumed-shape array, an interface body would be required anyway.

In Figure 13.6b, the function is invoked to find the logarithm of the array constant (/ 10.0, 100.0, 0.1 /) to the base 10.0. Of course, the intrinisic function LOG10 could have been employed to find this logarithm directly, but the purpose of the test driver is to check log_to_arb_base. When the program consisting of the main program of Figure 13.6b and the external function of Figure 13.6a is executed, log_to_arb_base returns a rank 1 array of three elements, and the following is displayed:

```
1.000  2.000 -1.000
```

13.8 CHARACTER FUNCTION RESULT OF NONCONSTANT LENGTH

In much the same way that the size of an array returned by a function is permitted to depend on values that may not become available until entry to the function, the length of the result of a function of type CHARACTER is permitted to depend on such values. In particular, the length of the result of a CHARACTER function can be specified in terms of quantities in the function's argument list, and an example of such a function is presented in this section. The function given here returns the concatenation of a user-specified number of copies of a user-specified string. However, the presentation in this section is only for tutorial purposes since the capabilities provided by the example function are the same as those of the new standard intrinsic function REPEAT.

Figure 13.7a gives the listing for a CHARACTER function named concat_copies that returns a result whose length is computed from properties of the function's arguments. Note that the first of the dummy arguments, string, is a CHARACTER variable whose length is specified by an asterisk (*), meaning its length is taken from its associated actual argument when concat_copies is invoked. Recall that such a CHARACTER variable is said to have an "assumed length." The second dummy argument is the INTEGER variable ncopies. Now examine the type declaration in Figure 13.7a for the result variable copies:

```
CHARACTER(ncopies*LEN(string)) :: copies
```

```
        ! function that returns the character string
        ! obtained by concatenating ncopies of string

FUNCTION concat_copies (string, ncopies) RESULT (copies)

    CHARACTER(*), INTENT (IN)        :: string    ! Dummy arg
                                                  ! assumes
                                                  ! length from
                                                  ! actual arg.

    INTEGER,       INTENT (IN)       :: ncopies   ! dummy arg

    CHARACTER(ncopies*LEN(string)) :: copies      ! Length of
                                                  ! result
                                                  ! depends on
                                                  ! length of
                                                  ! one dummy
                                                  ! arg & value
                                                  ! of other.

    INTEGER :: i

    copies = string    ! Set result variable to initial value.

    DO i = 2, ncopies
       copies = string // copies   ! Build rest of result.
    END DO

END FUNCTION concat_copies
```

FIGURE 13.7A. Function returning string of nonconstant length.

Here LEN is the standard intrinsic function that determines the length
of a character string, so the length of the result returned by the function
is the value of the second argument, ncopies, multiplied times the length
of the first argument, string.

Figure 13.7b lists a main program that invokes the function of Figure
13.7a twice. The first time that concat_copies is invoked, a string of
length 12 consisting of 4 copies of the string abc is returned. The second time that concat_copies is invoked, a string of length 6 consisting of
6 copies of the string X is returned. Thus, when the program made
up of the main program of Figure 13.7b and the external function
subprogram of Figure 13.7a is executed, the following is displayed

abcabcabcabc
XXXXXX

```
PROGRAM demo_nonconstant_len_char_func

   INTERFACE

      ! Interface body is mandatory because result of
      ! concat_copies is CHARACTER with neither
      ! constant length nor assumed length.

      FUNCTION concat_copies (string, ncopies)                    &
                                          RESULT (copies)
         CHARACTER(*), INTENT (IN)      :: string
         INTEGER,      INTENT (IN)      :: ncopies
         CHARACTER(ncopies*LEN(string)) :: copies
      END FUNCTION concat_copies

   END INTERFACE

   ! Invoke external function concat_copies twice.
   PRINT "(1X, A)", concat_copies ("abc", 4)
   PRINT "(1X, A)", concat_copies ("X", 6)

END PROGRAM demo_nonconstant_len_char_func
```

FIGURE 13.7B.   Test driver for external function of Figure 13.7a.

Note in Figure 13.7a that the first assignment statement assigns one copy of the input string to the result variable copies. Then, the DO loop will append one copy of string to the result variable each time through the loop. A little thought and/or experimentation will reveal that concat_copies is well behaved if ncopies is zero or string has zero length, returning a zero-length string in either case. However, unless string has zero length, associating a negative actual argument with ncopies will cause an error condition since a negative length would then be specified for a CHARACTER variable.

Observe the presence of the interface body for concat_copies in the main program of Figure 13.7b. As mentioned in Section 13.5, the interface body is mandatory since concat_copies is a function returning a result of type CHARACTER whose length is specified neither by a constant nor by an asterisk.

Traditionally, Fortran has provided no mechanism for dealing with the situation illustrated by the example of this section. However, the FORTRAN 77 standard does support FUNCTION statements such as the following:

```
CHARACTER*(*) FUNCTION func (arg)
```

This means that the effective length of the result returned by func will be determined at compile time by the mandatory declaration given for func in each routine that invokes it. This mechanism is, of course, still available in Fortran 90, but it is less flexible than the approach illustrated earlier in this section and offers no advantage. Therefore, the author recommends avoidance of CHARACTER functions with assumed-length results.

This section presented an example of an external function returning a CHARACTER result whose length depends on values that do not become available until entry to the function, but module and internal functions offer this capability as well. Of course, a module or internal function would ordinarily be somewhat easier to use in this situation since no interface body would be involved.

13.9 ARGUMENT KEYWORDS

In traditional Fortran, the association of actual arguments with dummy arguments has always been accomplished by positional correspondence. This method of associating actual and dummy arguments remains popular in Fortran 90, but the new standard also supports a mechanism known as "argument keywords" for handling this. The use of argument keywords can improve the readability of long argument lists, and as will be discussed in the next section, their use plays a role in the way that Fortran 90 deals with optional arguments. The Fortran 90 argument keyword mechanism is rather similar to what is called "named parameter association" in Ada. Argument keywords can be used with module, external, or internal subprograms, although their use with internal subprograms would be a little unusual. This section will illustrate the use of argument keywords with an external subprogram; thus, as indicated in Section 13.5, the availability of an interface body is compulsory.

The main program of Figure 13.8a calls external subroutine copy_ with_subst twice, the first time employing the traditional positional arguments and the second time using argument keywords. Figure 13.8b gives the listing for the subroutine, which copies one character string named source to another named target, substituting one user-specified character named new for another named old. In the example of Figure 13.8a, the source string s, containing "dada", is copied to the target t, except the letter "o" is substituted each time the letter "a" occurs. When the program consisting of the main program of Figure 13.8a and the subroutine of Figure 13.8b is executed, the following is displayed:

```
PROGRAM demo_arg_keywords

  INTERFACE

    ! Interface body is mandatory because copy_with_subst is
    ! called later using argument keywords.

    SUBROUTINE copy_with_subst (source, target, old, new)
       CHARACTER(*), INTENT (IN)   :: source
       CHARACTER(*), INTENT (OUT)  :: target
       CHARACTER(1), INTENT (IN)   :: old, new
    END SUBROUTINE copy_with_subst

  END INTERFACE

  CHARACTER(4) :: s, t

  s = "dada"

  ! Call external subroutine using positional arguments.
  ! Interface body is not required for this call.
  CALL copy_with_subst (s, t, "a", "o")

  PRINT "(A)", " positional: " // t

  s = "dada"

  ! Call external subroutine using argument keywords.
  ! Interface body is required for this call.
  CALL copy_with_subst (target = t, source = s,   &
                        new = "o",  old = "a")

  PRINT "(A)", "    keyword: " // t

END PROGRAM demo_arg_keywords
```

FIGURE 13.8A. An example of the use of argument keywords.

```
positional: dodo
   keyword: dodo
```

Pay particular attention in Figure 13.8a to the second CALL to the subroutine:

```
CALL copy_with_subst (target = t, source = s,   &
                      new = "o",  old = "a")
```

```
! copies a character string from source to target,
! substituting the character specified by new for
! any occurrence of the character specified by old

SUBROUTINE copy_with_subst (source, target, old, new)

   CHARACTER(*), INTENT (IN)   :: source
   CHARACTER(*), INTENT (OUT) :: target
   CHARACTER(1), INTENT (IN)   :: old, new

   INTEGER :: i

   DO i = 1, MIN (LEN (source), LEN (target))

      IF (source(i:i) == old) THEN
         target(i:i) = new              ! substitute
      ELSE
         target(i:i) = source(i:i)   ! don't substitute
      END IF

   END DO

END SUBROUTINE copy_with_subst
```

FIGURE 13.8B. Subroutine called in Figures 13.8a, 13.8c, and 13.8d.

This CALL statement illustrates the argument keyword mechanism. With respect to an external procedure, an **argument keyword** is a dummy argument name in the procedure's interface body which may be used ahead of the equal sign (=) in a reference to the procedure. The argument keywords in the above CALL statement are then target, source, new, and old. Note that when an argument keyword is specified for each argument in a procedure reference, the actual arguments may be arbitrarily ordered.

A careful comparison of the subroutine listing of Figure 13.8b with the rules of Section 13.5 reveals that there is nothing in the subroutine itself that makes the use of an interface body mandatory under any circumstances. Also, in Figure 13.8a, the first CALL statement, which uses positional arguments, does not force the use of an interface body. The requirement for the interface body arises, then, from the second CALL in Figure 13.8a since it manifests a reference to an external procedure with argument keywords specified.

As indicated in Section 13.2, the variable names in an interface body may be different from those in the procedure whose interface it specifies. This presents no difficulties with respect to argument keywords, as shown by the main program of Figure 13.8c, which behaves exactly the same as that of Figure 13.8a. The only important distinction between the two main programs is that different names are chosen for the dummy arguments in the interface bodies. But observe that in both Figures 13.8a and 13.8c, the argument keywords used in the

```
        ! Note: This main program behaves exactly the
        !       same as the main program of Figure 13.8a.

PROGRAM demo_alt_arg_keywords

   INTERFACE

        ! Dummy argument names in interface body may
        ! differ from dummy argument names in subprogram.

        SUBROUTINE copy_with_subst (string_in, string_out,  &
                                    old_letter, new_letter)
           CHARACTER(*), INTENT (IN)  :: string_in
           CHARACTER(*), INTENT (OUT) :: string_out
           CHARACTER(1), INTENT (IN)  :: old_letter,        &
                                         new_letter
        END SUBROUTINE copy_with_subst

   END INTERFACE

   CHARACTER(4) :: s, t

   s = "dada"
   CALL copy_with_subst (s, t, "a", "o")
   PRINT "(A)", " positional: " // t

   s = "dada"

   ! Argument keywords in CALL may differ from dummy
   ! argument names in subprogram, but must be same as
   ! dummy argument names in interface body.
   CALL copy_with_subst (string_out = t,  string_in = s,  &
                   new_letter = "o", old_letter = "a")

   PRINT "(A)", "    keyword: " // t

END PROGRAM demo_alt_arg_keywords
```

FIGURE 13.8c. Argument keywords are those in the interface body.

CALL statement are the dummy argument names in the corresponding interface body. However, note that in Figure 13.8c, the argument keywords are different from the dummy argument names in the subroutine of Figure 13.8b. The point being made here is that, for an external procedure, an argument keyword must be the same as a dummy argument name in the procedure's interface body, but it may or may not match a dummy argument name in the subprogram itself.

Observe that if a dummy argument name is employed as an argument keyword, it could happen that the argument keyword is the same as a variable name outside the interface body. However, this causes no particular difficulties, because argument keywords are in a class by themselves. An example of where this occurs is illustrated by the main program of Figure 13.8d.

```
PROGRAM demo_var_name_dupes_arg_keyword

  INTERFACE

    SUBROUTINE copy_with_subst (source, target, old, new)

      CHARACTER(*), INTENT (IN)  :: source  ! arg keyword

      CHARACTER(*), INTENT (OUT) :: target  ! arg keyword

      CHARACTER(1), INTENT (IN)  :: old, new

    END SUBROUTINE copy_with_subst

  END INTERFACE

  CHARACTER(4) :: source, target  ! variable names

  source = "dada"

  ! in CALL, arg keyword to left of =, var name to right
  CALL copy_with_subst (target = target, source = source,  &
                                new = "o",  old = "a")

  PRINT "(A)", " source = " // source   ! variable name

  PRINT "(A)", " target = " // target   ! variable name

END PROGRAM demo_var_name_dupes_arg_keyword
```

FIGURE 13.8D. A variable name may duplicate an argument keyword.

In Figure 13.8d, take particular note of the CALL statement:

```
CALL copy_with_subst (target = target, source = source,  &
                             new = "o",   old = "a")
```

In this statement, the name target to the left of the equal sign is an argument keyword while the name target to the right of the equal sign is the variable declared in the statement

```
CHARACTER(4) :: source, target
```

The name source is treated in an analogous manner. Hence, there is no ambiguity, and in fact, given the close relationship between an argument keyword and its corresponding actual argument, choosing the same name for both as in Figure 13.8d is often a good idea, although this notion probably takes some getting used to.

When the program consisting of the main program of Figure 13.8d and the subroutine of Figure 13.8b is executed, the following is displayed:

```
source = dada
target = dodo
```

By the way, it is permissible to begin an actual argument list using positional arguments and then switch to argument keywords later in the list. However, once an argument keyword appears in an actual argument list, an argument keyword must be used for each of the remaining arguments in the list. For example, in Figure 13.8a, it is permissible to code the second CALL statement as follows:

```
CALL copy_with_subst (s, t, new = "o", old = "a")
```

13.10 OPTIONAL ARGUMENTS

It is not unusual for a procedure to have an argument list where some of the arguments are often not needed. But a procedure reference that conforms to the FORTRAN 77 standard must always specify an actual argument to correspond to each dummy argument, whether any use of the actual argument other than as a place holder is made or not. Moreover, the requirement to fill every position in the actual argument list rules out providing the mechanism of indicating acceptance of a default by omitting an actual argument. The Fortran 90 standard addresses these issues by permitting an actual argument to be omitted, provided that the corresponding dummy argument is specified as having the OPTIONAL attribute. The new standard intrinsic function PRESENT is supplied to permit a determination of whether an actual argument corresponding to such a dummy argument is present when the procedure is invoked. However, as mentioned in Section 13.5, an interface body is mandatory for an external procedure having a dummy argument with the OPTIONAL attribute.

At this point in the discussion, some readers may envision being able to code subroutine calls such as

```
CALL sub_with_optional_args (arg_1, , arg_3)  ! not standard
```

or

```
CALL sub_with_optional_args ( , arg_2)  ! not standard
```

However, standard Fortran 90 syntax rules do not permit consecutive commas, leading commas, or trailing commas in actual argument lists, although some implementations may support calls similar to the above. But as will be shown below, the availability of the argument keyword mechanism, described in the preceding section, makes it unnecessary to use syntax such as that illustrated in the two CALL statements above.

Figure 13.9a lists a subroutine named get_date_and_time, each of whose arguments has been declared to have the OPTIONAL attribute. The subroutine is coded in such a way that a caller may get either the current date or the time of day, or both. Also, the caller may specify that the date be returned in one of the three styles shown in Table 13.1. If the caller omits the argument that specifies a style for the date, the default is Style 1, which is the form usually used in the United States.

Various ways of using get_date_and_time are illustrated by the main program of Figure 13.9b. In the first CALL statement, positional correspondence of actual and dummy arguments is used, although the last two actual arguments are omitted. This CALL asks for only the date in the default style, which is Style 1. The second CALL asks for both the current date in the default style and the time of day and also uses positional correspondence although here only the last argument is omitted. The third CALL requests only the date in Style 3, using positional correspondence for the first argument, and then switching to an argument keyword to specify a value for the third argument while bypassing the second. The fourth CALL uses argument keywords to ask for only the date in Style 2. Finally, the fifth CALL uses an argument keyword to bypass the first argument and obtain only the local time of day.

When the program consisting of the main program of Figure 13.9b and the subroutine of Figure 13.9a is executed, something like the following is displayed:

```
SUBROUTINE get_date_and_time (date, time, date_style)

  CHARACTER(8), INTENT (OUT), OPTIONAL :: date
  CHARACTER(5), INTENT (OUT), OPTIONAL :: time
  INTEGER     , INTENT (IN),  OPTIONAL :: date_style

  INTEGER                  :: local_date_style
  INTEGER, DIMENSION(8) :: values
  INTRINSIC DATE_AND_TIME, MOD, PRESENT

  ! Use new intrinsic subroutine to get system date & time.
  CALL DATE_AND_TIME (VALUES = values)

  IF (PRESENT (date)) THEN

    IF (PRESENT (date_style)) THEN
       local_date_style = date_style   ! caller specified
                                       ! a date style
    ELSE
       local_date_style = 1            ! Default to Style 1.
    END IF

    values(1) = MOD (values(1), 100)   ! Abbreviate year.

    SELECT CASE (local_date_style)
    CASE (1)
       WRITE (date, "(I2.2, A1, I2.2, A1, I2.2)")          &
                 values(2), "/", values(3), "/", values(1)
    CASE (2)
       WRITE (date, "(I2.2, A1, I2.2, A1, I2.2)")          &
                 values(3), "/", values(2), "/", values(1)
    CASE (3)
       WRITE (date, "(I2.2, A1, I2.2, A1, I2.2)")          &
                 values(1), "/", values(2), "/", values(3)
    END SELECT

  END IF

  IF (PRESENT (time)) WRITE (time, "(I2.2, A1, I2.2)")     &
                              values(5), ":", values(6)

END SUBROUTINE get_date_and_time
```

FIGURE 13.9A. Subroutine that may be called with arguments omitted.

TABLE 13.1   Three styles for
specifying a date

Style	Example Date
1	03/21/94
2	21/03/94
3	94/03/21

```
03/21/94
03/21/94   16:31
94/03/21
21/03/94
16:31
```

Observe in Figure 13.9a that the standard intrinsic function PRESENT is used to check for the presence of each of the three optional arguments. The lone argument of PRESENT must be a dummy argument with the OPTIONAL attribute. PRESENT returns .TRUE. if the argument is present and .FALSE. if it is omitted.

The subroutine of Figure 13.9a calls the intrinsic subroutine DATE_AND_TIME to fetch the computer system's idea of the local time and current date. Like many of the new standard intrinsic procedures, DATE_AND_TIME has optional arguments, and the argument keyword mechanism may be used to skip past arguments not needed. The fourth argument for DATE_AND_TIME is a rank 1 INTEGER array named VALUES such that VALUES(1) is the year (for example, 1992), VALUES(2) is the month of the year, VALUES(3) is the day of the month, VALUES(5) is the hour of the day (range 0 through 23), and VALUES(6) is the minutes past the hour. The VALUES array also contains other information not needed for this example.

Since get_date_and_time is an external procedure having optional arguments, the interface body in the main program of Figure 13.9b is mandatory. Also, the last three CALL statements in Figure 13.9b would force the use of an interface body anyway because of the appearance of argument keywords. Note also in Figure 13.9b that, as discussed in the preceding section, the names time and date both appear in the fourth and fifth CALL statements in the roles of variable names as well as argument keywords.

Perhaps a few general remarks are in order about optional arguments in standard Fortran 90. Of course, exactly one actual argument must be associated with each nonoptional dummy argument, and at most one actual argument may be associated with each optional dummy argument. Naturally, the OPTIONAL attribute may be specified only for a

```
PROGRAM demo_optional_args

   INTERFACE

      ! Interface body is mandatory because
      ! get_date_and_time has optional arguments.

      SUBROUTINE get_date_and_time (date, time, date_style)
         CHARACTER(8), INTENT (OUT), OPTIONAL :: date
         CHARACTER(5), INTENT (OUT), OPTIONAL :: time
         INTEGER,      INTENT (IN),  OPTIONAL :: date_style
      END SUBROUTINE get_date_and_time

   END INTERFACE

   CHARACTER(8) :: date
   CHARACTER(5) :: time

   CALL get_date_and_time (date)
   PRINT "(1X, A)", date

   CALL get_date_and_time (date, time)
   PRINT "(1X, A, 2X, A)", date, time

   CALL get_date_and_time (date, date_style = 3)
   PRINT "(1X, A)", date

   CALL get_date_and_time (date_style = 2, date = date)
   PRINT "(1X, A)", date

   CALL get_date_and_time (time = time)
   PRINT "(1X, A)", time

END PROGRAM demo_optional_args
```

FIGURE 13.9B.   Test driver for subroutine of Figure 13.9a.

dummy argument. But it is perhaps not so obvious at first that, aside from appearing as the argument in a reference to the intrinsic function PRESENT, there is almost no valid use of an optional dummy argument whose corresponding actual argument is not present. This is the fundamental reason that the local variable local_date_style is employed in Figure 13.9a. However, it is permitted to use an optional dummy argument that is not present as an actual argument in a reference to another

procedure, provided that, in this role, it corresponds to an optional
dummy argument of that procedure.

13.11 GENERIC NAME IMPLEMENTED USING EXTERNAL PROCEDURES

In Section 9.2, a generic name was specified for a family of functions implemented as module procedures. It is also possible to specify a generic
name for external procedures. However, as was mentioned in Section
13.5, an interface block is mandatory when an external procedure is invoked by a generic name. The example of arranging things so that the
generic name sin_in_deg can be used to invoke any function in a family,
which was presented in Section 9.2, will be repeated in this section, except that here the family of functions will be implemented as external
procedures rather than as module procedures.

For the approach used in this section, it turns out to be convenient
to have the named constants Dble, Deg_to_rad_real, and Deg_to_rad_dble
available for use in various scoping units. Hence, they are placed in a
module named sin_in_deg_decls, as shown in Figure 13.10a. Then, any
scoping unit requiring these named constants can access them by using
the module.

The four external functions listed in Figure 13.10b are equivalents
to the four functions contained in the module of Figure 9.1a. Note in
Figure 13.10b that the external functions access the named constants
Dble, Deg_to_rad_real, and Deg_to_rad_dble by using the module of Figure
13.10a. This is different from the module procedures of Figure 9.1a,
which access these named constants by host association.

```
MODULE sin_in_deg_decls

   INTEGER, PARAMETER :: Dble = KIND (0D0)

   REAL, PARAMETER :: Deg_to_rad_real = 0.1745329E-1

   REAL(Dble), PARAMETER ::                                    &
                     Deg_to_rad_dble = 0.17453292519943D-1

END MODULE sin_in_deg_decls
```

FIGURE 13.10A. Module specifying named constants for sine functions.

```
FUNCTION sin_in_deg_for_real_scalar (x) RESULT (sine)

   USE sin_in_deg_decls
   REAL, INTENT (IN) :: x
   REAL              :: sine

   sine = SIN (Deg_to_rad_real * x)

END FUNCTION sin_in_deg_for_real_scalar

FUNCTION sin_in_deg_for_real_rank1 (x) RESULT (sine)

   USE sin_in_deg_decls
   REAL, DIMENSION(:), INTENT (IN) :: x
   REAL, DIMENSION(SIZE (x))       :: sine

   sine = SIN (Deg_to_rad_real * x)

END FUNCTION sin_in_deg_for_real_rank1

FUNCTION sin_in_deg_for_dble_scalar (x) RESULT (sine)

   USE sin_in_deg_decls
   REAL(Dble), INTENT (IN) :: x
   REAL(Dble)              :: sine

   sine = SIN (Deg_to_rad_dble * x)

END FUNCTION sin_in_deg_for_dble_scalar

FUNCTION sin_in_deg_for_dble_rank1 (x) RESULT (sine)

   USE sin_in_deg_decls
   REAL(Dble), DIMENSION(:), INTENT (IN) :: x
   REAL(Dble), DIMENSION(SIZE (x))       :: sine

   sine = SIN (Deg_to_rad_dble * x)

END FUNCTION sin_in_deg_for_dble_rank1
```

FIGURE 13.10B. External functions that find sines of angles in degrees.

The Fortran 90 mechanism for associating a generic name with the names of external procedures is to specify an interface block with the generic name in the INTERFACE statement and to place an interface body for each of the external procedures inside the interface block. This is

```
MODULE sin_in_deg_interface

    INTERFACE sin_in_deg ! Name sin_in_deg may be used to
                         ! invoke any function named in this
                         ! interface block.

        FUNCTION sin_in_deg_for_real_scalar (x) RESULT (sine)
            REAL, INTENT (IN) :: x
            REAL              :: sine
        END FUNCTION sin_in_deg_for_real_scalar

        FUNCTION sin_in_deg_for_real_rank1 (x) RESULT (sine)
            REAL, DIMENSION(:), INTENT (IN) :: x
            REAL, DIMENSION(SIZE (x))       :: sine
        END FUNCTION sin_in_deg_for_real_rank1

        FUNCTION sin_in_deg_for_dble_scalar (x) RESULT (sine)
            USE sin_in_deg_decls
            REAL(Dble), INTENT (IN) :: x
            REAL(Dble)              :: sine
        END FUNCTION sin_in_deg_for_dble_scalar

        FUNCTION sin_in_deg_for_dble_rank1 (x) RESULT (sine)
            USE sin_in_deg_decls
            REAL(Dble), DIMENSION(:), INTENT (IN) :: x
            REAL(Dble), DIMENSION(SIZE (x))       :: sine
        END FUNCTION sin_in_deg_for_dble_rank1

    END INTERFACE

END MODULE sin_in_deg_interface
```

FIGURE 13.10c. A generic name for a family of external procedures.

illustrated for the generic name sin_in_deg in Figure 13.10c, where the interface block is placed in a module for user convenience. Observe that when a generic name is specified for an external procedure, it is compulsory to specify an interface body for that external procedure, while when a generic name is specified for a module procedure, that procedure name must appear in a MODULE PROCEDURE statement. In this connection, recall that an interface body is never used for a module procedure.

Figure 13.10d lists a main program that uses the module of Figure 13.10c. The main program of Figure 13.10d is the same as that of Figure 9.1b, except that the two main programs use different modules. When

```
PROGRAM demo_generic_name

   USE sin_in_deg_interface

   REAL                                :: sine_of_real_scalar
   REAL,              DIMENSION(3) :: sine_of_real_array
   REAL(KIND (0D0))                    :: sine_of_dble_scalar
   REAL(KIND (0D0)), DIMENSION(2) :: sine_of_dble_array

   sine_of_real_scalar = sin_in_deg (30.0)
   PRINT "(E20.12)", sine_of_real_scalar

   sine_of_real_array = sin_in_deg ( (/ 30.0, 60.0, 90.0 /) )
   PRINT "(3E20.12)", sine_of_real_array

   sine_of_dble_scalar = sin_in_deg (30D0)
   PRINT "(E20.12)", sine_of_dble_scalar

   sine_of_dble_array = sin_in_deg ( (/ 30D0, 60D0 /) )
   PRINT "(2E20.12)", sine_of_dble_array

END PROGRAM demo_generic_name
```

FIGURE 13.10D.   Main program that uses the module of Figure 13.10c.

the program consisting of the code of Figures 13.10a, 13.10b, 13.10c, and 13.10d is executed, the display is identical to that of the example program of Section 9.2.

It is worthwhile to compare the approach of implementing the generic name sin_in_deg using external functions given in this section against that using module functions in Section 9.2. Note that for the module developer, the module function approach is ordinarily preferable since it is more straightforward, requiring less code and fewer program units. However, there may be some situations in which the external function approach is desirable. For example, code for a family of external procedures may already exist, and it may be undesirable to convert them into module functions for operational reasons. In any event, it is always possible to implement a generic identifier using either module procedures or external procedures with an interface block.

A situation arises in the example discussed in this section concerning the handling of the named constant Deg_per_rad_dble that illustrates a subtle difference between the FORTRAN 77 and Fortran 90 standards. In establishing the value of a double-precision named constant, the FORTRAN 77 standard permits an implementation to choose whether to treat an initialization expression such as 0.017453292519943 as single precision or as double precision, and many popular implementations have chosen the latter treatment. However, the Fortran 90 standard requires that a literal constant such as 0.017453292519943 always be treated as single precision, even when used as the initialization expression for a named constant. Hence, it is significant in Figures 13.10a and 9.1a that the initialization expression is specified as 0.17453292519943D-1 since this way of coding the value forces a Fortran 90 compiler to treat it as double precision. It should perhaps be mentioned that the issue discussed in this paragraph is, strictly speaking, not considered to reflect an incompatibility between the FORTRAN 77 and Fortran 90 standards. Nevertheless, it should be understood that an implication of the foregoing discussion is that it is possible under some circumstances for the same source code executed on the same computer system to yield different results, depending on whether the source code is compiled by a Fortran 90 or a FORTRAN 77 compiler, even when each compiler adheres strictly to its respective standard.

13.12 ISSUES OF SCOPE RELATED TO INTERFACE BODIES

As can be seen from the preceding sections of this chapter, the name of, say, a dummy argument or a result variable used inside an interface body has a different interpretation from the use of that same name outside the interface body. Thus, it is no surprise that the interface body plays a role in the formal definition of the term "scoping unit," which refers to a part of a program containing a collection of names sharing the same scope. Recall that Fortran 90 standard defines a **scoping unit** to be any one of the following:

(1) a derived-type definition;

(2) an interface body, excluding any derived-type definitions and interface bodies contained within it;

(3) a subprogram, excluding derived-type definitions, interface bodies, and subprograms contained within it; or

(4) a main program, module, or block data program unit, excluding derived-type definitions, interface bodies, and subprograms contained within it.

Note that any interface body that contains no derived-type definition and has no interface body nested within it constitutes a scoping unit.

```
! Program unit 1: main program
PROGRAM demo_scope              ! scoping unit 1
  IMPLICIT NONE                 ! scoping unit 1

  TYPE :: derived_type          ! scoping unit 2
    SEQUENCE                    ! scoping unit 2
    INTEGER :: x                ! scoping unit 2
  END TYPE derived_type         ! scoping unit 2

  INTEGER          :: x = 1     ! scoping unit 1
  TYPE (derived_type) :: y      ! scoping unit 1
  INTERFACE                     ! scoping unit 1

    SUBROUTINE sub (y, x)       ! scoping unit 3
      IMPLICIT NONE             ! scoping unit 3

      TYPE :: derived_type      ! scoping unit 2'
        SEQUENCE                ! scoping unit 2'
        INTEGER :: x            ! scoping unit 2'
      END TYPE derived_type     ! scoping unit 2'

      INTEGER          :: y     ! scoping unit 3
      TYPE (derived_type) :: x  ! scoping unit 3
    END SUBROUTINE sub          ! scoping unit 3

  END INTERFACE                 ! scoping unit 1
  y%x = 2                       ! scoping unit 1
  CALL sub (x, y)               ! scoping unit 1
END PROGRAM demo_scope          ! scoping unit 1

! Program unit 2: external subprogram
SUBROUTINE sub (y, x)           ! scoping unit 4
  IMPLICIT NONE                 ! scoping unit 4

  TYPE :: derived_type          ! scoping unit 2''
    SEQUENCE                    ! scoping unit 2''
    INTEGER :: x                ! scoping unit 2''
  END TYPE derived_type         ! scoping unit 2''

  INTEGER          :: y         ! scoping unit 4
  TYPE (derived_type) :: x      ! scoping unit 4
  PRINT "(2I3)", y, x%x         ! scoping unit 4
END SUBROUTINE sub              ! scoping unit 4
```

FIGURE 13.11.   Program broken down into its scoping units.

The circumstances under which one interface body contains another are somewhat unusual, and an example is given in Section G.4 of Appendix G.

An example program decomposed into its scoping units is shown in Figure 13.11. The program consists of two program units, namely a main program and an external subroutine subprogram. Observe that the above definition of a scoping unit has been applied to the program, and each scoping unit has been identified in the comments. The program turns out to be made up of six scoping units, and as always, the scoping units are nonoverlapping. It is worth noting that scoping unit 1 in Figure 13.11 is in three noncontiguous pieces. When this program is executed, the following is displayed:

    1   2

In Figure 13.11, the derived-type definition for derived_type is repeated in three different scoping units for the purpose of better illustrating scoping units. Requirements of the Fortran 90 standard are met since the SEQUENCE statement is present in each definition. However, in general, it is recommended that such a derived-type definition be placed in a module, and then each scoping unit needing access to the definition should use the module.

Fortran 90 has four varieties of scoping units that always reside inside another scoping unit: derived-type definition, interface body, internal subprogram, and module subprogram. It is important to understand that a derived-type definition, an internal subprogram, or a module subprogram always has access to the names in its host scoping unit via host association. However, an interface body does not have access to the names in its host scoping unit, and in fact, the Fortran 90 standard requires that the data environment for an interface body be completely independent from that of its host scoping unit. This independence is so complete that if an interface body is contained within a scoping unit where an IMPLICIT statement is operative, that IMPLICIT statement has no effect on the interface body. It follows then that the data type of any undeclared variable in an interface body not containing an IMPLICIT statement is determined by the usual Fortran rule: If the name starts with one of the letters i through n, the type defaults to INTEGER, while if the name starts with any other letter, the type defaults to REAL.

CHAPTER 14

Input/Output

14.1 Overview of New I/O Features

The Fortran 90 standard provides a handful of minor enhancements to the I/O features delineated in the FORTRAN 77 standard. The new standard I/O features supply capabilities that are generally available in one way or another in most computing environments supporting a FORTRAN 77 implementation. Even so, the Fortran 90 features described in this chapter improve the ease of use of the language and the portability of programs written in it.

The most important of the new standard features is a form of I/O known as "nonadvancing I/O." Traditionally, all Fortran I/O has been record oriented, but nonadvancing I/O permits character oriented data transfer. The hallmark of nonadvancing I/O is the presence of the new ADVANCE = "NO" specifier in a READ or WRITE statement. In addition, a READ statement with ADVANCE = "NO" specified may also contain the new SIZE= specifier to determine how many characters were read and/or the new EOR= specifier indicating a statement label to branch to if end of record is detected. Furthermore, if such a READ statement contains an IOSTAT= specifier, the variable specified will be assigned an implementation-dependent negative value upon detection of end of record. Nonadvancing I/O, whose use is limited to sequential formatted I/O, will be discussed in Sections 14.7 and 14.8.

The primary purpose of the OPEN statement is, of course, to associate a unit number with an external file, and after successful execution of such an OPEN, the file is said to be **connected** to the unit. Also, an auxiliary purpose of the OPEN statement is to allow the programmer to indicate some properties of the file that is being connected to a unit. The Fortran 90 standard supports four specifiers in the OPEN statement that were not present in standard FORTRAN 77: ACTION=, POSITION=, PAD=, and DELIM=. In addition, the new standard permits STATUS ="REPLACE" to be specified in the OPEN, but "REPLACE" is not a permissible value for the STATUS= specifier in standard FORTRAN 77.

The new features in the OPEN statement will be described in Sections 14.2 through 14.6.

The Fortran 90 standard enhances the standard FORTRAN 77 version of the INQUIRE statement in two different ways: (1) The list of standard specifiers is expanded by adding ACTION=, READ=, WRITE=, READWRITE=, POSITION=, PAD=, and DELIM= to accommodate the enlarged list of standard specifiers in the OPEN statement; and (2) a new form of the INQUIRE, featuring the IOLENGTH= specifier, permits the length of an unformatted output list to be determined for use in the RECL= specifier of the OPEN for a direct access file. Sections 14.11 and 14.12 discuss the new features of the INQUIRE statement.

In addition to continuing support for standard FORTRAN 77 format edit descriptors, such as I3 and E12.5, the Fortran 90 standard provides five new edit descriptors. The new standard provides the ES and EN edit descriptors, which are variants of the traditional E edit descriptor, for outputting real values in scientific notation and engineering notation, respectively. Details of the ES and EN edit descriptors will be given in Section 14.9. Also, the B, O, and Z edit descriptors are standardized for I/O of integral values in binary, octal, and hexadecimal forms, respectively. These three edit descriptors are described in Appendix E.

For years, a rudimentary mechanism known as "namelist" has been provided in many versions of Fortran as a vehicle for performing simple I/O. For example, the heart of an input data file in namelist form might look like

```
START = 976.3, INTVAL = 4, TITLE = 'VOLTAGE VS. TIME'
```

where START, INTVAL, and TITLE are names of variables in a program that will read this data file, and the values to the right of the equal signs are to be assigned to these variables when the data file is read. A number of FORTRAN 77 implementations support a NAMELIST statement along with special forms of READ and WRITE statements that make it very easy to write code to handle namelist I/O, and many programmers have found this form of I/O to be quite handy, particularly for program testing. However, there was no standard governing the namelist mechanism prior to Fortran 90, and the rules specified in the new standard differ somewhat from those of most of the earlier popular implementations of this capability. Section 14.10 will present namelist I/O as mandated by the Fortran 90 standard.

14.2   THE STATUS = "REPLACE" SPECIFIER IN THE OPEN

The FORTRAN 77 standard supports the STATUS= specifier in the OPEN statement, but the only permissible values on the right-hand side of the equal sign evaluate to one of the strings OLD, NEW, SCRATCH, or UNKNOWN when trailing blanks are trimmed. If OLD is specified, it is an error if the file does not exist before the OPEN is executed. If NEW is specified, the OPEN attempts to create the file, and it is an error if the file already exists before the execution of the OPEN. If SCRATCH is specified, the file, which must not be named, is created for use by the program, but it is deleted upon being closed (or when the program terminates execution). The FORTRAN 77 standard also permits STATUS = "UNKNOWN" to be specified, but the meaning of this specification is implementation-dependent.

The Fortran 90 standard carries over all four of the STATUS= specifiers supported by standard FORTRAN 77, and it adds a fifth possibility, STATUS = "REPLACE", with the following meaning: If the file does not already exist, it is created; if the file does exist, it is deleted and a new file is created with the same name. Actually, the meaning of STATUS = "REPLACE" in standard Fortran 90 is essentially the same as the meaning of STATUS = "UNKNOWN" implemented in most of the popular versions of FORTRAN 77, and thus, these two STATUS= specifiers will be synonymous in many situations in most Fortran 90 implementations. However, for reasons of portability, it is wise to avoid the use of STATUS = "UNKNOWN" in Fortran 90. Incidentally, if the STATUS= specifier is omitted from an OPEN, the default is STATUS = "UNKNOWN" in both the FORTRAN 77 and Fortran 90 standards.

The STATUS = "REPLACE" specifier is illustrated in the first OPEN statement in the program given in Figure 14.1. When the program is executed, the user inputs a sequence of REAL values at the terminal, one value per line, and the program writes these values to the file named REALS.DAT. The user signals the end of the sequence of REAL values by inputting an end-of-file indication, which varies from implementation to implementation but is typically something like CTRL-Z or CTRL-D. After the end-of-file indication is input, the program displays the contents of the file REALS.DAT on the screen, one value per line.

Observe in Figure 14.1 that the first OPEN statement for file REALS.DAT specifies STATUS = "REPLACE", which means that an attempt will be made to create a fresh file with this name, whether a file with the name REALS.DAT already exists or not. If a file with this name exists prior to the execution of the OPEN statement, it will be deleted before being replaced with the fresh REALS.DAT. Note that this implies that if no file named REALS.DAT exists before the first OPEN is executed, the effect of the specifier STATUS = "REPLACE" is identical to that of the specifier STATUS = "NEW". However, if STATUS = "NEW" were specified instead of STATUS = "REPLACE" in the program of Figure 14.1, it would be necessary to delete the file REALS.DAT before running the program a second time; otherwise, an error would occur on the first OPEN statement during the second execution of the program.

```
PROGRAM demo_status_equals_replace

   REAL    :: data_val
   INTEGER :: read_stat

   ! Create new file REALS.DAT & connect unit 10 to new file.
   ! If file named REALS.DAT already exists, delete it
   ! before creating the new file.
   OPEN (UNIT = 10, FILE = "REALS.DAT", STATUS = "REPLACE")

   ! Read values from keyboard and write to file REALS.DAT.
   DO
      READ (*, *, IOSTAT = read_stat) data_val
      IF (read_stat /= 0) EXIT    ! Exit loop if EOF or error.
      WRITE (10, "(F12.5)") data_val
   END DO

   CLOSE (UNIT = 10)  ! unit 10 no longer connected to file

   ! If loop exited because of error, display message & stop.
   IF (read_stat > 0) THEN
      PRINT "(A)", " Error reading input."
      STOP
   END IF

   ! Connect unit 11 to existing file REALS.DAT.
   OPEN (UNIT = 11, FILE = "REALS.DAT", STATUS = "OLD")

   REWIND (UNIT = 11)    ! Make sure the file is
                         ! positioned at its beginning.

   ! Read values from file REALS.DAT and display on screen.
   DO
      READ (11, "(F12.5)", IOSTAT = read_stat) data_val
      IF (read_stat /= 0) EXIT
      PRINT "(F13.5)", data_val
   END DO

   CLOSE (UNIT = 11)  ! unit 11 no longer connected to file

END PROGRAM demo_status_equals_replace
```

FIGURE 14.1. Program with STATUS = "REPLACE" specifier in the OPEN statement.

The standard Fortran 90 rules governing the range of values allowed for read_stat, the variable used with the IOSTAT= specifier in Figure 14.1, are the same as those in standard FORTRAN 77. If an error occurs, read_stat must be set to some positive value, but the compiler vendor is free to choose which positive values indicate which sorts of errors. If an end of file is detected, both standards require that read_stat be set to some implementation-dependent negative value. And if there is no error and end of file is not detected, read_stat must be set to zero. Thus, either DO loop in Figure 14.1 will be exited when end of file is detected or when an error occurs during a read. Note that if an error is detected during the first READ statement, then a message will notify the user and the STOP statement will terminate program execution.

Observe in the first READ statement in Figure 14.1 that the format is specified as an asterisk (*). The asterisk format specification is the hallmark of the form of I/O known as "list-directed I/O," which is essentially the same in Fortran 90 as it is in FORTRAN 77. In list-directed input, the form of the input value must be acceptable for the type of the input list item, so each input value to the first READ statement in Figure 14.1 must be numeric since data_val is declared to be REAL.

Note in Figure 14.1 that the file REALS.DAT is connected to unit 10 when the first OPEN is successfully executed, and later REALS.DAT is connected to unit 11 if no error occurs when the second OPEN is executed. Since the execution of the first CLOSE statement terminates the connection of unit 10 to REALS.DAT, the program would behave in exactly the same manner if unit number 10 were substituted everywhere for unit number 11. However, this was not done in Figure 14.1 in the interest of making the example easy to follow.

The REWIND statement in Figure 14.1 guarantees that the file REALS.DAT is positioned at its initial point when reading begins, but this statement can be omitted in all currently available versions of Fortran known to the author. For years, the default behavior of virtually all Fortran implementations has been to open an existing disk file positioned at its beginning, but this is not required by either the FORTRAN 77 standard or the Fortran 90 standard. Nevertheless, when it is desired to connect an existing sequential disk file for processing to begin at its first record, the author recommends, for purposes of readability and portability, that the OPEN statement be followed immediately by a REWIND statement as in Figure 14.1 or, better yet, that POSITION = "REWIND" be specified in the OPEN statement as discussed in the next section.

14.3   THE POSITION= SPECIFIER IN THE OPEN

When an existing file is opened for sequential access, it is usually, though not always, desirable that it be positioned at its initial point. The Fortran 90 standard introduces the POSITION= specifier in the OPEN statement to provide the programmer with some control over the positioning of a file at the time it is opened. The standard permits only three values to appear to the right of the equal sign in the POSITION= specifier: APPEND, REWIND, and ASIS. The specifier POSITION = "APPEND" positions the file so that the next output will be appended to the end of any records that the file already contains. The specifier POSITION = "REWIND" positions the file at its initial point. The specifier POSITION = "ASIS" leaves the position unchanged if the file exists and is already connected, but the position is unspecified by the standard if the file exists but is not already connected. If the POSITION= specifier is omitted from an OPEN, the default is POSITION = "ASIS". Note that for an existing file that is not connected, if POSITION = "ASIS" is specified or, equivalently, the POSITION= specifier is omitted, the Fortran 90 standard does not require that the file be positioned at its beginning, but in practice, virtually all implementations can be expected to do this anyway.

The program of Figure 14.2 illustrates the use of the OPEN statement POSITION= specifier. For concreteness, suppose that a file named INTS.DAT, which is intended to contain a sequence of one-digit values, already exists and contains the following data:

```
1
2
```

Assume that each of the two lines above represents one record, and that the file contains no blanks. Since the file INTS.DAT is opened with specifier POSITION = "APPEND" present, the WRITE statements add records at the end of the file.

In the second OPEN statement in Figure 14.2, the POSITION = "REWIND" specifier guarantees that the file INTS.DAT will be positioned at its initial point. Of course, for any fresh connection of a unit number with an ordinary disk file, the file will be positioned at its initial point anyway in nearly all implementations, so the POSITION = "REWIND" specifier in Figure 14.2 could ordinarily be omitted in practice without affecting the behavior of the program. However, neither the FORTRAN 77 standard nor the Fortran 90 standard requires that the connection of an existing file automatically result in its being positioned at its beginning.

The DO loop in Figure 14.2 will read through the file INTS.DAT and display its contents. For the example file described above, the program will display the following:

```
1
2
3
4
```

Lazy programmers may not find much use for the POSITION = "REWIND" specifier in the OPEN statement. Because of the long-standing

```
PROGRAM demo_position_equals

    INTEGER :: int_in
    INTEGER :: ios

    ! Append two records to the file INTS.DAT.

    OPEN (UNIT = 10, FILE = "INTS.DAT", STATUS = "OLD",  &
                                POSITION = "APPEND")

    WRITE (10, "(I1)") 3
    WRITE (10, "(I1)") 4

    CLOSE (UNIT = 10)

    ! Read & display all records in the file INTS.DAT.

    OPEN (UNIT = 11, FILE = "INTS.DAT", STATUS = "OLD",  &
                                POSITION = "REWIND")

    DO
        READ (11, "(I1)", IOSTAT = ios) int_in
        IF (ios < 0) EXIT
        PRINT *, int_in
    END DO

    CLOSE (UNIT = 11)

END PROGRAM demo_position_equals
```

FIGURE 14.2. Program illustrating POSITION= specifier in the OPEN.

tradition that an existing disk file is automatically positioned at its initial point at the time of connection, POSITION = "REWIND" can nearly always be omitted with impunity in practice. Nevertheless, the author recommends use of the POSITION = "REWIND" specifier where appropriate to improve readability and portability.

As to the POSITION = "ASIS" specifier, it seems to the author that there is no situation covered by the Fortran 90 standard where its explicit specification offers any advantage. In this regard, it may be helpful to recognize that, for purposes of backward compatibility, a Fortran 90 OPEN with POSITION= specifier omitted is required to behave the same as an equivalent FORTRAN 77 OPEN, which, since ASIS is the default value for the new POSITION= specifier, implies that a Fortran 90 OPEN with POSITION = "ASIS" specified must also behave the same as an equivalent

FORTRAN 77 OPEN. Thus, ASIS is perhaps best thought of as the value of the POSITION= specifier that permits the Fortran 90 OPEN to duplicate the behavior of the FORTRAN 77 OPEN, while the APPEND and REWIND values of the new specifier provide the Fortran 90 OPEN with capabilities not available in the FORTRAN 77 OPEN.

14.4 THE ACTION= SPECIFIER IN THE OPEN

It is often desirable for a file to be opened only for reading to prevent accidental overwriting of data in the file, but FORTRAN 77 provides no standard way of accomplishing this. However, extensions supporting this sort of capability are available in many versions of FORTRAN 77, but implementation details vary from compiler to compiler. In Fortran 90, one of the most widely available treatments of this capability has been adopted as standard: In the OPEN statement for a file, the programmer can specify ACTION = "READ" to prevent the file from being written to, ACTION = "WRITE" to prevent the file from being read from, and ACTION = "READWRITE" if the file may be either

```
PROGRAM demo_read_only_and_write_only

    ! file opened in such a way that it may not be read from
    OPEN (UNIT = 10, FILE = "INFO.DAT",              &
          STATUS = "REPLACE", ACTION = "WRITE")


    CALL write_file (10)


    CLOSE (UNIT = 10)


    ! file opened in such a way that it may not be written to
    OPEN (UNIT = 11, FILE = "INFO.DAT", STATUS = "OLD",  &
                    POSITION = "REWIND", ACTION = "READ")


    CALL read_file (11)


    CLOSE (UNIT = 11)


END PROGRAM demo_read_only_and_write_only
```

FIGURE 14.3A. A write-only file that is changed to read only.

```fortran
! Read lines of input from keyboard and write to file.

SUBROUTINE write_file (unit_no)

   INTEGER, INTENT (IN) :: unit_no
   CHARACTER(132)        :: buffer
   INTEGER               :: read_stat

   DO
      READ (*, "(A)", IOSTAT = read_stat) buffer
      IF (read_stat /= 0) EXIT
      WRITE (unit_no, "(A)") TRIM (buffer)
   END DO

END SUBROUTINE write_file

! Read lines of input from file and write to screen.

SUBROUTINE read_file (unit_no)

   INTEGER, INTENT (IN) :: unit_no
   CHARACTER(132)        :: buffer
   INTEGER               :: read_stat

   DO
      READ (unit_no, "(A)", IOSTAT = read_stat) buffer
      IF (read_stat /= 0) EXIT
      PRINT *, TRIM (buffer)
   END DO

END SUBROUTINE read_file
```

FIGURE 14.3B. Subroutines called by code of Figures 14.3a and 14.3c.

written to or read from. If a file is opened with the ACTION= specifier omitted, the standard permits the default to be implementation dependent, but ACTION = "READWRITE" will be the default for most implementations.

Two of the ACTION= specifiers discussed above are illustrated in the main program of Figure 14.3a. An external file named INFO.DAT is connected to unit 10 for writing only as indicated by the ACTION = "WRITE" specifier in the first OPEN statement. The external subroutine write_file, whose listing is given in Figure 14.3b, is called to get keyboard input and write it to the file. The first CLOSE statement terminates the connection

```
PROGRAM demo_action_equals_readwrite

    ! file opened so that it may be read from or written to
    OPEN (UNIT = 12, FILE = "INFO.DAT",                      &
          STATUS = "REPLACE", ACTION = "READWRITE")

    CALL write_file (12)

    REWIND (UNIT = 12)    ! Reposition file to its beginning.

    CALL read_file (12)

    CLOSE (UNIT = 12)

END PROGRAM demo_action_equals_readwrite
```

FIGURE 14.3c. A file that may be read from or written to.

of INFO.DAT with unit 10. The second OPEN statement connects INFO.DAT
to unit 11 for reading only as indicated by the ACTION = "READ" specifier.
The external subroutine read_file, whose listing is also given in Figure
14.3b, is called to read the file and display the contents on the terminal
screen.

The third standard ACTION= specifier, ACTION = "READWRITE", is illustrated by the main program of Figure 14.3c, which also calls the
subroutines given in Figure 14.3b. Note in Figure 14.3c that the file
INFO.DAT is opened only once and closed only once. After the file is
written, the REWIND statement is used to reposition the file to its beginning before reading begins. Observe that the main programs of Figures
14.3a and 14.3c represent two approaches to accomplishing the same
final result. However, the approach of Figure 14.3a is safer because the
chance of accidentally performing an undesired I/O operation on the
file is reduced. This element of safety becomes more important in large
programs that are worked on by several programmers.

Some miscellaneous points of discussion arise in the example programs given in this section. First, since write_file and read_file are external
subprograms, it might be better style if Figures 14.3a and 14.3c contained interface bodies for these two subroutines, but this is not done
here for purposes of clarity of exposition. Second, the test of read_stat
in both subroutines in Figure 14.3b fails to distinguish between detection of end of file and the occurrence of an error during a read, and
again this is for tutorial simplicity. Finally, both subroutines in Figure
14.3b invoke the new standard intrinsic function TRIM to trim any trailing blanks from the variable named buffer. As a consequence of this,

records in the file INFO.DAT will typically be trimmed to a length shorter than the length of the variable buffer. But this causes no difficulty in any standard-conforming implementation of Fortran 90 because execution of the READ statement in read_file transfers a copy of such a record to the left portion of buffer and pads blanks on the right. The issue of input records that are shorter than the length demanded by an input list and its associated format will be discussed in detail in the next section.

14.5 THE PAD= SPECIFIER IN THE OPEN

A situation frequently encountered when performing sequential, formatted reads of an external file is that a record contains less data than is necessary to satisfy all the items in the input list and its associated format. There are two sensible ways of dealing with this situation: (1) treat it as an error; or (2) treat the record as if it were padded on the right with enough blanks to satisfy the input list/format combination. The FORTRAN 77 standard requires adherence to the first alternative, but most of the popular implementations of that standard ignore this requirement and follow the second alternative. The Fortran 90 programmer has the capability of specifying which of these two alternative treatments is to be followed by means of the PAD= specifier in the OPEN statement.

The PAD= specifier is illustrated in the program of Figure 14.4. Observe that the file VARLEN.DAT is opened, read through, and closed; then it is reopened and read through a second time. The PAD = "YES" specifier appears in the first OPEN statement, and PAD = "NO" is specified in the second OPEN. For concreteness, suppose that the file VARLEN.DAT contains the following:

```
12345
ABCDEF
GHIJK
LMNO
PQRST
```

Each line above represents one record, and there are no blanks in the file. If the program of Figure 14.4 is executed with this file as input, the following will be displayed:

```
12345
ABCDE
GHIJK
```

```
PROGRAM demo_short_record_handling

   CHARACTER(5) :: buffer
   INTEGER      :: ios

   ! Open existing file, specifying PAD = "YES".
   OPEN (UNIT = 15, FILE = "VARLEN.DAT", STATUS = "OLD",     &
                         POSITION = "REWIND", PAD = "YES")

   ! Read file, displaying data transferred for each record.
   DO
      READ (15, "(A5)", IOSTAT = ios) buffer
      IF (ios /= 0) EXIT    ! exit loop if EOF or error
      PRINT *, buffer
   END DO

   ! If EOF is detected on attempted read, display a message.
   IF (ios < 0)                                              &
            PRINT "(A)", ' No read errors with PAD = "YES"'

   CLOSE (UNIT = 15)

   ! Reopen the file, this time specifying PAD = "NO".
   OPEN (UNIT = 16, FILE = "VARLEN.DAT", STATUS = "OLD",     &
                         POSITION = "REWIND", PAD = "NO")

   ! Again read file, displaying data transferred for each
   ! record.
   DO
      READ (16, "(A5)", IOSTAT = ios) buffer
      IF (ios /= 0) EXIT    ! exit loop if EOF or error
      PRINT *, buffer
   END DO

   ! If error is detected on attempted read, display a message.
   IF (ios > 0) PRINT "(A)", ' Read error with PAD = "NO"'

   CLOSE (UNIT = 16)

END PROGRAM demo_short_record_handling
```

Figure 14.4. Program illustrating the OPEN statement PAD= specifier.

```
LMNO
PQRST
No read errors with PAD = "YES"
12345
ABCDE
GHIJK
Read error with PAD = "NO"
```

Note that both READ statements in Figure 14.4 read a record into buffer, a CHARACTER variable of length 5, under an A5 edit descriptor. Thus, records of length 5 are simply read in and displayed. Observe that the second record, ABCDEF, contains six characters, but only the first five are read in and displayed for both passes through the file. This follows both the FORTRAN 77 and Fortran 90 standards, which require that if a record contains more data than is necessary to satisfy the input list/format combination, the remaining data are ignored. (However, Fortran 90 has provisions for altering this treatment as well, as will be described in Sections 14.7 and 14.8.) But note that the fourth record, LMNO, in VARLEN.DAT contains only four characters, and it is treated differently in the two passes through the file. In the first pass, with PAD = "YES", there is no error and a blank is padded to the right of this input record, while in the second pass, with PAD = "NO", an error condition is raised. Hence, the Fortran 90 programmer has some control over how the situation is handled when a formatted read requires more data than the record contains.

For the PAD= specifier, the Fortran 90 standard permits only the character strings YES or NO (possibly in lower case and possibly with trailing blanks) to appear on the right-hand side of the equal sign. If the PAD= specifier is omitted in an OPEN, PAD = "YES" is the default. Note that this Fortran 90 default conflicts with the FORTRAN 77 standard but is in agreement with most actual implementations of that earlier standard.

14.6 THE DELIM= SPECIFIER IN THE OPEN

List-directed output, that is, output from a WRITE or PRINT statement whose format is specified by an asterisk (*), is essentially the same in standard Fortran 90 as it is in standard FORTRAN 77. However, the FORTRAN 77 standard specifies that in this form of output, values of type CHARACTER will be output without delimiters. The Fortran 90 standard permits the programmer to indicate whether such values will be output-delimited by apostrophes ('), output-delimited by quote marks ("), or output without delimiters. Also, Fortran 90 permits the same three choices for outputting CHARACTER values in namelist output, a form of output not supported in standard FORTRAN 77. Namelist I/O will be discussed in Section 14.10.

The Fortran 90 mechanism for controlling the appearance of delimiters surrounding character constants written with list-directed or namelist formatting is the DELIM= specifier in the OPEN statement, and the use of this specifier is illustrated in the program of Figure 14.5. The

```
      ! Note: The DELIM= specifier in the OPEN statement
      !       affects only list-directed and namelist output.

PROGRAM demo_delim_equals

   CHARACTER(25) :: buffer

   OPEN (UNIT = 10, FILE = 'LIST.OUT', &   ! DELIM= specifier
                    STATUS = 'REPLACE')    ! omitted, so same
                                           ! as DELIM = 'NONE'

   buffer = 'The first output record.'
   WRITE (10, *) buffer                ! no delimiters

   OPEN (UNIT = 10, STATUS = 'OLD',  &     ! Change delimiters
              DELIM = 'APOSTROPHE')        ! to apostrophes.

   buffer = "Second output record."
   WRITE (10, *) buffer                    ! apostrophe delimiters

   OPEN (UNIT = 10, STATUS = "OLD",  &     ! Change delimiters
                    DELIM = "QUOTE")       ! to quotes.

   buffer = 'Output record number 3.'
   WRITE (10, *) buffer                    ! quote mark delimiters

   OPEN (UNIT = 10, STATUS = 'OLD',  &     ! Change delimiters
                    DELIM = 'NONE')        ! to none.

   buffer = "Fourth output record."
   WRITE (10, *) buffer                    ! no delimiters

   CLOSE (UNIT = 10)

END PROGRAM demo_delim_equals
```

FIGURE 14.5. Program illustrating OPEN statement DELIM= specifier.

possible standard values for the DELIM= specifier are APOSTROPHE, QUOTE, and NONE. If the DELIM= specifier is omitted, the default value is NONE. Note in the first OPEN statement in Figure 14.5 that DELIM= does not appear, and so, by default, any character constant written will not be delimited by either apostrophes or quote marks. In the second OPEN statement, the specifier DELIM = 'APOSTROPHE' indicates that in list-directed and namelist output, character constants are to be surrounded by apostrophes. The specifier DELIM = "QUOTE" in the third OPEN signifies that character constants are to be surrounded by quote marks in list-directed and namelist output. Finally, the specifier DELIM = 'NONE' in the last OPEN means that character constants will not be output surrounded by either apostrophes or quote marks.

When the program of Figure 14.5 is executed, the following is written to file LIST.OUT:

```
The first output record.
'Second output record.      '
"Output record number 3.    "
Fourth output record.
```

Observe that the choice of delimiter employed inside the program of Figure 14.5 has no bearing on the delimiter appearing in the output. Note also that trailing blanks are output to the file, so the first output record has one trailing blank and the fourth output record has four trailing blanks.

Observe in Figure 14.5 that no file name appears in the last three OPEN statements. This illustrates a carryover from standard FORTRAN 77 that is sometimes called "open-by-unit." If a unit is already connected to a file, issuing an OPEN for that unit without specifying a file indicates that the file to be connected to the unit is the same as the file to which the unit is already connected. Figure 14.5 shows how to use such an OPEN to change the value of the DELIM= specifier, and the same approach may also be used to change the value of the PAD= specifier (Section 14.5) and the BLANK= specifier (a carryover from FORTRAN 77). Execution of an open-by-unit does not affect the position of a file.

When an OPEN is given for a file that is already connected, the only specifiers permitted to take values different from those already in effect are the DELIM=, PAD=, BLANK=, IOSTAT=, and ERR= specifiers, and this rule applies to specifiers whose values are assumed by default as well as to those whose values are specified explicitly. In particular, the STATUS= specifier in such an OPEN is not permitted to take a value different from that already in effect, and this dictates the explicit specification of the value OLD for the STATUS= specifier in each of the last three OPEN statements in Figure 14.5. This comes about because of the following behavior: After successful execution of an OPEN statement with a STATUS = "REPLACE" specifier, the Fortran 90 standard requires that the status of the newly opened file be automatically updated to reflect its current status, so the status of the file is changed to OLD upon completion of its creation. Hence, in each of the last three OPENs in Figure 14.5, conformance to the standard requires that the STATUS= specifier must take on the value OLD. It should be noted that, according to the standard, the STATUS= specifier may not be omitted in any of the last three OPENs in Figure 14.5 since this would be the equivalent of specifying the default value of UNKNOWN for the STATUS= specifier and thus would constitute an illegal attempt to implicitly specify a value for the STATUS= specifier different from that currently in effect.

14.7 NONADVANCING I/O

Traditionally, all Fortran I/O has been record-oriented. In record-oriented input, a read of as little as the first character of a long record automatically causes the file to be positioned all the way to the beginning of the next record. And in record-oriented output, a write automatically causes an end-of-record indicator to follow any data that are written. While record-oriented I/O works well in most situations of practical interest to Fortran programmers, it is sometimes desirable to be able to read or write only a part of a record and leave the file positioned wherever the I/O operation left off. For example, in a file containing mixed records written in different formats, the first character in a record might be a code indicating which of several formats should be employed to read the rest of the record. In such a situation it would be convenient to be able to use one READ statement to read the first character and another to read the rest of the record in the appropriate format. In order to address such requirements, Fortran 90 introduces a character-oriented I/O, which the new standard calls **nonadvancing I/O** to distinguish it from the traditional record-oriented I/O, which has now been designated as **advancing I/O**. Some literature uses the descriptive term "partial record I/O" as a synonym for nonadvancing I/O. Also, some people characterize nonadvancing I/O as "stream I/O," but this suggests an insensitivity to end of record not exhibited by Fortran 90 nonadvancing I/O.

To understand how nonadvancing I/O works, consider the problem of writing a program to make a character-by-character copy of an arbitrary file. A general solution to this problem, which is so easily handled in most other popular languages, is not readily available in standard FORTRAN 77. A program illustrating a Fortran 90 approach to this

```
              ! Make a copy of a file, one character at a time.

PROGRAM copy_file

   ! End-of-file and end-of-record values
   ! are implementation dependent.
   INTEGER, PARAMETER :: Eof = -1,  Eor = -2

   CHARACTER(1) :: one_char
   INTEGER      :: read_stat

   OPEN (UNIT = 10, FILE = "INFILE.DAT", STATUS = "OLD",  &
                                      POSITION = "REWIND")

   OPEN (UNIT = 11, FILE = "OUTFILE.DAT", STATUS = "NEW")

   DO
      READ (UNIT = 10, FMT = "(A1)",        &   ! Read one
               IOSTAT = read_stat,          &   ! char from
                  ADVANCE = "NO") one_char       ! input file.

      IF (read_stat == Eof) EXIT   ! Exit DO if end of file.

      IF (read_stat == 0) THEN
         ! Write character just read to output file.
         WRITE (UNIT = 11, FMT = "(A1)", ADVANCE = "NO")   &
                                             one_char
      ELSE IF (read_stat == Eor) THEN
         ! End of record input -- output end of record.
         WRITE (UNIT = 11, FMT = "()", ADVANCE = "YES")
      ELSE
         PRINT "(A)", " Error reading input file."
         STOP
      END IF
   END DO

   CLOSE (UNIT = 10)
   CLOSE (UNIT = 11)

END PROGRAM copy_file
```

FIGURE 14.6. Program illustrating nonadvancing I/O.

problem is given in Figure 14.6, where the most important thing to note is the appearance of the ADVANCE = "NO" specifier in both the READ statement and the first WRITE statement. The READ statement reads only one character, and the ADVANCE = "NO" specifier causes the input file to remain positioned immediately after that character at the completion of the read, suppressing the automatic skip to the beginning of the next record that accompanies execution of a traditional record-oriented READ statement. Similarly, the first WRITE statement writes only one character, and the presence of the ADVANCE = "NO" specifier causes the output file to remain positioned immediately after that character at the completion of the write, suppressing the automatic output of an end-of-record indicator that accompanies execution of a traditional record-oriented WRITE statement.

After each execution of the READ statement in Figure 14.6, read_stat takes on a value indicating whether any special conditions arose during the read. The Fortran 90 standard requires that the read_stat values must obey the following rules:

(1) The value must be zero if there is no error and neither end of file nor end of record is detected.
(2) The value must be positive if an error occurs, and implementation-specific meanings are ordinarily associated with specific positive values by compiler vendors.
(3) The value must be negative if end of file is detected and no error occurs. The standard permits the value indicating end of file to be implementation-dependent, but many compilers use -1 for this purpose.
(4) If there is no error and end of file is not detected, but end of record is detected, the value must be negative and different from that indicating end of file. Again, the standard permits the value indicating end of record to be implementation-dependent, but many compilers use -2 for this purpose.

These rules are backwardly compatible with those in the FORTRAN 77 standard, the only difference being that the Fortran 90 rules allow for the possibility of an end-of-record indication on nonadvancing reads, a capability not available in standard FORTRAN 77.

If read_stat has the end-of-file value after the READ in Figure 14.6, the simple DO construct is exited, and the input and output files are closed. If read_stat has the value zero, there was no error and neither end of file nor end of record was detected, so the character just read is written to the output file using a nonadvancing WRITE. If read_stat has the end-of-record value, an end of record is written to the output file using an advancing WRITE. Finally, if read_stat is neither zero nor the end-of-file value nor the end-of-record value, it must be some positive value, and a message indicating that a read error occurred is displayed.

In Figure 14.6, the WRITE statement that writes the end-of-record indication to the output file is coded as follows:

```
WRITE (UNIT = 11, FMT = "()", ADVANCE = "YES")
```

However, since I/O is by default advancing and UNIT= and FMT= may be omitted, this statement could be coded as

```
WRITE (11, '()')
```

by using apostrophes as delimiters instead of quote marks. The latter version of this WRITE statement is a valid way to write an empty record in standard FORTRAN 77, although most programmers seem unaware of this. Incidentally, note that Fortran 90 permits both advancing and nonadvancing I/O to be performed on the same file.

The standard provides no way to specify nonadvancing I/O in a PRINT statement. The ADVANCE = "NO" specifier may appear only in a formatted sequential READ or WRITE statement where the format is not specified by an asterisk (*). The only time it makes sense to test the value returned by the IOSTAT= specifier for end of record is after the execution of a READ statement having the ADVANCE = "NO" specifier. Also, the Fortran 90 standard supports READ statements such as the following:

```
READ (UNIT = 10, FMT = "(A)", ADVANCE = "NO",  &
                EOR = 500, END = 999)
```

This means that if an end of file is detected during the READ, branch to the statement labeled 999, and if an end of record is detected, branch to the statement labeled 500.

14.8 THE SIZE= SPECIFIER IN A NONADVANCING READ

The preceding section introduced the principal ideas surrounding the use of nonadvancing I/O, and this section will extend that discussion slightly by describing the SIZE= specifier, which may appear only in a READ statement that contains an ADVANCE= specifier with the value NO. When execution of a nonadvancing READ statement terminates, the value of the variable specified in the SIZE= specifier is set to the count of the characters transferred from the input file during execution of the READ. One use for a nonadvancing READ with a SIZE= specifier is to read varying-length records and determine their lengths.

A simple program that illustrates the use of the SIZE= specifier is given in Figure 14.7. The program is intended to read sequentially a

```
PROGRAM demo_size_equals

   INTEGER, PARAMETER :: Max_rec_len = 9

   CHARACTER(Max_rec_len+1) :: buffer

   INTEGER :: read_stat
   INTEGER :: num_chars
   INTEGER, PARAMETER :: Eof = -1, Eor = -2

   OPEN (UNIT = 15, FILE = "FILEDATA.TXT", STATUS = "OLD",    &
                                        POSITION = "REWIND")

   DO
       READ (UNIT = 15, FMT = "(A)", ADVANCE = "NO",          &
                  IOSTAT = read_stat, SIZE = num_chars) buffer

       IF (read_stat == Eor) THEN
           PRINT "(A, I5)", " Number characters read = ",     &
                                                    num_chars
       ELSE IF (read_stat == Eof) THEN
           PRINT "(A)", " Input file read successfully."
           EXIT
       ELSE IF (read_stat == 0) THEN
           PRINT "(A)", " Input record too long."
           EXIT
       ELSE
           PRINT "(A)", " Error on read."
           EXIT
       END IF
   END DO

   CLOSE (UNIT = 15)

END PROGRAM demo_size_equals
```

FIGURE 14.7. Program that demonstrates the SIZE= specifier.

file having variable-length records where the length of an input record is not expected to exceed nine characters. The unrealistically short record length limit has been chosen for tutorial purposes and can be increased by changing the value of the named constant Max_rec_len. Each time the READ statement is executed, the value of the variable num_chars will be set to the number of characters transferred to buffer from the input file and the value of the variable read_stat will be set as discussed in the preceding section.

Now suppose that the file input to the program of Figure 14.7 contains the following:

```
ABCDE
F

IJKLMNOPQ
1234567890
abcde
```

Each line above represents one record in the input file, and each record has no trailing blanks. The third line above is blank and represents a zero-length record. Executing the program of Figure 14.7 with this file as input will result in the following display:

```
Number of characters read =    5
Number of characters read =    1
Number of characters read =    0
Number of characters read =    9
Input record too long.
```

Note that each execution of the READ statement causes one record to be input if the record contains nine or fewer characters, and that even a zero-length record causes no difficulty. After each of the first four executions of the READ, read_stat takes on the value Eor and num_chars takes on the values 5, 1, 0, and 9, respectively. After the fifth execution of the READ, read_stat takes on the value zero and num_chars takes on the value 10.

Each of the first four executions of the nonadvancing READ in Figure 14.7 for the sample input file listed above attempts to read 10 characters from a record that contains fewer than 10 characters. Thus, end of record is detected, all the characters in that record are transferred to the beginning of buffer, and blanks are padded on the right of buffer. Note that the count of characters transferred in num_chars does not include the blank padding. The fifth execution of the nonadvancing READ in Figure 14.7 for the sample input file listed above transfers all 10 characters in the record to buffer and leaves the file positioned just in front of the end-of-record indication, so end of record is not detected by this READ.

An important point illustrated by the preceding example program is this: Unlike some other languages, the Fortran 90 nonadvancing READ does **not** treat the end-of-record indicator as simply another character in the stream of input. The portrayal of the nonadvancing READ as character oriented is applicable only when no end of record is encountered during the execution of the READ. A Fortran 90 READ, whether advancing or nonadvancing, always gives special treatment to an end-of-record indicator.

14.9   ES AND EN DATA EDIT DESCRIPTORS

For years Fortran has provided the E edit descriptor for use in outputting floating-point values. For example, executing a statement such as

```
PRINT "(E11.3)", 12300.0
```

will display something like

```
0.123E+05
```

preceded by two blanks. The output is, of course, a computer-peculiar way of representing 0.123×10^5, where the quantity 0.123 is known as the "significand" and the quantity 5 (or 05) is called the "exponent." The standards permit some minor variations in the form of the output controlled by an E edit descriptor (for example, the leading zero of the significand may be replaced by a blank), but the significand must always be greater than or equal to 0 and less than 1.

Because the output produced by the E edit descriptor has been around for so many years, it is perhaps no longer obvious that its form does not reflect any representation of numerical quantities in general use in the technical world. In order to provide more flexibility, the Fortran 90 standard supports two alternative edit descriptors, ES and EN, for outputting floating-point values. The ES edit descriptor produces an output field in a scientific notation where the magnitude of the significand is always greater than or equal to 1 and less than 10, except when the output value is 0. Thus, executing a statement such as

```
PRINT "(ES11.3)", 12300.0
```

will display something like

```
1.230E+04
```

preceded by two blanks. Similarly, the EN edit descriptor produces an output field in an engineering notation where the exponent is divisible by 3 and the magnitude of the significand is greater than or equal to 1 and less than 1000, except when the output value is 0. Hence, executing a statement such as

```
PRINT "(EN11.3)", 12300.0
```

will display something like

```
12.300E+03
```

preceded by one blank

The program of Figure 14.8 displays various floating-point values under the control of the F, E, ES, and EN edit descriptors. When the program is executed, the following is displayed:

```
    F              E            ES            EN
----------     ----------   ----------   ------------

   4.56        0.456E+01    4.560E+00      4.560E+00
   0.00001     0.100E-04    1.000E-05     10.000E-06
4567.8         0.457E+04    4.568E+03      4.568E+03
  -0.4        -0.400E+00   -4.000E-01   -400.000E-03
```

The Fortran 90 standard permits minor variations in the form of the output produced by the ES and EN edit descriptors analogous to the minor variations permitted for the E edit descriptor.

In addition to the Ew.d form of the E edit descriptor, the FORTRAN 77 standard supports an Ew.dEe form, which specifies that the exponent part of the output is to consist of e digits. Of course, the Fortran 90 standard also supports this latter form of the E edit descriptor and, by analogy, provides ESw.dEe and ENw.dEe forms of the ES and EN edit

```
PROGRAM es_and_en_edit_descriptors

   PRINT "(A)",                                                        &
        "      F          E           ES            EN       "
   PRINT "(A)",                                                        &
        " ----------   ----------   ----------   ------------"

   PRINT "( F8.2, 3X, E12.3,     ES12.3,     EN14.3)",  &
             4.56,       4.56,      4.56,       4.56

   PRINT "(F11.5,      E12.3,     ES12.3,     EN14.3)",  &
           0.00001,    0.00001,   0.00001,    0.00001

   PRINT "( F7.1, 4X, E12.3,     ES12.3,     EN14.3)",  &
            4567.8,     4567.8,    4567.8,     4567.8

   PRINT "( F7.1, 4X, E12.3,     ES12.3,     EN14.3)",  &
             -0.4,       -0.4,      -0.4,       -0.4

END PROGRAM es_and_en_edit_descriptors
```

FIGURE 14.8. Program illustrating use of ES and EN edit descriptors.

descriptors as well. In addition, the FORTRAN 77 standard supports a P edit descriptor, which specifies a scale factor that may affect output produced under an E edit descriptor. Again, the Fortran 90 standard maintains support for the P edit descriptor, but output produced under ES or EN edit descriptors is unaffected by the presence of such a scale factor.

It is permissible to embed one or more blanks in an ES or EN edit descriptor. The Fortran 90 standard permits blanks to appear anywhere within a format specification, even in the free source form. Such blanks have no effect on the interpretation of the format specification unless, of course, they are contained within a character string to be output.

14.10   NAMELIST I/O

For a Fortran programmer, developing a first-rate user interface, complete with forms, menus, default input values, and the like, can be tedious and time-consuming. Thus, it sometimes makes good sense for at least some phases of program development to settle for an interface that is easy to program, even if that interface is less than ideal from a user's point of view. For years, many versions of Fortran have addressed this issue by supporting a rough and ready capability known as **namelist**, which is a collection of variable names for which the programmer specifies a group name for purposes of I/O. However, there was no standard governing this form of I/O prior to the Fortran 90 standard, so it seems likely that variations of this capability will be around for a long time.

Figure 14.9 gives a Fortran 90 program illustrating the use of a namelist. The NAMELIST statement specifies that the group name engr_ rept may be used for purposes of I/O to refer to the collection of names made up of the variables rept_option, print_option, ref, ring_pressures, and rept_heading. Then, when the READ statement is executed, data are transferred from the external file connected to unit 15 into variables grouped under the name engr_rept.

Now, suppose that the external file, whose name is specified to be ENGRREPT.CTL in the OPEN statement, looks as follows:

```
&engr_rept print_option = T,
           rept_heading = "Pressure Analysis",
           ring_pressures = 0.51, 0.48, 0.50, 0.52,
           ref = 0.50, "psi"                              /
```

```
PROGRAM demo_namelist

   INTEGER                :: rept_option = 2
   CHARACTER(20)          :: rept_heading
   REAL, DIMENSION(4) :: ring_pressures
   LOGICAL                :: print_option = .FALSE.

   TYPE :: ref_type
      REAL            :: pressure
      CHARACTER(3) :: units
   END TYPE ref_type

   TYPE (ref_type) :: ref

   ! engr_rept is group name for var names after 2nd slash.
   NAMELIST / engr_rept / rept_option, print_option, ref,  &
                          ring_pressures, rept_heading

   OPEN (UNIT = 15, FILE = "ENGRREPT.CTL",            &
            STATUS = "OLD", POSITION = "REWIND")

   READ (UNIT = 15, NML = engr_rept)    ! Read namelist input
                                        ! from external file.

   CLOSE (UNIT = 15)

   PRINT "(1X, A)", rept_heading

   IF (print_option) THEN
      PRINT "(A, I1)", " Report Option = ", rept_option
   END IF

   PRINT "(A, 4F7.2)", " Ring Pressures = ", ring_pressures
   PRINT "(A, F7.2, 1X, A)", " Reference Pressure = ", ref

END PROGRAM demo_namelist
```

FIGURE 14.9. Program demonstrating the use of namelist input.

Ordinarily, such a file is created using a text editor. The entry &engr_rept
indicates the beginning of the namelist input and the slash (/) indicates
its end. Between these delimiters appear entries of the form

   var = value(s)

separated by commas. Each var is a variable name in the NAMELIST
statement in Figure 14.9. If var is a simple, nonaggregate variable, a

single value appears to the right of the equal sign. If *var* is an array or a structure, a list of values may appear to the right of the equal sign.

Observe that the order of the variable names in the input file need not be the same as that in the NAMELIST statement. Further note that not all variables in the NAMELIST statement need appear in the file. For example, rept_option is absent in the input file, so it is unaffected by the execution of the READ statement. However, all variables whose names appear in the input file have their values set or changed. Observe that values may be set for LOGICAL variables by inputting T or F on the right-hand side of the equal sign. Also, note that a CHARACTER value must be enclosed within quote marks (or apostrophes) in the input file. When the program of Figure 14.9 is executed, the following is displayed:

```
Pressure Analysis
Report Option = 2
Ring Pressures =     0.51    0.48    0.50    0.52
Reference Pressure =    0.50 psi
```

The form of a NAMELIST statement for specifying one namelist is

NAMELIST / *group-name* / *variable-name-list*

The *group-name* is chosen by the programmer, subject to the usual rules for a Fortran 90 name. There may be any number of NAMELIST statements. Note that the form above for the NAMELIST statement is quite similar to that of a COMMON statement specifying a named common block. In the same manner that more than one named common block may be specified in a single statement, it is also permitted to specify more than one namelist in a NAMELIST statement.

Consider the READ statement in Figure 14.9:

```
READ (UNIT = 15, NML = engr_rept)
```

This may be coded more succinctly as

```
READ (15, engr_rept)
```

If NML= is omitted in a namelist READ statement, then the first item in the control information list must be the unit specified without the optional characters UNIT= and the second item in the list must be the group name of the namelist. A namelist READ statement never has a list of input quantities following its final right parenthesis, and its parenthesized control information list never contains a format.

Although not illustrated in Figure 14.9, there is also a namelist WRITE statement. For example, the values of the variables in the namelist engr_rept could be output using the statement

```
WRITE (15, engr_rept)
```

The values of all variables in the namelist are output in a format that may vary slightly from implementation to implementation. However, the Fortran 90 standard requires that the output of the variable names be in the same order as they appear in the NAMELIST statement.

The format of the external text file containing namelist input data dictated by the Fortran 90 standard is slightly different from most of the older popular versions of Fortran that supported a namelist capability, but compiler vendors are likely to maintain at least partial backward compatibility. The new standard demands that the first nonblank character in the namelist input be an ampersand (&) followed immediately by the group name of the namelist with no intervening space. The ampersand is permitted to be the very first character in the file, although it may be preceded by any number of blanks. The occurrence of a slash outside of a character string terminates the namelist input. As illustrated above, commas may be used as value separators in the namelist input, but it is acceptable simply to use blanks to separate the values.

As illustrated in the example input given above for engr_rept, an array name with no parenthesis following may appear on the left-hand side of the equal sign to signify the whole array. Also, values for individual array elements and/or array sections may be specified in namelist input. For example, suppose that the following declaration appears for an array named nums:

```
INTEGER, DIMENSION(10) :: nums
```

Then, if nums is specified to be in a namelist, the following would be valid input for that namelist:

```
nums(8) = 88, nums(1:5:2) = 11, 33, 55
```

When a READ statement is executed for this namelist, nums(1) is set to 11, nums(3) is set to 33, nums(5) is set to 55, nums(8) is set to 88, and the rest of the elements of nums are unaffected.

Also as illustrated in the example input given above for engr_rept, the name of a variable of derived type with no percent sign (%) following may appear on the left-hand side of the equal sign to signify the entire structure. In addition, component selection may be specified in namelist input. For example, suppose the following specifications are established:

```
TYPE :: singer
   CHARACTER(10) :: first_name
   CHARACTER(20) :: last_name
END TYPE singer
TYPE (singer) :: pop_male, pop_female
```

Then, if pop_male and pop_female appear in a namelist, the following would be valid input for that namelist:

```
pop_male%first_name = "Michael",
pop_male%last_name = "Jackson",
pop_female%first_name = "Madonna"
```

When a READ statement is executed for this namelist, both components of pop_male would be set, pop_female%first_name would be set, and pop_female%last_name would be unaffected.

Namelist I/O is considered to be formatted even though no format is specified. This form of I/O bears some kinship to list-directed I/O, which, recall, is characterized by the use of an asterisk (*) as the format specifier. The forms of input acceptable in value lists in namelist input are basically the same as those acceptable for list-directed input, except that delimiting apostrophes or quote marks are always required for character strings in namelist input while there are some circumstances under which these delimiters may be omitted for character strings in list-directed input.

14.11   THE NEW SPECIFIERS IN THE INQUIRE STATEMENT

The INQUIRE statement enables the programmer to determine the current status of a file attribute. Standard FORTRAN 77 supports two forms of this statement, inquiry by file and inquiry by unit. Both of these forms of the INQUIRE statement remain the same in standard Fortran 90, except that the new standard provides seven additional INQUIRE specifiers to accommodate the new OPEN statement specifiers as described in Sections 14.3 through 14.6.

The possible values that may be assigned to the seven Fortran 90 INQUIRE specifiers not carried over from FORTRAN 77 are as follows:

POSITION = pos If the file is connected by an OPEN statement and is not repositioned before the INQUIRE is executed, pos will be assigned the value REWIND, APPEND, or ASIS, depending on the explicit or default value of the POSITION= specifier in the OPEN. If the file has been repositioned since its connection, pos is assigned an implementation-dependent value which is not REWIND unless the file is positioned at its initial point and not APPEND unless the file is positioned at its terminal point. If there is no connection or the file is connected for direct access, pos is assigned the value UNDEFINED.

DELIM = del If the file is connected for formatted I/O, del will be assigned the value APOSTROPHE, QUOTE, or NONE, depending on whether the apostrophe is used as the character string delimiter in list-directed and namelist output, the quote is used as the delimiter in list-directed and namelist output, or no delimiting character is to be used for character strings in such output. If there is no connection or if the file is not connected for formatted I/O, del will be assigned the value UNDEFINED.

PAD = pad If the connection of the file to the unit included the PAD= specifier and its value was NO, pad will be assigned the value NO. Otherwise, pad will be assigned the value YES.

ACTION = act If the file is connected for input only, act is assigned the value READ. If the file is connected for output only, act is assigned the value WRITE. If the file is connected for both input and output, act is assigned the value READWRITE. If there is no connection, act is assigned the value UNDEFINED.

READ = rd If READ is an allowed action for the file, rd is assigned the value YES. If the implementation determines that READ is not an allowed action, rd is assigned the value NO. If the implementation leaves undetermined whether READ is an allowed action for the file, rd is assigned the value UNKNOWN.

WRITE = wr If WRITE is an allowed action for the file, wr is assigned the value YES. If the implementation determines that WRITE is not an allowed action, wr is assigned the value NO. If the implementation leaves undetermined whether WRITE is an allowed action for the file, wr is assigned the value UNKNOWN.

READWRITE = rw If READWRITE is an allowed action for the file, rw is assigned the value YES. If the implementation determines that READWRITE is not an allowed action, rw is assigned the value NO. If the implementation leaves undetermined whether READWRITE is an allowed action for the file, rw is assigned the value UNKNOWN.

The program of Figure 14.10 illustrates all seven of the INQUIRE statement specifiers that are supported by the Fortran 90 standard but not by the FORTRAN 77 standard. First, an OPEN statement is issued that gives a file named TESTFILE.DAT a variety of attributes. Then, the INQUIRE statement makes an inquiry by file to determine some of those

```
PROGRAM demo_new_inquire_specifiers

    CHARACTER( 9) :: act, pos
    CHARACTER( 7) :: rd, wr, rw
    CHARACTER(10) :: del
    CHARACTER( 3) :: pad

    OPEN (UNIT = 20, FILE = 'TESTFILE.DAT', STATUS = "OLD",  &
                    POSITION = "APPEND",  DELIM = 'APOSTROPHE', &
                                    PAD = 'NO', ACTION = "WRITE")

    INQUIRE (FILE = "TESTFILE.DAT", POSITION = pos,       &
                    DELIM = del, PAD = pad, ACTION = act,  &
                    WRITE = wr, READ = rd, READWRITE = rw)

    PRINT "(A)", " POSITION  = " // pos
    PRINT "(A)", " DELIM     = " // del
    PRINT "(A)", " PAD       = " // pad
    PRINT "(A)", " ACTION    = " // act
    PRINT "(A)", " WRITE     = " // wr
    PRINT "(A)", " READ      = " // rd
    PRINT "(A)", " READWRITE = " // rw

    CLOSE (UNIT = 20)

END PROGRAM demo_new_inquire_specifiers
```

FIGURE 14.10. Program illustrating the new specifiers in the INQUIRE statement.

attributes. Finally, a sequence of seven PRINT statements displays the values of those file attributes. In Figure 14.10, each variable whose value may be set when the INQUIRE statement is executed is declared to be of sufficient length to hold all characters in any standard value that theoretically may be assigned to it. For example, the length of act is declared to be 9 characters to accommodate the possible value READWRITE, even though in the example act takes on the value WRITE padded with four blanks on the right.

When the program of Figure 14.10 is executed, the output is along the following lines:

```
POSITION  = APPEND
DELIM     = APOSTROPHE
PAD       = NO
ACTION    = WRITE
WRITE     = YES
```

```
READ       = UNKNOWN
READWRITE = UNKNOWN
```

The display above is self-explanatory, except for the output of the value UNKNOWN for the variables rd and rw: Since it is possible to deduce from the code of Figure 14.10 that reading from the file is not permitted, one might expect the value NO to appear in place of UNKNOWN in the above display. However, this expectation is not guaranteed to be met since, if ACTION = "WRITE" is specified in the OPEN for a file, the standard allows an implementation to leave the permissible actions undetermined for purposes of the READ= and READWRITE= specifiers in an INQUIRE. Similarly, if ACTION = "READ" is specified in the OPEN for a file, the standard allows an implementation to leave the permissible actions undetermined for purposes of the WRITE= and READWRITE= specifiers in an INQUIRE. Thus, use of the READ=, WRITE=, and READWRITE= specifiers may not be completely straightforward under all circumstances. However, a programmer always has the alternative of obtaining the allowed actions for a connected file by way of the ACTION= specifier of the INQUIRE.

14.12 INQUIRE-BY-OUTPUT-LIST FORM OF THE INQUIRE STATEMENT

Standard FORTRAN 77 supports two forms of the INQUIRE statement, inquire by file and inquire by unit, and both forms remain the same in Fortran 90, except that the set of standard specifiers available for use is enlarged slightly as discussed in the preceding section. But Fortran 90 also supports a third form of the INQUIRE statement, inquire by output list, that features the new IOLENGTH= specifier. The inquire-by-output-list capability is intended primarily to improve the portability of programs that perform unformatted direct access I/O.

When an OPEN is issued for a direct access file, the standards dictate that the record length must be given by the RECL= specifier, and each record in the file will be of this length. But the standards permit the internal representation of data to be implementation dependent, so the length of the output resulting from a particular unformatted write may vary from implementation to implementation. The problem then is this: How can a value be given in the RECL= specifier in a way that guarantees the portability of the source code to other standard-conforming implementations? In standard Fortran 90, this problem is solved by first using inquire by output list to determine the length of the record

```
PROGRAM demo_inquire_by_output_list

    INTEGER, PARAMETER :: Num_vals = 5   ! # of array elements
    REAL, DIMENSION(Num_vals) :: a, b    ! arrays to hold data

    INTEGER :: i          ! DO loop index
    INTEGER :: rec_len    ! record len for direct access file

    DO i = 1, Num_vals
        a(i) =  i            ! Load positive values into array a.
        b(i) = -i            ! Load negative values into array b.
    END DO

    INQUIRE (IOLENGTH = rec_len) a, b   ! Determine len of I/O
                                        ! list consisting of
                                        ! arrays a and b and
                                        ! store result in
                                        ! rec_len.

    ! Use rec_len as record length of direct access file.
    OPEN (UNIT = 12, FILE = "DATAVALS.DAT",                    &
                   STATUS = "REPLACE",                         &
                         ACCESS = "DIRECT", RECL = rec_len)


    WRITE (UNIT = 12, REC = 17) a, b    ! Write to record 17.

    a = 0.0; b = 0.0   ! Zero all elements of both a and b.

    READ (UNIT = 12, REC = 17) a, b     ! Read from record 17.

    DO i = 1, Num_vals
        PRINT "(2F8.2)", a(i), b(i)  ! display values just read
    END DO

    CLOSE (UNIT = 12)

END PROGRAM demo_inquire_by_output_list
```

FIGURE 14.11. Program illustrating inquire by output list.

that would result from executing an unformatted WRITE having the output list of interest, and then using this length in the RECL= specifier of the OPEN for the file.

The contrived program of Figure 14.11 illustrates the use of the inquire-by-output-list form of the INQUIRE statement. The program opens a file named DATAVALS.DAT for direct access, performs an unformatted write to a record in the file, and then reads back the data in that record. The output list for the unformatted write consists of two REAL arrays named a and b. The INQUIRE statement determines the length of this output list, no matter what internal representation the implementation employs for REAL values, and assigns that length to rec_len. Then rec_len is used as the value for RECL= in the OPEN statement for DATAVALS.DAT. Incidentally, the OPEN connects DATAVALS.DAT for unformatted I/O because the default form of I/O for a direct access file, unlike that for a sequential file, is unformatted.

The first DO loop in the program of Figure 14.11 loads nonzero values into the arrays a and b, and then the WRITE statement writes the internal representation of those values to record 17. Next, all elements of a and b are cleared to zero, and then the values in record 17 are read back into a and b. Finally, the second DO loop displays the values that were read back into a and b. When the program of Figure 14.11 is executed, the following is displayed:

```
1.00    -1.00
2.00    -2.00
3.00    -3.00
4.00    -4.00
5.00    -5.00
```

The general form of the inquire by output list is

INQUIRE (IOLENGTH = *length*) *output-item-list*

where *output-item-list* is an unformatted output list and *length* is a scalar INTEGER variable of default kind. When the INQUIRE is executed, *length* is assigned a value that represents the length in implementation dependent units of a record that would result from the use of *output-item-list* in an unformatted output statement. The value assigned to *length* is required by the standard to be suitable as a RECL= specifier in an OPEN statement connecting a file for unformatted direct access so that I/O can be performed on the file by statements whose I/O lists are the same as *output-item-list*.

APPENDIX A

FORTRAN 90 STANDARD STATEMENT KEYWORDS

For a given dialect of Fortran, there is normally some sort of reference document that formally specifies the valid syntax for each variety of statement. For most categories of statements, the syntax rules dictate the appearance of fixed sequences of letters, traditionally known as **keywords**, at specified places in the statement. In particular, most statements are required to begin with a keyword made up of a sequence of letters that constitute an ordinary word in the English language. Examples of such words are DO, END, and INTEGER. Some statements begin with a pair of keywords (for example, GO TO, DOUBLE PRECISION, ELSE IF). Furthermore, the term "keyword" encompasses certain sequences of letters appearing to the left of an equal sign (=) in a parenthesized list in certain (mostly I/O) statements. Consider, for example, the following statement:

```
READ (UNIT = 15, FMT = "(A)", IOSTAT = ios) buf
```

Here, the initial sequence of letters READ is, of course, a keyword, but also UNIT, FMT, and IOSTAT are considered to be keywords, even though FMT and IOSTAT are not English words. And, there are additional situations in Fortran where a particular sequence of letters appearing in a particular context is characterized as being a keyword.

In Fortran 90, the sort of sequence of letters that has traditionally been called a "keyword" has been redesignated as a **statement keyword**. The modifier "statement" has been prepended to distinguish the traditional sort of keyword from the Fortran 90 "argument keyword" as described in Section 13.9. But even in a Fortran 90 context, when not preceded by the word "argument," the term "keyword" is usually taken to mean "statement keyword."

Table A.1 presents a list of Fortran 90 statement keywords. The list was extracted from the syntax rules in the new standard. Of course, all FORTRAN 77 keywords are statement keywords in Fortran 90, so

bold typeface is employed in Table A.1 to highlight those statement keywords in Fortran 90 that are not keywords in FORTRAN 77. Also, the valid contexts in which each statement keyword is permitted to appear are summarized in Table A.1, and Fortran 90 statement keyword contexts that are not carried over from FORTRAN 77 are indicated by **bold typeface**. Always bear in mind that Table A.1 is based on the Fortran 90 and FORTRAN 77 standards, while popular implementations are likely to feature additional keywords and/or contexts for keywords that are not reflected in this table.

From the viewpoint of a Fortran applications programmer, the distinction between a (statement) keyword and other sequences of letters that are built into the language may not be obvious. Note, however, that edit descriptors, such as A, TR, and BZ, are not considered to be keywords. Also, operators, such as .AND. and .NOT., are not keywords, and the logical constants .TRUE. and .FALSE. are not keywords. Of course, intrinsic procedure names are not keywords, although there are a few instances where the sequence of letters in the name of an intrinsic function is the same as that of a statement keyword (for example, REAL, LEN, and SIZE).

TABLE A.1   Fortran 90 Standard Statement Keywords

Keyword	Context(s)
ACCESS	ACCESS= specifier in OPEN or INQUIRE statement
ACTION	**ACTION= specifier in OPEN or INQUIRE statement**
ADVANCE	**ADVANCE= specifier in READ or WRITE statement**
ALLOCATABLE	**Array specification**
ALLOCATE	**Dynamically allocate storage.**
ASSIGN	Assign label (statement number) to variable.
ASSIGNMENT	**Interface block for defined assignment**
	PUBLIC or PRIVATE statement
	ONLY clause of USE statement
BACKSPACE	Position data file.
BLANK	BLANK= specifier in OPEN or INQUIRE statement
BLOCK	BLOCK DATA statement
	END BLOCK DATA statement
CALL	Invoke a subroutine.
CASE	**CASE construct**
CHARACTER	Type declaration statement
CLOSE	Terminate connection of a unit to an external file.
COMMON	Specify block of physical storage that can be accessed by separately compiled scoping units.
COMPLEX	Type declaration statement

TABLE A.1   Continued

Keyword	Context(s)
CONTAINS	**Indicates presence of internal subprograms or module subprograms**
CONTINUE	Statement indicating no action to be performed
CYCLE	**Curtail execution of an iteration of a DO construct.**
DATA	DATA statement to specify initial value for variable
	BLOCK DATA statement
	END BLOCK DATA statement
DEALLOCATE	**Release storage obtained by ALLOCATE statement.**
DEFAULT	Case selector in a CASE construct
DELIM	DELIM= specifier in OPEN or INQUIRE statement
DIMENSION	Array specification
DIRECT	DIRECT= specifier in INQUIRE statement
DO	Indexed DO statement
	DO construct
DOUBLE	DOUBLE PRECISION specification in type declaration statement
ELSE	IF construct
ELSEWHERE	**WHERE construct**
END	**IF, DO, CASE, or WHERE construct**
	Derived-type defintion
	Interface block
	END PROGRAM, END MODULE,
	END SUBROUTINE, END FUNCTION, or
	END BLOCK DATA statement
	Traditional one-word END statement
	END= specifier in READ or WRITE statement
ENDFILE	Write an endfile record.
ENTRY	Specify entry point in subprogram.
EOR	**EOR= specifier in READ statement**
EQUIVALENCE	Permit two or more local names to refer to same storage area.
ERR	ERR= specifier in I/O statements
EXIST	EXIST= specifier in INQUIRE statement
EXIT	**Cause termination of execution of a DO construct.**
EXTERNAL	Identifies names of external and dummy procedures and block data program units
FILE	FILE= specifier in OPEN or INQUIRE statement
FMT	FMT= specifier in READ or WRITE statement
FORM	FORM= specifier in OPEN or INQUIRE statement
FORMAT	FORMAT statement
FORMATTED	FORMATTED= specifier in INQUIRE statement
FUNCTION	First statement of a function subprogram
	END FUNCTION statement
GO	(Unconditional) GO TO, computed GO TO, assigned GO TO statements

Table A.1   Continued

Keyword	Context(s)
IF	IF construct, (logical) IF statement, arithmetic IF statement
IMPLICIT	Indicate type and kind for implicitly typed data entities whose names begin with one of the letters specified.
	IMPLICIT NONE statement
IN	**INTENT specification for dummy argument**
INOUT	**INTENT specification for dummy argument**
INQUIRE	Inquire about status and attributes of a file.
INTEGER	Type declaration statement
INTENT	**Specify intended use of dummy argument.**
INTERFACE	**First statement of an interface block**
	END INTERFACE statement
INTRINSIC	Identifies names of intrinsic procedures
IOLENGTH	**IOLENGTH= specifier in INQUIRE statement**
IOSTAT	IOSTAT= specifier in I/O statement
KIND	**KIND= specifier in type declaration statement**
LEN	**LEN= specifier in CHARACTER type specifications**
LOGICAL	Type declaration statement
MODULE	**First statement of a module program unit**
	END MODULE statement
	MODULE PROCEDURE statement in interface block
NAME	NAME= specifier in INQUIRE statement
NAMED	NAMED= specifier in INQUIRE statement
NAMELIST	**Specifies names of variables to be grouped for I/O**
NEXTREC	NEXTREC= specifier in INQUIRE statement
NML	**NML= specifier in READ or WRITE statement**
NONE	**IMPLICIT NONE statement**
NULLIFY	**Give pointer a verifiable status of having no target.**
NUMBER	NUMBER= specifier in INQUIRE statement
ONLY	**USE statement**
OPEN	Initiate or modify connection between external file and unit.
OPENED	OPENED= specifier in INQUIRE statement
OPERATOR	**Interface block for defined operation**
	PUBLIC or PRIVATE statement
	ONLY clause of USE statement
OPTIONAL	**Dummy argument specification**
OUT	**INTENT specification for dummy argument**
PAD	**PAD= specifier in OPEN or INQUIRE statement**
PARAMETER	Specify name representing a constant value.
PAUSE	Cease execution, but leave program in resumable state.
POINTER	**Indicates name may refer to different storage areas at different times**
POSITION	**POSITION= specifier in OPEN or INQUIRE statement**
PRECISION	DOUBLE PRECISION specification in type declaration statement

TABLE A.1   Continued

Keyword	Context(s)
PRINT	Perform output to default output unit.
PRIVATE	**Indicates names in module which are not to be accessible outside the module**
PROCEDURE	**MODULE PROCEDURE statement in interface block**
PROGRAM	First statement in main program
	END PROGRAM statement
PUBLIC	**Indicates names in module which are to be accessible outside the module**
READ	Perform input
	READ= specifier in INQUIRE statement
READWRITE	**READWRITE= specifier in INQUIRE statement**
REAL	Type declaration statement
REC	REC= specifier in READ or WRITE statement
RECL	RECL= specifier in OPEN or INQUIRE statement
RECURSIVE	**FUNCTION or SUBROUTINE statement**
RESULT	**FUNCTION or ENTRY statement**
RETURN	Complete execution of instance of a subprogram.
REWIND	Position a file at its intial point.
SAVE	Indicates local variables in a subprogram whose values and statuses are to be retained after exit from that subprogram
	Indicates names of common blocks whose values are to be retained after exit from subprograms specifying those named common blocks
	Indicates variables in a module whose values and statuses are to be retained after exit from subprograms using that module
SELECT	**CASE construct**
SEQUENCE	**In derived-type definition to impose a storage order for values of components of that derived type**
SEQUENTIAL	SEQUENTIAL= specifier in INQUIRE statement
SIZE	**SIZE= specifier in READ statement**
STAT	**STAT= specifier in ALLOCATE or DEALLOCATE statement**
STATUS	STATUS= specifier in OPEN or CLOSE statement
STOP	Terminate program execution.
SUBROUTINE	First statement of a subroutine subprogram
	END SUBROUTINE statement
TARGET	**Specifies that all or part of named data object can be pointed to**
THEN	IF construct
TO	ASSIGN statement or any form of GO TO statement
TYPE	**Derived-type definition**
	Type declaration statement

Table A.1   Continued

Keyword	Context(s)
UNFORMATTED	UNFORMATTED= specifier in INQUIRE statement
UNIT	UNIT= specifier in I/O statements
USE	**Access a module.**
WHERE	**Masked array assignment**
WHILE	**DO WHILE statement**
WRITE	Perform output.
	WRITE= specifier in INQUIRE statement

ORDER OF STATEMENTS

Figure B.1 shows the order of statements as required by the Fortran 90 standard. Vertical lines indicate varieties of statements that may be interspersed, while horizontal lines denote varieties of statements that may not be interspersed. The required order of those statements that also exist in FORTRAN 77 remains essentially the same, except that the Fortran 90 standard relaxes the FORTRAN 77 requirement that all DATA

PROGRAM, SUBROUTINE, FUNCTION, MODULE, or BLOCK DATA Statement		
USE Statements		
	IMPLICIT NONE	
FORMAT and ENTRY Statements	PARAMETER Statements	IMPLICIT Statements
	PARAMETER and DATA Statements	Type Declaration Statements, Derived-Type Definitions, Interface Blocks, Statement Functions, and Specification Statements
	DATA Statements	Executable Constructs
CONTAINS Statement		
Internal Subprograms or Module Subprograms		
END Statement		

FIGURE B.1. Required order of Fortran 90 statements.

455

statements follow all type declaration statements and all specification statements.

A **specification statement** is one of the following:

ALLOCATABLE statement
COMMON statement
DATA statement
DIMENSION statement
EQUIVALENCE statement
EXTERNAL statement
INTENT statement
INTRINSIC statement
NAMELIST statement
OPTIONAL statement
POINTER statement
PRIVATE statement
PUBLIC statement
SAVE statement
TARGET statement

An **executable construct** is one of the following:

ALLOCATE statement
ASSIGN statement
assignment statement
BACKSPACE statement
CALL statement
CASE Construct
CLOSE statement
CONTINUE statement
CYCLE statement
DEALLOCATE statement
DO Construct
ENDFILE statement
EXIT statement
GO TO statement (any form)
IF construct
IF statement (any form)
INQUIRE statement
NULLIFY statement
OPEN statement
PAUSE statement
pointer assignment statement
PRINT statement
READ statement
RETURN statement
REWIND statement
STOP statement
WHERE construct
WHERE statement
WRITE statement

APPENDIX C

FORTRAN 90 STANDARD GENERIC INTRINSIC PROCEDURES

In Fortran, an **intrinsic function** is a function that is automatically provided as part of the language. Consider, for example, SQRT, which has long been a Fortran intrinsic function. The name SQRT is built into the language with a predefined meaning so that a Fortran programmer can code, without taking any special action, an expression such as SQRT (x) to represent the square root of x.

The Fortran 90 standard requires implementations to supply not only certain functions as part of the language, but also certain subroutines. The subroutines that must be automatically provided as part of an implementation conforming to the new standard are known as **intrinsic subroutines**. Since "procedure" has been for some time the Fortran term for either a function or a subroutine, it is natural that the term **intrinsic procedure** is employed in Fortran 90 to refer to either an intrinsic function or an intrinsic subroutine.

Table C.1 lists 113 names for intrinsic procedures that must be supported by a compiler conforming to the Fortran 90 standard. One hundred eight of these intrinsic procedures are functions, while only five are subroutines. The FORTRAN 77 standard does not support intrinsic subroutines, but 38 of the intrinsic function names in Table C.1 are carried over from the older standard. The names of Fortran 90 intrinsic procedures that are not standard in FORTRAN 77 are highlighted by **boldface type** in Table C.1. But even for those intrinsic functions whose names have been carried forward from the older standard, the Fortran 90 versions generally provide enhanced capabilities, which are also indicated by **boldface type** in the table.

Of course, some of the intrinsic procedure names indicated as new in Table C.1 have been widely available for a long time as extensions to the FORTRAN 77 standard. Noteworthy among these are the MIL-STD-1753 bit manipulation procedures, such as ISHFT, MVBITS, and so forth.

The author recommends that intrinsic procedures be referenced using only the names in Table C.1. However, for purposes of backward compatibility, the new standard permits some intrinsic functions to be invoked by names not found in this table. Examples of such names are IABS, ALOG, and AMIN0, and the complete list of 47 such names can be extracted from the list of specific names for intrinsic functions given in the Fortran 90 standard. But for these 47 specific names, all of which are carried over from FORTRAN 77, the new standard dictates that the arguments must be of default kind—a restriction not generally shared by the names in Table C.1 (although this restriction is likely to be relaxed sometimes in Fortran 90 implementations). Of course, source code that references any of these 47 names in a manner conforming to the FORTRAN 77 standard will still conform to the Fortran 90 standard. Nevertheless, it is always possible to avoid references to standard intrinsic procedures by names other than those in Table C.1, and in the opinion of the author, it is almost always best to do so.

It should be noted that all of the names for intrinsic procedures listed in Table C.1 are characterized as generic names in Fortran 90. This may be mildly surprising to those readers who recognize that there are a few intrinsic function names in the table (for example, CHAR, INDEX, LEN, LGE) that are not considered to be generic in FORTRAN 77. In FORTRAN 77, an intrinsic function name is said to be generic only if its argument is permitted to be of more than one data type, but this implication of the term "generic" is not perfectly preserved in Fortran 90—without explanation, the new standard slightly alters the traditional meaning of the term in this context. But in spite of the slightly altered terminology, any source code using an intrinsic function in a manner that conforms to the FORTRAN 77 standard will still conform to the Fortran 90 standard. In practice, the only thing that needs to be understood about the new standard's terminology here is that some intrinsic procedure names are classified as generic while others are classified as specific, and these two classes are governed by somewhat different language rules. Actually, the characterization of intrinsic procedure names in terms of generic and specific classes is rather unimportant in Fortran 90 and could have been avoided altogether in the new standard if it were not for backward compatibility requirements. If intrinsic procedures are referenced only by the names in Table C.1 and intrinsic procedure names are never referenced in argument lists, the Fortran 90 programmer does not care whether an intrinsic procedure name is generic or specific. A little more discussion of the rather unusual special case of referencing an intrinsic procedure name in an argument list is given in Section G.5 of Appendix G.

A new Fortran 90 feature that is reflected in Table C.1 is that the keyword argument mechanism may be used in invoking intrinsic procedures. Each name given in the table inside the parentheses following an intrinsic procedure name is an argument keyword that may be specified to the left of an equal sign when this mechanism is employed. Observe also in Table C.1 that some intrinsic procedures have one or more arguments that may sometimes be omitted. The programmer can use the keyword argument mechanism to skip over any optional arguments that are not needed.

Table C.1 follows the Fortran 90 standard in placing each intrinsic procedure in one of four classes, based on behavioral characteristics of the procedure:

a. *Elemental function*: a function whose principal argument may be either a scalar or an array. If the argument is an array, the function acts separately on each element to produce a result having the same shape as the argument. For example, if the argument of SQRT is a scalar, the result is the square root of that scalar; but if the argument is a 2 × 3 array, the result is a 2 × 3 array, each element of which is the square root of the corresponding element of the argument.

b. *Inquiry function*: a function whose result does not depend on the value of its principal argument, but rather depends on some other property of that argument. For example, if the argument of LEN is a scalar expression of type CHARACTER, then the result is the maximum number of characters that the argument can contain, irrespective of what character value(s) the argument contains when LEN is applied. In fact, it is permissible to apply an inquiry function to an argument that has never been given any value.

c. *Transformational function*: a catch-all class for any intrinsic function that fails to qualify as either an elemental function or an inquiry function. For example, MAXVAL returns the maximum value of the elements of an array. Most, but not all, transformational functions have at least one array-valued argument.

d. *Subroutine*: an intrinsic procedure that must be invoked using a CALL statement. For example, DATE_AND_TIME may be called to obtain the computer system current date and time of day. Only 5 of the 113 standard intrinsic procedures are subroutines.

Table C.1   Fortran 90 Standard Generic Intrinsic Procedures

Subprogram Name and Arguments	Optional Arguments	Class	Imprecise Description
ABS (A)		Elemental function	Take absolute value.
ACHAR (I)		**Elemental function**	**Return character in position I of ASCII collating sequence.**
ACOS (X)		Elemental function	Find arccosine (inverse cosine).
ADJUSTL (STRING)		**Elemental function**	**Left-justify string, removing leading blanks and inserting trailing blanks.**
ADJUSTR (STRING)		**Elemental function**	**Right-justify string, removing trailing blanks and inserting leading blanks.**
AIMAG (Z)		Elemental function	Return imaginary part of a complex number.
AINT (A, **KIND**)	**KIND**	Elemental function	Truncate to a whole number.
ALL (MASK, DIM)	**DIM**	**Transformational function**	**Determine whether all values along dimension DIM of array MASK are true.**
ALLOCATED (ARRAY)		**Inquiry function**	**Indicate whether storage is currently allocated for an allocatable array.**
ANINT (A, KIND)	**KIND**	Elemental function	Find nearest whole number.
ANY (MASK, DIM)	**DIM**	**Transformational function**	**Determine whether any value along dimension DIM of array MASK is true.**
ASIN (X)		Elemental function	Find arcsine (inverse sine).
ASSOCIATED (POINTER, TARGET)	**TARGET**	**Inquiry function**	**Indicate whether a pointer currently points to a target.**
ATAN (X)		Elemental function	Find arctangent (inverse tangent) of X.
ATAN2 (Y, X)		Elemental function	Find arctangent of complex number (X, Y).
BIT_SIZE (I)		**Inquiry function**	**Return number of bits used by implementation to represent an integer of same kind as I.**
BTEST (I, POS)		**Elemental function**	**Test a bit of an integer value.**
CEILING (A)		**Elemental function**	**Find least integer greater than or equal to A.**
CHAR (I, **KIND**)	**KIND**	Elemental function	Return character in position I of the implementation's collating sequence.
CMPLX (X, Y, **KIND**)	Y, **KIND**	Elemental function	Convert to complex type.

TABLE C.1   Continued

Subprogram Name and Arguments	Optional Arguments	Class	Imprecise Description
CONJG (Z)		Elemental function	Find conjugate of a complex number.
COS (X)		Elemental function	Find cosine.
COSH (X)		Elemental function	Find hyperbolic cosine.
COUNT (MASK, DIM)	**DIM**	**Transformational function**	**Count number of true elements of array MASK along dimension DIM.**
CSHIFT (ARRAY, SHIFT, DIM)	**DIM**	**Transformational function**	**Perform circular shift of elements of rank 1 sections.**
DATE_AND_TIME (DATE, TIME, ZONE, VALUES)	**DATE, TIME, ZONE, VALUES**	**Subroutine**	**Return system date and time.**
DBLE (A)		Elemental function	Convert to double precision.
DIGITS (X)		**Inquiry function**	**Return number of significant digits (usually binary or hexadecimal digits) used by implementation to represent a number of type and kind of argument.**
DIM (X, Y)		Elemental function	Return maximum of $X - Y$ and 0.
DOT_PRODUCT (VECTOR_A, VECTOR B)		**Transformational function**	**Perform dot product multiplication of vectors.**
DPROD (X, Y)		Elemental function	Return double-precision product of two values of type default real.
EOSHIFT (ARRAY, SHIFT, BOUNDARY, DIM)	**BOUNDARY, DIM**	**Transformational function**	**Perform end-off shift of elements of rank 1 sections.**
EPSILON (X)		**Inquiry function**	**Return a very small positive number of the same type and kind as X.**
EXP (X)		Elemental function	Raise $e = 2.718\ldots$ to the power X.
EXPONENT (X)		**Elemental function**	**Return value of implementation's exponent part of argument when represented as a real number.**
FLOOR (A)		**Elemental function**	**Find greatest integer less than or equal to A.**
FRACTION (X)		**Elemental function**	**Return approximation to value of implementation's fractional part of argument when represented as a real number.**

Table C.1   Continued

Subprogram Name and Arguments	Optional Arguments	Class	Imprecise Description
HUGE (X)		**Inquiry function**	**Return approximation to implementation's largest number of same type and kind as X.**
IACHAR (C)		**Elemental function**	**Return position of character in ASCII collating sequence.**
IAND (I, J)		**Elemental function**	**Perform a logical AND.**
IBCLR (I, POS)		**Elemental function**	**Clear bit at position POS in I.**
IBITS (I, POS, LEN)		**Elemental function**	**Extract LEN bits from I, starting at position POS.**
IBSET (I, POS)		**Elemental function**	**Set bit at position POS in I.**
ICHAR (C)		Elemental function	Return position of character in implementation's collating sequence for characters whose kind is same as that of argument.
IEOR (I, J)		**Elemental function**	**Perform an exclusive OR.**
INDEX (STRING, SUBSTRING, **BACK**)	**BACK**	Elemental function	Return the starting position of a substring within a string.
INT (A, **KIND**)	**KIND**	Elemental function	Convert to integer type.
IOR (I, J)		**Elemental function**	**Perform an inclusive OR.**
ISHFT (I, SHIFT)		**Elemental function**	**Perform an end-off bit shift.**
ISHFTC (I, SHIFT, SIZE)	**SIZE**	**Elemental function**	**Perform a circular it shift.**
KIND (X)		**Inquiry function**	**Return implementation's value of kind type parameter of X.**
LBOUND (ARRAY, DIM)	**DIM**	**Inquiry function**	**Return lower bounds of an array.**
LEN (STRING)		Inquiry function	Return the length of character argument.
LEN_TRIM (STRING)		**Elemental function**	**Return length of character argument without counting trailing blanks.**
LGE (STRING_A, STRING_B)		Elemental function	Test whether one string is greater than or equal to another, based on the ASCII collating sequence.
LGT (STRING_A, STRING_B)		Elemental function	Test whether one string is greater than another, based on the ASCII collating sequence.

TABLE C.1 Continued

Subprogram Name and Arguments	Optional Arguments	Class	Imprecise Description
LLE (STRING_A, STRING_B)		Elemental function	Test whether one string is less than or equal to another, based on the ASCII collating sequence.
LLT (STRING_A, STRING_B)		Elemental function	Test whether one string is less than another, based on the ASCII collating sequence.
LOG (X)		Elemental function	Take natural logarithm (base $e = 2.718...$).
LOG10 (X)		Elemental function	Take common logarithm (base 10).
LOGICAL (L, KIND)	**KIND**	**Elemental function**	**Convert between kinds of logical.**
MATMUL (MATRIX_A, MATRIX_B)		**Transformational function**	**Perform matrix multiplication as usually described in mathematics texts.**
MAX (A1, A2, A3, ...)	A3, ...	Elemental function	Find maximum value in a list of values.
MAXEXPONENT (X)		**Inquiry function**	**Return approximation to maximum exponent used by implementation in representing real number of same type and kind as argument.**
MAXLOC (ARRAY, MASK)	**MASK**	**Transformational function**	**Find location in array of element having max value.**
MAXVAL (ARRAY, DIM, MASK)	**DIM, MASK**	**Transformational function**	**Find max value of elements of array.**
MERGE (TSOURCE, FSOURCE, MASK)		**Elemental function**	**Choose between value in TSOURCE and value in FSOURCE based on value of MASK.**
MIN (A1, A2, A3, ...)	A3, ...	Elemental function	Find minimum value in a list of values.
MINEXPONENT (X)		**Inquiry function**	**Return approximation to most negative exponent used by implementation in representing real number of same type and kind as argument.**
MINLOC (ARRAY, MASK)	**MASK**	**Transformational function**	**Find location in array of element having min value.**
MINVAL (ARRAY, DIM, MASK)	**DIM, MASK**	**Transformational function**	**Find min value of elements of array.**
MOD (A, P)		Elemental function	Return remainder of A divided by P, having same sign as A.
MODULO (A, P)		**Elemental function**	**Return remainder of A divided by P, having same sign as P.**

TABLE C.1   Continued

Subprogram Name and Arguments	Optional Arguments	Class	Imprecise Description
MVBITS (FROM FROMPOS, LEN, TO, TOPOS)		**Subroutine**	**Copy a sequence of bits from one data object to another.**
NEAREST (X, S)		**Elemental function**	**Return value of machine representable real number nearest to (but distinct from) X in direction indicated by sign of S.**
NINT (A, KIND)	**KIND**	Elemental function	Return integer nearest to A, where A is type real.
NOT (I)		**Elemental function**	**Flip value of each bit in I.**
PACK (ARRAY, MASK, VECTOR)	**VECTOR**	**Transformational function**	**Construct a rank one array by copying from ARRAY those elements specified by MASK, while optionally copying additional elements from VECTOR.**
PRECISION (X)		**Inquiry function**	**Return number of decimal digits of precision with which implementation can represent a real number with same kind type parameter as X.**
PRESENT (A)		**Inquiry function**	**Determine whether an optional argument is present.**
PRODUCT (ARRAY, DIM, MASK)	**DIM, MASK**	**Transformational function**	**Find product of all elements of array along dimension DIM under control of a mask.**
RADIX (X)		**Inquiry function**	**Return base used by implementation in representing numbers of same type and kind as X.**
RANDOM_NUMBER (HARVEST)[1]		**Subroutine**	**Return pseudorandom number(s) in unit interval.**
RANDOM_SEED (SIZE, PUT, GET)	**SIZE, PUT, GET**	**Subroutine**	**Get or set seed for pseudorandom number generator.**
RANGE (X)		**Inquiry function**	**Return approximation to largest integer N such that implementation can represent values of same type and kind as X whose magnitudes are in range 10^{-N} to 10^{N}.**
REAL (A, KIND)	**KIND**	Elemental function	Convert to real type.

[1] A bit of trivia regarding RANDOM_NUMBER revolves around the choice of HARVEST as the name of its keyword argument. If something sounds familiar here, it is probably because of the classic 1942 MGM movie "Random Harvest," starring Ronald Colman and Greer Garson. The film was based on the popular 1941 novel of the same name by James Hilton.

Table C.1   Continued

Subprogram Name and Arguments	Optional Arguments	Class	Imprecise Description
REPEAT (STRING, NCOPIES)		Transformational function	Concatenate copies of a string.
RESHAPE (SOURCE, SHAPE, PAD, ORDER)	PAD, ORDER	Transformational function	Construct an array of specified shape from elements of a given array.
RRSPACING (X)		Elemental function	Return approximation to reciprocal of implementation's relative spacing of real numbers near the argument value.
SCALE (X, I)		Elemental function	Return X times b^I, where b is the base (usually 2 or 16) used by the implementation in representing real values of same kind as X.
SCAN (STRING, SET, BACK)	BACK	Elemental function	Return position in a string of the first occurrence of any one of the characters in SET.
SELECTED_INT_KIND (R)		Transformational function	Return implementation's value of kind type parameter for kind of integer capable of representing all integral values n such that $-10^R < n < 10^R$.
SELECTED_REAL_KIND (P, R)		Transformational function	Return implementation's value of kind type parameter for kind of real capable of representing real values with decimal precision of at least P digits and a decimal exponent range of at least R.
SET_EXPONENT (X, I)		Elemental function	Return real number of same kind as X whose fractional part is same as that of X and whose exponent part is I.
SHAPE (SOURCE)		Inquiry function	Return shape of an array or scalar.
SIGN (A, B)		Elemental function	Return absolute value of A times the sign of B.
SIN (X)		Elemental function	Find sine.
SINH (X)		Elemental function	Find hyperbolic sine.
SIZE (ARRAY, DIM)	DIM	Inquiry function	Return number of elements in ARRAY along dimension DIM.
SPACING (X)		Elemental function	Return approximation to implementation's absolute spacing of real numbers near the argument value.
SPREAD (SOURCE, DIM, NCOPIES)		Transformational function	Construct an array consisting of NCOPIES of array SOURCE along dimension DIM.

TABLE C.1   Continued

Subprogram Name and Arguments	Optional Arguments	Class	Imprecise Description
SQRT (X)		Elemental function	Take square root.
SUM (ARRAY, DIM, MASK)	DIM, MASK	Transformational function	**Sum elements of an array along dimension DIM under the control of a mask.**
SYSTEM_CLOCK (COUNT, COUNT_RATE, COUNT_MAX)	COUNT, COUNT_ RATE, COUNT_ MAX	Subroutine	**Return implementation-dependent clock count data from system clock.**
TAN (X)		Elemental function	Find tangent.
TANH (X)		Elemental function	Find hyperbolic tangent.
TINY (X)		Inquiry function	**Return approximation to implementation's smallest positive real number of same kind as X.**
TRANSFER (SOURCE, MOLD, SIZE)	SIZE	Transformational function	**Return result with physical representation identical to SOURCE, but treated as if its type and kind were those of MOLD.**
TRANSPOSE (MATRIX)		Transformational function	**Transpose an array of rank 2.**
TRIM (STRING)		Transformational function	**Return argument with trailing blanks removed.**
UBOUND (ARRAY, DIM)	DIM	Inquiry function	**Return upper bounds of an array.**
UNPACK (VECTOR, MASK, FIELD)		Transformational function	**Construct an array with shape same as MASK by copying some elements from rank 1 array VECTOR and other elements from FIELD.**
VERIFY (STRING, SET, BACK)	BACK	Elemental function	**Identify position of first character in a string that does not appear in a given set of characters.**

FIXED SOURCE FORM

The Fortran 90 standard supports two source forms, free and fixed. The free source form is described in Section 2.3, and all of the example programs in this tutorial have been presented in that form. The Fortran 90 standard fixed source form will be described in this appendix. The two source forms are fundamentally incompatible, and the new standard prohibits the mixing of free and fixed source forms in the same program unit. Each Fortran 90 implementation must provide some means for the programmer to specify which of the two source forms is being used for each program unit. Of course, the default will ordinarily be the free source form—the fixed source form is provided primarily for reasons of backward compatibility with FORTRAN 77 implementations. The idea is that all new program units will be developed using the free source form while old subprograms that are subject to only minor revisions can be maintained in the fixed source form. In cases where an old subprogram requires a major change, it will usually be advantageous to translate it to the new free source form, and there is software available to aid in the translation.

The Fortran 90 standard fixed source form is essentially the same as the FORTRAN 77 standard source form with minor extensions. The syntactically significant part of each line is confined to the first 72 positions; the first 5 positions are used only for labels (statement numbers), continuation is indicated by a character other than blank or zero in position 6, and the statements themselves are confined to positions 7 through 72. A Fortran 90 compiler is not required to permit more than 19 continuation lines in the fixed source form. The ampersand (&) is not used for continuation.

As in FORTRAN 77, blanks (outside character strings) are not significant, and an asterisk (*) or a C in character position 1 indicates that the entire line is a comment. However, unlike standard FORTRAN 77, an exclamation mark (!) in any position other than 6 indicates that the rest of the line is a comment (provided, of course, that the exclamation mark is not somehow part of a character string). Also, more than one statement may appear on a line, but adjacent statements must be separated by a semicolon (;).

Under some unusual circumstances, someone may wish to produce Fortran 90 code for use in either free or fixed source form. This can be accomplished by staying within the following guidelines:

1. Limit the appearance of all statements to character positions 7 through 72.
2. Confine all labels to positions 1 through 5.
3. To continue a statement, place one ampersand in position 73 of a line to be continued and another ampersand in position 6 of the following line.
4. Always treat blanks as significant.
5. Indicate all comments by using the exclamation mark, but never place an exclamation mark in position 6.

APPENDIX E

BINARY, OCTAL, AND HEXADECIMAL VALUES

The FORTRAN 77 standard provides no mechanism at all for binary, octal, and hexadecimal literal constants (collectively known as "BOZ literal constants"), but for some time most popular FORTRAN 77 implementations have in some manner supported octal and hexadecimal constants, and quite a few have supported binary constants as well. BOZ literal constants are supported by the Fortran 90 standard, although not very well since the new standard limits their appearance to DATA statements. Figure E.1 gives a complete program that demonstrates how BOZ literal constants are dealt with in standard Fortran 90.

When executed, the program of Figure E.1 displays the following:

```
00101   0027   003A
```

The Fortran 90 standard specifies that BOZ constants can be used to initialize only INTEGER variables. It is ordinarily preferable as a matter

```
PROGRAM demo_boz_constants

   INTEGER :: bin_val, oct_val, hex_val

   DATA bin_val / B'101' /    ! Fortran 90 standard
   DATA oct_val / O"27" /     ! limits appearance of BOZ
   DATA hex_val / Z"3A" /     ! constants to DATA stmts.

   ! Edit descriptors in following stmt are standard.
   PRINT '(B6.5, O6.4, Z6.4)', bin_val, oct_val, hex_val

END PROGRAM demo_boz_constants
```

FIGURE E.1. Program illustrating binary, octal, and hexadecimal constants.

of Fortran 90 style to initialize a variable by using the equal sign in its type declaration, but the standard does not permit this for a BOZ constant. Of course, alternative syntax for binary, octal, and/or hexadecimal values will be supported in many Fortran 90 implementations, and some or all of the restrictions described here may be relaxed.

The Fortran 90 standard dictates that each BOZ literal constant must consist of the appropriate letter B, O, or Z followed by a string enclosed by either apostrophes (') or quote marks ("). For a binary constant, the string can contain only the digits 0 or 1; for an octal constant, the string can contain only the digits 0 through 7; and for a hexadecimal constant, the string can contain only digits and letters A through F. As always in Fortran 90, the letters B, O, or Z and/or the letters A through F may appear in upper case and, if an implementation supports lower case in the source at all, any of these letters may appear in either upper or lower case.

In the format specification in the PRINT statement in Figure E.1, note the edit descriptors B, O, and Z for outputting data in binary, octal, and hexadecimal form, respectively. These edit descriptors are standard in Fortran 90, but they were not part of the FORTRAN 77 standard. The usage of the B, O, and Z edit descriptors is similar to that of the I edit descriptor in either FORTRAN 77 or Fortran 90. For example, if it were desired to suppress display of the leading zeros by the program of Figure E.1, the PRINT statement could be changed to the following:

```
PRINT '(B6, O6, Z6)', bin_val, oct_val, hex_val
```

OBSOLESCENT FEATURES

F.1 The Nature of Obsolescent Features

The Fortran 90 standard identifies a small group of features, known as **obsolescent features**, which it recommends that programmers avoid using. All of these features are standard in FORTRAN 77, and they are still supported by the Fortran 90 standard, but all references to them in the new standard are printed in a very small type size to emphasize their second-class status. The Fortran 90 standard recommends that support for the obsolescent features eventually be dropped in future standards, but thoughtful observers believe that most popular Fortran implementations will continue to support these features indefinitely because of their widespread presence in existing programs. Nevertheless, the classification of these features as obsolescent indicates a broad-based disapproval, and careful programmers should avoid using them except under exceptional circumstances. The remainder of this appendix gives brief descriptions of all of the obsolescent features.

F.2 DO Control Variable of Type REAL

The Fortran 90 standard categorizes the use of a control variable of type REAL in a DO construct as obsolescent. Thus, code such as the following should be avoided:

```
REAL :: x
DO x = 0.1, 0.5, 0.1      ! obsolescent
    PRINT "(F5.1)", x
END DO
```

Presumably, the intention is that the PRINT statement be executed five times, but because of rounding problems, the PRINT will execute only four times in some implementations. An alternate way of achieving the same result in a reliable and portable fashion would be

```
INTEGER :: i
DO i = 1, 5                    ! not obsolescent
    PRINT "(F5.1)", 0.1 * i
END DO
```

The recommendation that a variable of type REAL not be used as a DO control variable applies to DOUBLE PRECISION as well, since in Fortran 90, DOUBLE PRECISION is considered to be a kind of type REAL.

F.3 DO Termination Other Than END DO or CONTINUE

Almost any sort of statement is permitted to be the last statement in a DO construct, but the Fortran 90 standard classifies as obsolescent the practice of terminating a DO with anything other than an END DO or a CONTINUE. Hence, code such as the following should be avoided:

```
      REAL, DIMENSION(5) :: x
      INTEGER            :: i
      DO 100 i = 1, 5
100     x(i) = i                 ! obsolescent
```

Of course, a nonobsolescent alternate for the above code fragment would be

```
REAL, DIMENSION(5) :: x
INTEGER            :: i
DO i = 1, 5
    x(i) = i
END DO                     ! not obsolescent
```

Also, the Fortran 90 standard considers the following alternate to be nonobsolescent:

```
      REAL, DIMENSION(5) :: x
      INTEGER            :: i
      DO 100 i = 1, 5
          x(i) = i
100 CONTINUE                   ! not obsolescent
```

In terms of readability, the END DO should ordinarily be preferred over the CONTINUE as a DO construct terminator because END DO has no other purpose in the language, while CONTINUE may be used for many purposes.

F.4 SHARED DO TERMINATION

It is permissible to employ the same statement to terminate more than one DO construct, but this practice is classified as obsolescent by the Fortran 90 standard. Therefore, code such as the following should be avoided:

```
        REAL, DIMENSION(5,5) :: y
        INTEGER               :: i, j
        DO 100 i = 1, 5
           DO 100 j = 1, 5
              y(i,j) = i * j
    100 CONTINUE                        ! obsolescent
```

Each DO construct should be coded with its own terminating statement, which should be either END DO or CONTINUE as discussed in the preceding section. A nonobsolescent way of achieving the same results as the above code fragment is as follows:

```
    REAL, DIMENSION(5,5) :: y
    INTEGER               :: i, j
    DO i = 1, 5
       DO j = 1, 5
          y(i,j) = i * j
       END DO                    ! not obsolescent
    END DO                       ! not obsolescent
```

F.5 ARITHMETIC IF STATEMENT

Careful programmers have rejected the general use of the arithmetic IF statement for years, and so it is no surprise that the Fortran 90 standard places this statement in the obsolescent category. Thus, code such as the following is to be avoided:

```
        INTEGER :: n = 1
        IF (n - 1) 10, 20, 30          ! obsolescent
    10 PRINT *, 'n is less than 1.'
        GO TO 40
    20 PRINT *, 'n is equal to 1.'
        GO TO 40
    30 PRINT *, 'n is greater than 1.'
    40 CONTINUE
```

Except under exceptional circumstances, control structures based on either the logical IF statement, the IF construct, or the SELECT CASE construct should be preferred over control structures based on the arithmetic IF statement. For example, an alternate way of coding the preceding fragment using the IF construct is as follows:

```
INTEGER :: n = 1
IF (n < 1) THEN                          ! not obsolescent
    PRINT *, 'n is less than 1.'
ELSE IF (n == 1) THEN
    PRINT *, 'n is equal to 1.'
ELSE IF (n > 1) THEN
    PRINT *, 'n is greater than 1.'
END IF
```

F.6 BRANCH TO END IF FROM OUTSIDE IF CONSTRUCT

For purposes of backward compatibility with the FORTRAN 77 standard, Fortran permits branching to an END IF statement from outside its IF construct but designates this feature as obsolescent. Hence, code such as the following should be avoided:

```
      IF (n == -1) GO TO 100
      IF (n /= 0) THEN
          PRINT *, 'n is not zero.'
100 END IF                              ! obsolescent
```

A nonobsolescent way of recoding the preceding fragment is simply to branch to the statement following the END IF:

```
      IF (n == -1) GO TO 100
      IF (n /= 0) THEN
          PRINT *, 'n is not zero.'
      END IF
100 CONTINUE                            ! not obsolescent
```

Of course, the preceding code fragment, while avoiding obsolescent features, is not exemplary in terms of style.

F.7 H EDIT DESCRIPTOR

Formats such as the one in the following PRINT statement are classified as obsolescent and should be avoided:

```
PRINT "(32H Don't use obsolescent features!)"   ! obsolescent
```

An alternative, nonobsolescent way of coding the above PRINT statement is

```
PRINT "(' Don''t use obsolescent features!')"   ! OK
```

Better yet, in the opinion of the author, would be

```
PRINT "(A)", " Don't use obsolescent features!"   ! OK
```

F.8   PAUSE STATEMENT

The PAUSE statement causes the execution of a program to be suspended
until some implementation-dependent external command is entered at
a terminal keyboard, causing execution to be resumed at the statement
immediately following the PAUSE. However, the new standard categorizes the PAUSE statement as obsolescent, so code such as the following
should be avoided:

```
PAUSE   ! obsolescent
```

The effect that programmers ordinarily intend to achieve by using a
PAUSE statement can be realized in a more portable way by code such
as the following:

```
CHARACTER :: ignored_input

! The following code uses no obsolescent features.
WRITE (*, "(A)", ADVANCE = "NO")                          &
                    " Press <Return> to continue."
READ (*, "(A)") ignored_input
```

F.9   THE ASSIGN STATEMENT AND THE ASSIGNED GO TO STATEMENT

For many years, Fortran programmers have been able to employ the
ASSIGN statement to assign a statement label to an ordinary INTEGER
variable, and then later use that INTEGER variable in a form of the GO
TO statement to specify the label to branch to. This form of the GO TO
statement is known as the "assigned GO TO." The ASSIGN statement and
the assigned GO TO statement, both of which are supported as obsolescent features in standard Fortran 90, are illustrated in the program of

```
PROGRAM demo_assigned_go_to

     INTEGER :: place_to_go_back_to

     sum = 0.0

     WRITE (*, "(A)", ADVANCE = "NO") " Enter a number: "
     ASSIGN 100 TO place_to_go_back_to          ! obsolescent
     GO TO 500

 100 WRITE (*, "(A)", ADVANCE = "NO")                          &
                          " Enter a second number: "
     ASSIGN 200 TO place_to_go_back_to          ! obsolescent
     GO TO 500

 200 WRITE (*, "(A)", ADVANCE = "NO")                          &
                          " Enter a third number: "
     ASSIGN 300 TO place_to_go_back_to          ! obsolescent
     GO TO 500

 300 WRITE (*, "(/A, F13.5)") " Sum of 3 numbers = ", sum
     STOP

 500 READ *, x
     sum = sum + x
     GO TO place_to_go_back_to (100, 200, 300)     ! obso-
                                                   ! lescent

END PROGRAM demo_assigned_go_to
```

FIGURE F.1A.   Examples of ASSIGN and assigned GO TO statements.

Figure F.1a. The GO TO statement just before the END PROGRAM statement causes control to be transferred back to either 100, 200, or 300,
depending on which of the three ASSIGN statements was most recently
executed.

   In Fortran 90, it is usually not difficult to think of a simpler control
structure to replace code employing an assigned GO TO. For example,
the program of Figure F.1b uses an internal subroutine named get_and_
add to achieve the same results as the program of Figure F.1a. Note that
the program of Figure F.1b avoids the use of any obsolescent features,
and certainly the code of Figure F.1b is more readable than that of
Figure F.1a. Some veteran Fortran programmers are likely to assert
that the execution efficiency of the program of Figure F.1b will not be
as good as that of the program of Figure F.1a, but studies would be

```
PROGRAM demo_avoid_assigned_go_to

  sum = 0.0

  WRITE (*, "(A)", ADVANCE = "NO") " Enter a number: "
  CALL get_and_add                              ! not obsolescent

  WRITE (*, "(A)", ADVANCE = "NO") " Enter a second number: "
  CALL get_and_add                              ! not obsolescent

  WRITE (*, "(A)", ADVANCE = "NO") " Enter a third number: "
  CALL get_and_add                              ! not obsolescent

  WRITE (*, "(/A, F13.5)") " Sum of 3 numbers = ", sum

CONTAINS

  SUBROUTINE get_and_add                        ! not obsolescent

    READ *, x
    sum = sum + x

  END SUBROUTINE get_and_add

END PROGRAM demo_avoid_assigned_go_to
```

FIGURE F.1B. Alternate for Figure F.1a with no obsolescent features.

required to determine the truth of this claim. Even if this assertion should be true, marginal improvements in execution efficiency should seldom be made at the expense of program readability.

F.10 ASSIGNED FORMAT

The ASSIGN statement was illustrated in the preceding section in the context of the assigned GO TO, but the FORTRAN 77 standard also supports using the ASSIGN statement to assign the label of a FORMAT statement to an ordinary INTEGER variable, and then later using that INTEGER variable to specify that format in a READ, WRITE, or PRINT statement. This is illustrated for the INTEGER variable ifmt in the following code fragment:

```
      INTEGER :: ifmt
1000 FORMAT (' This is output 1.')
2000 FORMAT (' This is output 2.')

      ASSIGN 2000 TO ifmt          ! obsolescent
      PRINT ifmt                   ! obsolescent
```

The Fortran 90 standard continues support for the assigned format but classifies it as an obsolescent feature. The assigned format can be avoided by using a CHARACTER expression to specify the format. For example, the preceding code fragment could be replaced with the following:

```
CHARACTER(80) :: fmt
CHARACTER(80), PARAMETER ::                                    &
              fmt1 = "(' This is output 1.')", &
              fmt2 = "(' This is output 2.')"

fmt = fmt2    ! not obsolescent
PRINT fmt     ! not obsolescent
```

```
PROGRAM demo_alt_return

      CALL divide (0.0, 1.0, q, *999)     ! obsolescent

      PRINT *, q

      STOP

  999 PRINT *, "Zero divisor detected."

END PROGRAM demo_alt_return

SUBROUTINE divide (divisor, dividend, quotient, *)  ! obso-
                                                    ! lescent

      IF (divisor == 0.0) RETURN 1      ! obsolescent

      quotient = dividend / divisor

END SUBROUTINE divide
```

FIGURE F.2A. Program illustrating the alternate return mechanism.

```
! Note: This program behaves the same as the program of
!        Figure F.2a but uses no obsolescent features.

PROGRAM demo_avoid_alt_return

   CALL divide (0.0, 1.0, q, istat)

   IF (istat == 0) THEN
      PRINT *, q
   ELSE
      PRINT *, "Zero divisor detected."
   END IF

END PROGRAM demo_avoid_alt_return

SUBROUTINE divide (divisor, dividend, quotient, istat)

   IF (divisor /= 0.0) THEN
      quotient = dividend / divisor
      istat = 0
   ELSE
      istat = 1
   END IF

END SUBROUTINE divide
```

FIGURE F.2B. Program avoiding use of alternate return mechanism.

F.11 ALTERNATE RETURN

Upon return from a call to a subroutine, it is often handy to resume execution somewhere other than at the statement immediately following the CALL statement, particularly in the event of an error being detected in the subroutine. The FORTRAN 77 standard supports such a capability by way of the alternate return mechanism, which is illustrated by the program of Figure F.2a. Upon completion of execution of the subroutine divide, execution will continue at one of two places: If execution of divide reaches the END SUBROUTINE statement, the next statement to be executed will be the PRINT statement immediately following the CALL statement; but if the variable divisor is equal to zero, then the statement

```
RETURN 1
```

is executed, and the next statement to be executed is the statement labeled 999 in the main program.

Of course, the use of alternate returns can always be avoided. For example, the program of Figure F.2b, which uses no obsolescent features, achieves the same effect as that of Figure F.2a. Actually, it seems to the author that the code of Figure F.2a is arguably more readable than that of Figure F.2b. Nevertheless, the use of statement labels does not fit in well with Fortran 90 style, so on balance, it is wise to forgo the use of alternate returns.

SPECIAL-PURPOSE VARIETIES OF PROCEDURES

G.1 OVERVIEW OF THE APPENDIX

The FORTRAN 77 standard supports three varieties of procedures that are used only in special situations:

1. procedures defined by statement functions;
2. procedures defined by multiple-entry subprograms;
3. dummy procedures.

Of course, all of these are supported by the Fortran 90 standard as well, but there are some aspects of their treatment in the new standard that may not be altogether obvious. This appendix will present a brief discussion of each of the three varieties of procedures.

In connection with dummy procedures, it is possible in FORTRAN 77 that intrinsic procedure names might be used as actual arguments. For purposes of backward compatibility, Fortran 90 maintains support for this capability, but only under circumstances similar to those that might arise in FORTRAN 77. The final section of this appendix discusses the use of intrinsic procedure names as actual arguments.

G.2 STATEMENT FUNCTIONS

A **statement function** is a function defined by a single statement, and that single statement is rather similar in form to an assignment statement. When present, a statement function appears in the specification

part of a main program or a subprogram, and the statement is classified
as nonexecutable. There are situations in which a statement function
provides the programmer with an intuitive, convenient way to code
a simple procedure. However, it should be borne in mind that anything that can be done by a statement function can also be done by the
Fortran 90 internal function subprogram, and the latter offers greater
flexibility and better readability.

The main program of Figure G.1 contains a statement function
named f that expresses the mathematical equation

$$f(x) = x^3 + 2x^2 - x - 2$$

in Fortran. The DO loop causes the function to be evaluated for a
sequence of values. When the program is executed, the following is
displayed:

```
0.800   -1.008
0.900   -0.551
1.000    0.000
1.100    0.651
1.200    1.408
```

The Fortran 90 standard imposes a number of restrictions on statement functions. Each dummy argument must be a scalar, and the
expression to the right of the equal sign (=) must contain only intrinsic

```
PROGRAM demo_statement_function

    REAL :: f    ! type declaration for result of stmt function

    REAL :: x    ! type declaration for dummy arg of stmt func

    f (x) = x ** 3 + 2.0 * x ** 2 - x - 2.0   ! stmt function

    INTEGER :: i
    REAL    :: val

    DO i = 8, 12
       val = 0.1 * i
       PRINT "(2F8.3)", val, f (val)   ! Invoke stmt function.
    END DO

END PROGRAM demo_statement_function
```

FIGURE G.1. Main program containing a statement function.

operations where each term is composed of only scalar-valued quantities. The interface for a statement function is considered to be implicit,
so the Fortran 90 features requiring an explicit interface are unavailable
with a statement function: The result cannot be array-valued; a dummy
argument cannot be a pointer or a target; the result cannot be a pointer;
argument keywords cannot be used in referencing the function; and so
on. These limitations are not shared by internal function subprograms,
which always have explicit interfaces. Also, a statement function must
never be invoked recursively, another limitation not shared by an internal function subprogram. Finally, the name of a function defined by
a statement function must not appear in an argument list, but this is
also true for the name of an internal subprogram.

G.3 MULTIPLE-ENTRY SUBPROGRAMS

A **multiple-entry subprogram** is a subprogram that contains one or
more ENTRY statements. Each ENTRY statement marks a place where the
subprogram can be entered and is thought of as marking the beginning
of the definition of a new procedure. A popular use of a multiple-entry
subprogram is to package together a group of closely related procedures
that share data specifications. Since a general understanding of the
main ideas surrounding the use of this variety of subprogram lends
insight into the terminology and concepts of the Fortran language, a
brief discussion of it will be presented in this section. However, it should
be kept in mind that, in Fortran 90, the module provides a mechanism
for packaging groups of related procedures that is generally superior
to that of the multiple-entry subprogram.

Figure G.2a gives an example of a multiple-entry function subprogram named sin_in_deg. However, the subprogram sin_in_deg can be
entered not only at its top, but also at the alternate entry points cos_
in_deg and tan_in_deg, which are indicated by ENTRY statements. Thus,
the function subprogram sin_in_deg is considered to define three procedures: sin_in_deg, cos_in_deg, and tan_in_deg. Observe in Figure G.2a that
the data specifications at the top of the function sin_in_deg are shared by
all three entry points. Also, while the ENTRY statement itself is available
in standard FORTRAN 77, the RESULT clause of this statement is not.
In Fortran 90, the RESULT clause is used in the ENTRY statement in a
manner similar to its use in the FUNCTION statement, as is discussed in
Section 6.4.

Figure G.2b gives a main program that can serve as a test driver for
the function subprogram of Figure G.2a. When the main program and

```
! collection of trig funcs for use with angles in degrees

FUNCTION sin_in_deg (x) RESULT (sin_val)    ! 1st entry point

   REAL :: sin_val, cos_val, tan_val    ! result variables

   REAL, INTENT (IN) :: x               ! angle in degrees

   REAL, PARAMETER :: Deg_to_rad = 0.0174533

   sin_val = SIN (Deg_to_rad * x)

   RETURN    ! required to avoid falling through

ENTRY cos_in_deg (x) RESULT (cos_val)       ! 2nd entry point

   cos_val = COS (Deg_to_rad * x)

   RETURN    ! required to avoid falling through

ENTRY tan_in_deg (x) RESULT (tan_val)       ! 3rd entry point

   tan_val = TAN (Deg_to_rad * x)

END FUNCTION sin_in_deg
```

Figure G.2a. A multiple-entry function subprogram.

the function subprogram are compiled and linked, executing the resulting program causes the following display:

```
0.50000
0.86603
0.57735
```

Note that in the main program of Figure G.2b, each of the names sin_in_deg, cos_in_deg, and tan_in_deg is treated as if it were the name of an external subprogram. But, strictly speaking, only sin_in_deg meets the definition of function subprogram as given in Section 6.1. This example helps to sharpen the distinction, drawn in Section 6.11, between a subprogram and a procedure since there is only one subprogram (sin_in_deg), but there are three procedures (sin_in_deg, cos_in_deg, and tan_in_deg). Note that the main program deals only with external procedures, rather than subprograms, and is unaware of the implementations of the procedures.

```
PROGRAM demo_multiple_entry_function

    INTERFACE    ! interface bodies for 3 external procedures

        FUNCTION sin_in_deg (x) RESULT (sin_val)
            REAL                :: sin_val
            REAL, INTENT (IN) :: x
        END FUNCTION sin_in_deg

        FUNCTION cos_in_deg (x) RESULT (cos_val)
            REAL                :: cos_val
            REAL, INTENT (IN) :: x
        END FUNCTION cos_in_deg

        FUNCTION tan_in_deg (x) RESULT (tan_val)
            REAL                :: tan_val
            REAL, INTENT (IN) :: x
        END FUNCTION tan_in_deg

    END INTERFACE

    PRINT "(F8.5)", sin_in_deg (30.0)
    PRINT "(F8.5)", cos_in_deg (30.0)
    PRINT "(F8.5)", tan_in_deg (30.0)

END PROGRAM demo_multiple_entry_function
```

FIGURE G.2B.   Test driver for the function subprogram of Figure G.2a.

Observe in Figure G.2b that an interface body is provided for each of the three external procedures. Thus, an interface body is provided for a procedure, rather than for a subprogram. Actually, in this example, none of the three interface bodies is mandatory. However, if the interface bodies are omitted, it is desirable at least to declare the data types of the procedure names in some manner such as the following:

```
REAL :: sin_in_deg, cos_in_deg, tan_in_deg
```

G.4 DUMMY PROCEDURES

A dummy argument whose corresponding actual argument is a procedure name is known as a **dummy procedure**. Even though dummy procedures have been a feature of Fortran for many years, few program-mers feel entirely comfortable with them, so this section will illustrate the use of a dummy procedure in a Fortran 90 program. The context in which a dummy procedure usually arises is that of one programmer developing a subprogram that will be used by other programmers.

Figure G.3a shows a function subprogram find_zero, which has been developed to find a root of an arbitrary continuous (mathematical) function of one real variable. More specifically, if $f(x)$ is any continuous function and a and b are the left and right end points, respectively, of an interval where $f(a)$ is negative and $f(b)$ is positive, then find_zero is designed to determine a value x between a and b such that $f(x)$ is 0.

```
FUNCTION find_zero (a, b, f) RESULT (x)

   REAL                 :: x          ! result variable
   REAL, INTENT (IN) :: a, b          ! dummy arguments

   INTERFACE
      FUNCTION f (x) RESULT (y)
         REAL                 :: y     ! interface body for
         REAL, INTENT (IN) :: x        ! dummy procedure f
      END FUNCTION f
   END INTERFACE

   REAL :: left, right                 ! local variables

   left = a;  right = b

   DO
      x = (left + right) / 2.0

      IF (f (x) < 0.0) THEN            ! dummy proc f invoked
         left = x
      ELSE IF (f (x) > 0.0) THEN       ! dummy proc f invoked
         right = x
      ELSE
         EXIT
      END IF

      IF ((right - left) < 2.0 * SPACING (x)) EXIT
   END DO

END FUNCTION find_zero
```

FIGURE G.3A. Example of a subprogram featuring a dummy procedure.

Note in Figure G.3a the name f in the list of dummy arguments for find_zero. This is the same name f that later appears in the expression f (x), which initially occurs just after the first use of the keyword IF and again after the keywords ELSE IF. The name f is simply a dummy name that stands for a name to be supplied as an actual argument when find_zero is invoked.

Assuming that find_zero works as advertised, another programmer may wish to use it to locate a root between 0.0 and 1.0 of the fifth-order polynomial p(x) given by

$$p(x) = x^5 + 2x^3 - 1.$$

The programmer can accomplish this by first writing the function subprogram p shown in Figure G.3b, which evaluates the above fifth-order polynomial for any input value of the argument x. Then the programmer can pull all this together by writing the main program of Figure G.3c, which invokes find_zero. Note in Figure G.3c that the actual argument p corresponds to the dummy argument f in Figure G.3a. Thus, when the expression f (x) in find_zero is executed, the function subprogram named p of Figure G.3b will be invoked. When the complete program made up of the program units in Figures G.3a, G.3b, and G.3c is executed, something like the following will be displayed:

```
0.733157E+00
```

This value is a root of the fifth-order polynomial whose equation is given above.

An important, and perhaps unexpected, requirement is that in order to use an external procedure name as an actual argument, the programmer must explicitly indicate to the compiler in some manner that the procedure is external. This requirement is met in the main program of

```
!       function to evaluate
!       fifth-order polynomial

FUNCTION p (x) RESULT (y)

    REAL                :: y
    REAL, INTENT (IN) :: x

    y = x ** 5 + 2.0 * x ** 3 - 1.0

END FUNCTION p
```

FIGURE G.3B. Subprogram defining polynomial whose root is desired.

```
PROGRAM demo_dummy_proc

    ! Interface block containing interface bodies follows.
    INTERFACE

        ! interface body for external proc find_zero:
        FUNCTION find_zero (a, b, f) RESULT (x)
            REAL               :: x
            REAL, INTENT (IN) :: a, b

            INTERFACE                   ! Interface bodies may nest.
                ! interface body for dummy proc f:
                FUNCTION f (x) RESULT (y)
                    REAL               :: y
                    REAL, INTENT (IN) :: x
                END FUNCTION f
            END INTERFACE

        END FUNCTION find_zero

        ! interface body for external proc p:
        FUNCTION p (x) RESULT (y)
            REAL               :: y
            REAL, INTENT (IN) :: x
        END FUNCTION p

    END INTERFACE

    REAL :: root

    root = find_zero (0.0, 1.0, p)    ! find_zero invoked,
                                      ! external func p
                                      ! passed as arg
    PRINT "(E14.6)", root

END PROGRAM demo_dummy_proc
```

FIGURE G.3C. Main program that invokes subprogram of Figure G.3a.

Figure G.3c by supplying the interface body for the procedure name
p, which is later used as an actual argument when find_zero is invoked.
However, it should be mentioned that an interface body is not required
to accomplish this—as in FORTRAN 77, an EXTERNAL statement may
be employed for this purpose. Also, Fortran 90 provides the EXTERNAL
attribute for use in the type declaration of a function. Thus, in Figure
G.3c, the interface body for p may be omitted, provided that something

like the following appears somewhere outside the interface block in the
specification part of the main program:

```
REAL, EXTERNAL :: p
```

If this approach is used and the interface body for find_zero is retained, the interface block containing the interface body for f should
be replaced with something like the following in Figure G.3c:

```
REAL, EXTERNAL :: f
```

Actually, none of the interface bodies in Figure G.3c is mandatory, and it is permissible in this example to omit the entire interface
block, although, if this is done, something like the following should be
substituted:

```
REAL, EXTERNAL :: p, find_zero
```

Similarly, the interface block in Figure G.3a may be omitted, in which
case it would be desirable at least to substitute a type declaration for f
such as

```
REAL :: f
```

By the way, it is forbidden to specify an INTENT attribute for a dummy
procedure.

The foregoing completes the general discussion of the use of dummy
procedures, but some readers might like to have some explanation of
the particular technique used in the subprogram find_zero of Figure G.3a
to determine a root. The method used in find_zero is based on the the-
orem that if a continuous function $f(x)$ changes sign from point a to
point b, where a is to the left of b, then there is a root in the interval
$[a, b]$. The approach then is to bisect the interval and check the sign
of the function at the midpoint x. For concreteness, assume that $f(a)$ is
negative while $f(b)$ is positive. Then if $f(x) < 0$, there is a root in $[x, b]$;
if $f(x) > 0$, there is a root in $[a, x]$; and if $f(x) = 0$, x is a root. Unless the
midpoint happens to be a root, the bisection is repeated on the half-
interval known to contain a root. The bisection is performed repeatedly
until either a midpoint turns out to be a root or the interval known to
contain a root becomes so small that the root can be considered to have
been determined with sufficient precision.

The judgment as to when a root has been determined with sufficient
precision is somewhat subjective. The length of an interval [left,right] is
(right – left), and clearly the magnitude of this difference must be small
in some sense when the root is considered to have been determined.
The criterion used in the function of Figure G.3a is that the interval
must be small relative to how closely, utilizing the default kind of data
type REAL, the implementation on which execution is taking place approximates real numbers near the midpoint of the interval. The new

standard intrinsic function SPACING, which returns the implementation's spacing between numbers of the kind of its REAL argument near the argument value, provides the tool needed to apply this criterion.

G.5   INTRINSIC PROCEDURE NAME AS AN ACTUAL ARGUMENT

In Figure G.3c of the preceding section, the procedure name p is used as an actual argument, where p is defined by the external function subprogram of Figure G.3b. But it is also permissible for the name of an intrinsic procedure to be used as an actual argument. This is illustrated by the main program of Figure G.4, which invokes the function find_zero of Figure G.3a with the intrinsic function SIN as an actual argument. The program of Figure G.4 expects find_zero to determine the value of x in radians such that the trigonometric sine of x is zero, where x is between 6.0 and 7.0. When the complete program made up of the program units in Figures G.4 and G.3a is executed, something like the following will be displayed:

```
0.628319E+01
```

The function find_zero has behaved as expected, since the value displayed is an approximation to 2π, and the sine of 2π radians is zero.

```
PROGRAM demo_intrinsic_actual_arg

   REAL, EXTERNAL :: find_zero

   INTRINSIC SIN    ! mandatory for name SIN
                    ! since appears as actual arg

   REAL :: root

   root = find_zero (6.0, 7.0, SIN)    ! find_zero invoked
                                       ! with specific name
                                       ! of intrinsic func
                                       ! used as actual arg

   PRINT "(E14.6)", root

END PROGRAM demo_intrinsic_actual_arg
```

FIGURE G.4. An intrinsic function name used as an actual argument.

The Fortran 90 standard imposes rather severe restrictions on the use of intrinsic procedure names as actual arguments. First, not just any name for an intrinsic procedure can be used as an actual argument, but only those names listed in the new standard as specific names for intrinsic functions, a set of names carried over from the FORTRAN 77 standard without change. Second, the usage of the dummy procedure corresponding to an intrinsic procedure actual argument must be consistent with the usage of that intrinsic procedure in FORTRAN 77, and in particular, such a dummy procedure must be referenced only with scalar arguments. And finally, the name of an intrinsic procedure used as an actual argument must be specified as INTRINSIC.

Even though the use of a specific name for an intrinsic procedure is illustrated in this section, the author recommends the avoidance of all uses of specific names for intrinsic procedures. In the opinion of the author, it is best to reference intrinsic procedures only by generic names in Fortran 90. It should be noted, however, that adherence to this policy means that an intrinsic procedure name can never be used as an actual argument, but this limitation can be easily worked around as follows: Instead of using a specific name of an intrinsic procedure as the actual argument, a short subprogram can be written that references the intrinsic procedure by its generic name, and it is the name of this subprogram that is then used as the actual argument. Hence, it is always possible to avoid referencing intrinsic procedures by specific names.

INDEX

Printed in Great Britain
by Amazon.co.uk, Ltd.,
Marston Gate.